Teaching the Catholic Faith Today

RESOURCES FOR CATECHETICAL TEACHERS

General Editor: REV. MSGR. EUGENE KEVANE, PH.D.

1. *The Holy See.*   TEACHING THE CATHOLIC FAITH TODAY

Teaching the Catholic Faith Today

TWENTIETH CENTURY CATECHETICAL
DOCUMENTS OF THE HOLY SEE

Pope St. Pius X, Handing on Christian Doctrine by Teaching, 1905
Pope Pius XI, On Better Care for Catechetical Instruction, 1935
Pope Paul VI, The Creed of the People of God, 1968
Pope Paul VI, General Catechetical Directory, 1971
Pope Paul VI, Evangelization in the Modern World, 1975
Pope John Paul II, On Catechesis in Our Time, 1979
Pope John Paul II, Metanoia: Letters on the Eucharist, 1979, 1980

With an Introduction and Topical Index by
Eugene Kevane

And a Preface by
Silvio Cardinal Oddi, *Prefect*
Sacred Congregation for the Clergy

ST. PAUL EDITIONS   BOSTON, MASSACHUSETTS

NIHIL OBSTAT
    Richard V. Lawlor, S.J.
    Censor Deputatus

IMPRIMATUR
    ✠ Humberto Cardinal Medeiros
    Archbishop of Boston

Acknowledgments

Handing on Christian Doctrine by Teaching: The text of *Handing on Christian Doctrine by Teaching* is reprinted from *Catechetical Documents of Pope Pius X*, translated and edited by Joseph B. Collins, S.S., D.D., Ph.D. Copyright © 1946, by Joseph B. Collins, S.S., and used with the kind permission of Helen Collins Gibbons.

On Better Care for Catechetical Teaching: Official Vatican Translation.

The Creed of the People of God: NC News Service Translation.

General Catechetical Directory: The text of the *General Catechetical Directory* copyright © 1971, by the United States Catholic Conference, Washington, D.C., is reproduced by license of copyright owner. All rights reserved.

Evangelization in the Modern World: Reprinted with permission from *L'Osservatore Romano* (English Edition).

On Catechesis in Our Time: Reprinted with permission from *L'Osservatore Romano* (English Edition).

To All the Bishops of the Church and to All the Priests of the Church: Vatican Translation from Vatican Polyglot Press.

The Mystery and Worship of the Eucharist: Reprinted with permission from *L'Osservatore Romano* (English Edition).

Instruction On Worship of the Eucharistic Mystery: Reprinted with permission from *L'Osservatore Romano* (English Edition).

ISBN 0-8198-7319-5 cloth
      0-8198-7320-9 paper

Copyright © 1982, by the Daughters of St. Paul

Printed in the U.S.A. by the Daughters of St. Paul
50 St. Paul's Ave., Boston, MA 02130

The Daughters of St. Paul are an international congregation of religious women serving the Church with the communications media.

CONTENTS

Preface xi
Introduction xiii
Pope St. Pius X,
  Handing on Christian Doctrine by Teaching, 1905 1
Pope Pius XI,
  On Better Care for Catechetical Teaching, 1935 15
Pope Paul VI,
  The Creed of the People of God, 1968 29
Pope Paul VI,
  General Catechetical Directory, 1971 41
Pope Paul VI,
  Evangelization in the Modern World, 1975 145
Pope John Paul II,
  On Catechesis in Our Time, 1979 209
Pope John Paul II,
  Metanoia: The Mystery and Worship of the
    Eucharist, 1979, 1980 271
Topical Index 339
General Index 351

PREFACE

This handy collection of 20th century papal documents concerning the teaching of Christian doctrine to children and adults alike will be welcomed by English-speaking catechists everywhere for it is the first such collection in this language of which I have heard. Priests, particularly, will find a bonus in the collection because there are included the beautiful letters of our present Holy Father on the Eucharist, which he wrote for Holy Thursday of the years 1979 and 1980.

Msgr. Eugene Kevane sets the documents in historical perspective in his Introduction, thus helping the reader to understand the human scene against which a particular document was written, which often helps to explain why a given Pope chose one subject rather than another to emphasize, or why he approached a certain topic in one way rather than in another.

The Topical Index, also prepared by Msgr. Kevane, provides a practical key to the whole collection and will enable the observant catechist to note how Catholic teaching remains consistent while not ceasing to develop.

Teaching the Catholic Faith Today will serve to help root catechesis in Catholic Tradition so that catechists can more confidently adapt the adaptable to the times while holding firm on the deposit of faith.

The Daughters of St. Paul are to be congratulated on this publication and I wish it a wide distribution and study.

SILVIO CARDINAL ODDI, *Prefect*
Sacred Congregation for the Clergy

Rome, September 14, 1981

INTRODUCTION

Pope John XXIII gives the context for the set of documents on Evangelization and Catechesis published by the Supreme Magisterium of the Catholic Church in the decade which has followed the closing of Vatican II. Speaking to the pastors of his Diocese of Rome, he says, "The Catechism is the constant preoccupation of the Church.... This solicitude takes on innumerable forms according to the demands and conditions of various times, but these forms are always one and the same in their basic concern. It is that of breaking the bread of truth for the Christian people in a simple and understandable form which can be retained in the memory and meditated upon, and which can be handed on in the families as their precious heritage."[1]

Since the "Catechism" of which he speaks is the official elementary-level explanation of the Apostles' Creed and of its application to Christian living, Pope John XXIII is actually voicing concern for the deposit of faith. This concern has motivated the Catholic Church since the Apostles; but the concentration of documents expressing it in the Twentieth Century, and especially in the decade after Vatican II, is altogether unprecedented.

The purpose of the present volume is to gather under one cover these post-conciliar documents together with the two earlier catechetical milestones of the present century, the *Acerbo nimis* of St. Pius X and the *Provido sane* of Pope Pius XI, for the convenience both of students and of catechists busy in the field. It should also contribute toward the authentic interpretation of these documents by the light each throws upon the rest.[2] No commen-

---

1. John XXIII, "L'incontro coi parroci," *Acta Apostolicae Sedis* (March 31, 1962), pp. 169-170.

2. In his Prologue to the *Ascent of Mount Carmel*, St. John of the Cross admits that his readers will find his treatise difficult at the beginning. "But as the reader passes on, he will find himself understanding the first part better, since one part will explain another." See E. Allison Peers (transl.), *The Complete works of St. John of the Cross* (Westminster: The Newman Press, 1964), p. 14. This illustrates the point.

tary will be given; the footnote references are exclusively those official in the documents themselves. The topical index is designed to assist in this comparative study of the documents for their mutual illumination.

These documents, furthermore, should not be taken in a contemporary isolation, as if they were somehow different from the previous life of the Church since the Apostles. For full intelligibility, they need to be seen in the larger perspective of the constant catechetical concern of the Church since Jesus sent his Apostles on their worldwide mission to teach all nations. Before presenting the Twentieth Century documents, therefore, it seems proper to review briefly this more general background.

THE DEPOSIT OF FAITH

From the very beginning described in the New Testament, the Catholic Church has treasured the faith which she teaches as a divine deposit entrusted to her by the Supreme Being of the universe. The very idea of catechesis always has been that of a teaching process which is abidingly faithful to this divine deposit. What, exactly, is this deposit? Where can it be found officially stated and formulated? Why is it treasured? The answers are contained in the Person and the teaching of Jesus Christ.

These catechetical documents of the Holy See in the present century illuminate and interpret each other in a similar way. There is of course the further fact that all the documents of the Supreme Magisterium form one luminous and self-interpreting whole, reflecting the one, unified mind of Jesus Christ, the Divine Teacher, in his Body which is the Church. The documents of his Church interpret each other, comment upon each other, throw light upon each other. No one of them or group of them can be taken in isolation as having a meaning apart from or different than the whole. The mind of Christ is a seamless robe of unified meaning, of divine truth, expressed for specific topics and purposes in the various documents. For instance, whenever philosophical dimensions, implications or presuppositions come up in documents that are theological or catechetical or scriptural or social in purpose, then the documents on the renewal of Christian Philosophy must be kept in mind. This is the source of illumination, of authentic interpretation, of the abiding and eternal hermeneutic. To give one example, it is entirely mistaken to take *Catechesi tradendae* in isolation and then to "interpret" it in the light of a vague philosophy picked up by osmosis from a decadent religious environment and its light theological literature popular at the moment.

Jesus Christ, the Divine Teacher

While Jesus was indeed a carpenter in Nazareth until he was about thirty years of age, the recognition has been growing as a result of the more recent scriptural studies that he presented himself in his public life as a recognized *Rabbi* or Teacher of the Torah in Israel.[3] This is of basic importance for the self-image of the catechist today. It is the avenue, furthermore, by which younger Catholics are re-discovering the Magisterium and a sense of personal loyalty to it born of their characteristic new interest in Jesus Christ and faith in him as a person.

Pope John Paul II has made these newer insights official in *Catechesi tradendae*, nos. 7-8. "The Gospels clearly relate occasions when Jesus taught," he writes. "It is the witness that Jesus gives of himself: 'Day after day I sat in the temple teaching' (Mt. 26:55). ...'Crowds gathered to him again; and again, as his custom was, he taught them' (Mk. 10:1). ...One who teaches in this way has a unique title to the name of 'Teacher'.... This image of Christ the Teacher is at once majestic and familiar, impressive and reassuring. It comes from the pen of the evangelists and it has often been evoked subsequently in iconography since earliest Christian times, so captivating is it. And I am pleased to evoke it at the beginning of these considerations on catechesis in the modern world."

This insight illuminates and unifies all of these Twentieth Century catechetical documents published by the Supreme Magisterium of the Church which Jesus sent to catechize all nations. They implement his own teaching for they specify the way by which catechists are his instruments in continuing that same teaching today.

What was the content of Jesus' teaching? How did he form the minds of his disciples? A catechetical reading of the Gospels shows that he taught them to understand who he himself is, and what the religion is by which mankind is to respond to this central

---

3. For the comprehensive study of the matter, see Friedrich Normann, *Christos Didáskalos: Die Vorstellung von Christus als Lehrer in der christlichen Literatur des ersten und zweiten Jahrhunderts* (Muenster: Achendorffsche Verlagsbuchhandlung, 1966); for Jesus' methods as a teacher, see William H. Russell, *Jesus the Divine Teacher* (New York: Kenedy, 1944).

doctrine.⁴ So that they would know who he himself is, he taught them the mystery of the Trinity. Within the Godhead of Yahweh, the One God of the Hebrew revelation, there are three equal divine Persons. Gradually, with the utmost skill as a teacher, he brings them to know and to profess the faith in the divine Trinity which will characterize the Church he is building upon this foundation, these specially-chosen full-time disciples or students, who have come to be called his Apostles because he sent them to the whole world with his own identical teaching mission and doctrine.⁵

With regard to God the Father Almighty, Creator of heaven and earth, he taught them that he was not come to destroy the prophets but to fulfill them. The substance of the Hebrew religion continues in this new universal Church which he is building: its revealed concept of God, his attributes, his almighty creating power and his Providence over his creation, will be handed on to all the gentile nations.

In their life with him, the disciples came to know Jesus well, coming gradually to recognize him as the only begotten son of God, their Lord: One in his divine Person, but possessing two natures, the nature of Yahweh, the Supreme Being, and the human nature he received by being born of the Virgin Mary, his mother. Thus, as a result of the program of their Teacher, the Apostles became able to celebrate his death in charity, to proclaim his resurrection with living faith, and to look forward with firm hope to his Second Coming in glory as the Judge of the living and the dead.

He taught them that there is a third divine Person, the Holy Spirit of God, whom he promised to send to them as the Spirit of Truth to support their teaching of their faith, as the Spirit of Life to animate the Sacraments of his religion, and as the Spirit of Holiness to sustain the life of prayer and Gospel morality in his Church.

Thus Jesus' teaching fulfilled in a divinely simple yet masterful way his own first call when he began his public life, summarized in Mark 1:14-15: "After John had been delivered up, Jesus came into

---

4. Hence the basic principle of catechetical method stated in the *General Catechetical Directory*, no. 40: "Catechesis must necessarily be Christocentric"; see below, p. 74.

5. In the original Greek text of the Gospels, Jesus' inner circle of specially-chosen disciples are customarily called his *mathetai*, the ordinary word at that time for "students." See Kittel-Bromiley, *Theological Dictionary of the New Testament* (Grand Rapids: Eerdmans, 1967), Vol. IV, pp. 390-461.

Galilee, preaching the gospel of the Kingdom of God, and saying, 'The time is fulfilled, and the Kingdom of God is at hand. Repent and believe the gospel.' " He taught them the essential content or "articles" of this Gospel which they were to believe with divine faith; and he helped them take up in response this repentance or *metanoia*, the Christian way of life with its three fundamental aspects: personal prayer, Gospel morality, and the practice of the Seven Sacraments which he taught them to administer in his Church.

Such, then, is the "deposit of faith" which the Apostles received from Jesus Christ, their Divine Teacher.

Since the Person who taught these disciples with his human voice and lips and language was the Second Person of the divine Trinity, his teaching is the culmination and fulfillment of the revelation begun with Moses and the Prophets. Concluding his study of the privileges of the Apostles, who lived with Jesus and learned from him, the theologian Charles Journet summarizes the constant teaching of the Church regarding the deposit of faith: "Besides the exceptional knowledge they had of the revealed deposit, the Apostles enjoyed the privilege of a miraculous assistance which enabled them to give it an *oral or written expression* (his emphasis) so faithful that God himself must be said to speak by their mouths."[6]

The Divine Teacher accomplished his purpose. He taught and formed these disciples so that he could send them as Apostles with his own mission to teach divine revelation, the very Word of God. "My teaching is not from myself: it comes from the one who sent me" (Jn. 7:16). "As the Father sent me, so I am sending you" (Jn. 20:21). "You will be my witnesses not only in Jerusalem..., but to the ends of the earth" (Acts 1:8).

The Trinitarian pattern of this teaching that witnesses to him is clear from his final mandate to his Apostles as founders of his

---

6. Charles Journet, *The Church of the Word Incarnate*, Vol. I, *The Apostolic Hierarchy* (London: Sheed and Ward, 1955), p. 142. See the *General Catechetical Directory*, no. 12, on "Jesus Christ: Mediator and Fullness of all Revelation"; and no. 13: "The divine revelation which constitutes the object of the Catholic Faith, and which was completed at the time of the Apostles, must be clearly distinguished from the grace of the Holy Spirit, without whose inspiration and illumination no one can believe." Below, pp. 55-56.

worldwide Teaching Church: "Go, therefore, make disciples of all the nations; baptize them in the name of the Father and of the Son and of the Holy Spirit, and teach them to observe all the commands I gave you. And know that I am with you always; yes, to the end of time" (Mt. 28:19-20).

The Catechetical Teaching of the Apostles

The concern of the Apostles to hand on the deposit of faith by teaching is clear in the book of the Acts and in the Epistles which the Apostles wrote. The Apostolic Church was a teaching Church. Every early Christian community had *didáskaloi,* "teachers": parish catechists, one would say today, or CCD teachers. Paul himself was one of them before he was sent on his missions by the Church: "In the Church at Antioch the following were prophets and teachers: Barnabas, Simeon called Niger..., and Saul" (Acts 13:1).[7]

The writings of the New Testament do not report directly on this first teaching by which new converts were initiated into the Mystery of Christ and helped to deepen their conversion. But they reflect it indirectly in many places, and they constantly presuppose its existence. How else could the Epistles of St. Paul have been understood when received and read in the communities? To begin with, there is an elementary level proper to children and to adults who come like little children seeking entrance into the Kingdom of God. "Let us leave behind us then all the elementary teaching about Christ and concentrate on its completion, without going over the fundamental doctrines again" (Heb. 6:1).[8] After this elementary instruction which prepares for Christian initiation, there is a higher level of Christian doctrine which builds upon the deposit of faith.[9] The existence and practical nature of this first catechetical

---

7. For the many other references to "teachers" in the New Testament writings, see "The *didáskaloi* of the early Christian community," in Kittel-Bromiley, *Theological Dictionary of the New Testament, op. cit.,* Vol. II, pp. 157-159.

8. J. N. D. Kelly, *Early Christian Creeds* (London: Longmans, 1972; third edition), p. 8: This passage "refers unmistakably to an elementary stage in Christian education which includes instruction in doctrine as well as in ethics and the Sacraments.... The passage is concerned with catechetical practice."

9. For the contemporary continuation of this instruction in Christian Doctrine which distinguishes between the elementary and secondary levels, see the *General*

instruction is everywhere presupposed. "Brothers," St. Paul writes to his community of predilection, "we urge you and appeal to you in the Lord Jesus to make more and more progress in the kind of life that you are meant to live: the life that God wants, as you learned from us, and as you are already living it. You have not forgotten the instructions we gave you on the authority of the Lord Jesus" (1 Thes. 4:1-2).

This first catechetical instruction had a definite form or pattern or "syllabus" to which St. Paul alludes in a striking passage. "You were once slaves of sin, but thank God you submitted without reservation to the creed you were taught" (Rom. 6:17). In the original Greek, "the creed you were taught" (translation of the Jerusalem Bible) reads *typon didaches*, the "form" or "pattern" or "standard" of "the teaching." When the catechumenate of the Early Church becomes visible in the historical records of the early Christian writers, it will be massively clear that this pattern or syllabus is the Trinitarian faith and the corresponding *metanoia* given to his Church by Jesus the Divine Teacher. The Jerusalem Bible is therefore quite correct in rendering *typos didaches* into the English of today as "the creed you were taught."[10]

This brings the content of the first catechetical teaching into view. It is the deposit of faith. This content can be studied in the "Jerusalem *Kerygma*," the first discourses of St. Peter as recorded in the Acts of the Apostles. St. Paul's Epistles bear witness to the extension of this same deposit of faith to the gentiles. "As soon as you heard the message we brought you as God's message, you accepted it for what it really is, God's message, and not some human thinking" (1 Thes. 2:13). "You must be rooted in Christ," he

---

Catechetical Directory, no. 83, which speaks of "the simple and objective kind of instruction which is appropriate for children"; and no. 88 on the change of method necessary with adolescents who need help in "the formation of a religious way of thinking"...by a "catechesis...which provides the rational foundations for faith." Below, pp. 108 and 110.

10. See F. Prat, S.J., *La théologie de Saint Paul* (Paris: Beauchesne, 1933), Vol. II, pp. 32-42, *"La catéchèse apostolique"*; esp. p. 35 on Rom. 6:17: *"Three* conclusions result from this text. First, the *typos didaches* is a fixed and uniform teaching, because *typos* means an 'exemplar' and a 'model'...; secondly, it is authoritative, containing God's Will for a new way of life...; thirdly, it is a rule that binds all the Churches, the preachers and teachers being obliged to conform to it in their work."

tells the Galatians, "and be built on him and held firm by the faith you have been taught" (Col. 2:6-7).

What this faith, this content of the deposit, is, becomes quite explicit in First Corinthians. "Brothers," St. Paul writes, "I want to remind you of the gospel I preached to you, the gospel that you received.... I taught you what I had been taught myself, namely that Christ died for our sins, in accordance with the Scriptures; that he was buried; and that he was raised to life on the third day, in accordance with the Scriptures; that he appeared first to Cephas and secondly to the Twelve...and last of all he appeared to me, too" (1 Cor. 15:1-8).

"I taught you what I had been taught myself."[11] Concern for this deposit of faith is the hallmark of the Church of the Apostles.

---

11. See J. N. D. Kelly, *op. cit.*, p. 10: "St. Paul...had a healthy regard for the objective body of teaching authoritatively handed down in the Church." These words of the non-Catholic professor at Oxford can be taken to specify in a general way what is meant by "the deposit of faith." This "deposit of faith," as Cardinal Joseph Ratzinger points out, is the source and origin of content in catechetical teaching. "The baptismal questioning with its Interrogatory Creed," he writes, "...is the very heart of the Roman Rite of Baptism, and corresponds to the very essence of the baptismal event as witnessed by the oldest formulas of the Sacrament which have been handed down...(Hippolytus, Ambrose, Augustine, and the Oriental Church before Gregory of Nyssa). The sacramental formula, itself based on Mt. 28:19, is the original 'Short Formulation of the Faith,' a concentrated statement of the basic structure and substantial content of the Faith which the Creed professes." J. Ratzinger, "Taufe und Formulierung des Glaubens," *Ephemerides Theologicae Lovanienses* (May 1973), p. 81. Ratzinger takes issue with Karl Rahner's view of "Short Formulations of the Faith" in his *Schriften zur Theologie*, Vol. 8, pp. 153-164. For Rahner, a "Creed" is a mere abstract summary of a theology, a doctrinal structure contrived out of mere human thinking of today. This, Ratzinger points out, "is to lose all perceptiveness regarding the original meaning of the Profession of Faith by means of the Symbol or Creed," p. 82. The relationship to the *metanoia*, the new Christian way of living, Ratzinger concludes, tends to be missing from this kind of contemporary discussion, and thus the way is barred to the renewal both of catechetical teaching and of the Sacraments: "The contemporary discussion is confined to summaries of this or that theology, and not that of the short summary of the Faith," Ratzinger, *ibid.*, p. 82. Ratzinger goes on to link this baptismal Creed with the content of catechetical instruction, with the very heart of catechetical practice in the Early Church, and with the correct procedure for the renewal of contemporary catechetical teaching. It is clear that the concept "deposit of faith" is basic and central in catechesis as the instrument and means for its Christocentrism. Cf. the *General Catechetical Directory*, no. 40. Hence it is also the

Since it is the very Word of God, since it is Jesus' own teaching both in content and in pattern, concern for fidelity in teaching it is a self-evidence. The Apostles do not go forth to "inculcate their own personal opinions and options."[12] They have a quite different concern, one which forms the very substance of the Apostolic Succession, as the Pastoral Epistles bear witness. Timothy, already ordained by the Apostle (2 Tm. 1:6), is to guard and keep safe the deposit of faith which has been entrusted to him (1 Tm. 6:20), handing it on to men fit to teach others (2 Tm. 2:2), on whom he in turn is to lay hands (1 Tm. 5:22).[13]

"It is impossible," J. N. D. Kelly concludes, "to overlook the emphasis on the transmission of authoritative doctrine which is found everywhere in the New Testament.... The references to an inherited corpus of teaching are clear enough."[14]

"Rule of Faith" in St. Irenaeus' sense, the norm of authenticity in Catechetics, and the chief criterion for evaluating syllabi and textbooks in religious education. The concept of the "deposit" is in the original Greek of the inspired text where it is denoted by the word *parathéke*, the ordinary word for something valuable committed to a trustee. For further study, see Kittel-Bromiley, *Theological Dictionary of the New Testament* (Grand Rapids: Eerdmans, 1972), Vol. 8, pp. 152-168, and for the word *parathéke*, "deposit," in particular, pp. 162-164. For the specific use of this word in the New Testament, see the exegetical studies of the Pastoral Epistles, e.g., Norbert Brox, *Le lettere pastorali* (Brescia: Morcelliana, 1970), who states his conclusion as follows, p. 348: "The *parathéke* designates the Faith insofar as it is a heritage which is handed on. It is the substance of the orthodox teaching." For helpful leads in relating the concept to contemporary catechetics, see Gino Concetti (ed.) *Evangelizzazione e Catechesi* (Milano: Massimo, 1980); Jean Galot, "Cristo Evangelizzatore e Maestro," pp. 215-227; Martino Conti, "La Chiesa, Communità Evangelizzatrice," pp. 228-251; and *passim*. See also the post-conciliar Rites for Adult and Infant Baptism, and for the Ordination of Deacons, Priests and Bishops.

12. John Paul II, *Catechesi tradendae*, no. 6; "In catechesis," he continues in the same place, "it is Christ, the Incarnate Word and Son of God, who is taught—everything else is taught with reference to him—and it is Christ alone who teaches." These words which are a directive for the last two decades of the Twentieth Century express with wonderful accuracy the way the Apostles saw and practiced the teaching of the deposit of faith in the First Century. See below, p. 213.

13. See Charles Journet, *op. cit.*, "The Apostolic Hierarchy," pp. 16-49, esp. pp. 16-17, "The Chain of Apostolicity."

14. J. N. D. Kelly, *op. cit.*, p. 8. See *ibid.*, pp.10-11: "...the documents themselves testify to the existence of a corpus of distinctively Christian teaching. In this sense at any rate it is legitimate to speak of the Creed of the Primitive Church. Nor was it something vague and nebulous: its main features were clearly enough defined. The Epistles and Gospels are, of course, rarely if ever concerned to set out

In fact, the word *Katechein*, meaning an elementary form of oral instruction, is found frequently in the Greek text of the New Testament: "catechetics," "catechism," "catechesis" and "catechumenate" derive from it. Apparently it was St. Paul who adopted this comparatively rare Greek word to denote this distinctively Christian teaching of the deposit of revelation coming from Jesus the Divine Teacher. "Paul uses this word exclusively in the sense of 'giving instruction concerning the content of the faith'.... He uses not only the common *didáskein* but also this much rarer word, hardly known at all in the religious vocabulary of Judaism, as a technical term for Christian instruction. He desires thereby to emphasize the particular nature of instruction on the basis of the Gospel. The word selected was in fact very apt to assume the exclusive sense of Christian instruction, and it finds an echo today in the word 'catechism.' "[15]

The Church of the Apostles, then, had a definite program of catechetical teaching. It held to the standard procedures of oral teaching and a form or pattern for guarding the integrity of the content. The content was divine revelation itself, received from Jesus Christ the Divine Teacher as a deposit of faith. He entrusted this divine deposit to his Church to be guarded, to be handed on by a faithful teaching, and to be developed by infallible explanations — and this all days, even to the end of time.[16]

The Successors of the Apostles and Their Catechumenate

The death of the last Apostle, sixty or seventy years after the crucifixion of Jesus, saw the Church busily carrying out its man-

---

the faith in its fullness: they rather presuppose and hint at it. Even so, it is possible to reconstruct, with a fair degree of confidence, what must have been its chief constituents." And he cites the works of C. H. Dodd together with the *Symbolforschung* of the German scholars A. Seeberg and Paul Feine.

15. J. W. Beyer, in Kittel-Bromiley, *Theological Dictionary of the New Testament, op. cit.*, Vol. III, 638-639.

16. For the official teaching of the Catholic Church on the concept of divine revelation and the process of its transmission, see the two Dogmatic Constitutions of Vatican I, *Dei Filius* (April 24, 1870), "On the Catholic Faith," and *Pastor Aeternus* (July 18, 1870), "On the Church of Christ"; and the two Dogmatic Constitutions of Vatican II, *Lumen Gentium* (November 24, 1964), "On the Church," and *Dei Ver-*

date. Its catechetical teaching program was already well established in the chief centers of the pagan Empire of Rome: from Jerusalem the Church went early to Antioch, and on to St. Paul's missionary foundations; to Rome itself, where St. Peter organized the Church; to Ephesus in the person of St. John. St. Mark, Peter's younger associate at Rome, built up the Church at Alexandria in Egypt. In each of these apostolic centers, this same program for teaching the deposit of faith was organized, wonderfully unified both in structure and in content. This "Catechumenate," as it was called, was everywhere the same, the same as it had been back to its origin in the teaching of Jesus. Wherever the Catholic Church reached and branched out from these original apostolic centers, it took root and grew by means of this same catechetical program for handing on the faith by teaching.

By late Second Century, this same Catechumenate was flourishing in secondary centers like Lyons in southern Gaul. The works of Irenaeus bear witness to its continuing fidelity in teaching the deposit of faith. Irenaeus was the spiritual grandson of St. John the Apostle. For St. John taught Polycarp in his Catechumenate at Ephesus. Polycarp became a priest himself and then bishop of neighboring Smyrna, where he as a matter of course organized his own Catechumenate. Among his catechumens was the young Greek Irenaeus, who decided upon the priesthood and the missions in the west.

In his book, *Against the Heresies,* Irenaeus gives a description of the deposit of faith which follows the doctrinal substance of what later on will be called "The Apostles' Creed." "The Church," he writes, "though dispersed throughout the whole world..., has received this faith from the Apostles and their disciples: (She believes) in one God, the Father Almighty, maker of heaven and earth, and the seas with all things that are in them; and in one Lord Jesus Christ, the Son of God, who became incarnate for our salvation; and in the Holy Spirit, who proclaimed through the prophets the dispensations of God, and the advent, and the birth from a Virgin, and the passion, and the resurrection from the dead, and the ascen-

---

bum (November 18, 1965), "On Divine Revelation." This official teaching is fundamental to the field of Catechetics and basic for understanding correctly the nature and the unity of the catechetical documents of the same Supreme Magisterium gathered into the present volume.

sion into heaven in the flesh, of the well-beloved Christ Jesus our Lord, and his Second Coming from the heavens in the glory of the Father to gather all things into one (Eph. 1:10), and to raise up anew all flesh of the whole human race."[17]

Irenaeus is firmly convinced that this deposit of faith is being handed on unaltered in the catechetical teaching of the Catholic Church. This deposit of faith constitutes the on-going Apostolicity of this same Catholic Church and provides the catechists with their Rule of Faith and Canon of Truth, concepts which Irenaeus developed to meet Gnosticism, the first great heretical challenge in the life of the Church. Irenaeus says that Christians receive this Rule of Faith in their baptism, a clear indication that he means the interrogatory form of the Apostles' Creed.[18]

Irenaeus continues in his famous passage on the deposit of faith. "The Church," he writes, "having received this preaching and this faith, although scattered throughout the whole world, yet, as if occupying but one house, carefully preserves it. She also believes these points just as if she had but one soul and one and the same heart; and she proclaims them, and teaches them, and hands them down with perfect harmony, as if she possessed only one mouth. For, although the languages of the world are dissimilar, yet the import of the tradition is one and the same.... As the sun, that creature of God, is one and the same throughout the whole world, so also the preaching of the truth shines everywhere and enlightens all men that are willing to come to a knowledge of the truth."[19]

For St. Irenaeus the catechetical teaching which hands on the deposit of faith is what later times will call "the Ordinary and Universal Magisterium." For him, there was as yet no other form of the Magisterium, for the actions of the Extraordinary Magisterium, taken to explain, defend and develop the Articles of Faith which constitute the deposit, belonged to the future in the great Ecumenical Councils still to come.[20] For St. Irenaeus and the Fathers of the Early Church generally, this Magisterium of the

---

17. Irenaeus, *Against the Heresies*, I, 10, 1; in Roberts-Donaldson (eds.) *The Ante-Nicene Fathers* (Grand Rapids: Eerdmans, 1973; reprint), Vol. I, p. 330.
18. Irenaeus, *ibid.*, I, 9, 4; p. 330.
19. Irenaeus, *ibid.*, I, 10, 2; p. 331.
20. Cf. John Paul II, *Catechesi tradendae*, no. 52: "It is on the basis of revelation that catechesis will try to set its course, revelation as transmitted by the universal magisterium of the Church, in its solemn or ordinary form." Below, p. 249.

Catechumenate, handing on the divine deposit, was Jesus Christ continuing to teach in his Body, which is the Church. It is not surprising, then, that devotion to Jesus Christ the Divine Teacher, to which Pope John Paul II alludes in the passage cited above, characterized this Early Church in a special way.

The Catechumenate becomes fully visible in the writings of the Fathers of the Church. It is everywhere the same, whether in the East with St. Cyril of Jerusalem, in Northern Italy with Saint Ambrose of Milan, or in Africa with St. Augustine. It is always an organized teaching which explains the Apostles' Creed article by article and then teaches how to deepen the threefold personal response of *metanoia* in prayer, Gospel morality and sacramental living. Let St. Augustine, in one of his homilies to his catechumens, speak for all the Fathers.

"Receive, my sons, the rule of faith which is called the Creed. When you have received it, write it on your hearts. Recite it daily to yourselves. Before you go to sleep, before you go forth, fortify yourselves with your Creed.... This is the Creed that you will be going over in your thoughts and repeating from memory. These words that you have heard are scattered throughout the divine Scriptures. They have been assembled and unified to facilitate the memory of dull mankind in order that everyone will be able to say the Creed and adhere to what he believes."[21]

Based directly on the original call of Jesus Christ to mankind, (Mk. 1:14-15), the Catechumenate of the Early Church is his teaching of the faith and its corresponding *metanoia*, extended now to the nations. It is the vital activity of Evangelization and Catechesis, the very life of the Church organized and functioning. It is the deposit of faith taught and applied in the formation of persons for living the new Christian way of life.

---

21. St. Augustine, "The Creed," translated by Sister Marie Liguori, I.H.M., in St. Augustine: *Treatises on Marriage and Other Subjects* (New York: Fathers of the Church, 1955), p. 289. For the original text, see R. Vander Plaetse (ed.) *S. Aurelii Augustini: Sermo de Symbolo ad Catechumenos*, in *Corpus Christianorum* (Turnholti: Brepols, 1969), Vol. 46, pp. 179-199; on p. 181, the editor reconstructs the Latin text of the "Apostles' Creed" used in the Church of Augustine's day, identical in pattern and substance with the formulation familiar in English today. For a convenient collection of Augustine's catechetical homilies and discourses, see Suzanne Poque, *Augustin d'Hippone: Sermons Pour la Pâque* (Paris: Cerf, 1966), in the series *Sources Chrétiennes*.

Shortly after Augustine's time St. Vincent of Lerins produced his famous "Vincentian Canon," the summational principle of the Early Church by which it expressed and implemented its concern to keep its precious deposit intact, unadulterated by human innovations, and hence faithful to Jesus Christ. For human opinions drawn from ambient philosophies and cultures do indeed come up, producing doctrinal novelties which impact upon Evangelization and Catechesis. In such a case, St. Vincent identifies the authentic and original deposit of faith as that which has been taught *everywhere* in the Church, held by *all* in the Church, from the very *origin* of the Church in Jesus' teaching of his Apostles. "In the Catholic Church," he writes, "every care should be taken to hold fast to what has been believed everywhere, always and by all." *Quod ubique, quod semper, quod ab omnibus.*[22] Commenting on this "canon," St. Vincent recalls the anxious words of the Apostolic Church to Timothy: "O Timothy, keep the deposit, avoiding profane novelties." Then he asks, "Is then religion in the Church of Christ to be incapable of progress? But surely, there must be progress and that not a little.... We must make this reservation, however, that the progress shall be a genuine progress and not an alteration of the faith. We have progress when a thing grows and yet remains itself: we have alteration when a thing becomes something else."[23] "Let, then," he continues, completing his formulation of his Canon, "understanding, knowledge and wisdom grow and advance mightily and strongly in individuals as well as in the community, in one man as well as in the Church as a whole, according to the degree proper to each age and time; but only within their own domain, that is, with the same dogma, the same meaning, the same sense."[24]

---

22. Vincent of Lerins, *The Commonitories*, I, 2; in Rudolph E. Morris transl.) *The Fathers of the Church* (New York: The Fathers of the Church, 1949), Vol. 7, p. 270.

23. *Ibid.*, I, 23; translation by Charles Journet, *op. cit.*, pp. 536-537.

24. *Ibid.*, I, 23; this is the passage quoted within Chapter IV of the Constitution *Dei Filius* of Vatican I; see John F. Broderick, S.J. (transl.), *Documents of Vatican Council I* (Collegeville: The Liturgical Press, 1971), p. 48. Beginning in 1835, the Supreme Magisterium has been making the "Vincentian Canon" more and more its own to express its growing concern in recent times for the deposit of faith. To cite only a few additional examples: Pope Leo XIII recalls it in his document (1899) on "False Americanism in Religion," the tendency to introduce new opinions into the very "doctrines in which the *deposit of faith* is contained"; St. Pius X makes signifi-

The Catechumenate did not end with the end of the Patristic Age. It changed its form, quite naturally, and continued for over a thousand years to teach and to form Catholic children by means of this same original deposit believed everywhere, always and by all. And adults beyond Christendom, from St. Boniface crossing the Rhine in the Eighth Century to St. Francis Xavier crossing the Pacific Ocean in the Sixteenth, continued to be received into the Church in the age-old way of the Catechumenate. They learned the same rudiments of the same doctrine.

Always and everywhere this Ordinary and Universal Magisterium proceeded under the supervision of the men in Holy Orders, helped by the religious and the lay catechists, and especially by the parents in family catechetics. At his ordination each bishop affirmed his resolution "to maintain the content of faith, entire and uncorrupted, as handed down by the apostles and professed by the Church at all times and places," words which clearly echo the practice of the Early Church summarized in the Vincentian Canon. Each priest likewise expresses his resolution "to exercise the Ministry of the Word worthily and with wisdom, preaching the gospel and explaining the Catholic faith." The deacons, although primarily concerned with the Ministry of Charity, likewise profess their intention to participate in this same catechetical ministry, resolving "to hold with a clear conscience to the Mystery of Faith, as the Apostle calls it, and to proclaim this faith in word and action taught by the gospel and the Church's tradition."[25]

---

cant reference to it in *Pascendi* (1908); Pope John XXIII uses its very words in his discourse (1962) opening Vatican II and giving it its orientation; as to Pope Paul VI, there is not only frequent allusion, but the *Creed of the People of God* in particular; and Pope John Paul II may be said to cite the Vincentian Canon implicitly wherever in his many discourses in various parts of the world he stresses the abiding character of the deposit of faith.

25. These quotations are taken from the present post-conciliar Rites of Ordination of bishops, priests and deacons; the Church of today, however, has received these concepts from the Early Church and has used them faithfully across all the Christian centuries. See The Roman Pontifical, *The Ordination of Deacons, Priests and Bishops* (Washington: NCCB, 1969), p. 37, p. 26 and p. 14. The fact that the very rite of ordination contains the "Vincentian Canon" of the Early Church regarding the deposit of faith is even more visible in the Latin: *Vultis depositum fidei, secundum traditionem inde ab Apostolis in Ecclesia semper et ubique servatam, purum et integrum custodire?* And the answer: *Volo.*

Always and everywhere, furthermore, the substance of this teaching has been one and the same since its origin in the call of Jesus Christ: "The time has come, and the Kingdom of God is close at hand. Repent and believe the Good News" (Mk. 1:14-15). It is first a teaching of what is to be believed, namely the Articles of Faith summarized in the Apostolic Profession; and then it is a teaching that helps them to repent and deepen their *metanoia* or conversion to God Incarnate. This repentance or *metanoia* is the new Christian way of life with its three principal activities: personal prayer, Gospel morality and Sacramental living. Thus the four areas of catechetical content, classical in the Catechumenate, come into view together with their roots in the life and work of the Divine Teacher.

The Catechumenate, carrying out the Ordinary and Universal Magisterium of the Catholic Church, is a magnificent teaching program. It is divine in origin, divine in both the simplicity and the power of its elements, and divine in its salvific purpose of forming persons unto the new way of life. At the same time, it is carried forward by frail humans who at times do not see or accomplish effectively its work and its mission. Children were sometimes given baptism as a perfunctory social enrollment, but not the reality of Christian formation based on the doctrine of the Catholic faith. Religious illiteracy, defined correctly as ignorance with respect to the very Articles of Faith which are the elements and rudiments of Christian Doctrine, sometimes affected minds over even wide regions of Christendom. And this introduces a new phase in the concern of the Church for her divine deposit.

Concern for the Deposit in Modern Times

At the opening of the modern period of universal history in the Sixteenth Century, the concern of the Catholic Church for the deposit of faith took a new turn which continues into the present Twentieth Century and provides the immediate background for the catechetical documents gathered in the present volume.

The occasion was the Protestant movement led by Martin Luther. He made use of the newly-invented printing press to capture in print the centuries-long heritage of oral catechesis by question-and-answer. History credits him with initiating the booklet for children called ever since "The Catechism." He retained the same four classical areas of content and the Christocentrism which the Ecumenical Councils of the Early Church had defended and consolidated. In other words, he did not depart from the Ordinary and Universal Magisterium regarding the first and second Articles of the Apostles' Creed. But, seeing differently the presence and the work of the Holy Spirit, Luther introduced innovational changes in the third Article regarding the Church, its Magisterium and its Sacraments.

The Catholic Church called the Council of Trent to define the truth of the faith in the points challenged by the novel opinions and at the same time to see to a better pastoral and catechetical care of souls so that they might receive the Sacraments with accurate personal knowledge regarding their nature, purpose and power for the life of Grace. To this end the Council of Trent projected a "Catechism" to be used in pastoral care "so that the faithful may be mindful of the Christian Profession which they made in their baptism, and be prepared for reading and study of the Holy Bible."[26] Seventeen years later the Council of Trent gave this project final form by mandating a printed manual for use by the living pastor and his living adult catechists as a handbook and guide in giving instruction on the content of the Catholic faith. At its close, the Council of Trent committed this project to the Holy See. The Pope set up a Commission chaired by St. Charles Borromeo to produce this manual, known generally ever since as "The Roman Catechism."[27]

Both in quality of composition and in its authoritative character this *Roman Catechism* is a unique work. It prescinds in a remarkable way from the particular innovations of the Protestant movement, proceeding to put into print the positive catechetical

---

26. Cf. A. Thiener (ed.), *Acta genuina ss. Oecumenici Concilii Tridentini* (1874), Vol. I, p. 91.

27. Published at Rome in 1566, by order of Pope Pius V. In English-speaking lands, it has often been published under the title, "Catechism of the Council of Trent." It is noteworthy that this basic and authoritative catechetical masterpiece, summing up the heritage of the Catechumenate conducted by Jesus Christ the Divine Teacher in his Body which is the Church, was out of print and unavailable through normal channels in the United States in the years of catechetical confusion which followed Vatican II. This fact illustrates negatively the immediate situation of the catechetical documents gathered in the present volume.

heritage of the Ordinary and Universal Magisterium as a whole. This is reflected not only in the content of the doctrine, but also in its division into the four areas of teaching which had been the pattern in the Catechumenate since the Apostles. These four areas are the familiar ones noted already: the explanation of the Catholic faith professed in the Articles of the Apostles' Creed; and the teaching of the *metanoia*, the threefold response in personal life: the Seven Sacraments, the Ten Commandments, and the petitions of the Our Father as the syllabus for teaching the practice of personal prayer.

Published in Latin, the Holy See directed the bishops everywhere to have it translated faithfully into the vernaculars and to place it in the hands of the pastors and their catechetical teachers. It became in this way the basic instrument for renewal of the Church. As a later Council was to say, "the moral life of the Christian people was revitalized by a more thorough instruction given to the faithful and by the more frequent reception of the sacraments."[28]

It is clear from this that the Catholic Church refused to be dislodged from the historic primacy of the living catechist, never to be displaced by the various printed and non-printed media invented in the modern age. At the same time, the best Catholic minds recognized that the production of Catechisms for children could not be left as a monopoly of the Protestant movement. The very faith itself is at stake, for such a Catechism is intended to be an elementary explanation of the Apostles' Creed, implementing "the simple and objective kind of instruction which is appropriate for children."[29] Led by St. Peter Canisius (a *peritus* at the Council of Trent), St. Robert Bellarmine and others, national, regional and diocesan catechisms were composed and published by authority of the bishops. They were put into use together with the Roman Catechism, which sustained the living teaching and explanation of the points of doctrine communicated by the catechisms in the same question-and-answer form which Luther had retained, reflecting in print the method of oral teaching prior to the printing press.

All of this bears obvious witness to the ongoing concern of the Catholic Church for the deposit of faith. These new printed tools

---

28. Vatican I, Constitution *Dei Filius* (April 24, 1870); in John F. Broderick, S.J., *op. cit.*, p. 38.
29. *General Catechetical Directory*, no. 83. Below, p. 108.

are designed to serve the deposit, to communicate it ever more efficiently and more widely, and to secure it from doctrinal innovations or omissions. The Ordinary and Universal Magisterium proceeds as the dynamic apostolicity of the Church: it holds fast by these actions of the Holy See and the bishops "to what has been believed everywhere, always, and by all." The major catechetical Encyclical of Pope Benedict XIV, *Etsi minime* (February 7, 1742) illustrates the concern for the deposit at midpoint of the Church's journey from Trent to Vatican I, at the turn into the new problematic of Spinoza, Voltaire, Rousseau and the rise of philosophical atheism. This Encyclical is entirely devoted to confirming and extending the provisions of the Council of Trent for the teaching of "the rudiments of the Catholic faith, or, as they call it, Christian Doctrine,"[30] in the parishes by the pastors and under the supervision of the bishops. Noteworthy is the historic beginning of the special catechetical apostolate of the laity in this Pope's call for the enlisting of lay catechists to assist the pastors in the parishes, "who are to hear the boys and girls giving from memory their Lord's Prayer, Hail Mary, Apostles' Creed, and other similar points of doctrine."[31]

Even more striking, and pointing forward not only to Vatican I, but also to the catechetical documents of the Twentieth Century, especially *Catechesi tradendae*, is the recognition by Pope Benedict XIV of the problems arising from the multiplicity of children's Catechisms and hence the desirability of one unifying instrument for the elementary explanation of the Apostles' Creed. "Following the footsteps of Pope Clement VIII and others among our Predecessors," he writes, "We exhort in the Lord and earnestly recommend that the Catechism composed by Cardinal Bellarmine, under mandate of the same Clement VIII, be used in teaching Christian Doctrine. It is well known that this booklet was diligently examined and approved by a Congregation of the Holy See deputed for the purpose, and that Pope Clement VIII in a decision most salutary for souls ordered it to be published. For it was his intention to provide one and the same method of teaching and learning Christian Doctrine to be observed by all from that time

---

30. Benedict XIV, *Etsi minime* (February 7, 1742), no. 2; in *Magnum Bullarium Romanum* (Luxemburg: Gosse, 1752), Vol. XVI, p. 64.

31. Benedict XIV, *op. cit.*, no. 7; p. 65.

forward. There is nothing more desirable than this kind of uniformity. There is nothing more effective or opportune for guarding in advance against the errors which can creep into the situation of such a variety of Catechisms for children. If, however, because of peculiar necessities of particular regions, some other Catechism be used, strict and watchful care must be exercised to see that it not contain, or be changed so as to contain, anything out of harmony with Catholic truth. Care must be taken, furthermore, that in such a Catechism the teachings of the faith are explained in a clear and lucid manner. If any truths are omitted, they are to be added; if there is anything redundant or superfluous, it is to be removed from the text. For a method of teaching that is brief and unequivocal helps greatly in the learning, and it facilitates the questioning when the time comes to evaluate the progress which the children have made."[32]

This document of the Holy See, standing out among many others, bears a special witness to the constant concern of the Holy

---

32. Benedict XIV, *op. cit.*, no. 17; p. 66. In par. 18, *ibid.*, Pope Benedict continues in a passage which relates directly to what St. Pius X will call "the creation of an atmosphere of unbelief," an atmosphere that was in its first beginnings at 1740, but which has been mounting to a climax in the present century. Continuing on the minimum requirements of a Catechism substituting for the Bellarmine and discussing its practical use, Pope Benedict XIV writes: "This Catechism should also contain the Acts of Faith, Hope and Charity. There must be no doubt that it is wise and correct to compose and print these prayers. If a Catechism lacks them, a revised and corrected edition is to be printed. These Acts should be brief, not verbose. In the catechetical teaching their full meaning is to be explained, as well as the nature of the virtue which they express. Because the customary practice of making these Acts is in the highest degree necessary for each person who professes the Christian Religion, their use should not be restricted and limited to a few times each year. Let each Bishop, therefore, out of concern both for his own salvation and that of his flock, legislate carefully on this matter for the pastors of his city and his diocese, as follows. After Masses on Sundays and Holy Days, before the altar, let the pastors pray these Acts of Faith, Hope and Charity in a loud and clear voice, phrase by phrase, pausing for the people to repeat the phrases after him. This will cause the faithful gradually to commit these Acts to memory, and thus they will begin the devout use of them not only on the feast days but on the rest of the days as well." *Ibid.*, no. 18; p. 66. This clearly relates to concern for the deposit of faith; and it is in fact an early perception of the religious ignorance among Catholics which the Holy See in the Twentieth Century will call "an open wound in the side of the Church." All of this forms the background for the catechetical documents gathered in the present volume. In late Twentieth Century it has become rather a commonplace to find

See for the deposit of faith. This concern is now a matter of practical pastoral practice supervised by the Holy See and the Bishops acting in concert. It is a definite procedure of teaching that makes use of the printed media which fix the heritage of oral teaching of the deposit deriving from Jesus and his Apostles. It is clear from the evidence that the Catholic Church is teaching the deposit by placing the Roman Catechism in the hands of the living pastor and his teachers, together with the brief official statements of the elements or rudiments of Christian Doctrine called since Luther's time simply "The Catechism."

A century after Benedict XIV the Church reaches the times and events which led the Holy See to convene the First Vatican Council, meeting in Rome from December 8, 1869 to the Autumn of 1870, when the outbreak of the Franco-Prussian War caused its abrupt suspension with much of its agenda left unfinished.

The First Vatican Council was able to accomplish two far-reaching actions, both explicit expressions of concern for the deposit of faith.

The first of these actions which the Council was able to complete was the publication of its two Dogmatic Constitutions, *Dei Filius* (April 24, 1870), "On the Catholic Faith," and *Pastor aeternus* (July 18, 1870), "On the Church of Christ."[33] These two

---

young Catholics on the graduate level of universities who have never heard of the Acts of Faith, Hope and Charity after sixteen years of Catholic elementary, secondary and college education. In all innocence and good will, they ask where they can obtain a copy of these Acts.

33. The immediate occasion for the calling of Vatican I was a certain kind of teaching, first noted officially in 1835, on the part of a small number of priests, mostly in Germany, on the faculties of seminaries and universities. Misled by the metaphysical substrate of modern philosophical pantheism and atheism, thinking to use that metaphysical view of reality to make the Church more successful with modern man, they began to profess cultural and historical relativism of the dogmas of the Catholic faith. These dogmas are infallibly true (so they taught), but only with a truth relative to the philosophical and scientific progress of mankind at the time of the dogmatic definition by the Church. Thus the teaching of faith, which God has revealed (so they taught) has been proposed as a matter to be perfected by human ingenuity. Development of doctrine thus becomes changed in meaning. It is clear that such an opinion is a doctrinal novelty which violates the Vincentian Canon. For in such a view, the teaching of the faith is no longer seen as a divine deposit which Jesus Christ the Divine Teacher handed over to his Spouse, the Church, to be guarded faithfully and to be explained infallibly. See *Dei Filius*, chapter four, with its third canon; John F. Broderick, S.J., *op. cit.*, p. 48 and p. 51.

Constitutions secure the foundations of catechetical teaching by establishing the nature of Divine Revelation, in the first instance, and the infallibility of the Supreme Magisterium as its channel, in the second. For if there is no transcendent personal God to speak his Word by the lips of his divine and eternal Son incarnate, then there is no "deposit of faith" to hand on by teaching, guarding and treasuring it by doing so. This would be a direct threat to Catechetics, for quite naturally it would begin to have a different content, a different pattern and form, and even a different purpose in its teaching.[34] It is significant that the very concept "Ordinary and Universal Magisterium" received formal definition in *Dei Filius:* "All those matters must be believed with divine and Catholic faith that are contained in the Word of God, whether in Scripture or Tradition, and that are proposed by the Church, either by a solemn decision, or by the ordinary and universal magisterium, to be believed as divinely revealed."[35]

The second action of Vatican I relates to this universal magisterium in its ordinary form, carried out chiefly by the

---

34. In their discussions on the floor, the Council Fathers of Vatican I cited *The Religious Future of Modern Societies*, by Earnest Renan, for its attack upon the very idea of the Creed. Renan looked forward to a new and better religion which will unite mankind "no longer in the dead letter of Creeds but in the idea of pure religion" (p. 374). This idea is the Reign of the Spirit, characterized by non-dogmatic religious acts that are personal and spontaneous. The Council Fathers recognized this accurately as a religiosity of merely human opinions on the level of natural philosophizing, not the religion of supernatural revelation. Hence Renan rejected any Creed professing faith in such a revelation as basically harmful and divisive. See J. D. Mansi, *Sacrorum Conciliorum Collectio* (Leipzig: 1926), Vol. 51, cols. 541-542 and 571-573. Renan was a former priest who was appointed to a professorship at the now-secularized University of Paris by persons hostile to the Church. Among his students was the young Father Alfred Loisy, later to become "the Father of Catholic Modernism" under Popes Leo XIII and Pius X. Loisy died in 1940 in the most abject atheism, in formal apostasy from his God and his Church. All of this touches the shadow-side of the Twentieth Century; it forms an undeniably significant part of the background for its catechetical documents from *Acerbo nimis* to *Catechesi tradendae*. This aspect of the background calls for much research. But the study of this negative dimension is beyond the scope and the purpose of the present Introduction.

35. Vatican I, *Dei Filius*, chapter 3; John F. Broderick, S.J., *op. cit.*, p. 44. Pope John Paul II in *Catechesi tradendae*, no. 52, is explicit on the same twofold division of the Supreme Magisterium: "It is on the basis of revelation that catechesis will try to set its course, revelation as transmitted by the universal magisterium of the Church, in its solemn or ordinary form." See below, p. 249.

apostolate of Evangelization and Catechesis. This action concerned the composition of a uniform catechism for children with its use to be mandated throughout the Universal Church. Thus it intended to address and solve the problem attaching to the variety of national and even diocesan Catechisms, identified by Pope Benedict XIV in the previous century. In presenting this new dimension of concern for the deposit of faith there is an altogether special guide in the person of Pope John XXIII.

On the eve of Vatican II, Pope John XXIII gave a memorable address to the parish priests of his Diocese of Rome which linked the coming Council with the field of Catechetics in a remarkable way.[36] "The success of this Ecumenical Council," he stated, "will lie in the restoration and renewal of the Universal Church. This renewal is summarized in three points: a restored fervor of religious devotion; an extensive and deep renewal of catechetical teaching; and thus a noble, model and apostolic Christian life."[37] To this end Pope John XXIII, as so many of his predecessors had done, held up the Roman Catechism to his pastors, calling it "The Summa of Pastoral Theology." Then he turned to the action of Vatican I on behalf of a universal and uniform Catechism for children, quoting from the *schema* distributed to the Council Fathers on January 14, 1870.[38]

Presented to the Council Fathers of Vatican I by authority of the Holy See, this *schema* bears the title, "On the composition and use of one small Catechism for the Universal Church." "All the members of the Church of Christ diffused throughout the whole world," it begins, "should be of one heart and one soul; hence they must likewise be unified in their lips and their language. It must be recognized, however, that a variety in approach and method of teaching the rudiments of the faith to the faithful is no slight obstacle to this unity. Hence, with the approval of this Council, We shall take care to produce a Small Catechism by Our authority, which all are to use. Thus the variety of small Catechisms will be removed for the future. In composing this Small Catechism, the Catechism of St. Robert Bellarmine is hereby proposed as a model, the one composed at the command of this Holy See, and already

---

36. See John XXIII, "L'incontro coi parroci," *AAS* (March 31, 1962), 167-175.
37. John XXIII, *ibid.*, p. 168.
38. See John XXIII, *ibid.*, pp. 170-171.

recommended to all Ordinary Bishops of the world by Benedict XIV (February 7, 1742). In the use of it, it will be necessary that priests have it in hand for explanation to the Christian people. But more than this, it must be found also in the hands of the faithful in such a form that they will be able easily to commit it to memory, to form as it were their identification and pledge for the happiness of heaven, the happiness promised to those who live by the faith."[39]

Pope John XXIII singles out this final phrase for his pastors. "What words, venerable Brothers and beloved Sons! *Identification and pledge for the happiness of heaven!* It is impossible to define better the importance of the Catechism. As the sacred canons of the Councils have repeatedly legislated, this catechetical teaching must be accomplished ahead of time in order to have a worthy reception of the Sacraments. It must be sown in the hearts, in the hearts of all the faithful. We must do this teaching tirelessly, so that the faithful can comprehend the Bible and be instructed in the Law of the Lord."[40]

After some weeks of discussion on the floor of Vatican I, the project for the Small Catechism survived intact.[41] It was brought to formal vote at the 49th General Congregation of Vatican I on May 4, 1870. Of the 591 Council Fathers present, 491 voted *placet*, approval, 56 voted *non placet*, and 44 gave approval with qualification. Of the Cardinals participating, 31 voted approval, 3 voted *non placet*.[42]

This overwhelming formal vote stands as a fact in the life of the Catholic Church. After the vote the Council turned to its second Dogmatic Constitution, *Pastor aeternus*. In the vicissitudes of the coming months, with the darkening international situation, the disciplinary decree for the Small Catechism, completed in every other respect, was left without formal promulgation when the Council was suspended (October 20, 1870) at the outbreak of the Franco-Prussian War.

---

39. See J. D. Mansi, *Sacrorum Conciliorum Collectio* (Leipzig: 1924), Vol. 50, cols. 700-701.
40. John XXIII, *op. cit.*, p. 171.
41. For the record of this discussion, see J. D. Mansi, *op. cit.*, Vol. 50, cols. 699-866, and Vol. 51, cols. 454-500.
42. For the details on the voting, see J. D. Mansi, *op. cit.*, Vol. 51, cols. 493-512; for the tabulation by name and diocese, cols. 501-512.

Thus the pastors and the faithful continued after Vatican I with the Roman Catechism together with the several national and regional Catechisms for children as the ongoing teaching aids for handing on the elements and rudiments of the deposit of faith.[43] The Christian Era was at the eve of its Twentieth Century. The Ecumenical Councils, actions of the Extraordinary Magisterium, had safeguarded the deposit of faith taught by the Ordinary and Universal Magisterium, actions which perpetuate the same meaning which the deposit had for the Apostles. The uniform Small Catechism is suspended, indeed, but not forgotten. The Teaching Church, however, is faced with deeper issues as the new Twentieth Century opens. They turn about the Dogmatic Constitutions *Dei Filius* and *Pastor aeternus*. Will all the members of the Church obey their letter and spirit, especially those who are teachers in the Church? For these Dogmatic Constitutions are designed to protect the Church from an ambient atmosphere of unbelief, as St. Pius X will phrase it, which removes any idea of a transcendent God and hence any idea of a deposit of faith. The practical effect of this atmosphere is to generate religious ignorance, ignorance of the very Articles of Faith, illiteracy with regard to the very elements of Christian Doctrine: and the atmosphere then feeds upon this same religious ignorance, growing as it grows and deepens.

Such is the thought-provoking context of catechetical teaching in the Twentieth Century, with its new dimension of concern for the deposit of faith reflected in the number of its documents which bear directly upon catechetical teaching.

CATECHETICAL DOCUMENTS OF THE TWENTIETH CENTURY

Pope John XXIII summarizes all the efforts of the Successors of St. Peter across the centuries and the bishops in communion with them when he says, "The Catechism is the constant preoccupation

---

43. The idea of one uniform Small Catechism for Catholic children universally continues to preoccupy the Church at all levels of catechetical responsibility, despite the fact that the Twentieth Century will be challenged by even more fundamental concerns for the deposit of faith, linked with the four Dogmatic Constitutions of Vatican I and Vatican II; see note 16, above. For the ongoing question regarding the suspended "Small Catechism" project of Vatican I, the 1977 Synod of Bishops should be studied in detail; and cf. especially Pope John Paul II, *Catechesi tradendae*, no. 50, below, p. 248.

of the Church."[44] This preoccupation is actually one thing with the abiding concern for the deposit of faith, born of love for its doctrine, which has been sketched above from Jesus and His Apostles to the threshold of the present century.[45] It remains to present this same concern for the deposit and this same love for its doctrine as the essential nature of the catechetical documents of this Twentieth Century and as the bond of unity between them.

St. Pius X: Acerbo nimis, 1905

Ordained in 1858, Father Joseph Sarto spent his first nine years in the priesthood as the associate pastor of Tombolo in his native diocese. Then followed a lengthy tour of duty as the pastor of Salzano. Always he was the personal catechist of his people who took pastoral care of their souls by teaching them and their children the truths of the faith summarized in the official Catechism. His teaching was effective and practical. He explained the points of doctrine in an attractive way, rooting them in the minds, wills, imaginations and lives of his hearers. Named bishop of Mantua, he continued to teach: he taught both dogmatic theology in his Seminary and he continued teaching the Catechism to his people. His pastoral letters renewed catechesis in the entire diocese, and actually contain already the substance of the *Acerbo nimis*.

Elevated to the Holy See of St. Peter as Pope Pius X, he expressed the intention and program of his pontificate in the well-known motto, *Instaurare omnia in Christo*. He himself tells us that catechetical teaching is the chief means to achieve this "renewal of

---

44. John XXIII, "L'incontro coi parroci," *AAS* (March 31, 1962), p. 169: "Di fatto, il Catechismo è la preoccupazione costante della Chiesa." This famous and venerated Pope of the late Twentieth Century continues, pp. 169-170: "In the diocesan Synods as well as...above all in the Ecumenical Councils, this solicitude takes on innumerable forms which vary according to the needs and conditions of the times. But these forms are all one and the same in their underlying principle, which is that of breaking the bread of truth for the Christian people, in a form that is simple and understandable, that can be remembered, meditated upon, and handed on in the families as a precious heritage." It would be difficult to improve upon this as a definition of the nature and purpose of catechesis, and of the Catechism as its official instrument for explaining the content of its Creed and its *metanoia*. The "Catechism," of course, is simply the printed form of the older oral catechesis, used since the invention of printing.

45. See Pius XI, *Provido sane* (1935); p. 17, below.

all things in Christ."[46] It is logical, therefore, to find him turning immediately to *Acerbo nimis*, "Handing on Christian Doctrine by Teaching," published on April 15, 1905.[47]

Acerbo nimis, the comprehensive and programmatic treatment of Catechetics for the entire Twentieth Century, is remarkable as a statement of the new Pope's personal activity and experience through a lifetime of teaching the Faith in his pastoral care of souls. At the same time it contains the essence of the Church's activity and experience in catechesis since the divine command given to the Apostles, "Go, teach all nations" (Mt. 26:20). The plan of the Encyclical is simple and forthright. The chief cause for "the decline of religion," a phenomenon which the *General Catechetical Directory* will call "The Reality of the Problem," is "ignorance of things divine." Then the Pope explains what to do about the problem. The remedy is simply to see to the effective teaching of the truths of the Catholic Faith to the children, to the adolescents, and to the adult Catholics in the parishes. In other words, *Acerbo nimis* continues to state the historic concern for the deposit of faith, but now in the very practical way of showing how to hand it on by teaching it, and of giving directions for actually doing this teaching.

---

46. St. Pius X says more than once that the renewal of catechetics is the means for achieving the goal of his pontificate, *instaurare omnia in Christo*. See, for example, his reply to an Italian bishop approving and encouraging a projected national conference on Catechetics, *Acta Sanctae Sedis*, Vol. 37 (1904-1905), p. 487: "Your proposal aims at the very goal which we have urged repeatedly. For in order to achieve the restoration of all things in Christ, that is, the re-Christianization of moral customs in public and private life, it is absolutely necessary that the doctrine and the precepts of Christ once more fill the minds and hearts of the common people."

47. St. Pius X, *Acerbo nimis: De Christiana doctrina tradenda*. For the official Latin text, see *Acta S. Sedis*, Vol. 37 (1904-1905), pp. 613-625. The Latin word *tradere*, "to hand something to another person," became a standard technical term in the Roman educational system of the classical age with the meaning of "handing on a body of doctrine to others by teaching": hence the Latin title of *Acerbo nimis* is correctly rendered by the phrase, "Handing on Christian Doctrine by Teaching." This gives likewise the most fundamental meaning of "Tradition" in the Church sent by Christ to "teach all the nations" (Mt. 28:19). See the directly related passage in *Catechesi tradendae*, no. 22, p. 227 below, where *traditio* is for some reason left untranslated by the translator of the Pope's Latin text into English. The full meaning could have been rendered as "...communicated from one generation to the next by a living, active process of handing on Christian doctrine, the deposit of faith, by teaching."

"The task of the catechist," St. Pius X writes, "is to take up one or other of the truths of Faith or of Christian morality and then explain it in all its parts..., moving his hearers and clearly pointing out to them how they are to regulate their own conduct."[48] This is the abiding heart of catechetical purpose and method, and it expresses the constant practical concern of the Catholic Church for handing on the deposit of faith. This simple, clear and practical method, centered upon the truths of the deposit one by one, is specified in detail by the letter which the Pope caused to be sent a month after *Acerbo nimis* to each pastor of his own diocese of Rome: "Each catechetical instruction is to take up a point from the diocesan catechism, explaining it by making use of *The Roman Catechism*.... It is a pleasant duty to recommend to you as a pastor the careful study of this *Roman Catechism*, produced and published by mandate of the Council of Trent, which is always to be used by the pastors in teaching the doctrine of Jesus Christ to their faithful people."[49]

Such is the divinely simple means to the end he has set up for his government of the Universal Church: this effective way of teaching the truths of Creed and Catechism is the means for restoring and renewing all things in Christ. Catechetical teaching of the deposit of faith can accomplish this renewal worldwide—and only it can do so. Addressed primarily to the bishops and parish priests of the world, St. Pius X has a clear message: there is no authentic and effective care of souls apart from the deposit of faith. Without this divine deposit, they will neither know, love and follow Jesus the Good Shepherd nor be able to receive his Sacraments fruitfully.

---

48. St. Pius X, *Acerbo nimis*, "The Catechetical Lesson Plan," below, p. 8.

49. St. Pius X, through his Cardinal Vicar, "Circular Letter, May 18, 1905, to the pastors of the diocese of Rome "On the Teaching of Christian Doctrine," *Acta S. Sedis* (1904-1905), pp. 725-727. This letter gives a rare insight into catechetical methodology: "The pastor is to see to catechetical instruction which takes a point of doctrine from this diocesan Catechism and explains it by making use of *The Roman Catechism*," p. 727. For *The Roman Catechism*, see above, pp. xxix-xxx. This union of *The Roman Catechism* in the hands of the living catechists with the elements (or "points") of doctrine as stated in the official elementary Catechisms of the Church could well be termed the classical heritage of catechesis in the Church, constituting the basic teaching activity of the "Ordinary and Universal Magisterium." See Vatican I, *Dei Filius*, c.3 (D-S 3011); the GCD, no. 119; and *Catechesi tradendae*, nos. 22, 50 and 52; below, pp. 130, 226-227, 248 and 249-250.

St. Pius X continued the fundamentally catechetical orientation of his pontificate with many documents designed to implement or encourage the catechetical renewal which he had launched. Space permits mention of only two, the two most intrinsically linked with the purpose of *Acerbo nimis*.

The first is his *Catechism of Christian Doctrine* which he published in 1905, shortly after *Acerbo nimis*. In it he addressed himself to the matter left unfinished by Vatican I, the uniform catechism for explaining the Creed and the Christian *metanoia* in their first and most simple elements. He took up the catechism of Saint Robert Bellarmine which had descended in various dioceses of Italy, re-worked it and made it law for all the dioceses of Italy. It is remarkable that he continued to work on this *Catechism of Christian Doctrine* during his years as Pope, using it himself and listening to reports returning from catechists in the field.[50] On the basis of this experience, he caused a new and final edition of his *Catechism of Christian Doctrine* to be published in 1912, with fewer points of doctrine, and with the answers expressed still more briefly and simply.[51]

The second document is the famous *Quam singulari* on the first Confession and Holy Communion of Catholic children.[52] By this measure St. Pius X launched an ongoing movement of renewal in the spiritual life of Twentieth Century Catholics. This fundamental document is of course intrinsically linked with the *General Catechetical Directory* and with the well-being of the sacramental system of the Church, as its Addendum makes clear.[53]

---

50. St. Pius X taught his own Catechism regularly in the Piazza San Damaso at the Vatican throughout his years as Pope to children living near St. Peter's. His Secretary of State, Cardinal Merry del Val, did the same thing at S. Maria in Trastevere. Both were convinced that the struggle against religious ignorance is a question of life or death both for the Church and for civil society. See A. Zulueta Marigosta, in *Gran Enciclopedia Rialp*, Vol. V, p. 389.

51. See note 55, below.

52. See Pope St. Pius X, *Quam singulari*, AAS (1910, pp. 577-583; for the English translation, see Joseph B. Collins, S.S. (trans.), *Catechetical Documents of Pope Pius X* (Paterson, New Jersey: Saint Anthony Guild Press, 1946), pp. 54-62.

53. See Paul VI, *General Catechetical Directory* (1971), "Addendum: The First Reception of the Sacraments of Penance and the Eucharist"; below, pp. 139-143. With respect to no. 4 of this Addendum, "Certain New Experiments," see the joint *Declaration* of the Congregations for the Sacraments and for the Clergy, approved by Pope Paul VI, AAS (July 31, 1973), p. 410; for the English translation, see Austin

Concern for the purity and integrity of the deposit of faith motivated all the measures which St. Pius X was forced to take in order to stop the inroads of the Modernist movement within the Church. This movement was essentially against the deposit as such, holding that "the Articles of Faith did not have the same meaning for Christians of the Early Church as they do for Christians of today."[54] The Holy See maintains abidingly, from *Acerbo nimis* in 1905 through *Catechesi tradendae* in 1979, that the truth is exactly the opposite to this Modernist teaching. This is ongoing fidelity to the deposit in the present century.

Nearing the end of his life when he published the new and final edition of his *Catechism of Christian Doctrine*, St. Pius X stressed the positive side of catechetical teaching as the constant concern of his pontificate. "From the beginning," he writes, "we devoted the greatest care to the religious instruction of the Christian people, and in particular of the children, persuaded that the greatest part of the evils which afflict the Church arises from the ignorance of her teaching and her laws. Her enemies condemn them, blaspheming that of which they are ignorant, and many of her children, knowing her doctrines and her laws only imperfectly, live as if no laws existed. Hence we have insisted frequently upon the necessity of catechetical instruction and we have promoted it everywhere to the very best of our power."[55]

Flannery, O.P. (ed.) *Vatican Council II: The Conciliar and Post Conciliar Documents* (New York: Costello Publishing Company, 1975), p. 241. This *Declaration* concludes: "After mature consideration and having taken account of the views of the bishops, the Sacred Congregation for the Discipline of the Sacraments and for the Clergy declares by this present document, with the approval of the Sovereign Pontiff, Paul VI, that these experiments, which have lasted for two years up to the end of the school year 1972-1973, should cease and that everybody everywhere should conform to the decree *Quam singulari."*

54. See D-S 3462 for this erroneous proposition condemned by the Supreme Magisterium in its document of July 3, 1907. For a comprehensive and dispassionate summary of the efforts of St. Pius X to preserve the content of catechetical teaching against this negative phenomenon, see James M. Egan, O.P., "Pius X and the Integrity of Doctrine," in Joseph B. Collins, S.S. (ed.), *A Symposium on the Life and Work of Pope Pius X* (Washington: Confraternity of Christian Doctrine, 1946), pp. 50-67.

55. St. Pius X, Letter of October 18, 1912, to his Cardinal Vicar on the new edition of the Catechism, *AAS* (1912), p. 690. This new edition has been made

Pope Pius XI: *Provido sane consilio,* 1935

Elected to the Holy See of St. Peter after the ravages of World War I were ended at last, Pope Pius XI carried the catechetical program of St. Pius X forward lucidly and vigorously.[56] In his very first months as Pope he was writing on behalf of intensified catechetical teaching. "The content of the Catechism," he says, "must be given in the form of a true teaching, as in a school, with methods suitable for reaching the noble purpose for which this teaching takes place."[57] This summarizes the thinking of St. Pius X and contains already in germ the practical directives which he himself (Pius XI) will give in *Provido sane,* directions and regulations which rightly earn him the title, "Organizer of Catechetics in the Catholic Church."[58]

Pope Pius XI took the first step on June 29, 1923, "by his own initiative out of the fullness of the Apostolic Authority," with the document entitled "On Organizing the Teaching of Christian Doctrine in the Entire Catholic World."[59] His purpose is to implement a closer contact of the Holy See with each bishop of the world with

---

available again in the years after Vatican II in English translation: Pope St. Pius X, *Catechism of Christian Doctrine* (Arlington, Virginia: Center for Family Catechetics, 1980).

56. From the beginning of his pontificate Pope Pius XI was planning the measures necessary to carry forward the catechetical renewal begun by Pius X and to consolidate it. His predecessor, Pope Benedict XV could do little, for his years were absorbed in the problems created by World War I. He did, however, publish the Code of Canon Law, begun by Pius X, in which the canons on catechetics embody the directives given in *Acerbo nimis;* and he set up a commission to carry forward the uniform Catechism projected at the First Vatican Council. This commission seems to have disappeared in the throes of the war. Research is needed on the intentions of the Holy See in its regard.

57. Pius XI, Letter of June 19, 1922; for the text, see G. Frumento, *La catechesi nei documenti della Santa Sede* (Roma: Edizioni Paoline, 1965), pp. 38-39. This letter manifests the mind of Pope Pius XI regarding catechesis, reflecting *Acerbo nimis* accurately and looking forward already to *Provido sane consilio.*

58. Pope Pius XI is generally recognized as the "organizer" and "legislator" of catechetical teaching, fulfilling the logical step forward in the catechetical renewal launched by St. Pius X; see G. Frumento, *op. cit.,* pp. 38-55, with the references.

59. Pius XI, *Motu proprio: De christianae doctrinae institutione toto orbe catholico ordinanda, AAS* (1923), pp. 327-329. This document is dated on the Feast of Sts. Peter and Paul, June 29, 1923, a date which recurs frequently for actions of the Holy See which have a special reference to the deposit of faith. It follows immediately after the *Studiorum ducem* of Pius XI, which regulated the academic

regard to catechetical teaching. To this end he establishes "a special Catechetical Office which the Apostolic See will use as its instrument for fostering world-wide obedience to its laws on the teaching of Christian Doctrine to the people and for guiding and promoting catechetical activity in the universal Church."[60] Pope Pius XI calls for all lay associations and religious congregations to assist the parish clergy in catechetical teaching. In a striking passage he urges the Catholic schools and colleges to set up special post-graduate institutes for their own graduates where they can "obtain a Diploma attesting to their competence as teachers of Christian Doctrine, Bible History and Church History."[61]

All of this catechetical activity is to be "carefully supervised by the bishops," who are directed to make a detailed report every three years on all these matters, especially regarding the catechetical diploma programs in the Catholic schools and colleges of each diocese.[62]

"We have the happy hope," Pius XI says in concluding his letter, "that these measures will bring ever more thirsting souls ever

---

order of teaching in the Church. This present document regulates a separate and distinct order of teaching, *institutio*, in the Church, the catechetical teaching of the deposit of faith as such.

60. Pius XI, *ibid.*, pp. 327-328; the Latin of this basic passage reads: "Itaque, motu proprio ac de apostolicae potestatis plenitudine, Nos apud Sacram Congregationem Concilii peculiare Officium instituimus et per has Litteras declaramus, quo velut instrumento utitur Apostolica Sedes ad urgendam toto orbe terraum obtemperationem suis legibus de populo christianae doctrinae praeceptis erudiendo: cuius Officii sit universam in Ecclesia actionem catechisticam moderari ac provehere." For the current description of the functions and competency of this Catechetical Office at Rome, see Paul VI, *Motu proprio: Pro comperto sane, AAS* October 31, 1967, pp. 910-911. In the same document, Paul VI changed the name of the Sacred Congregation of the Council to "Sacred Congregation for the Clergy," as expressing better the purpose of the Congregation. It is noteworthy that the special relationship of catechetical teaching to the priesthood is reflected in the very structure of the Holy See.

61. Pius XI, *ibid.*, p. 328. This concept of special "Catechetical" Institutes and Centers, authorized to award "Catechetical Diplomas," points forward to the *General Catechetical Directory*, no. 109; see below, pp. 124-125.

62. See Pius XI, *ibid.*, p. 329; it is significant that the bishops, in their periodic catechetical reports to the Holy See, are to specify in particular what is being done on these catechetical diploma programs which the Holy See intends Catholic schools and colleges to organize for their graduates. The academic order of teaching is to minister in this way to the catechetical order.

more widely over the earth to the inexhaustible fountains of truth and Grace, 'the water...welling up to eternal life' (Jn. 4:14), so that religious ignorance, that greatest of all the stains upon the Catholic peoples, will be washed away."[63]

This new Catechetical Office of the Holy See embarked immediately upon the remarkable procedure which produced *Provido sane consilio*. By a letter dated June 24, 1924, Pius XI consulted every bishop of the world on the state of catechetical teaching in his diocese and on the needs of the Church for greater effectiveness in carrying out this teaching. Twenty questions asking for specific and detailed information were included in the letter. Seven years were taken to gather this data from the entire world, followed by two more years to analyze the results and to compose the final outcome: the *Provido sane consilio* published significantly on the Feast of the Holy Family, January 12, 1935.

This document is a masterpiece of catechetical wisdom, eminently practical, the fruit of the experience of the Catholic Church across all the centuries since the Apostles. The careful consultation with the bishops is striking: the resulting catechetical directives adapt the catechetical heritage to the great need of the Catholic Church in the present century for an effective catechesis specifically designed to overcome the stain and the wound of religious ignorance. That the document is intended to be an instrument for practical efficacy is clear from the list of twenty-four questions appended to it to serve the actual administration, supervision and evaluation of the catechetical programs in each diocese and in its parishes.

Practical although it indeed is, the *Provido sane consilio* fairly pulses with an animating spirit, nothing other than the same love for the doctrine of the Faith and concern for the purity and integrity of the deposit which has been the constant preoccupation of the Catholic Church across the ages.

Pope Pius XI followed up this major and central document of his pontificate with a constant flow of catechetical exhortation and

---

63. Pius XI, *ibid.*, p. 329. This expression of hope on the part of the Holy See carries the vision which animated St. Pius X forward toward mid-Twentieth Century. The vigorous and worldwide renewal of authentic catechesis, handing on the deposit of faith by teaching, is intended and hoped to be the instrument for general renewal in the Church and also in civil society: *Instaurare omnia in Christo*, together with *Pax Christi in Regno Christi*, the motto of Pope Pius XI.

direction. "The Catechism," he insists, "is to be taught using all the means which good methodology provides."[64] He stressed increasingly the primary role of the priest in Catechetics, especially the parish priest.[65] Toward this end, he gave recurring attention to the teaching of Catechetics as an ecclesiastical science in the seminaries of the world, a teaching with its own proper object and syllabus. Noteworthy is his enactment of a special and stern procedure for the approval of textbooks for use in teaching Christian doctrine. The faculties of the bishops for granting the *imprimatur* are restricted in this case: it is not to be granted without a previous examination of the books in question by the Catechetical Office of the Holy See.[66]

Provido sane consilio, it may safely be said, is a major catechetical document of the Catholic Church, one which carries *Acerbo nimis* forward and which remains the abidingly valid foundation for solving the catechetical problems of the later Twentieth Century and for implementing the catechetical documents which come after Vatican II. For knowledge and love for the deposit are always the purpose, and religious ignorance is always the problem. "It is incredible," Pius XI writes in a passage which summarizes all his catechetical work, "how great is the ignorance of Christian Doctrine which the Church suffers in the present time. This is true of the faithful in whatever age group or social rank. Hence the Catechism must be given with renewed dedication, lest in a time of so much education in other fields, religious knowledge, the most important of all, alone suffer neglect."[67]

Pope Pius XII, close to Pius XI as his Secretary of State, succeeded him and ruled the Church from 1938 across the difficult years of World War II up to 1958: to John XXIII and Vatican II. In these decades of mid-Twentieth Century, Pius XII issued no major cate-

---

64. Pius XI, Circular Letter of the Catechetical Office (November 30, 1925); in G. Frumento, *op. cit.*, p. 50.

65. See G. Frumento, *op. cit.*, p. 50: "It is necessary to bear in mind that the Church, and the Church alone, has the divine mission to teach Religion, and that the priest, commissioned by the Church for this task, has a special grace from God to do this teaching fruitfully."

66. See G. Frumento, *op. cit.*, pp. 50-51, quoting the Circular Letters of the Catechetical Office dated February 20, 1925, and June 21, 1930.

67. Pius XI, "Letter to the Cardinal Archbishop of Naples," *AAS* (1928), pp. 290-291.

chetical document as such. But the catechetical renewal was a constant theme of his administration. He gave encouragement and guidelines for initiatives everywhere, always with the purpose of confirming and consolidating the provisions of Pius X and Pius XI. Space permits only one typical example of his many catechetical allocutions and letters. "The world suffers from serious evils," he writes to a Catechetical Congress of the Church in Spain, "but few have such grave consequences as the religious ignorance which has become general. Society itself has urgent need for energetic remedies for this, and the most urgent of all is the diffusion of the Catechism."[68] The lament of his predecessors over the evil of religious ignorance becomes even more explicit in Pius XII. "Religious ignorance," he told the pastors of the City of Rome, "is an open wound in the side of the Church."[69] Again and again he returned to this problem in his letters and allocutions. There is only one remedy, he urges, and that is "to intensify by every intelligent means an efficacious catechetical activity."[70] Pope Pius XII calls upon catechetical teachers, the parents of the Catholic children, and the men in Holy Orders, in that order of ascending responsibility. It is the Catholic priest who renders "the incomparable service of handing on the treasures of Christian Doctrine to the on-coming generations by forming them with the Catechism."[71] For a priest, "no time is more precious than that which he dedicates to the teaching of the Catechism."[72] "Pastors, whenever it is possible, should personally prepare their children for First Penance and First Holy Communion.... The Catechism Hour offers each pastor a fruitful occasion for contact with the young generation of his parish."[73]

Pope Pius XII, it is clear, continues the concern of the Church for the deposit of faith in a most forceful and lucid way which

---

68. Pius XII, To the National Catechetical Congress of Spain; in G. Frumento, *op. cit.*, pp. 56-57.
69. Pius XII, Discourse of March 10, 1948; in G. Frumento, *op. cit.*, p. 57.
70. Pius XII, Letter of July 20, 1949; in G. Frumento, *op. cit.*, p. 57.
71. Pius XII, Letter to the Catechetical Congress of Spain; in G. Frumento, *op. cit.*, p. 58.
72. Pius XII, Letter to the Secretary of State, July 20, 1949; in G. Frumento, *op. cit.*, p. 59.
73. Pius XII, Lenten Discourse to the Pastors of Rome, February 6, 1940; in G. Frumento, *op. cit.*, p. 59.

deserves special study in his documents. In fact, as his pontificate nears its end, he becomes ever more "catechetical," so to speak, calling for a "pastoral updating," a renewal of pastoral activity in the Church which will make catechetics ever more fruitful. Using the phrase *aggiornamento pastorale* when addressing the priests of Italy in 1956, Pope Piux XII calls for an "adaptation" of the pastoral ministry to the modern sciences, to the mentality and the problems of modern man, but above all to the living Magisterium, all, as he says explicitly, at the service of "the deposit of faith." "Our concern in this matter," he states, "is to clarify and to strengthen personal convictions on the necessity of maintaining this contact with the Magisterium of the Church in order to keep the pastoral ministry adapted to the times and to contemporary man. The Church possesses from Christ himself the resources for this ministry, namely his own truth and the presence of the Holy Spirit. Thus armed, the Church has its finger on the pulse of the times, and the faithful in turn must keep their fingers on the pulse of the Church for correct orientation, diagnosis and prognosis in our times in relationship to eternity."[74]

It is precisely this program of *aggiornamento pastorale* which Pope John XXIII took in hand from his predecessor and charged Vatican II to realize, as his opening discourse on October 11, 1962 explicitly states.[75] With this the remarkable group of catechetical documents associated with the Second Vatican Council come into view.

Pope Paul VI: The Creed of the People of God, 1968

This unique document of the living and contemporary Magisterium is intrinsically catechetical in nature. The reason is its explicit and intrinsic connection with the deposit of faith which indefectibly since the Apostles has been the formal object and the ongoing content of catechetical teaching. Pope Paul VI could not be more clear: this solemn Profession of Faith comes from "Our stead-

---

74. Pius XII, "Allocution to the Italian Clergy on the Pastoral Ministry," *AAS* (1956), pp. 707-708.
75. See John XXIII, Allocution *Gaudet Mater Ecclesia*, October 11, 1962, the official opening of Vatican II, in *AAS* (November 26, 1962), pp. 786-795.

fast will to *guard the deposit* of faith from corruption."⁷⁶ And he cites St. Paul, 1 Timothy 6:20, an explicit inspired source for the use of the phrase, "deposit of faith."

"In making this Profession," the Vicar of Christ continues, "we are aware of the disquiet which agitates certain groups of men at the present time with regard to the Faith.... We see even Catholics allowing themselves to be seized by a kind of passion for change and novelty...[giving] rise, as is unfortunately seen in these days, to disturbance and doubt in many faithful souls."⁷⁷

To understand the nature and post-conciliar catechetical importance of this document its occasion and setting must be noted. Pope John XXIII has convened Vatican II and it has already ended on December 8, 1965. The Catholic Church and indeed the world itself have had an exhilarating moment of hope for a new springtime of spiritual renewal upon this earth. Hardly had the Council ended, however, when a discordant and even ominous note sounded: in 1966 the Dutch bishops approved the publication of *The New Catechism*. Appearing immediately in several translations, it promised to catechize the whole world. But the catechesis was a subtle deviation from the Ordinary and Universal Magisterium which the Teaching Church has been carrying on since the Apostles. Faithful use of "the Catechism" had been urged frequently by all the Popes of the Twentieth Century, not for its own sake, nor because of its humble format, but because it explains the Creed in "the simple and objective kind of instruction which is appropriate for children."⁷⁸ The Dutch Catechism, however, does not explain the Creed; it sets it aside by subtly deviating its mean-

---

76. Paul VI, *The Creed of the People of God*, no. 1; see below, p. 29. For the official Latin text of this "Sollemnis Professio Fidei," see *AAS* (August 10, 1968), pp. 433-445.

77. Paul VI, *ibid.*, no. 4; see below, p. 30.

78. Paul VI, *General Catechetical Directory*, no. 83; see below, pp. 107-108. Since catechesis is the handing on of the deposit of faith by teaching, it must have an elementary level proper to children, for otherwise it could not be authentic as a form of teaching on the human scene. The elements of content on this level are the very Articles of Faith. Jesus himself stresses that adults who come to his Religion must be like the children, receiving these same elements with childlike faith. Saint Pius X in *Quam singulari* takes the predilection of Jesus for the children as his point of departure. These elements of doctrine proper to children, since they are the Articles of Faith, are the means whereby children come to him, their Creator,

ing. Since the Creed is the profession of the Apostles' faith in Jesus as our Lord, the Redeemer and Savior of all, the issue is clear. Catholics of Holland recognized it perceptively and appealed by letter to Pope Paul VI. With equal perceptiveness the Pope called for a world-wide Year of Faith in which Catholics everywhere were to renew their baptismal faith by a new and concerted use of the Apostles' Creed in teaching and in prayer. He closed this Year of Faith on June 30, 1968, by his own solemn profession of the Creed of the People of God, "in the name of all the Pastors and all the faithful..., in full communion with you all."[79]

"Without being strictly speaking a dogmatic definition," the Pope states, [this] "Solemn Profession of Faith...repeats in substance, with some developments called for by the spiritual condition of our time, the Creed of Nicea, the Creed of the immortal Tradition of the holy Church of God.... As once at Caesarea Philippi the Apostle Peter spoke on behalf of the Twelve to make a true confession, beyond human opinions, of Christ as Son of the Living God, so today his humble Successor, Pastor of the Universal Church, raises his voice to give, on behalf of all the People of God, a firm witness to the divine Truth entrusted to the Church to be announced to all nations."[80]

Thus the Pope himself clarifies the nature of this developed and contemporary Creed of the People of God. As an oak tree grows out of the small acorn, so it is that the Nicene Creed developed, just as the Nicene Creed was itself a development of the original substance of the "Apostles' Creed," the baptismal profession which the Church was sent to teach to all nations. In other words, the Creed of the People of God is the deposit of faith, stated with a

---

Redeemer and Savior. For Jesus' own forceful insistence on this matter, see Mark 10:13-14. Children appear frequently in the Gospels: Mark 9:35-36; Mt. 19:13; Mark 10:16; Mt. 15:38; Mt. 21:16; Mt. 18:2-4; Mt. 18:6; Mt. 11:25 and Luke 10:21-22.

79. Paul VI, *Creed of the People of God*, no. 7; see below, p. 31.

80. Paul VI, *ibid.*, nos. 3 and 7; see below, p. 30 and 31. Once again these catechetical documents contain the best explanation of their nature and purpose, as nos. 1-7 of this *Creed* bear witness. For a detailed theological commentary, see Candido Pozo, S.J., *Creed of the People of God* (Chicago, Illinois: Franciscan Herald Press, 1980), and for a catechetical commentary, see Eugene Kevane, *Creed and Catechetics: A Catechetical Commentary on the Creed of the People of God* (Westminster, Maryland: Christian Classics, 1978).

developed comprehensiveness in order to counter and to eliminate the errors which were beginning to spread in catechetical teaching. Putting this another way, the Creed of the People of God summarizes the content taught by the Church in her "Ordinary and Universal Magisterium."[81] It is the historic concern of the Catholic Church for her treasured deposit of faith, expressed in the times after Vatican II in the most explicit way. In a sense, it is the absolutely basic catechetical document, the one which states the doctrinal content presupposed by all the other catechetical documents of the Twentieth Century. This is why Pope John Paul II writes as follows in *Catechesi tradendae:* "In the Creed of the People of God, proclaimed at the close of the Nineteenth Century of the martyrdom of the Apostles Peter and Paul, my predecessor Paul VI decided to bring together the essential elements of the Catholic Faith, especially those that presented greater difficulty or risked being ignored. This is a sure point of reference for the content of Catechesis."[82]

Pope Paul VI affirmed the same in his allocutions, pointing to the Creed as the abiding canon of truth and rule of faith for catechists. "Do not think," he teaches in a typical passage, "that you have the Faith if you do not adhere to the content of the Faith, namely, to the Symbol or Creed which is the Church's synthetic summary of the truths of the Faith. Do not think you can renew religious life or approach those who stand afar by minimizing or deforming this precise teaching of the Church. Do not believe that a docile acceptance of this teaching humiliates thinking or stops research or closes the door to progress in Christian knowledge. Today mention is often made of the *kerygma,* namely the proclamation of the Gospel truths which bear Christian salvation to mankind. Know how to see the unity of that proclamation with the Catechism taught by your parish priest, the unity of divine revelation and the Creed which professes divine faith: and hold yourself jealously and joyfully attached to that didactic and liturgical formulation of the doctrine of the Church. To summarize all that we want to say to you we shall borrow the words of that incomparable

---

81. For the defined doctrine of the Church on "the Ordinary and Universal Magisterium," see Vatican I, Constitution *Dei Filius,* Chapter III (D-S, no. 3011); and see John Paul II, *Catechesi tradendae,* no. 52, below, p. 249.

82. John Paul II, *Catechesi tradendae,* no. 28; see below, pp. 230-231.

bishop, teacher and pastor, St. Ambrose, when he was explaining the Creed to his catechumens just as every good catechist does: 'In this teaching we are to add nothing and subtract nothing. For this is the Creed which the Holy Roman Church holds and professes, that Roman See of the first of the Apostles from which he continues to hand on our common and universal faith.' "[83]

Shortly after giving the Church this Creed of the People of God, Pope Paul VI reflected upon its very idea in a masterful summary. "A profession of faith cannot be other than a summary, a 'symbol' as it is called in traditional theological language, a formula, a *regula fidei* ("rule of faith") containing the main truths of faith in terms authoritative yet as far as possible condensed and abbreviated. From the earliest days of the Church there was a synthesis of fundamental dogmas of doctrinal teaching which the candidates for Baptism had to learn and recite from memory. The use of this teaching method probably originated in Rome; we have a record of it at the beginning of the third century in the so-called 'apostolic tradition' of Hippolytus which consisted in a kind of interrogation such as is still used in the baptismal liturgy (cf. DS 10). It was believed that this text went back to the Apostles, whence our 'Apostles' Creed,' as it is called, and therefore it enjoyed great credit. St. Ambrose saw in it the authentic tradition as being what the Roman Church always safeguards and preserves."[84]

This fundamental catechetical document, the Creed of the People of God, especially when taken together with the explanatory allocutions of Pope Paul VI and the *Catechesi tradendae* of John Paul II, makes it clear that the deposit of faith is the very substance and content of catechesis. This deposit *is* the Creed together with the *metanoia* or conversion which applies the Catholic Faith to life

---

83. Paul VI, General Audience (May 31, 1967); in Discours du Pape, *Le Catéchisme: Comment l'enseigner?* (Saint Cénéré, France: "Éditions Saint-Michel, 1972), pp. 150-151.

84. Paul VI, General Audience (July 3, 1968); in E. Kevane, *op. cit.*, pp. 171-172. In this same allocution, the Pope states what he wishes the result of the *Creed of the People of God* to be in the Catholic Church: "We must all set ourselves to renewed serious study of our religion, and we hope that in every country there will be a new and original flowering of religious literature." See *ibid.*, p. 173. For the identity of Pope Paul's concern for the deposit of faith with that of St. Pius X, see the allocution of January 19, 1972, *ibid.*, p. 205-208, especially p. 207 where the documents of St. Pius X are cited.

by personal prayer, Gospel morality and sacramental living. The Creed *is* the deposit of faith, expressed by the Church and professed by the Church. It is the source of content and at the same time the basic syllabus or pattern for the catechetical teaching which all the other catechetical documents of the Twentieth Century specify and guide. It is that abiding doctrine, taught by the Ordinary and Universal Magisterium, to which Pope John XXIII alluded explicitly when he opened Vatican II and gave it its orientation and purpose. This provides the link with the next document, the one which came directly from Vatican II.

Pope Paul VI: General Catechetical Directory, 1971

The *General Catechetical Directory* stands at the center of this cluster of Twentieth Century catechetical documents of the Supreme Magisterium of the Catholic Church. It is the most basic of them, the one to which all the others relate. It came into existence by mandate of Vatican II through a process much like that which produced *Provido sane consilio.* The very mention of Vatican II evokes the figure of Pope John XXIII, the most "catechetical" of all contemporary Popes, St. Pius X and perhaps John Paul II alone excluded.[85] In a very real sense the *General Catechetical Directory* belongs to John XXIII and his Council, even though it was completed and published by Paul VI. It derives most directly from the original inspiration of John XXIII in calling Vatican II, and reflects with precision the pastoral character which he wished the Council to have. To place the *General Catechetical Directory* properly in its setting, therefore, one must first see John XXIII as the great catechetical priest which he was, and then look into the manner and purpose with which the *Directory* came out of Vatican II.

The short five-year pontificate of John XXIII was full of concern for the deposit of faith; his numerous documents on the teaching of the faith are abidingly practical and helpful for catechists, as a sampling will show. "The bishop and all his priests working with him," he said at the opening of his pontificate,

---

85. See G. Frumento, *op. cit.,* pp. 263-271 for a chronological listing of the catechetical documents of Popes in the present century. For Pius XI, 40 are listed in 17 years; for Pius XII, 32 in 19 years; for John XXIII, 40 in 5 years.

"express the first characteristic of the pastoral mission of Church, the teaching of Sacred Doctrine. And this takes place by means of a catechesis that is strong, illuminating and attractive to those who receive it."[86] "The first and weightiest responsibility of the Sacred Hierarchy is that of securing the continuing presence of the Word of God in the world. This is done by means of the proclamation and the teaching of revealed truth."[87] These words look forward to the Synods of Bishops and the documents on Evangelization and Catechesis. John XXIII held up the Curé of Ars as "the tireless catechist" who fulfilled what Trent calls "the first and greatest duty of the priest," the point so stressed by Pius X.[88] At the canonization of St. Gregory Barbarigo, Pope John XXIII praises the new Saint as the apostle of catechesis. "His Catechism was that of St. Robert Bellarmine," he says, "and he saved souls by breaking the bread of Christian Doctrine for them.... The Catechism was for him an exquisite form of charity for the people."[89] A year later he gives the same praise to a Religious Sister, at the canonization of St. Bertilla, "who treasured the Catechism given her by her pastor when she was a child, reading and studying it continually and becoming a lifelong teacher of it to others.... The learned Cardinal St. Gregory Barbarigo and this humble daughter of the same Venetian soil complement each other in their love for the Catechism."[90]

Pope John XXIII has no reluctance about the Catechism. He wants it to be used, used properly with the latest and best methodology, because its doctrine witnesses to Jesus. He knows that children cannot come to Jesus apart from this doctrine which witnesses to him. He speaks of the Catechism with remarkable frequency, defines its nature and function lucidly and encourages its proper use throughout the documents which record his daily ministry. He connects it directly with the concern of the Church for

---

86. John XXIII, Discourse at the Lateran Basilica (November 23, 1958); in G. Frumento, *op cit.*, p. 68.

87. John XXIII, Allocution (September 25, 1960); in G. Frumento, *op. cit.*, p. 69.

88. See John XXIII, Encyclical Letter on the Centenary of the Curé of Ars (August 1, 1959); in G. Frumento, *op. cit.*, p. 92.

89. John XXIII, Discourse at the Canonization of St. Gregory Barbarigo (May 26, 1960); in G. Frumento, *op. cit.*, p. 93.

90. John XXIII, Discourse at the Canonization of St. Bertilla Boscardin (May 11, 1961); in G. Frumento, *op. cit.*, pp. 94-95.

the deposit of faith: "The Catechism is the constant preoccupation of the Church," he explains to the Pastors of Rome in a passage cited at the outset of this Introduction to the Twentieth Century catechetical documents.[91] Catechesis, he tells his Pastors on another occasion, means "explaining the truths contained in the Catechism in an organic and persuasive way.... It must embrace the whole: faith, morality and sacramental liturgy, in order to give solid nourishment to the people so that from intellectual conviction each person passes to the practical living of the teaching."[92] As St. Pius X before him, John XXIII wants the best and most effective methods to be put into service when teaching the truths of Creed and Catechism. "An instruction which would limit itself to a mere learning of the formulas of the Catechism and the fundamental precepts of Christian morality, without moving the soul and the will to live according to that doctrine, would run the grave risk of giving inert members to the Church, whereas the true profession of the Faith creates a new man who gives a supernatural meaning to all the activities of his life."[93] Christian doctrine and Christian life are never separated by John XXIII, let alone placed in some kind of artificial opposition, a point which John Paul II will stress in *Catechesi tradendae*. It is this same intrinsic correlation of doctrine and life that John XXIII urges upon priests: "Every homily and sermon should be a form of catechism, of catechetical teaching."[94] Writing to a catechetical Congress in his own former Archdiocese of Venice, John XXIII gives the definition and purpose of catechesis and refers to its instrument as "The golden book, the Catechism." "Catechesis is the systematic and complete teaching of the divine revelation handed on in the Church, in order to make it ever better known and applied ever more deeply in personal living.... It aims at forming convinced Christians who know their faith and put it into practice.... Reflection on the great realities of Christianity,

---

91. See note 1, p. xiii, above.

92. John XXIII, Discourse to the Pastors of Rome (February 13, 1961); in G. Frumento, *op. cit.*, pp. 70-71. John XXIII insists in his various catechetical discourses on "a systematic and organic teaching," the same as John Paul II in *Catechesi tradendae*, nos. 21 and 22; see below, pp. 226-227.

93. John XXIII, Encyclical *Principes pastorum*, dated November 28, 1959, *AAS* (December 10, 1959), pp. 833-864; for the passage quoted, p. 850.

94. John XXIII, Discourse to the Pastors of Rome (February 22, 1962); in G. Frumento, *op. cit.*, pp. 72-73.

summarized in that golden book called the Catechism, will certainly lead to the fruit of interior renewal."[95] Hence in his weekly allocutions John XXIII persistently urges the study of the Catechism. "Beloved sons! The Catechism, that small book, I love to stress, is the summa of divine truth and divine love. For each one of you it is your guide in the present and the future.... All my life I have encouraged the study of the Catechism...always urging both priests and laity to fulfill this sacred duty, the duty of teaching and instructing in the doctrine of Christ."[96]

Many additional instances could be cited. But perhaps these suffice to reveal the pastoral heart of John XXIII, a pastor who brings souls to Christ by means of the deposit of faith, expressed in the Creed which professes him, and communicated by use of the Catechism which explains this same credal deposit and applies it to life. It is this dimension of John XXIII which led to the calling of Vatican II as a pastoral Council and which inspired his now-famous opening discourse on October 11, 1962.[97]

"The greatest concern of the Ecumenical Council is this," Pope John XXIII told the assembled Council Fathers, "that the sacred deposit of Christian doctrine should be guarded and taught more efficaciously.... The salient point of this Council is not, therefore, a discussion of one article or another of the fundamental doctrine of the Church...which is presumed to be well known and familiar to all. For this a Council was not necessary...[but] it is necessary that this certain and unchangeable doctrine, to which the obedience of Faith must be given, be studied thoroughly and explained in the way for which our times are calling. For the deposit of faith in itself, namely the truths which form the content of our venerable

---

95. John XXIII, Letter to the Catechetical Congress of Venice (April 22, 1961); in G. Frumento, *op. cit.*, pp. 86-87.

96. John XXIII, Allocution to pilgrims at St. Peter's (December 8, 1958); in G. Frumento, *op. cit.*, pp. 74-75.

97. Pope John XXIII composed a prayer for all the Catholics of the world to use together with himself in preparing for Vatican II. See G. Frumento, *op. cit.*, p. 79. This prayer beseeches God that the Council "will lead to a diffusion of the light and power of the Gospel in human society; and that through the Council all men may come to a deeper knowledge of the doctrine taught by the Church." These two aspirations are the essence of evangelization and catechesis, the subject of the future Synods of Bishops and the documents *Evangelii nuntiandi* and *Catechesi tradendae*. See above, p. xxxv, for the way John XXIII linked Vatican II as a whole with the catechetical apostolate.

doctrine, is one thing, and the way in which it is expressed is another thing, *eodem tamen sensu eademque sententia*, but nevertheless with the same meaning and the same sense."[98]

These words bind Vatican II to Vatican I, which uses the same phrase in its solemn definition against historical relativism, and to the Rule of Faith in the catechumenate of the Early Church which St. Vincent of Lerius summarized in his canon.[99] It is clear that Pope John XXIII intended Vatican II to minister to a more effective teaching of the deposit of faith to contemporary man. There is to be no change in the Faith itself, no change in its interpretation: the meaning is to abide so that the Apostolicity of the Church may remain intact. John XXIII reflects to a high degree the ongoing concern of the Catholic Church for the deposit of faith.[100]

The Second Vatican Council addresses itself to catechetical teaching in *Christus Dominus*, the "Decree on the Bishop's Pastoral Office in the Church," no. 44: "A Directory...should be compiled for the catechetical instruction of the Christian people in which the fundamental principles of this instruction and its organization will be dealt with and the preparation of books relating to it."[101]

---

98. John XXIII, "Gaudet Mater Ecclesia," *AAS* (November 26, 1962), p. 792.
99. See above, notes 22, 23, and 24.
100. When he closed the Council, Pope Paul VI referred to the fact that the Documents of Vatican II had come through the stresses and crosscurrents of the four years 1962-1965 unblemished in their fidelity to the deposit of faith. See his allocution *Publica haec sessio* to the Council Fathers on November 18, 1965; in *L'Osservatore Romano—Italian Edition* (November 19, 1965), p. 1: "Fidelity is their characteristic.... This word...*aggiornamento*, which described the goal of Pope John XXIII, certainly did not have the meaning for him which some try to give it, as if it allowed for the 'relativization,' according to the spirit of the world, of everything in the Church—dogmas, laws, structures, traditions." The key phrase of this passage in the Latin spoken by Pope Paul VI reads: *quasi accommodatione illa liceret secundum "relativismi" placita.*
101. *Christus Dominus*, no. 44, "Decree on the Pastoral Office of Bishops in the Church;" in Austin Flannery, O.P. (ed.) *Vatican Council II: the Conciliar and Post Conciliar Documents* (Collegeville, Minnesota: The Liturgical Press, 1975), p. 590. For the basic statement on the apostolate of a bishop in catechetical teaching, see *Christus Dominus*, no. 14, with the *General Catechetical Directory*, no. 17, where this key catechetical concept of Vatican II is quoted: "The catechetical form...of the ministry of the word...'is intended to make men's faith become living, conscious and active, through the light of instruction.'" See below, p. 60.

This mandate was taken up promptly after the Council ended by the Catechetical Office of the Holy See, now well established since the pontificate of Pius XI. The methods which produced *Provido sane* were followed again: consultations with the bishops of the entire world, linked with intensive and expert revisions by special commissions.[102] The resulting *General Catechetical Directory* was made public in Rome on Easter Sunday, April 11, 1971: "The Supreme Pontiff, Paul VI, approved this *General Directory* together with the Addendum, confirmed it by his authority and ordered it to be published."[103]

Once again, the document itself is its own best evidence regarding its nature and purpose. What is its authority? The passage just cited provides the answer. Is it binding? The "Foreword" gives the answer: "Those things which are said about divine revelation, the criteria according to which the Christian message is to be expounded, and the more outstanding elements of that same message, are to be held by all. On the other hand, those things which are said about the present situation, methodology, and the form of catechesis for people of differing ages, are to be taken rather as suggestions and guides, for a number of them are of necessity taken from the human sciences, theoretical as well as practical, and these are indeed subject to some evolution."[104]

In other words, the *General Catechetical Directory* is exactly what its title indicates: it is a *directory* on the methods of carrying out "the catechetical instruction of the Christian people." It tells how to do this instruction, as a telephone directory tells how to find a number or a city directory an address. It states "the fundamental principles of this instruction," and it outlines "the fundamental principles of its organization." These are precisely the points mandated by Vatican II.[105]

It follows from the "Foreword," furthermore, that the *General Catechetical Directory* contains within itself two distinct levels of catechetical methodology. The first functions on a higher spiritual

---

102. This process was completed under the supervision of the American Cardinal, John J. Wright, as Prefect of the Sacred Congregation of the Clergy and its Catechetical Office of the Holy See.
103. Paul VI, *General Catechetical Directory*; see below, p. 144.
104. Paul VI, *General Catechetical Directory*, "Foreword"; see below, p. 42.
105. Vatican II, *Christus Dominus*, no. 44; see note 101, above.

level, actually supernatural, for it consists of methodological principles which are intrinsic to the revealed deposit as such: if these are disregarded or used ineptly, the deposit of faith is not handed on intact. It is not communicated in its own proper supernatural mode. Such a catechesis fails in the precise function defined by Vatican II: "The function...of catechetical instruction is to develop in men a living, explicit and active faith."[106] This faith, of course, is *divine* faith, in the full theological meaning of the term. This is the dimension of catechesis to which this first, or supernatural dimension of methodology ministers. The *General Catechetical Directory* treats of it in Parts Two and Three, on the principles governing "The Ministry of the Word" and the handing on of "The Christian Message."[107] These aspects of method, the *General Catechetical Directory* says pointedly, "are to be held by all."

The second dimension of catechetical methodology functions on the natural level. Here it makes use of all the principles, methods and organizational procedures of human teaching in the natural sciences and disciplines, calling them into the service of a higher body of content, the revealed deposit itself. The *General Catechetical Directory* discusses this natural level of catechetical methodology in Parts Four, Five and Six.[108]

What then of content? Does the *General Catechetical Directory* contain the content which is to be taught, namely the Articles of Faith together with their application to life in the triple *metanoia* of personal prayer, Gospel morality and sacramental living? The answer must be studied carefully, given precisely and applied correctly, lest catechesis suffer from ambiguity and minister to religious ignorance instead of dispelling it. Again it is the document itself which bears the needed witness. Some elements of the deposit

---

106. Vatican II, *Christus Dominus*, no. 14; see Flannery, *op. cit.*, p. 571.
107. See Paul VI, *General Catechetical Directory*, nos. 10-16; below, pp. 54-96.
108. *Ibid.*, nos. 70-134; below, pp. 97-138. It should be noted that Part One, "The Reality of the Problem," *General Catechetical Directory*, nos. 1-9, is likewise devoted fundamentally to methodology, that of "fostering an appropriate re-evangelization of men" (*General Catechetical Directory*, no. 6; see *General Catechetical Directory*, no. 2). St. Pius X in his seminal and pioneering way recognized this special challenge to catechetical methodology, as a perusal of his *Catechism of Christian Doctrine* makes clear. There is furthermore a direct correlation between this Part One of the *General Catechetical Directory* and the *Evangelii nuntiandi* of Pope Paul VI.

of faith are indeed present in the *General Catechetical Directory*, in Part Three, Chapter II, "The More Outstanding Elements of the Christian Message."[109] But in no. 36, the *Directory* is clear and explicit. "The content of the faith" is indeed dealt with, but "this second chapter is by no means intended to set forth each and every one of the Christian truths which constitute the object of faith and of catechesis."[110] The point of view is methodological: this chapter identifies "features...of the saving message...which must be brought out more clearly in a new, adapted catechesis which pursues its goal faithfully."[111] The *General Catechetical Directory* knows where "the Christian truths which constitute the object of faith and of catechesis" are to be found: "The ordinary or extraordinary Magisterium of the Church provides for this point authoritatively by its public pronouncements."[112]

---

109. See Paul VI, *General Catechetical Directory*, nos. 47-69; below, pp. 79-96.

110. *Ibid.*, no. 36; below, pp. 70-71.

111. *Ibid.*

112. Paul VI, *General Catechetical Directory*, ibid. This Ordinary and Universal Magisterium also provides the light for catechists to follow regarding "the truths of the faith which today are being more sharply denied or neglected." See also the "Foreword" (below, p. 42): "the errors which are not infrequently noted in catechesis today." Perhaps the most subtle of these errors arises from a failure to take proper account of the intrinsic relationship between a "Catechetical Directory" and "the deposit of faith" and its " Articles of Faith" professed at Baptism and taught in catechesis by the Church. Do the Articles of Faith have to be in a Catechetical Directory? Here one must distinguish between the theoretical and the practical order. For purposes of study and to assist in the preparation of catechisms, a "Catechetical Directory" can of course be prepared, abstracting from the deposit of faith which other documents, such as the *Creed of the People of God* contain *per se* and *ex professo*. Since catechesis is a form of teaching, it is a practical process that unites a specific content with a proper method. In the practical order of catechetical teaching, therefore, the methods treated in the *General Catechetical Directory* must be united with the Articles of Faith and must function at their service. What can be separated in the abstract and theoretical order must be kept united in the concrete and practical order. "Distinguish in order to unite," as Jacques Maritain stated it in the title of his masterpiece on *The Degrees of Knowledge*. Once again, therefore, it is clear that the catechetical documents of the Holy See must be seen in union with each other and not isolation from each other. Otherwise, the *General Catechetical Directory* can be diverted to a great bustle of methodological activity which does not minister effectively to the handing on of the deposit, the Articles of Faith, by teaching. In such a case it would be used, or rather abused, as an umbrella for approaches in religious education characterized by the real absence instead of the

It is clear, then, that the *General Catechetical Directory* was never intended to be taken in isolation. [113] It gives the principles and methods for the ministry of the word: it specifies the "ministry," but presupposes that the Word of God, the deposit of faith, will be received from its own sources in order to be served in all its purity and integrity by "a new, adapted catechesis which pursues its goal faithfully." The operative word here is *faithfully:* from the beginning to end, the *General Catechetical Directory* is part of one seamless robe in catechetical doctrine and practice in the Catholic Church. It points to the Creed of the People of God for its doctrinal content, to *Acerbo nimis* for its heritage, to *Provido sane* for its organization, to *Evangelii nuntiandi* and *Catechesi tradendae* for right attitudes on the part of those who implement its methods. It does not stand catechetically alone in the present century. Quite the contrary. It stands fully in the line of all these documents, and bears witness once more to that constant concern of the Church since the Apostles that the deposit of faith be handed on by "catechesis which pursues its goal faithfully." Quite simply, the *General Catechetical Directory* is worthy of John XXIII and of his Council's mandate. It ought to be used with understanding of its nature and purpose, and with love for the content which it wishes to serve.

Pope Paul VI: Evangelii nuntiandi (1975)

This document came forth from the Synod of Bishops, a new organ of the Holy See for the government of the Universal Church. To understand the background and significance of this official treatise on Evangelization for the deposit of faith, it is necessary to consider briefly the Synod itself.

---

real presence of the deposit of faith. In such a situation, religious ignorance and religious illiteracy must necessarily result, especially among children. The *General Catechetical Directory*, no. 36, indicates the remedy briefly in its golden rule for catechists: "The ordinary or extraordinary Magisterium of the Church provides for this point authoritatively by its public pronouncements." See below, p. 71.

113. Even worse than isolating the *General Catechetical Directory* from the other catechetical documents of the Holy See would be the supplanting of it by ambiguous or incomplete national directories, themselves in turn supplanted by "commentaries" slanted away from the handing on of the deposit of faith by teaching. Such a phenomenon would frustrate the renewal of catechesis in the Twentieth Century by a positive deepening of religious ignorance and illiteracy.

Pope Paul VI had conducted two sessions of Vatican II in 1963 and 1964, a matchless experience of the need of the Universal Church for an organ to help implement her world-wide unity of purpose and teaching. To this end, as the fourth and final session of Vatican II approached, he constituted the Synod of Bishops by the document *Apostolica Sollicitudo* dated September 15, 1965.[114]

The very title, "Apostolic Solicitude" seems to point toward the constant concern for the deposit of faith which characterizes the catechetical life of the Church. This comes clearly into view when the two documents on Evangelization and Catechesis are seen as the first fruits of the Synod of Bishops.

But this concern for the deposit is linked even more explicitly to the Synod by Pope Paul VI in his allocution on September 29, 1967, addressing this historic first meeting of the new entity in the life and government of the Church. Calling the Synod of Bishops "an admirable sign of that communion" which unites the Churches governed by the Pastors assembled before him, Paul VI sees "the Holy Catholic Church coalescing from this communion in a hidden but true way into one firm, closely-knit structure."[115] Although the Synod of Bishops is not endowed with the solemn authority proper to the Ecumenical Council, Paul VI continues, it does nevertheless carry into practice certain of the more important proposals of Vatican II. "And the first of these concerned the Catholic Faith itself, that it be safeguarded and confirmed in its integrity, its power, its progress and its internal coherence, with account taken of its historic teaching process. Furthermore, the Council intended that the Catholic Faith be recognized as the necessary foundation of the Christian life, and as the very cause and supreme attribute of the Church herself."[116] Then Paul VI cites the words of John XXIII when he opened Vatican II and gave it its orientation and purpose.[117] "This concern for the faithful preservation of Christian doctrine," Paul VI continues, "which was given such a solemn declaration at the beginning of Vatican II, must continue abidingly in these times which have followed upon the same Council. Indeed,

---

114. See Paul VI, *Apostolica sollicitudo*, *AAS* (October 30, 1965), pp. 775-780.

115. Paul VI, Discourse opening the first Synod of Bishops, *AAS* (November 20, 1967), p. 963.

116. Paul VI, *ibid.*, p. 965.

117. See above, note 98.

those who have received the mandate in the Church of God to propagate the Gospel message and to teach and guard the deposit of faith must do so even more vigilantly because the dangers for this same deposit have become both more numerous and more serious. In fact, we must say these dangers have become immense because the general mentality of the day is alienated from religion. But even more so because of a particular reason full of deceit: the fact that in the very bosom of the Church works of not a few teachers and writers have been published, which, while proposing to express Catholic teaching in new ways and modes, nevertheless frequently desire more to accommodate the dogmas of the Faith to profane patterns of thought and speech than to obey the norms of the Church's Magisterium. It results from this, and it is an opinion widely disseminated, that the principles of the true doctrine may be neglected, and that each person by private judgment and according to natural propensity may select what each one wishes from the truths of the Faith, and reject the rest."[118]

The Successor of St. Peter continues this explicit expression of concern for the deposit of faith by rejecting "this kind of review of the sacred heritage of the Church's doctrine" in terms of a new hermeneutic producing a new meaning "far from the genuine tradition of the Church, with its reverence for the Word of God." Paul VI reasserts the formal motive of faith, namely the assent to the teaching of the Church on the authority of God revealing, and not on the basis either of philosophy, or of the behavioral sciences, or of a consultation regarding current opinion. And he cites St. Paul, Galatians, 1:6-9: "Even if an angel from heaven...."[119]

Then Paul VI gives the Synod of Bishops its specific purpose and charge. "We wish to confirm our own faith, insofar as we are teachers, witnesses and pastors in the Church of God, so that our faith may appear humble, sincere and authentic in the sight of the one Supreme Head of the Church who is the living invisible Christ. And we want to confirm the faith of all our sons in Christ, but especially the faith of those who study religion and theology. May they come to a renewed and vigilant insight regarding the certitude

---

118. Paul VI, *AAS* (November 30, 1967), pp. 965-966.

119. See Paul VI, *ibid.*, p. 966. This statement by the Pope seems to raise a serious question about certain types of "consultation" when the deposit of faith is concerned.

and the changelessness of the doctrine of the Church. May they thus give wise assistance in developing the sacred sciences and at the same time in keeping Catholic teaching firmly inviolate."[120]

It has seemed necessary to quote this lucid expression of concern for the deposit of faith at some length, for it is as it were the founding charter of the Synod of Bishops, the necessary background for understanding both *Evangelii nuntiandi* and *Catechesi tradendae,* and the prerequisite for recognizing the bond of unity between all the catechetical documents of the Church in the present century. The Synod of Bishops becomes visible as a standing and organized manifestation of the concern of the Holy See for the deposit of faith. It is intended to be a practical instrument for teaching and guarding the Catholic Faith on an effective world-wide basis. The unity of the Church is its precious deposit, and the deposit effects and manifests the unity. The living unity of the Church results from the ongoing communication of the deposit of faith by the mutually interrelated dynamic processes of Evangelization and Catechesis.

The document *Evangelii nuntiandi* becomes fully intelligible in the light of the foregoing. Its very nature as an "Apostolic Exhortation" fulfills the primary function of the Petrine office in the Church: "Confirm your brethren" (Luke 22:32). Once again, the document itself contains the best explanation of its nature and purpose in nos. 1-5.[121]

Concern for the deposit of faith is implicit throughout, and explicit in no. 15: "The Church is the depositary of the Good News to be proclaimed..., the teaching of the Lord and the Apostles.... The sources of grace have been entrusted to her. It is the content of the Gospel, and therefore of evangelization, that she preserves as a precious living heritage, not in order to keep it hidden but to communicate it."[122]

---

120. Paul VI, *ibid.,* pp. 966-967.
121. See Paul VI, *Evangelii nuntiandi,* nos. 1-5; below, pp. 145-148.
122. See Paul VI, *Evangelii nuntiandi,* no. 15; below, pp. 154-155. In his text the Pope cites 2 Cor. 11:28; 1 Tm. 5:17; 2 Tm. 2:15; 1 Cor. 2:5. These passages are central to "the deposit of faith" as a biblical concept. For this same concern in succinct contemporary statement, see *Evangelii nuntiandi,* no. 65, "The Unchangeable Deposit of Faith," p. 189 below; and *ibid.,* no. 25, p. 161 below.

At the very heart of this document is Part III, "The Content of Evangelization," nos. 25-39.[123] This is a comprehensive and authoritative statement of what the deposit of faith is. But it is not given in the form of the Creed. It is rather the substance of the Creed restated for modern man, the content of Evangelization and Catechesis as the basis for true social justice and authentic human promotion. Only the Catholic Church can realize the integral promotion of human persons, for only the Church has and gives Jesus Christ, "the mediator and fullness of all revelation."[124] Thus in these paragraphs the Church is the true Prophet for modern man, standing as God's authorized Witness to "The Redeemer of Man," over against the false prophets who politicize the Christian message, reduce it to the merely horizontal and temporal, and subject it to the dialectic of the dichotomies.[125]

Evangelii nuntiandi, in summary, presents the deposit of faith in the mode of a herald of the revealed message, addressing modern man at the point where his needs are most acute and his temptation is most deceptive. The deposit is given descriptively in relationship to these needs and to this horizontalist temptation, so as to beget among men, even among Catholics, the good and the better attitude toward the formulated Apostles' Creed, toward the Creed of the People of God and thus toward that authentic kind of catechesis for which the next document calls.

Pope John Paul II: Catechesi tradendae (1979)

The fourth convocation of the Synod of Bishops met in Rome under Pope Paul VI in the Autumn of 1977 with Cardinal Karol Wojtyla, Archbishop of Krakow, Poland, participating. The subject was catechesis, with a significant specific reference to children and young people.[126]

---

123. See Paul VI, *Evangelii nuntiandi*, nos. 25-39, "The Content of Evangelization;" below, pp. 161-168.
124. Paul VI, *General Catechetical Directory*, no. 12; see below, pp. 55-56.
125. See the initial and programmatic Encyclical of Pope John Paul II, *Redemptor hominis*, "The Redeemer of Man," dated March 4, 1979, *AAS* (March 15, 1979), pp. 257-354; and *Catechesi tradendae*, nos. 30, 31, 49 and especially 52; see below, pp. 233-235, 247-248 and 249-250.
126. For the official oral and written interventions of the bishops at the Synod, see *L'Osservatore Romano—English Edition*, the weekly issues from October 6,

Pope Paul VI in his discourse closing the Synod summarized the remarkably perceptive and unified interventions of the bishops assembled from every continent of the world. "We express our joy," the Pope says, "that the members of the Synod have found themselves in agreement on the principal aspects of catechesis, and that at the conclusion of their work they have submitted to us very useful suggestions contained in thirty-four propositions."[127] Then the Pope gives these headings to his summary.

First: "Integrity of Doctrine." "We rejoice over the emphasis placed on the bishop's responsibility to be vigilant and to see to it that full fidelity to the Word of God, as it has been manifested to us by Divine Revelation and transmitted in the course of the centuries by the Magisterium of the Church, be always preserved in catechesis.... Faithfulness to the deposit of Revelation clearly demands that no essential truth of the Faith should be passed over in silence.... The people entrusted to our care has the sacred and

---

1977, through November 17, 1977. The official topic of the Synod for "children and youth" is significant because of a current aberration in adult catechesis which sees it as the teaching of a new philosophical interpretation of Christianity on the adult level. This approach is designed to persuade parents to acquiesce with regard to programs which withhold the deposit of faith from Catholic children during their childhood years when they are of course too young to philosophize, but at the right age to learn the elements of Christian Doctrine. The Synod of Bishops is quite different: it proceeds in the context of the concern, constant since the Apostles, that the deposit of faith be handed on to the Catholics of the future, the same deposit which makes their parents Catholics in the present. The question is the same one which has preoccupied the Church ceaselessly since St. Pius X: religious ignorance as the problem and authentic catechesis as its solution. The then Cardinal Wojtyla made an insightful written intervention which actually solves the problematic of this aberrational adult "catechesis." It is reported in *L'Osservatore Romano—English Edition* (November 10, 1977), p. 13: "His Eminence recalled the need to establish a close link between the catechesis of young people and the catechesis of adults, especially of the family.... One must have a program of catechesis which is directly related to the progress of their children. This helps to form a common religious language within the family and to avoid parents feeling estranged from the catechesis of their children." He will return to the principles in this matter as Pope John Paul II in *Catechesi tradendae*, nos. 58, 59, 60, 61 and 68; see below, pp. 254-258 and 263-264.

127. Paul VI, "Discourse at the Conclusion of the Synod of Bishops, October 30, 1977," *L'Osservatore Romano—English Edition* (November 10, 1977), pp. 1 and 16.

inalienable right to receive the Word of God, the entire Word of God."[128]

Second: "Necessity of a Systematic Catechesis." "In the second place, it was a great comfort to us to see how everyone noted the extreme necessity of a systematic catechesis, precisely because this orderly study of the Christian mystery is what distinguishes catechesis from all other forms of presentation of the Word of God.... No one can arrive at the whole truth on the basis of some simple experience, that is, without an adequate explanation of the message of Christ.... The complete presentation of the Christian message obviously comprises also its moral principles.... To educate in the Faith also the children and young people of our Christian communities will mean, therefore, educating them to follow Christ."[129]

Third: "Usefulness of Formulas." "In the third place, we fully agree with you when you authoritatively recall the necessity of some fundamental formulas which will make it possible to express more easily, in a suitable and accurate way, the truths of the Faith and of Christian moral doctrine. These formulas, if learned by heart, greatly aid the stable possession of these truths...and make the profession of the Faith easier."[130]

On the basis of this world-wide catechetical unity of the Catholic bishops, Pope Paul VI began work on the catechetical document which the members of the Synod asked the Holy See to produce. Anyone who studies the text of *Catechesi tradendae* attentively will agree that the three summary headings of Pope Paul VI are the most accurate short synthesis of the future document that could be devised. It is well known in Rome that Paul VI had given final approval to *Catechesi tradendae* but that his death prevented him from publishing it. It is likewise known that his successor, John Paul I, himself a remarkably able and experienced

---

128. Paul VI, *ibid*. Here the Pope cites his own *Exhortation* on the fifth anniversary of the closing of Vatican II, *AAS* (1970), 97-106, an important expression of concern for the deposit in the very depths of the post-conciliar confusion. For the text, see E. Kevane, *op. cit.*, pp. 195-204.

129. Paul VI, *ibid*. The Pope cites 1 John 2:24 on the following of Christ. For the chief forms in which the Word of God is presented, see the *General Catechetical Directory*, no. 17; below, p. 60.

130. Paul VI, *ibid*.

priestly catechist, approved the document in his turn before his death after a few short weeks in office. Pope John Paul II, also a deeply experienced catechist, took the document in hand, gave it his own finalization, and published it on October 16, 1979.

Coming to the document itself, it should be noted that, like *Evangelii nuntiandi*, it is an "Apostolic Exhortation." The documents of the Holy See fall into several categories: Apostolic Constitutions, Encyclical Letters, actions taken *motu proprio*, and several others shown in the contents of the *Acta Apostolicae Sedis*. The Apostolic Exhortation is a genre which has been used increasingly in this Twentieth Century.[131] The Holy See always has encouraged, urged and exhorted not only the men in Holy Orders but also all religious and all the laity toward apostolic zeal for communicating the Gospel and handing on the deposit of faith. Pope Paul VI is explicit: "The duty of confirming the brethren [is] a duty which with the office of being the Successor of Peter we have received from the Lord, and [it] is for us a daily preoccupation."[132] And he cites the words of Jesus: "I have prayed to you, Simon, that your faith may not fail, and once you have recovered, you in your turn must strengthen your brothers" (Luke 22:32).

But it is Pope John Paul II who is making this divinely-mandated function of Peter the hallmark of his pontificate. This is the meaning of his pastoral journeys to the countries and continents of the whole world and the substance of his addresses to the various Episcopal Conferences and to the throngs of the faithful. It is his conscious and avowed intention, as one instance will witness. "Carrying out the mission received through Peter and his Suc-

---

131. In the Latin, *Adhortatio Apostolica*, where the word since classical times always has meant "To urge persons strongly to do a thing"; hence, "to encourage, to urge, or to exhort." The persons who are envisaged in these two documents begun by the Synods of Bishops and completed by Paul VI and John Paul II are not exactly the same. *Evangelii nuntiandi* has the bishops of the entire world primarily in view, for they hold the basic responsibility in the proclamation of the Gospel. "This is the special duty of the bishops," the Council of Trent teaches (Fifth Session, "On Reform," Chapter 2); and hence it orders "that all bishops,...and also all priests who in any way have charge of churches to which is attached the care of souls, are obliged personally, if not lawfully impeded, to preach the Holy Gospel of Jesus Christ." *Catechesi tradendae* has the persons of the catechists primarily in view: it is intended to give the same encouragement to all who help the bishops and pastors as catechetical teachers.

132. *Evangelii nuntiandi*, no. 1; see below, pp. 145-146.

cessors," he said at Porto Alegre, Brazil, "I have come to strengthen you in the Faith.... St. Paul travelled through cities already evangelized, exhorting Christians to persevere in the apostolic teaching and strengthening them in the faith received (See Acts 16:4-5). I ask God that this apostolic journey of mine may have the same meaning for you and obtain the same result."[133]

This is the meaning, the intention, the nature and the purpose of *Catechesi tradendae*. It gives no new doctrine or practice. It does not alter the content and method of catechesis. It encourages and urges catechists to be persons of the Apostolic Church, doing what Jesus himself commanded the Apostles to do, to teach all nations the deposit of faith. Upon reading this document, an experienced teaching Sister observed: All the aberrations in current religious education are specified and the right attitude is given in each case. These aberrations would disappear if those responsible for catechetical teaching would pay it heed.

This characterizes *Catechesi tradendae* aptly. It is concerned with attitude. Attitude first toward the content, explicitly discussed and urged throughout the document as nothing else than that same deposit of faith, the Divine Revelation taught to his Apostles by Jesus Christ the Divine Teacher. Only the attitude of the living catechist can assure that "integrity of content" for which no. 30 calls, and which catechumens have "the right to receive." And attitude secondly toward methods, the attitude which keeps methodology always in its rightful place, serving the content, "inspired by the humble concern to stay closer to a content that must remain intact" (no. 31).

Catechesi tradendae, as a matter of fact, stands close to *Acerbo nimis*, just as Pope John Paul II recalls the pastoral and catechetical personality of St. Pius X.[134] Concern for the deposit of

---

133. John Paul II, Homily at Porto Alegre, Brazil, *L'Osservatore Romano—Edition* (July 28, 1980), p. 4.

134. Fernando Salvestrini of the Lateran University makes this point well. See his "I caratteri distintivi degli operatori della catechesi," in Gino Concetti (ed.), *Evangelizzazione e Catechesi* (Milano: Massimo, 1980), pp. 280-281. For other commentaries on *Catechesi tradendae*, see Raimondo Spiazzi, O.P., *La catechesi nel nostro tempo* (Rovigo: Istituto Padano di Arti Grafiche, 1980); Cesare Bonivento, PIME, *"Going, Teach...."* (Boston, Massachusetts: St. Paul Editions, 1980); and Robert J. Levis and Michael J. Wrenn (eds.), *Pope John Paul II: Catechist* (Chicago, Illinois: Franciscan Herald Press, 1980).

faith is sustained throughout *Catechesi tradendae*, relentlessly, one might say. But it is not different from *Evangelii nuntiandi*, nos. 25-39, nor from Parts Two and Three of the *General Catechetical Directory*, nor from the clean-cut procedures enacted by *Provido sane*, nor from the holy zeal which animates *Acerbo nimis*. Concern for the deposit of faith, that it be handed on, especially to the young, and handed on in full purity and integrity, is the unifying bond between all the catechetical documents of the present century. "The integrity of the content," Pope John Paul II says, "deserves special attention today." And he proceeds to summarize the main points of doctrine in the Ordinary and Universal Magisterium of the Church, points which constitute what he explicitly calls "the deposit of faith."[135]

It remains to ask for the reason which underlies this determined, unremitting and ongoing concern for the deposit which has characterized the Catholic Church since the Apostles but which never before has needed such a cluster of catechetical documents devoted to it as these of the Twentieth Century. The answer is contained in the Eucharistic teaching of the present Pope, summarized in his Holy Thursday letters of 1979 and 1980.

Pope John Paul II: Metanoia (1979, 1980)

This final section of the present volume contains three remarkable documents of Pope John Paul II on the Mystery and the Worship of the Eucharist: the Holy Thursday letters of 1979 and 1980 to bishops, priests and deacons, and the *Inaestimabile donum* of April 17, 1980, on the liturgical norms, all three a unified whole addressed primarily to the bishops, priests and deacons of the Catholic Church.[136]

But, it may be asked, why are they given here among the catechetical documents? Are they not liturgical rather than catechetical?

These are perhaps the most basic questions in the field of catechetics today. When answered wrongly, the underlying reason emerges into view for the confusion and even chaos which besets this field in these post-conciliar times. In so delicate and at the same

---

135. *Catechesi tradendae*, no. 30; see below, pp. 233-234.
136. See Pope John Paul II, Letter of Holy Thursday, 1980; below, p. 307.

time urgent a matter, the authoritative teaching of the Church must be consulted, in order to answer these questions rightly.

The truth is that these documents of the *metanoia* are absolutely catechetical, because they contain the reason and the purpose of all catechetical teaching, and because they demonstrate in their own way the need of the Church for a catechesis that is faithful to the deposit by seeing rigorously to "integrity of content."[137] Pope John Paul II proceeds toward the right answer: "In order that the sacrificial offering of his or her faith (see Phil. 2:17) should be perfect, the person who becomes a disciple of Christ has the right to receive 'the word of faith' (Rom. 10:8) not in mutilated, falsified or diminished form, but whole and entire, in all its rigor and vigor. Unfaithfulness on some point to the integrity of the message means a dangerous weakening of catechesis and putting at risk the results that Christ and the ecclesial community have a right to expect from it."[138]

This passage of *Catechesi tradendae* actually contains the correct answer in full to the questions above. It remains only to explain its dense substance. For its full meaning bears on the doctrine of the Real Presence of the Victim of the Sacrifice of the New Testament in the Holy Eucharist. "The Mystery and Worship of the Eucharist" is the heart of the same deposit of faith which is the very content of catechetical teaching. It is catechetical teaching which makes the following passage a living reality in Catholic parishes: "All who participate with faith in the Eucharist become aware that it is a 'sacrifice,' that is to say, a 'consecrated Offering.' For the bread and wine presented at the altar and accompanied by the devotion and the spiritual sacrifices of the participants are finally consecrated, so as to become *truly, really and substantially* Christ's own body that is given up and his blood that is shed."[139]

Let John Paul II carry the explanation further. The following words, spoken on the Feast of the Apostles Peter and Paul, June 29, 1980, to the Cardinals and other collaborators in the central

---

137. John Paul II, *Catechesi tradendae*, no. 30; see below, pp. 233-234; this could be termed the constantly recurring theme of *Catechesi tradendae* as a whole.

138. John Paul II, *ibid.*, no. 30; see below, pp. 233-234.

139. John Paul II, Letter of Holy Thursday, 1980, no. 9; see below, p. 313. The words italicized in the Pope's letter are those of the solemn *de fide* definition of the Catholic Church regarding the doctrine of the Real Presence. See the *Creed of the People of God*, no. 24, with its reference to the conciliar definition; below, p. 37.

government of the Church, are actually the comprehensive "introduction" to these three documents of the *metanoia*.

"To love God! Liturgical life is the very special place where this exchange between God and man takes place: and the altar of the Eucharist, where Christ Jesus, the true and eternal Priest, offers himself as a victim to the Father for mankind, is the meeting point between heaven and earth. The Second Vatican Council gave a magnificent impetus to liturgical renewal, which had been prepared by a whole movement that had flourished all over the world since the innovations introduced by St. Pius X. The Constitution *Sacrosanctum Concilium* was the first document solemnly approved by the Council Fathers [of Vatican II], from which there started that constant work of reform, carried on humbly and courageously by the great Pontiff Paul VI.

"It is well known, however, that—alongside the dangerous ecclesiology which I mentioned before—there have developed movements and mentalities, both of regression and of arbitrary experimentation, which have sometimes led to serious disturbance of the faithful, priests, and the whole Church. The most evident contradictions have come to light precisely concerning the Eucharist, precisely at the Altar, where the *regula fidei*, the Rule of Faith, must inspire, on the contrary, the utmost respect for him who, in the Mass, renews his sacrifice in a sacramental form, and leaves it to his Church as a perpetual memorial of his immolated love.

"This was the origin of the letters which I addressed to the bishops and, through them, to the priests, on Holy Thursday of last year and of the recent *Dominicae Cenae* [of this year]. There followed (April 17, 1980) the liturgical norms of the competent Sacred Congregation in regard to the cult of the Eucharistic Mystery.

"I ask the whole Church to live in that spirit of respect and love, which these documents wish to instill."[140]

It remains to place this appeal of the Vicar of Christ in its catechetical context, the context of the deposit of faith. Catechesis began when Jesus Christ opened his public ministry before the people as the Herald of God and the Teacher of the revealed religion of the Eucharistic Sacrifice. "After John had been arrested, Jesus went into Galilee. There he proclaimed the Good News from God. 'The

---

140. John Paul II, "Address to Collaborators in the Central Government of the Church," *L'Osservatore Romano—English Edition* (July 4, 1980), p. 17.

time has come,' he said, 'and the Kingdom of God is close at hand. Repent, and believe the Good News' " (Mark 1:14-15).

The two fundamental components both of Christian doctrine and of the Christian way of living, namely, of catechesis as a whole, are contained in these two verbs which call to action: the response of the faith which believes the Gospel and the *metanoia*—the repentance, the conversion—which practices the Gospel in the prayer, the sacramental participation and the Gospel morality of daily Christian living.

But faith in whom? Conversion to whom? To the vague and nebulous "god" of pantheistic religiosity? Far from it. It is the call of God himself, Yahweh, in the Person of the eternal divine Son, the transcendent and almighty Creator of heaven and earth, for conversion to himself incarnate, made flesh, living among us as the Good Shepherd visiting his people. It is this active and practical conversion to the One who, when sending his Apostles to teach all the nations, baptizing them in the name of the Father and of the Son and of the Holy Spirit, added these words: "And know that I am with you always; yes, to the end of time" (Mt. 28:20). Those who follow this Way of Christian living, persons of the *metanoia*, the conversion, will celebrate his death with love, will proclaim his resurrection with living faith, and will await with unwavering hope his return in glory.[141]

This is the conversion which is the purpose of catechetical teaching. "Faith is a gift of God which calls men to conversion.... Catechesis performs the function of disposing men to receive the action of the Holy Spirit and to deepen their conversion."[142] "We must all be converted anew every day.... Being converted means 'to pray continually and never lose heart' (Luke 18:1). In a certain way prayer is the first and last condition for conversion, spiritual progress and holiness."[143]

---

141. See the Fifth Weekday Preface in the Eucharistic Prayers of the postconciliar Roman Missal.

142. The *General Catechetical Directory*, no. 22; see below, pp. 62-63.

143. John Paul II, Letter of Holy Thursday, 1979, no. 10; see below, p. 291. Hence in the catechisms which are classical and official in the Church, catechumens are taught about prayer, taught how to pray and taught to pray; prayer is one of the four areas of content in *The Roman Catechism*.

This is a practical and concrete personal conversion to the Jesus of the sacramental Presence, to the *Mysterium Christi*, to him who stands among us in the mystery and the worship of the Eucharist.[144] Catechesis is in focus when it teaches in such a way as to "deepen this conversion." Catechesis, the "word of faith," is intrinsically related to the Sacraments, for which prayer and Gospel morality are the necessary subjective dispositions. Again it is John Paul II who explains lucidly: "Catechesis is intrinsically linked with the whole of liturgical and sacramental activity, for it is in the Sacraments, especially in the Eucharist, that Christ Jesus works in fullness for the transformation of human beings.... Catechesis always has reference to the Sacraments.... Every form of catechesis necessarily leads to the Sacraments of faith."[145]

The answer to those questions on the inclusion of these Holy Thursday letters with the catechetical documents is now clear. It is contained in the Christocentrism of catechesis. "Christ Jesus, the incarnate Word of God,...is the center of the Gospel message within salvation history.... Hence catechesis must necessarily be Christocentric."[146]

It follows once again that the deposit of faith, which is the content of catechesis, is itself central. And why? Because of the factor of witness. The Divine Teacher, the first Catechist, who sent his

---

144. St. Elizabeth Ann Seton, the first American Saint, happened to be visiting in Italy while still a Protestant. "These people," she writes in a letter sent back to the United States, "really believe they have Jesus Christ with them in their churches." It was a discovery which led to her conversion. And see *The Creed of the People of God*, no. 26; below, p. 38.
145. John Paul II, *Catechesi tradendae*, no. 23; see below, pp. 227-228. See *Evangelii nuntiandi*, no. 28 and no. 36, below, pp. 162-163 and 166; Vatican II, *The Church*, no. 10; and Vatican II, *Life of Priests*, no. 5: "But the other sacraments, and indeed all ecclesiastical ministries and works of the apostolate are bound up with the Eucharist and are directed towards it. For in the most blessed Eucharist is contained the whole spiritual good of the Church, namely Christ himself our Pasch and the living bread which gives life to men through his flesh—that flesh which is given life and gives life through the Holy Spirit." All of this depends upon catechetical teaching in order that it be known and loved and put into daily living. Hence the Holy Thursday documents belong with those of catechetics, for they specify the catechetical Ministry of the Word, bringing it into clear focus and doing away with confusion and chaos by giving it its purpose.
146. The *General Catechetical Directory*, no. 40; see below, p. 74.

Apostles to teach and baptize all the nations, was the same who said to them: "You will receive power when the Holy Spirit comes on you, and then you will be my witnesses not only in Jerusalem but throughout Judaea and Samaria, and indeed to the ends of the earth" (Acts 1:8). The doctrine, the content of the teaching, the deposit of faith, is the instrument for the witnessing. There is no other. The teaching is the witnessing. If the teaching fails, so will the witnessing. The concern for the deposit which is the unifying bond of all these documents is a Christocentric concern. Love for the doctrine is a part of love for Jesus, the true and real Jesus of the baptismal profession, of the Apostles' Creed, and of the Eucharistic Presence.

John Paul II does indeed answer fully the question about the catechetical bearing of his Holy Thursday documents. But it is Paul VI, whom he calls "that great Pontiff," who puts the answer into lapidary brevity. "The future of the Church depends on the wisdom and zeal shown in Catechetics. The world says to us today precisely what a group of individuals recorded in the Gospel once said to the Apostle Philip: 'We wish to see Jesus' (John 12:21). And it is Jesus we must show to the world—Jesus, and no substitute. Hence, Venerable Brethren, we exhort you to the utmost vigilance in the matter of catechetical content, as you endeavor to point out to children and adults the Way, the Truth and the Life, who is Christ."[147]

Feast of the Assumption　　　　　　　　　　　　　Eugene Kevane
August 15, 1981

---

147. Paul VI, "Letter, June 6, 1976, to the Bishops of the United States on the occasion of the Bicentennial," *L'Osservatore Romano*—English Edition (July 8, 1976), p. 7. Paul VI was a remarkably catechetical Pope because of his personal Christocentrism. See for example his words to the crowds at St. Peter's in a general audience, *L'Osservatore Romano*—*English Edition* (October 6, 1977), p. 3: "Jesus is the way, the truth and the life" (John 14:6). Jesus is the light of the world (John 8:12; 9:5). Jesus is the Good Shepherd (John 10:11-14). Jesus is the Son of Man (Mt. 16:13; 25:31; 26:24); the Son of Mary (Mt. 13:55); the Son of God (Mt. 14:33; 26:64; John 9:35; etc.). Jesus is the Alpha and the Omega (Rv. 22:13).... The Successor of Peter wishes to proclaim (this witness) here with certainty and with humility of faith.... In the history of the world today still more than ever, Christ is alive, Christ is real, in the exceeding dimension of his divine Being." For a convenient collection of such discourses of Pope Paul VI on Jesus, see the publication of the Daughters of St. Paul: Paul VI, *Who Is Jesus?* (Boston, Massachusetts: St. Paul Editions, 1972).

POPE ST. PIUS X

Acerbo Nimis: De Christiana doctrina tradenda, 1905

Handing on Christian Doctrine by Teaching

To the venerable brethren, patriarchs, primates, archbishops, bishops and other ordinaries having peace and communion with the Apostolic See.

At this very troublesome and difficult time, the hidden designs of God have conducted our poor strength to the office of Supreme Pastor, to rule the entire flock of Christ. The enemy has, indeed, long been prowling about the fold and attacking it with such subtle cunning that now, more than ever before, the prediction of the Apostle to the elders of the Church of Ephesus seems to be verified: "I know that...fierce wolves will get in among you, and will not spare the flock."[1]

Causes for the Decline in Religion

Those who still are zealous for the glory of God are seeking the causes and reasons for this decline in religion. Coming to a different explanation, each points out, according to his own view, a different

---

1. Acts 20:29.

plan for the protection and restoration of the kingdom of God on earth. But it seems to us, venerable brothers, that while we should not overlook other considerations, we are forced to agree with those who hold that the chief cause of the present indifference and, as it were, infirmity of soul, and the serious evils that result from it, is to be found above all in ignorance of things divine. This is fully in accord with what God Himself declared through the prophet Osee: "And there is no knowledge of God in the land. Cursing and lying and killing, and theft and adultery have overflowed, and blood has touched blood. Thereafter shall the land mourn, and everyone that dwells in it shall languish."[2]

RELIGIOUS ILLITERACY OF CATHOLICS—It is a common complaint, unfortunately too well founded, that there are large numbers of Christians in our own time who are entirely ignorant of those truths necessary for salvation. And when we mention Christians, we refer not only to the masses or to those in the lower walks of life—for these find some excuse for their ignorance in the fact that the demands of their harsh employers hardly leave them time to take care of themselves or of their dear ones—but we refer to those especially who do not lack culture or talents and, indeed, are possessed of abundant knowledge regarding things of the world, but they live rashly and imprudently with regard to religion. It is hard to find words to describe how profound is the darkness in which they are engulfed and, what is most deplorable of all, how tranquilly they repose there. They rarely give thought to God, the Supreme Author and Ruler of all things, or to the teachings of the Faith of Christ. They know nothing of the Incarnation of the Word of God, nothing of the perfect restoration of the human race which He accomplished. Grace, the greatest of the helps for attaining eternal things, the Holy Sacrifice and the sacraments by which we obtain grace, are entirely unknown to them. They have no conception of the malice and baseness of sin; and hence they show no anxiety to avoid sin or to renounce it.

And so they arrive at life's end in such a condition that, lest all hope of salvation be lost, the priest is obliged to give in the last few moments of life a summary teaching of religion, a time which

---

2. Osee 4:1-3.

should be devoted to stimulating the soul to greater love for God. And even this as too often happens only when the dying man is not so sinfully ignorant as to look upon the ministration of the priest as useless, and then calmly faces the fearful passage to eternity without making his peace with God. And so our Predecessor, Benedict XIV, had just cause to write: "We declare that a great number of those who are condemned to eternal punishment suffer that everlasting calamity because of ignorance of those mysteries of faith which must be known and believed in order to be numbered among the elect."[3]

There is then, venerable brothers, no reason for wonder that the corruption of morals and depravity of life is already so great, and ever increasingly greater, not only among uncivilized peoples but even in those very nations that are called Christian. The Apostle Paul, writing to the Ephesians, repeatedly admonished them in these words: "But immorality and every uncleanness or covetousness, let it not even be named among you, as becomes saints; or obscenity or foolish talk."[4] He also places the foundation of holiness and sound morals upon a knowledge of divine things—which holds in check evil desires: "See to it therefore, brethren, that you walk with care: not as unwise but as wise.... Therefore, do not become foolish, but understand what the will of the Lord is."[5] And rightly so. For the will of man retains but little of that divinely implanted love of virtue and righteousness by which it was, as it were, attracted strongly toward the real and not merely apparent good. Disordered by the stain of the first sin, and almost forgetful of God, its Author, it improperly turns every affection to a love of vanity and deceit. This erring will, blinded by its own evil desires, has need therefore of a guide to lead it back to the paths of justice whence it has so unfortunately strayed.

The intellect itself is this guide, which need not be sought elsewhere, but is provided by nature itself. It is a guide, though, that, if it lacks its companion light, the knowledge of divine things, will be only an instance of the blind leading the blind so that both will fall into the pit. The holy king David, praising God for the

---

3. *Instit.* XXVII, 18.
4. Eph. 5:3-4.
5. *Ibid.*, 15-16.

light of truth with which He had illumined the intellect, exclaimed: "The light of your countenance, O Lord, is signed upon us."[6] Then he described the effect of this light by adding: "You have given gladness in my heart," gladness, that is, which enlarges our heart so that it runs in the way of God's commandments.

IMPORTANCE OF REVEALED KNOWLEDGE—All this becomes evident on a little reflection. Christian teaching reveals God and His infinite perfection with far greater clarity than is possible by the human faculties alone. Nor is that all. This same Christian teaching also commands us to honor God by faith, which is of the mind, by hope, which is of the will, by love, which is of the heart; and thus the whole man is subjected to the supreme Maker and Ruler of all things. The truly remarkable dignity of man as the son of the heavenly Father, in whose image he is formed, and with whom he is destined to live in eternal happiness, is also revealed only by the doctrine of Jesus Christ. From this very dignity, and from man's knowledge of it, Christ showed that men should love one another as brothers, and should live here as becomes children of light, "Not in revelry and drunkenness, not in debauchery and wantonness, not in strife and jealousy."[7] He also bids us to place all our anxiety and care in the hands of God, for He will provide for us; He tells us to help the poor, to do good to those who hate us, and to prefer the eternal welfare of the soul to the temporal goods of this life.

Without wishing to touch on every detail, nevertheless is it not true that the proud man is urged and commanded by the teaching of Christ to strive for humility, the source of true glory? "Whoever, therefore, humbles himself...he is the greatest in the kingdom of heaven."[8] From that same teaching we learn prudence of the spirit, and thereby we avoid prudence of the flesh; we learn justice, by which we give to every man his due; fortitude which prepares us to endure all things and with steadfast heart suffer all things for the sake of God and eternal happiness; and, last of all, temperance through which we cherish even poverty borne out of love for God, nay, we even glory in the cross itself, unmindful of its shame.

---

6. Ps. 4:7.
7. Rom. 13:13.
8. Mt. 18:4.

In fine, Christian teaching not only bestows on the intellect the light by which it attains truth, but from it our will draws that ardor by which we are raised up to God and joined with Him in the practice of virtue.

We by no means wish to conclude that a perverse will and unbridled conduct may not be joined with a knowledge of religion. Would to God that facts did not too abundantly prove the contrary! But we do maintain that the will cannot be upright nor the conduct good when the mind is shrouded in the darkness of crass ignorance. A man who walks with open eyes may, indeed, turn aside from the right path, but a blind man is in much more imminent danger of wandering away. Furthermore, there is always some hope for a reform of perverse conduct so long as the light of faith is not entirely extinguished; but if lack of faith is added to depraved morality because of ignorance, the evil hardly admits of remedy, and the road to ruin lies open.

How many and how grave are the consequences of ignorance in matters of religion! And on the other hand, how necessary and how beneficial is religious instruction! It is indeed vain to expect a fulfillment of the duties of a Christian by one who does not even know them.

The Duty of the Pastor

We must now consider upon whom rests the obligation to dissipate this most pernicious ignorance and to impart in its stead the knowledge that is wholly indispensable. There can be no doubt, venerable brothers, that this most important duty rests upon all who are pastors of souls. On them, by command of Christ, rest the obligations of knowing and of feeding the flocks committed to their care; and to feed implies, first of all, to teach. "I will give you pastors after my own heart," God promised through Jeremias, "and they shall feed you with knowledge and doctrine."[9] Hence the Apostle Paul said: "Christ did not send me to baptize, but to preach the Gospel,"[10] thereby indicating that the first duty of all those

---

9. Jer. 3:15.
10. 1 Cor. 1:17.

who are entrusted in any way with the government of the Church is to instruct the faithful in the things of God.

We do not think it necessary to set forth here the praises of such instruction or to point out how meritorious it is in God's sight. If, assuredly, the alms with which we relieve the needs of the poor are highly praised by the Lord, how much more precious in His eyes, then, will be the zeal and labor expended in teaching and admonishing, by which we provide not for the passing needs of the body but for the eternal profit of the soul! Nothing, surely, is more desirable, nothing more acceptable to Jesus Christ, the Savior of souls, who testifies of Himself through Isaias: "To bring good news to the poor he has sent me."[11]

Here then it is well to emphasize and insist that for a priest there is no duty more grave or obligation more binding than this. Who, indeed, will deny that knowledge should be joined to holiness of life in the priest? "For the lips of the priest shall keep knowledge."[12] The Church demands this knowledge of those who are to be ordained to the priesthood. Why? Because the Christian people expect from them knowledge of the divine law, and it was for that end that they were sent by God. "And they shall seek the law at his mouth; because he is the messenger of the Lord of hosts."[13] Thus the bishop speaking to the candidates for the priesthood in the ordination ceremony says: "Let your teaching be a spiritual remedy for God's people; may they be worthy fellow workers of our order; and thus meditating day and night on His law, they may believe what they read, and teach what they shall believe."[14]

If what we have just said is applicable to all priests, does it not apply with much greater force to those who possess the title and the authority of parish priests, and who, by virtue of their rank and in a sense by virtue of a contract, hold the office of pastors of souls? These are, to a certain extent, the pastors and teachers appointed by Christ in order that the faithful might not be as "children, tossed to and fro, and carried about by every wind of doctrine devised in

---

11. Lk. 4:18.
12. Mal. 2:7.
13. *Ibid.*
14. *Roman Pontifical.*

the wickedness of men," but that, "practicing the truth in love," they may "grow up in all things in him who is the head, Christ."[15]

For this reason the Council of Trent, treating of the duties of pastors of souls, decreed that their first and most important work is the instruction of the faithful.[16] It therefore prescribes that they shall teach the truths of religion on Sundays and on the more solemn feast days; moreover, during the holy seasons of Advent and Lent they are to give such instruction every day or at least three times a week. This, however, was not considered enough. The Council provided for the instruction of youth by adding that the pastors, either personally or through others, must explain the truths of religion at least on Sundays and feast days to the children of the parish, and inculcate obedience to God and to their parents. When the sacraments are to be administered, it enjoins upon pastors the duty to explain their efficacy in plain and simple language.

These prescriptions of the Council of Trent have been summarized and still more clearly defined by our Predecessor Benedict XIV, in his Constitution *Etsi minime*. "Two chief obligations," he wrote, "have been imposed by the Council of Trent on those who have the care of souls: first, that of preaching the things of God to the people on the feast days; and the second, that of teaching the rudiments of faith and of the divine law to the youth and others who need such instruction."

Here the wise Pontiff rightly distinguishes between these two duties: one is what is commonly known as the explanation of the Gospel and the other is the teaching of Christian doctrine. Perhaps there are some who, wishing to lessen their labors, would believe that the homily on the Gospel can take the place of catechetical instruction. But for one who reflects a moment, such is obviously impossible. The sermon on the holy Gospel is addressed to those who should have already received knowledge of the elements of faith. It is, so to speak, bread broken for adults. Catechetical instruction, on the other hand, is that milk which the Apostle Peter wished the faithful to desire in all simplicity like newborn babes.

---

15. Eph. 4:14, 15.
16. *Sess. 5, cap. 2 de Reform; Sess. 22, cap. 8; Sess. 24, cap. 4 and 7 de Reform.*

The Catechetical Lesson Plan

The task of the catechist is to take up one or other of the truths of faith or of Christian morality and then explain it in all its parts; and since amendment of life is the chief aim of his instruction, the catechist must needs make a comparison between what God commands us to do and what is our actual conduct. After this, he will use examples appropriately taken from the Holy Scriptures, Church history, and the lives of the saints—thus moving his hearers and clearly pointing out to them how they are to regulate their own conduct. He should, in conclusion, earnestly exhort all present to dread and avoid vice and to practice virtue.

We are indeed aware that the work of teaching the catechism is unpopular with many because as a rule it is deemed of little account and for the reason that it does not lend itself easily to the winning of public praise. But this in our opinion is a judgment based on vanity and devoid of truth. We do not disapprove of those pulpit orators who, out of genuine zeal for the glory of God, devote themselves to defense of the Faith and to its spread, or who eulogize the saints of God. But their labor presupposes labor of another kind, that of the catechist. And so if this be lacking, then the foundation is wanting; and they labor in vain who build the house.

Too often it happens that ornate sermons which receive the applause of crowded congregations serve but to tickle the ears and fail utterly to touch the hearts of the hearers.

Catechetical instruction, on the other hand, plain and simple though it may be, is that word of which God Himself speaks through the lips of the prophet Isaias: "And as the rain and the snow come down from heaven and return no more thither, but soak the earth, and water it, and make it to spring and give seed to the sower and bread to the eater; so shall my word be which shall go forth from my mouth; it shall not return to me void, but it shall do whatsoever I please, and shall prosper in the things for which I sent it."[17]

We believe the same may be said of those priests who work hard to produce books which explain the truths of religion. They are surely to be commended for their zeal, but how many are there

---

17. Is. 55:10-11.

who read these works and take from them a fruit commensurate with the labor and intention of the writers?

The teaching of the catechism, on the other hand, when rightly done, never fails to profit those who listen to it.

In order to enkindle the zeal of the ministers of God, we again insist on the need to reach the ever-increasing number of those who know nothing at all of religion, or who possess at most only such knowledge of God and Christian truths as benefits idolaters. How many there are, alas, not only among the young, but among adults and those advanced in years, who know nothing of the chief mysteries of faith; who on hearing the name of Christ can only ask: "Who is he...that I may believe in him?"[18] In consequence of this ignorance, they do not consider it a crime to excite and nourish hatred against their neighbor, to enter into most unjust contracts, to do business in dishonest fashion, to hold the funds of others at an exorbitant interest rate, and to commit other iniquities not less reprehensible. They are, moreover, ignorant of the law of Christ which not only condemns immoral actions, but also forbids deliberate immoral thoughts and desires. Even when for some reason or other they avoid sensual pleasures, they nevertheless entertain evil thoughts without the least scruple, thereby multiplying their sins above the number of the hairs of the head. These persons are found, we deem it necessary to repeat, not merely among the poorer classes of the people or in sparsely settled districts, but also among those in higher walks of life, even, indeed, among those puffed up with learning, who, relying upon a vain erudition, feel free to ridicule religion and to "deride whatever they do not know."[19]

CULTIVATING THE BAPTISMAL SEED—Now, if we cannot expect to reap a harvest when no seed has been planted, how can we hope to have a people with sound morals if Christian doctrine has not been imparted to them in due time? It follows, too, that if faith languishes in our days, if among large numbers it has almost vanished, the reason is that the duty of catechetical teaching is either fulfilled very superficially or altogether neglected. It will not

---

18. Jn. 9:36.
19. Jude 10.

do to say, in excuse, that faith is a free gift of God bestowed upon each one at Baptism. True enough, when we are baptized in Christ, the habit of faith is given, but this most divine seed, if left entirely to itself, by its own power, so to speak, is not like the mustard seed which "grows up...and puts out great branches."[20] Man has the faculty of understanding at his birth, but he also has need of his mother's word to awaken it, as it were, and to make it active. So too, the Christian, born again of water and the Holy Spirit, has faith within him, but he requires the word of the teaching Church to nourish and develop it and to make it bear fruit. Thus wrote the Apostle: "Faith then depends on hearing, and hearing on the word of Christ";[21] and to show the necessity of instruction, he added, "How are they to hear, if no one preaches?"[22]

What we have said so far demonstrates the supreme importance of religious instruction. We ought, therefore, to do all that lies in our power to maintain the teaching of Christian doctrine with full vigor, and where such is neglected, to restore it; for in the words of our Predecessor, Benedict XIV, "There is nothing more effective than catechetical instruction to spread the glory of God and to secure the salvation of souls."[23]

Catechetical Regulations

We, therefore, venerable brothers, desirous of fulfilling this most important obligation of our teaching office, and likewise wishing to introduce uniformity everywhere in so weighty a matter, do by our supreme authority enact the following regulations and strictly command that they be observed and carried out in all dioceses of the world.

I. On every Sunday and holy day, with no exception, throughout the year, all parish priests and in general all those having the care of souls shall instruct the boys and girls for the space of an hour from the text of the catechism on those things they must believe and do in order to attain salvation.

---

20. Mk. 4:32.
21. Rom. 10:17.
22. *Ibid.*, 14.
23. Constitution *Etsi minime*, 13.

II. At certain times throughout the year, they shall prepare boys and girls to receive properly the sacraments of Penance and Confirmation, by a continued instruction over a period of days.

III. With a very special zeal, on every day in Lent and, if necessary, on the days following Easter, they shall instruct with the use of apt illustrations and exhortations the youth of both sexes to receive their First Communion in a holy manner.

IV. In each and every parish the society known as the Confraternity of Christian Doctrine is to be canonically established. Through this Confraternity, the pastors, especially in places where there is a scarcity of priests, will have lay helpers in the teaching of the catechism, who will take up the work of imparting knowledge both from a zeal for the glory of God and in order to gain the numerous indulgences granted by the Sovereign Pontiffs.

V. In the larger cities, and especially where universities, colleges and secondary schools are located, let classes in religion be organized to instruct in the truths of faith and in the practice of Christian life the youths who attend the public schools from which all religious teaching is banned.

VI. Since it is a fact that in these days adults need instruction no less than the young, all pastors and those having the care of souls shall explain the catechism to the people in a plain and simple style adapted to the intelligence of their hearers. This shall be carried out on all holy days of obligation, at such time as is most convenient for the people, but not during the same hour when the children are instructed, and this instruction must be in addition to the usual homily on the Gospel which is delivered at the parochial Mass on Sundays and holy days. The catechetical instruction shall be based on the Roman Catechism, sometimes also called the Catechism of the Council of Trent; and the matter is to be divided in such a way that in the space of four or five years, treatment will be given to the Apostles' Creed, the sacraments, the ten commandments, the Lord's Prayer and the Precepts of the Church.

Venerable brothers, we decree and command this by virtue of our apostolic authority. It now rests with you to put it into prompt and complete execution in your respective dioceses, and by the power of your authority to see to it that these prescriptions of ours be not neglected or, what amounts to the same thing, that they be not carried out carelessly or superficially.

NECESSITY OF PREPARATION—That this may be avoided, you must exhort and urge your pastors not to impart these instructions without having first prepared themselves in the work. Then they will not merely speak words of human wisdom, but "in simplicity and godly sincerity,"[24] imitating the example of Jesus Christ, who, though He revealed "things hidden since the foundation of the world,"[25] yet spoke "all...things to the crowds in parables, and without parables...did not speak to them."[26] We know that the Apostles, who were taught by the Lord, did the same; for of them Pope St. Gregory wrote: "They took supreme care to preach to the uninstructed simple truths easy to understand, not things deep and difficult."[27] In matters of religion, the majority of men in our times must be considered uninstructed.

We do not, however, wish to give the impression that this studied simplicity in imparting instruction does not require labor and meditation—on the contrary, it demands both more than any other kind of preaching. It is much easier to find a preacher capable of delivering an eloquent and elaborate discourse than a catechist who can impart a catechetical instruction which is praiseworthy in every detail. No matter what natural facility a person may have in ideas and language, let him always remember that he will never be able to teach Christian doctrine to children or to adults without first giving himself to very careful study and preparation. They are mistaken who think that, because of inexperience and lack of training of the people, the work of catechizing can be performed in a slipshod fashion. On the contrary, the less educated the hearers, the more zeal and diligence must be used to adapt the sublime truths to their untrained minds; these truths, indeed, far surpass the natural understanding of the people, yet must be known by all—the uneducated and the cultured—in order that they may arrive at eternal happiness.

ZEAL AND LOVE FOR CHRISTIAN DOCTRINE—And now, venerable brothers, permit us to close this letter by addressing to you

---

24. 2 Cor. 1:12.
25. Mt. 13:35.
26. *Ibid.*, 34.
27. *Morals*, I, 17, *cap.* 26.

these words of Moses: "If any man be on the Lord's side, let him join with me."[28] We pray and entreat you to reflect on the great loss of souls due solely to ignorance of divine things. You have doubtless accomplished many useful and most praiseworthy works in your respective dioceses for the good of the flock entrusted to your care, but before all else, and with all possible zeal and diligence and care, see to it and urge on others that the knowledge of Christian doctrine pervades and imbues fully and deeply the minds of all. Here, using the words of the Apostle Peter, we say, "According to the gift that each has received, administer it to one another as good stewards of the manifold grace of God."[29]

Through the intercession of the most blessed immaculate Virgin, may your diligent efforts be made fruitful by the apostolic blessing which, in token of our affection and as a pledge of heavenly favors, we wholeheartedly impart to you and to your clergy and people.

Given at Rome, at St. Peter's, on the 15th day of April, 1905, in the second year of our pontificate.

POPE PIUS X

---

28. Ex. 32:26.
29. 1 Pt. 4:10.

POPE PIUS XI

Provido Sane Consilio, 1935

On Better Care for Catechetical Teaching

With truly farseeing wisdom, the Catholic Church, the guardian and teacher of divinely revealed truth, undertaking to fulfill her most holy office and duty, has always held that the imparting of the heavenly knowledge necessary for salvation through catechetical instruction must be placed among her most serious obligations. This work of bringing all men—particularly children and the poorly instructed adults—to know Christ our Lord and to learn His teachings must be committed to the zeal and ministry of qualified teachers.

In this the Church surely acts with prudence. The knowledge of a Christian is wholly contained in the words of the divine Redeemer: "This is everlasting life, that they may know you, the only true God, and him whom you have sent, Jesus Christ."[1] This knowledge is correctly and aptly contained in catechetical instruction wherein a summary of truths concerning God, Jesus Christ and His teachings and precepts are explained and presented to students

---

1. Jn. 17:3.

according to their age, ability, and condition of life. Indeed, when this matter has been presented and clearly illustrated, no better way can be desired to provide a firm and certain norm of true belief and right living for the faithful.

"Let the Little Children Come to Me"

Thus it is that in the Catholic Church catechetical instruction has been and indeed should be held as that voice through which divine Wisdom cries aloud in the streets: "Whosoever is a little one, let him come to me";[2] or like that lamp "shining in a dark place until the day dawns and the morning star rises in your hearts,"[3] or that "seed" and "leaven" of the Gospel whereby the whole Christian life springs into being and is nourished. Each of the faithful because of this instruction receives with profit the light of divine truth, the norm of divine law, and the help of divine grace; and he is able both to see what must be done and to gain the strength for its accomplishment. Religious instruction of this kind offers great advantages for all, but it is of special help in the years of childhood and adolescence, wherein lies the hope of adult life. Above all, then, catechetical instruction must be provided for children and youth, and they must be urged to take advantage of it. This is all the more necessary in an age in which the secular education of children and youth is eagerly planned and carried forward through a widespread pursuit of knowledge, manifold means of teaching, and improved methods of presenting matters to be learned. In the midst of such facilities for learning and such zeal for teaching, it must never be that the science of God and the all-important content of religion suffer neglect or omission.

It is evident too that the welfare of the nation itself is bound up with the Catholic instruction and training of children and youths. It is equally of vital interest to the state and to religion that citizens imbibe the Christian spirit as well as merely human knowledge and secular training.

It can thus be clearly understood why the Church, the teacher of Catholic truth and practice, out of love as well as prudence,

---

2. Prov. 9:4.
3. 2 Pt. 1:19.

speaks in the person of Christ and exclaims: "Let the little children come to me, and do not hinder them, for of such is the kingdom of God."[4]

Concern of the Holy See

The Roman Pontiffs as the supreme teachers and leaders of the Catholic Faith have always been fully cognizant of and attentive to all this, and they accordingly have never relaxed their vigilance and zeal in such an important matter.

There exists in our own time (if we may pass over more ancient documents) a splendid proof of this diligence in the Encyclical Letter *Acerbo nimis* of Pope Pius X which appeared on April 15, 1905. In this encyclical the ever-vigilant Pontiff first set forth the advantages that flow properly and solely from catechetical instruction, and then he concluded that the Faith in our day grows weak and is almost dead chiefly because the work of teaching Christian doctrine is either performed carelessly or is entirely omitted. He thereupon enacted legislation to provide for the teaching of Christian doctrine not only to boys and girls but also to youths and to adults as well.

The Code of Canon Law (Book III, tit. XX, chap. I) contains these same prescriptions practically in their entirety as set forth in the canons (1329-1336). Here the provisions relating to catechetical instruction, made obligatory throughout the universal Church, are duly stated and proposed as law.

With the purpose of seeing how the catechetical provisions of the Code are being carried out and to stimulate their enforcement when needful, Pope Pius XI, in a Motu proprio *Orbem catholicum* (June 29, 1923), instituted within this Sacred Congregation of the Council a catechetical office, whose special work is to guide and to promote the catechetical movement everywhere throughout the Catholic Church.

The zealous activities of the bishops have been in complete harmony with the commands and pleadings of the Supreme Pontiffs. In plenary and provincial councils, in diocesan synods, as well

---

4. Mk. 10:14.

as in catechetical congresses both diocesan and national, they have earnestly endeavored to improve the teaching of the catechism.

Despite the initial success of early beginnings, however, it is clear from the reports of the bishops themselves that there are still many obstacles which prevent the full force and effectiveness of the teaching of Christian doctrine. We must surely deplore first of all the carelessness of parents, many of whom are ignorant of the things of God and who accordingly do little or nothing for the religious education of their children. This is indeed a serious situation; for when the parents are either neglectful or deliberately opposed, there is practically no hope that the children will receive a religious training.

The condition is even worse where, as is the case in some nations, the very right of the Church to direct the Christian education of children is called into question or even denied by reason of political policy. Then the parents, overcome by indifference or their own fickleness of mind or weakened by the pressure of circumstances, offer neither opposition to the unjust laws nor do they give attention or care to the catechetical instruction of their children.

In countries where Catholics and non-Catholics dwell together and mixed marriages among them are common, it often happens as a consequence of the intimate relationship of married life that both the parents and children grow to disdain religion or fall altogether from the Faith.

A further consideration is a general lack of interest on the part of the children and youth in religion. They are taken up with other things and are attracted by games and exercises of physical culture, or by worldly shows where not infrequently moral discipline is relaxed; and thus led away, even on feastdays, the result is failure to attend the parish catechetical instruction. Thereupon forgetfulness and neglect of the things of God, which we so much deplore, take root in early childhood and grow worse with the years.

This forgetfulness and neglect cause even greater harm to the Faith in view of the fact that ravening wolves have come into the world, not sparing the flock; likewise, pseudo-teachers given to atheism and the new paganism have made their appearance, giving expression to clever falsehoods and sheer nonsense by writings and by other means cunningly attempting to destroy the Catholic belief in God, in Jesus Christ, and in the divine work of the Church. With these are joined the individuals who possess a semblance of Christian learning and piety, yet burn with zeal to propagate unhappy Protestantism. And with an ease that is almost unbelievable, they deceive those who are ignorant of or weak in Catholic doctrine—even also the simple and unwary faithful.

Although the bishops and those having the care of souls are striving diligently to overcome these difficulties, nevertheless this Sacred Congregation is bound to stimulate their zeal again and again; and their efforts do not exempt them from even greater attention and labor to a work upon which depends the eternal welfare of the sheep committed to their charge.

Further Catechetical Regulations

It has, therefore, seemed opportune to this Sacred Congregation that all interested in religious education should be encouraged to new efforts, and that certain prescriptions should be enacted and promulgated which, if observed, will give grounds to hope that catechetical instruction will make greater progress in the future.

In the first place let the bishops, mindful of the duty and office entrusted to them, exert even greater care and diligence than heretofore has been their custom, to encourage greater efforts and labor to spread catechetical instruction. "Let them see to it," therefore, in accord with Canon 336:2, "that the food of Christian doctrine be given to the faithful, especially to children and to the uninstructed, and that in the schools the education of children and youth be carried on according to the principles of the Catholic religion." Moreover, as provided in Canon 1336, "the Ordinary of the place has the right to legislate in his diocese in all matters that pertain to the instruction of the people in Christian doctrine," and, therefore, each Ordinary should consider in the Lord what preparations are to be made, what laws should be laid down for this most holy and necessary work, and by what means he can most easily and effectively carry out his plans in this matter. He shall bear in mind that, if the occasion warrants, he can punish those who are negligent or who refuse to obey with the penalties prescribed in Canons 1332:2 and 2182, and at the same time, as a reward to the zealous, he can intimate that special care and diligence exercised in the work of teaching catechism will be of greatest weight and importance in the conferring of parishes and other benefices.

Pastors and others having the care of souls should ever bear in mind that catechetical instruction is the foundation of the whole Christian life, and to its proper performance all their plans, studies, and efforts should be directed. Let them, therefore, note well and put into effect all the prescriptions of Canons 1330, 1331, and 1332; thus in this work in particular they ought to become all things to all men that they may gain all men for Christ, and be able to show themselves as faithful ministers and dispensers of the mysteries of God. Let them carefully determine the souls who need to be nourished with milk, and those who have need of more solid food, but let all be offered that food of doctrine that gives growth to the soul and mind so that the Christian will not be ignorant of his religion, neither will he hold it merely as a gift from his forebears, but on the contrary he will possess it well understood and clearly analyzed in order that it enrich both himself and others.

In carrying out this most holy work, "let the pastor," in accord with Canon 1333:1, "employ the help of other clerics in the parish, and also if necessary, of devout lay persons, especially those who belong to the Confraternity of Christian Doctrine or a similar society established in the parish." All of these, whether asked or commanded, should freely, nay more, should most gladly give their assistance to this work—as joyful givers beloved of the Lord.

The help of members of religious communities, according to Canon 1334, should not be lacking in a work so helpful, so pleasing to God, and so necessary for souls, if the Ordinary of the place requires it. The religious themselves on being called should joyfully respond, and they should even desire to give assistance in order to gain the reward exceedingly great through the salvation of souls that is achieved also in this part of the Lord's field, where the harvest is great but the laborers are few.

Finally, effective help and loyal support in this matter is both expected and demanded from parents and guardians. The provision of Canon 1113 should be called to their attention that, "they are bound by a most strict obligation to provide to the best of their ability for the religious and moral as well as for the physical and civil education of their children," and this obligation is fulfilled, according to Canon 1335, when they see to it that their children receive catechetical instruction and also, by Canon 1372:2, in providing them with a Christian education.

All of the matters we have here treated in summary are already well known and evident; nevertheless the old adage, "repetition is useful," must not be overlooked, especially when the subject is one that cannot be insisted upon too much.

Specific Commands for the Catechetical Apostolate

In order, then, that all of this may more readily be carried out in the entire world, this Sacred Congregation, with the approval of His Holiness, Pope Pius XI, commands that in all dioceses the following be observed:

1. In every parish, besides the Confraternity of the Blessed Sacrament, the Confraternity of Christian Doctrine, as the most important of all others, must be established in accordance with Canon 711:2, and it should embrace all who are capable of teaching and promoting catechetical instruction, especially teachers in the schools and all who are skilled in the science of teaching children.

2. Using the Letter of this Sacred Congregation directed to the Bishops of Italy as a norm, parochial classes in Christian doctrine should be established if they do not already exist. With the pastors themselves in charge of these classes, and with the employment of approved methods of teaching, children and youth will have opportunity to learn the fundamentals of the divine law and of the Faith. In order, moreover, to overcome the indifference of parents already referred to, who think their children are not obliged to attend the catechism classes of the parish because they are receiving religious instruction either at home or in the public schools, let the following be carefully observed:

    a. Pastors shall not admit to reception of the sacraments of Penance and Confirmation, as prescribed in Canon 1330, children who have not acquired sufficient knowledge of the catechism according to directives of the Decree of the Sacred Congregation of the Sacraments on August 8, 1910; and after they have received their First Communion, they must endeavor to learn the catechism more perfectly and with greater profit.

b. Pastors, preachers, confessors, and rectors of churches shall take particular care to advise parents of the grave obligation which is theirs to see to it that, "all subject to them or under their care are given catechetical instruction" (Canon 1335). On this subject, Pope Benedict XIV wrote as follows in his Encyclical *Etsi minime*, of February 7, 1742: "It is evident that the Bishop can and should in all earnestness recommend to preachers that in their sermons they impress upon the ears and minds of parents the importance of teaching their children the truths of our religion; and that if they are not fully capable of so doing, they should bring their children to the church where the precepts of the divine law will be explained."

c. Furthermore, let pastors and their assistants endeavor so far as they can to make the children eager to attend the parish catechism classes. To this end the most successful and tried means should be employed, for example, the celebration of a Mass for the children on all holy days, catechetical competitions, offering of attractive prizes, and the use of suitable projects and moderate forms of amusement.

d. Finally, let pastors carefully prepare the children so that they may be examined on their knowledge of religion by the bishop when he makes his pastoral visitation. The bishop will take this opportunity to call attention to the condition of religious instruction in the parish: what he feels needs correction, improvement, or special commendation.

3. There is a danger that the religious training received in childhood will be forgotten with advancing age, for as Pope Benedict XIV has pointed out, "It is well known that not only the young and those reaching maturity are steeped in ignorance of the things of God, but also adults and old people are altogether destitute of the teachings of salvation; this is because they have never learned them, or having once learned them they have little by little forgotten them" *(loc. cit.)*. Bishops, therefore, should carefully see to it that the provisions of Canon 1332 be scrupulously observed by the pastors. They are bound, according to this Canon, "to explain the catechism on Sundays and holy days to adults among the faithful in words suited to their capacity to understand." With this in mind, Pope Pius X, in his celebrated encyclical *Acerbo nimis*, ordered that "the *catechism of the Council of Trent* should be used in such a way

that over a period of four or five years the entire material would be covered which treats of the Apostles' Creed, the sacraments, the commandments, prayer, and the precepts of the Church," and the same holds true of the evangelical counsels, grace, the virtues, sin, and the last things.

Practical Means To Be Adopted

In addition to the above measures incumbent upon all, this Sacred Congregation considers it opportune to point out to the Ordinaries some means which experience has proved to be well adapted to the end desired. The Ordinaries, therefore, will take care that all or at least some of the means which here follow are used according to the different needs and circumstances of each diocese.

1. As is already provided for Italy in the Letter of this Sacred Congregation on December 12, 1929, the Ordinaries will, if possible, set up a diocesan catechetical office, which under their supervision will direct all catechetical education in the diocese. The chief functions of this office will be to provide:

a. that in parishes, in schools, and in colleges, Christian doctrine be taught by qualified teachers employing the traditional form of the Church;

b. that at stated times catechetical conventions and other meetings in the interests of religious education shall be held for the purpose of discussion and study of the methods best suited for catechetical instruction, as has been noted in a decree of this Sacred Congregation on April 12, 1924;

c. that a special Course of Lectures on Religion be offered each year to those who teach Christian doctrine in parochial and public schools, in order that they will increase in the quality and depth of their knowledge.

2. The Ordinaries shall not fail to appoint competent priest-visitors each year to inspect all the schools of religion in the dioceses; they shall carefully report the results, the improvements, or the weaknesses in the religious instruction of the schools. Pope Benedict XIV wrote on this subject as follows: "It will be of greatest benefit for the education of the Christian people if visitors be chosen, some to visit in the city, others to go about in the diocese,

making careful and exhaustive inquiry and informing the bishop who, thus made aware of the work being done by the pastors, may place praise or blame where it is deserved" *(loc. cit.)*.

3. In order that the mind of the Christian people may be directed from time to time toward religious education, let a Catechetical Day be established in each parish, if this has not already been done. On this day, the Feast of Christian Doctrine is to be celebrated with as much solemnity as possible. On this occasion:

    a. The faithful should be called together in the parish church, and having received the Holy Eucharist, they should pray to obtain greater fruit from divine teaching;

    b. A special sermon should be preached to the people on the necessity of catechetical instruction. Parents are to be told about their duty to instruct their children in Christian doctrine and to send them to the parochial catechism classes, being mindful of the divine command: "And these words which I command you this day shall be in your heart. And you shall tell them to your children...."[5]

    c. Books, pamphlets, leaflets, and other material suitable for the purpose should be distributed to the people;

    d. A collection may be taken up for the promotion of catechetical works.

4. In places where the scarcity of priests is such that the clergy themselves cannot satisfactorily perform the work of teaching Christian doctrine, the Ordinary should take active steps to supply *capable catechists* of both sexes to help the pastors to impart religious instruction in the parochial or in the public schools, even in the remote parts of the parish. A leading part in this work should be undertaken by all members of Catholic Action groups. These associations have already done much commendable work in this direction, and certain of them have very wisely provided in their constitutions that lectures in religion are to be conducted each year at which all their members must be present.

Members of other Catholic organizations and associations should not fail in this work, especially the societies of religious of

---

5. Dt. 6:6-7.

both sexes that are specifically dedicated to the education of youth. To these His Holiness, Pope Pius XI, addressed his memorable Motu Proprio *Orbem catholicum:* "We earnestly desire that in all the principal centers of religious societies which are engaged in the teaching of youth, there be established, under the direction and guidance of the bishops, schools for select students of both sexes, where they shall be trained in a suitable course of studies, and upon examination be declared fit to undertake the teaching of Christian doctrine and Bible and Church History." This surely will be accomplished if, as reason itself persuades and demands, the study of religion holds first place among the subjects pursued by children and youth in our Catholic schools and colleges. Let such instruction be given by priests skilled in teaching and according to proved principles of pedagogy.

If these means and plans are used, and if all who are dutybound give themselves vigorously and perseveringly to this work —more holy and more necessary than any other—then it can be hoped that the Christian people will be made secure through holy and uncorrupt doctrine against the attacks of error, becoming an acceptable people, followers of good works. Then, too, they will produce those wholesome results which the Roman Pontiffs have repeatedly desired for the salvation of souls. Finally, with the approval of His Holiness, Pope Pius XI, this Sacred Congregation, derogating in this respect from the above-mentioned Motu Proprio *Orbem catholicum,* commands all bishops to submit an accurate report every five years to this same Sacred Congregation regarding catechetical instruction in their dioceses. They shall use the questionnaire which follows and shall observe the order prescribed in Canon 340:2 of the Code of Canon Law relating to the report which must be submitted by each bishop on the state of the diocese entrusted to him.

Given at Rome, on the Feast of the Holy Family of Nazareth, January 12, 1935.

I. CARD. SERAFINI, *Prefect*
I. BRUNO, *Secretary*

****

QUESTIONNAIRE REGARDING THE TEACHING OF CHRISTIAN DOCTRINE

I. For Children

(a) *In the Parishes:*

Q. 1. What is the number of the children in the individual parishes, and how many of these attend catechetical instruction?

Q. 2. What diligence do the pastors display in the fulfillment of their task of giving the children religious instruction, and what pastors neglect this duty?

Q. 3. Have *parochial schools* been instituted in these same parishes? With what result, and what method do they follow in teaching Christian doctrine?

Q. 4. Do the priests and other clerics living within the territory of the parish assist the pastor in teaching Christian doctrine? In what way is this assistance given? Have any been negligent or recalcitrant?

Q. 5. Do the religious of both sexes assist the pastor in teaching catechism to the children? Have any shown themselves negligent or recalcitrant?

Q. 6. Has the *Confraternity of Christian Doctrine* been established in the separate parishes, and in what way does it cooperate with the pastor in teaching Christian doctrine to the children?

Q. 7. Do other societies of the laity, especially of *Catholic Action*, assist the pastor in this same duty?

Q. 8. Has a *Catechetical Bureau (Officium catechisticum)* or some similar institute been established in the diocese, or is it possible to establish such?

Q. 9. Is a *Catechetical Day* celebrated? In what manner?

Q. 10. Are *catechetical gatherings (coetus catechistici)* held? With what fruits? Are other conventions for religion schools held?

Q. 11. Are any means employed to stimulate both parents and children, so that the latter will attend the parish catechism class? What means are employed?

Q. 12. Is there anything that interferes with the more abundant fruits of the teaching of Christian doctrine? What abuses have crept in, and what means are being employed, or may be employed, to remove them?

(b) *In Catholic Schools and Colleges:*

Q. 13. How many Catholic schools for boys and girls, especially of recent institution, are under the direction of the secular or regular clergy or of religious sisters?

Q. 14. How many pupils are there, day and boarders, in the individual Catholic schools and colleges?

Q. 15. How often during the week, and by what method and with what results, is religious instruction given in these schools?

Q. 16. How could this instruction be more efficaciously and usefully promoted?

(c) *In the Public Schools:*

Q. 17. Is Christian doctrine being taught in the public schools? In what schools, and with what success?

Q. 18. Is the religious instruction subject to the authority and inspection of the Church? In what way and in what public schools?

Q. 19. In what public schools, and for what reason, is Christian doctrine not taught? How is the religious instruction of the pupils of these schools being provided for?

Q. 20. Are any means employed, or can there be, to secure that Christian doctrine may be taught in these schools?

II. *Adults*

Q. 21. Besides the usual homily, is any catechetical instruction being given by the pastor to adults? When is this instruction given?

Q. 22. With what diligence, by what method, and at what time do the pastors fulfill this duty?

Q. 23. Do the faithful attend religious instruction in the individual parishes, and with what results?

Q. 24. In view of the circumstances of the time and place, what means are considered most suitable for promoting the more fruitful religious instruction of adults?

POPE PAUL VI

Sollemnis Professio Fidei, 1968

The Creed of the People of God

Venerable brothers and beloved sons:

1 With this solemn liturgy we end the celebration of the nineteenth centenary of the martyrdom of the holy Apostles Peter and Paul, and thus close the Year of Faith. We dedicated it to the commemoration of the holy Apostles in order that we might give witness to our steadfast will to *guard the deposit*[1] of faith from corruption, that deposit which they transmitted to us, and to demonstrate again our intention of relating this same faith to life at this time when the Church must continue her pilgrimage in this world.

2 We feel it our duty to give public thanks to all who responded to our invitation by bestowing on the Year of Faith a splendid completeness through the deepening of their personal adhesion to the Word of God, through the renewal in various gatherings of the Profession of Faith, and through the testimony of a Christian life. To our brothers in the episcopate especially, and to all the faithful of the holy Catholic Church, we express our appreciation and we grant our blessing.

---

1. Cf. 1 Tm. 6:20.

3 Likewise we deem that we must fulfill the mandate entrusted by Christ to Peter, whose Successor we are, the last in merit; namely, to confirm our brothers in the Faith.[2] With the awareness, certainly, of our human weakness, yet with all the strength impressed on our spirit by such a command, we shall accordingly make a Profession of Faith, pronounce a formula which begins with the word *Credo, I believe*. Without being strictly speaking a dogmatic definition, it repeats in substance, with some developments called for by the spiritual condition of our time, the Creed of Nicea, the Creed of the immortal Tradition of the holy Church of God.

4 In making this profession, we are aware of the disquiet which agitates certain groups of men at the present time with regard to the Faith. They do not escape the influence of a world being profoundly changed, in which so many truths are being denied outright or made objects of controversy. We see even Catholics allowing themselves to be seized by a kind of passion for change and novelty. The Church, most assuredly, has always the duty to carry on the effort to study more deeply and to present in a manner ever better adapted to successive generations the unfathomable mysteries of God, rich for all in fruits of salvation. But at the same time the greatest care must be taken, while fulfilling the indispensable duty of research, to do no injury to the truths of Christian doctrine. For that would be to give rise, as is unfortunately seen in these days, to disturbance and doubt in many faithful souls.

5 It is supremely important in this respect to recall that, beyond what is observable, analyzed by the work of the sciences, the intellect which God has given us reaches *that which is*, and not merely the subjective expression of the structures and development of consciousness. And, on the other hand, it is important to remember that the task of interpretation—of hermeneutics—is to try to understand and extricate, while respecting the word expressed, the sense conveyed by a text, and not to recreate, in some fashion, this sense in accordance with arbitrary hypotheses.

---

2. Lk. 22:32.

6   But above all, we place our unshakeable confidence in the Holy Spirit, the soul of the Church, and in theological faith upon which rests the life of the Mystical Body. We know that souls await the word of the Vicar of Christ, and we respond to that expectation with the instructions which we regularly give. But today we are given an opportunity to make a more solemn utterance.

7   On this day which is chosen to close the Year of Faith, on this feast of the blessed Apostles Peter and Paul, we have wished to offer to the living God the homage of a Profession of Faith. And as once at Caesarea Philippi the Apostle Peter spoke on behalf of the Twelve to make a true confession, beyond human opinions, of Christ as Son of the living God, so today his humble Successor, Pastor of the universal Church, raises his voice to give, on behalf of all the People of God, a firm witness to the divine truth entrusted to the Church to be announced to all nations.

We have wished our Profession of Faith to be to a high degree complete and explicit, in order that it may respond in a fitting way to the need of light felt by so many faithful souls, and by all those in the world to whatever spiritual family they belong, who are in search of the truth.

Therefore, to the glory of God most holy and of our Lord Jesus Christ, trusting in the aid of the Blessed Virgin Mary and of the holy Apostles Peter and Paul, for the profit and edification of the Church, in the name of all the pastors and all the faithful, we now pronounce this Profession of Faith, in full communion with you all, beloved brothers and sons.

Profession of Faith

8   We believe in one only God, Father, Son and Holy Spirit, Creator of things visible such as this world in which our brief life passes, and things invisible such as the pure spirits which are also called angels,[3] and Creator in each man of his spiritual and immortal soul.[4]

---

3. Cf. Conc. Vat. I, Const. dogm. *Dei Filius, DS.* 3002.
4. Cf. Litt. Enc. *Humani generis, AAS* 42 (1950), p. 575; Conc. Lateran., V, *DS.* 1440-1441.

9   We believe that this only God is absolutely one in His infinitely holy essence as also in all His perfections, in His omnipotence, His infinite knowledge, His Providence, His will and His love. He is *He Who Is*, as He revealed to Moses[5]; and He is *love*, as the Apostle John teaches us[6]: so that these two names, being and love, express ineffably the same divine reality of Him who has wished to make Himself known to us, and who "dwelling in light inaccessible,"[7] is in Himself above every name, above every thing and above every created intellect. God alone can give us right and full knowledge of this reality by revealing Himself as Father, Son and Holy Spirit, in whose eternal life we are by grace called to share, here below in the obscurity of faith and after death in eternal light. The mutual bonds which eternally constitute the Three Persons, who are each one and the same divine Being, are the blessed inmost life of God thrice holy, infinitely beyond all that we can conceive in human measure.[8] We give thanks, however, to the divine Goodness that very many believers can testify with us before men to the Unity of God, even though they know not the mystery of the most holy Trinity.

10   We believe then in God who eternally begets the Son, in the Son, the Word of God, who is eternally begotten, in the Holy Spirit, the uncreated Person, who proceeds from the Father and the Son as their eternal Love. Thus in the Three Divine Persons, *coaeternae sibi et coaequales*,[9] the life and beatitude of God perfectly One superabound and are consummated in the supreme excellence and glory proper to uncreated Being, and always "there should be venerated Unity in the Trinity and Trinity in the Unity."[10]

11   We believe in our Lord Jesus Christ, who is the Son of God. He is the eternal Word, born of the Father before time began, and consubstantial with the Father, *homoousios to Patri*, and through Him all things were made. He was incarnate of the Virgin

---

5. Cf. Ex. 3:14.
6. Cf. 1 Jn. 4:8.
7. Cf. 1 Tm. 6:16.
8. Cf. Conc. Vat. I, Const. dogm. *Dei Filius*, DS. 3016.
9. Symbolum *Quicumque*, DS. 75.
10. *Ibid*.

Mary by the power of the Holy Spirit, and was made man: equal therefore to the Father according to His divinity, and inferior to the Father according to His humanity,[11] and Himself one, not by some impossible confusion of His natures, but by the unity of His Person.[12]

12 He dwelt among us, full of grace and truth. He proclaimed and established the kingdom of God and made us know in Himself the Father. He gave us His new commandment to love one another as He loved us. He taught us the way of the beatitudes of the Gospel: poverty in spirit, meekness, suffering borne with patience, thirst after justice, mercy, purity of heart, will for peace, persecution suffered for justice' sake. He suffered under Pontius Pilate, the Lamb of God bearing on Himself the sins of the world, and He died for us on the cross, saving us by His redeeming blood. He was buried, and, of His own power, rose the third day, raising us by His resurrection to that sharing in the divine life which is the life of grace. He ascended to heaven, and He will come again, this time in glory, to judge the living and the dead: each according to his merits—those who have responded to the love and piety of God going to eternal life, those who have refused them to the end going to the fire that is not extinguished. And His kingdom will have no end.

13 We believe in the Holy Spirit, who is Lord, and Giver of life, who is adored and glorified together with the Father and the Son. He spoke to us by the prophets, He was sent by Christ after His resurrection and ascension to the Father; He illuminates, vivifies, protects and governs the Church; He purifies the Church's members if they do not shun His grace. His action, which penetrates to the inmost of the soul, enables man to respond to the call of Jesus: *Be perfect as your heavenly Father is perfect.*[13]

14 We believe that Mary is the Mother, who remained ever a Virgin, of the Incarnate Word, our God and Savior Jesus Christ,[14] and that by reason of this singular election, she was, in consideration of the merits of her Son, redeemed in a more eminent

---

11. *Ibid.*, no. 76.
12. *Ibid.*
13. Cf. Mt. 5:48.
14. Cf. Conc. Ephes. *DS.* 251-252.

manner,[15] preserved from all stain of original sin[16] and filled with the gift of grace more than all other creatures.[17]

15   Joined by a close and indissoluble bond to the mysteries of the Incarnation and Redemption,[18] the Blessed Virgin, the Immaculate, was at the end of her earthly life raised body and soul to heavenly glory and likened to her risen Son in anticipation of the future lot of all the just[19]; and we believe that the Blessed Mother of God, the New Eve, Mother of the Church,[20] continues in heaven her maternal role with regard to Christ's members, cooperating with the birth and growth of divine life in the souls of the redeemed.[21]

16   We believe that in Adam all have sinned, which means that the original offense committed by him caused human nature, common to all men, to fall to a state in which it bears the consequences of that offense, and which is not the state in which it was at first in our first parents, established as they were in holiness and justice, and in which man knew neither evil nor death. It is human nature so fallen, stripped of the grace that clothed it, injured in its own natural powers and subjected to the dominion of death, that is transmitted to all men, and it is in this sense that every man is born in sin. We therefore hold, with the Council of Trent, that original sin is transmitted with human nature, "not by imitation, but by propagation" and that it is thus "in each of us as his own."[22]

17   We believe that our Lord Jesus Christ, by the sacrifice of the cross, redeemed us from original sin and all the personal sins committed by each one of us, so that, in accordance with the word of the Apostle, "where sin abounded, grace did more abound."[23]

---

15. Cf. Conc. Vat. II, Const. dogm. *Lumen gentium*, no. 53.
16. Cf. Pius IX, *Ineffabilis Deus, Acta*, pars. I, vol. I, p. 616.
17. Cf. *Lumen gentium*, no. 53.
18. Cf. *Ibid.*, nos. 53, 58, 61.
19. Cf. Const. Ap. *Munificentissimus Deus, AAS* 42 (1950), p. 770.
20. *Lumen gentium*, nos. 53, 56, 61, 63; Paulus VI, Alloc in conclusione III Sessionis Concilii Vat. II, *AAS* 56 (1964), p. 1016; Exhort. Apost. *Signum magnum, AAS* 59 (1967), pp. 465 et 467.
21. Cf. *Lumen gentium* no. 62; Paulus VI, Exhort. Apost. *Signum magnum, AAS* 59 (1967), p. 468.
22. Cf. Conc. Trid. Sess. V, Decret. *De pecc. orig.*, DS. 1513.
23. Rom. 5:20.

18   We believe in one Baptism instituted by our Lord Jesus Christ for the remission of sins. Baptism should be administered even to little children who have not yet been able to be guilty of any personal sin, in order that, though born deprived of supernatural grace, they may be reborn "of water and the Holy Spirit" to the divine life in Christ Jesus.[24]

19   We believe in one, holy, catholic, and apostolic Church, built by Jesus Christ on that rock which is Peter. She is the Mystical Body of Christ; at the same time a visible society instituted with hierarchical organs, and a spiritual community; the Church on earth, the pilgrim People of God here below, and the Church filled with heavenly blessings; the germ and the first fruits of the kingdom of God, through which the work and the sufferings of redemption are continued throughout human history, and which looks for its perfect accomplishment beyond time in glory.[25] In the course of time, the Lord Jesus forms His Church by means of the sacraments emanating from His plenitude.[26] By these she makes her members participants in the mystery of the death and resurrection of Christ, in the grace of the Holy Spirit who gives her life and movement.[27] She is therefore holy, though she has sinners in her bosom, because she herself has no other life but that of grace: it is by living by her life that her members are sanctified; it is by removing themselves from her life that they fall into sins and disorders that prevent the radiation of her sanctity. This is why she suffers and does penance for these offenses, of which she has the power to heal her children through the blood of Christ and the gift of the Holy Spirit.

20   Heiress of the divine promises and daughter of Abraham according to the Spirit, through that Israel whose Scriptures she lovingly guards, and whose patriarchs and prophets she venerates; founded upon the Apostles and handing on from century to century their ever-living word and their powers as pastors in the Successor of Peter and the bishops in communion with him; perpet-

---

24. Cf. Conc. Trid., *ibid.*, DS. 1514.
25. Cf. *Lumen gentium*, nos. 8 et 5.
26. Cf. *ibid.*, nos. 7, 11.
27. Cf. Conc. Vat. II, Const. *Sacrosanctum concilium*, nos. 5, 6; *Lumen gentium*, nos. 7, 12, 50.

ually assisted by the Holy Spirit, she has the charge of guarding, teaching, explaining and spreading the truth which God revealed in a then veiled manner by the prophets, and fully by the Lord Jesus. We believe *all that is contained in the Word of God written or handed down, and that the Church proposes for belief as divinely revealed, whether by a solemn judgment or by the ordinary and universal Magisterium.*[28] We believe in the infallibility enjoyed by the Successor of Peter when he teaches ex cathedra as Pastor and Teacher of all the faithful,[29] and which is assured also to the episcopal body when it exercises with him the supreme Magisterium.[30]

21 We believe that the Church founded by Jesus Christ and for which He prayed is indefectibly one in faith, worship and the bond of hierarchical communion.[31] In the bosom of this Church, the rich variety of liturgical rites and the legitimate diversity of theological and spiritual heritages and special disciplines, far from injuring her unity, make it more manifest.[32]

22 Recognizing also the existence, outside the organism of the Church of Christ, of numerous elements of truth and sanctification which belong to her as her own and tend to Catholic unity,[33] and believing in the action of the Holy Spirit who stirs up in the heart of the disciples of Christ love of this unity,[34] we entertain the hope that Christians who are not yet in the full communion of the one only Church will one day be reunited in one flock with one only Shepherd.

23 We believe that the Church is *necessary for salvation, because Christ, who is the sole Mediator and Way of salvation, renders Himself present for us in His Body which is the Church.*[35] But the divine design of salvation embraces all men; and those *who*

---

28. Cf. Conc. Vat. I, Const. *Dei Filius, DS.* 3011.
29. Cf. *ibid.*, Const. *Pastor aeternus, DS.* 3074.
30. Cf. *Lumen gentium*, no. 25.
31. Cf. *ibid.*, nos. 8, 18-23; Decret. *Unitatis redintegratio*, no. 2.
32. Cf. *Lumen gentium*, no. 23; Decret. Orientalium ecclesiarum, nos. 2, 3, 5, 6.
33. Cf. *Lumen gentium*, no. 8.
34. Cf. *ibid.*, no. 15.
35. Cf. *ibid.*, no. 14.

without fault on their part do not know the Gospel of Christ and His Church, but seek God sincerely, and under the influence of grace endeavor to do His will as recognized through the promptings of their conscience, they, in a number known only to God, *can obtain salvation.*[36]

24   We believe that the Mass, celebrated by the priest representing the person of Christ by virtue of the power received through the sacrament of Orders, and offered by him in the name of Christ and the members of His Mystical Body, is in true reality the sacrifice of Calvary, rendered sacramentally present on our altars. We believe that as the bread and wine consecrated by the Lord at the Last Supper where changed into His body and His blood which were to be offered for us on the cross, likewise the bread and wine consecrated by the priest are changed into the body and blood of Christ enthroned gloriously in heaven, and we believe that the mysterious presence of the Lord, under what continues to appear to our sense as before, is a true, real and substantial presence.[37]

25   Christ cannot be thus present in this sacrament except by the change into His body of the reality itself of the bread and the change into His blood of the reality itself of the wine, leaving unchanged only the properties of the bread and wine which our senses perceive. This mysterious change is very appropriately called by the Church *transubstantiation*. Every theological explanation which seeks some understanding of this mystery must, in order to be in accord with Catholic Faith, maintain that in the reality itself, independently of our mind, the bread and wine have ceased to exist after the Consecration, so that it is the adorable body and blood of the Lord Jesus that from then on are really before us under the sacramental species of bread and wine,[38] as the Lord willed it, in order to give Himself to us as food and to associate us with the unity of His Mystical Body.[39]

---

36. Cf. *ibid.*, no. 16.
37. Cf. Conc. Trid., Sess. XIII, Decret. *De Eucharistia*, DS. 1651.
38. Cf. *ibid.*, DS. 1642, 1651; Paulus VI, Litt. Enc. *Mysterium Fidei*, AAS 57 (1965), p. 766.
39. Cf. *S. Th.*, III, 73, 3.

26   The unique and indivisible existence of the Lord glorious in heaven is not multiplied, but is rendered present by the sacrament in the many places on earth where Mass is celebrated. And this existence remains present, after the sacrifice, in the Blessed Sacrament which is, in the tabernacle, the living heart of each of our churches. And it is our very sweet duty to honor and adore in the Blessed Host which our eyes see, the Incarnate Word whom they cannot see, and who, without leaving heaven, is made present before us.

27   We confess that the kingdom of God begun here below in the Church of Christ *is not of this world*[40] *whose form is passing*,[41] and that its proper growth cannot be confounded with the progress of civilization, of science or of human technology, but that it consists in an ever more profound knowledge of the unfathomable riches of Christ, an ever stronger hope in eternal blessings, an ever more ardent response to the love of God, and an ever more generous bestowal of grace and holiness among men. But it is this same love which induces the Church to concern herself constantly about the true temporal welfare of men. Without ceasing to recall to her children that *they have not here a lasting dwelling*,[42] she also urges them to contribute, each according to his vocation and his means, to the welfare of their earthly city, to promote justice, peace and brotherhood among men, to give their aid freely to their brothers, especially to the poorest and most unfortunate. The deep solicitude of the Church, the Spouse of Christ, for the needs of men, for their joys and hopes, their griefs and efforts, is therefore nothing other than her great desire to be present to them, in order to illuminate them with the light of Christ and to gather them all in Him, their only Savior. This solicitude can never mean that the Church conform herself to the things of this world, or that she lessen the ardor of her expectation of her Lord and of the eternal kingdom.

28   We believe in the life eternal. We believe that the souls of all those who die in the grace of Christ, whether they must still be purified in purgatory, or whether from the moment they leave their

---

40. Cf. Jn. 18:36.
41. Cf. 1 Cor. 1:31.
42. Cf. Heb. 13:14.

bodies Jesus takes them to paradise as He did for the Good Thief, are the People of God in the eternity beyond death, which will be finally conquered on the day of the resurrection when these souls will be reunited with their bodies.

29   We believe that the multitude of those gathered around Jesus and Mary in paradise forms the Church of heaven, where in eternal beatitude they see God as He is,[43] and where they also, in different degrees, are associated with the holy angels in the divine rule exercised by Christ in glory, interceding for us and helping our weakness by their brotherly care.[44]

30   We believe in the communion of all the faithful of Christ, those who are pilgrims on earth, the dead who are attaining their purification, and the blessed in heaven, all together forming one Church; and we believe that in this communion the merciful love of God and His saints is ever listening to our prayers, as Jesus told us: Ask and you will receive.[45] Thus it is with faith and in hope that we look forward to the resurrection of the dead, and the life of the world to come.

Blessed be God thrice holy. Amen.

Pronounced in front of the Basilica of St. Peter, on June 30, 1968, the sixth year of our pontificate.

POPE PAUL VI

---

43. 1 Jn. 3:2; Benedictus XII, Const. *Benedictus Deus*, DS. 1000.
44. Cf. *Lumen gentium*, no. 49.
45. Cf. Lk. 10:9-10; Jn. 16:24.

POPE PAUL VI

Directorium Catechisticum Generale, 1971

General Catechetical Directory

FOREWORD

This *General Catechetical Directory* is published in accord with the directive in the *Decree on the Bishops' Pastoral Office in the Church*, n. 44.

Considerable time was spent in the preparation of this document, not only because of the difficulties involved in a work of this sort, but also because of the method which was used in producing it.

Thus, after a special commission was set up consisting of men truly expert in catechesis—they were of various nationalities and had been selected after consultation with certain episcopates—the first thing done was to seek the advice and opinions of the various episcopates.

With that advice and those opinions in mind, a first draft of the *Directory* was worked up in an outline form showing only the principal features. This was examined at a special plenary session of the Sacred Congregation for the Clergy. After that, a longer draft was prepared, and once again the Conferences of Bishops were queried so that they might express their opinion about it. In accord with the advice and observations given by the bishops in this second consultation, a definitive draft of the *Directory* was prepared. Even so, before this was published, it was reviewed by a special theological commission and by the Sacred Congregation for the Doctrine of the Faith.

The intent of this *Directory* is to provide the basic principles of pastoral theology—these principles have been taken from the Magisterium of the Church, and in a special way from the Second General Vatican Council—by which pastoral action in the ministry of the word can be more fittingly directed and governed. This explains why the theoretical aspect is given primary emphasis in this *Directory*, although, as will be evident, the practical aspect is by no means neglected. Such a course of action was adopted especially for the following reason: the errors which are not infrequently noted in catechesis today can be avoided only if one starts with the correct way of understanding the nature and purposes of catechesis and also the truths which are to be taught by it, with due account being taken of those to whom catechesis is directed and of the conditions in which they live. Moreover, the specific task of applying the principles and declarations contained in this *Directory* to concrete situations properly belongs to the various episcopates, and they do this by means of national and regional directories, and by means of catechisms and the other aids which are suitable for effectively promoting the work of the ministry of the word.

It is clear that not all parts of the *Directory* are of the same importance. Those things which are said about divine revelation, the criteria according to which the Christian message is to be expounded, and the more outstanding elements of that same message, are to be held by all. On the other hand, those things which are said about the present situation, methodology, and the form of catechesis for people of differing ages, are to be taken rather as suggestions and guides, for a number of them are of necessity taken from the human sciences, theoretical as well as practical, and these are indeed subject to some evolution.

The *Directory* is chiefly intended for bishops, Conferences of Bishops, and in general all who under their leadership and direction have responsibility in the catechetical field. The immediate purpose of the *Directory* is to provide assistance in the production of catechetical directories and catechisms. Indeed, it is for this reason, that is, to help in the preparation of these tools, that the following have been done. Some basic features of present-day conditions have been set forth, so as to stimulate studies in the various parts of the Church, studies which should be carried out with careful and diligent effort, with regard to local conditions and local pastoral needs. Some general principles of methodology and catechesis for different age groups have been noted, so as to highlight how necessary it is to learn the art and wisdom of education. Special pains have been taken in the composition of Part Three, where the criteria which should govern the presentation of the truths to be taught through catechesis are set forth and where a summary of essential elements of the Christian faith is also given, so as to make fully clear the goal which catechesis must of necessity have, namely, the presentation of the Christian faith in its entirety.

Since the *Directory* is intended for countries which differ greatly in their conditions and pastoral needs, it is obvious that only common or average conditions could be considered in it. Therefore, in judging and evaluating the *Directory*, one will have to give due consideration to this particular feature as well as to the structure. The same thing must be said about the description of pastoral work given in Part Six. It deals with the plan of pastoral action that is to be promoted, and this is described only in general outlines. This will perhaps be inadequate for those areas in which catechesis has already made great strides, while, on the other hand, in those places where catechesis has not yet advanced very far, it will perhaps seem to demand too much.

With the publication of this document the Church gives new evidence of her concern for a ministry which is absolutely necessary for proper fulfillment of her mission in the world. It is prayerfully hoped that this document will be accepted and be carefully studied and weighed, with attention to the pastoral needs of the individual ecclesial communities. It is similarly hoped that this document will be able to stimulate new and more vigorous studies that faithfully respond to the needs of the ministry of the word and to the norms of the Magisterium of the Church.

ABBREVIATIONS

(Documents of Vatican Council II)

AA = Decree on the Apostolate of the Laity
  (*Apostolicam actuositatem*)
AG = Decree on the Missionary Activity of the Church
  (*Ad gentes*)
CD = Decree on the Bishops' Pastoral Office in the Church
  (*Christus Dominus*)
DH = Declaration on Religious Freedom
  (*Dignitatis humanae*)
DV = Dogmatic Constitution on Divine Revelation
  (*Dei Verbum*)
GE = Declaration on Christian Education
  (*Gravissimum educationis*)
GS = Pastoral Constitution on the Church in the Modern World
  (*Gaudium et spes*)
IM = Decree on the Instruments of Social Communication
  (*Inter mirifica*)
LG = Dogmatic Constitution on the Church
  (*Lumen gentium*)
NA = Declaration on the Relationship of the Church to Non-Christian Religions (*Nostra aetate*)
OT = Decree on Priestly Formation (*Optatam totius*)
PC = Decree on the Appropriate Renewal of the Religious Life
  (*Perfectae caritatis*)
PO = Decree on the Ministry and Life of Priests
  (*Presbyterorum ordinis*)
SC = Constitution on the Sacred Liturgy
  (*Sacrosanctum Concilium*)
UR = Decree on Ecumenism (*Unitatis redintegratio*)

Part One
The Reality of the Problem

Nature and Purpose of This Part

1 Since the essential mission of the Church is to proclaim and promote the faith in contemporary human society, a society disturbed by very great sociocultural changes, it is appropriate here, with the declarations of the Second Vatican Council in mind, to sketch some features and characteristics of the present situation by pointing out the spiritual repercussions they have and the new obligations the Church has as a result. The discussion here is not meant to be exhaustive, because the subject covers points which are unique and often very much different in the various parts of the Church. National directories will have the task of filling out this outline and applying it to the circumstances of individual countries and regions.

THE WORLD

The Modern World in Continual Development

2 "Today, the human race is passing through a new stage of its history. Profound and rapid changes are spreading by degrees around the world.... Hence we can already speak of a true social and cultural transformation, one which has repercussions on man's religious life as well" (GS, 4).

As examples, two repercussions on the life of faith which more directly affect catechesis can be cited:

a) In times past, the cultural tradition favored the transmission of the faith to a greater extent than it does today; in our times, however, the cultural tradition has undergone considerable change, with the result that less and less can one depend on continued transmission by means of it. Because of this, some renewal in evangelization is needed for transmitting the same faith to new generations.

b) It should be noted that the Christian faith requires explanations and new forms of expression so that it may take root in all successive cultures. Though the aspirations and basic needs peculiar to human nature and the human condition remain essentially the same, nevertheless, men of our era are posing new questions about the meaning and importance of life.

Believers of our time are certainly not in all respects like believers of the past. This is why it becomes necessary to affirm the permanence of the faith and to present the message of salvation in renewed ways.

Today one must also keep in mind the very great diffusion of the instruments of social communication, the influence of which extends beyond national boundaries and makes individual persons citizens as it were of human society as a whole (cf. IM, 22).

Such instruments exert very great influence on the lives of Christians, whether because of the things they teach or because of the style of thinking and mode of behavior they introduce among these same Christians. It is necessary to take account of this fact and to give it all due attention.

Pluralism Today

3 "By this very circumstance, the traditional local communities such as father-centered families, clans, tribes, villages, various groups and associations stemming from social contacts experience more thorough changes every day" (GS, 6).

In Christianity of old, religion was regarded as the chief principle of unity among peoples. Things are otherwise now. The cohesion of peoples which stems from the phenomenon of democratization promotes harmony among various spiritual families. "Pluralism," as it is called, is no longer viewed as an evil to be eliminated, but rather as a fact which must be taken into account; anyone can make his own decisions known without becoming or being regarded as alien to society.

Therefore, those engaged in the ministry of the word should never forget that faith is a free response to the grace of the revealing God. And to an even greater extent than this was done in the past, they should present the good news of Christ in its remarkable character both as the mysterious key to understanding of the whole human condition and as a free gift of God which is to be received by means of heavenly grace upon admission of one's own insufficiency (cf. GS, 10).

The Dynamism of Our Age

4 The building up of human society, human progress, and the ongoing execution of human plans stimulate the concern of the men of our era (cf. GS, 4). Faith should by no means keep itself as it were outside that human progress. Joined with that progress there are indeed even now serious aberrations. Accordingly, the Gospel message should pass judgment on this state of affairs and tell men what it means.

The ministry of the word, through an ever-deeper study of the divine and human calling of man, must permit the Gospel to spread its own vital seeds of genuine freedom and progress (cf. AG, 8, 12) and to stimulate a desire for promoting the growth of the human person and for contending against that way of acting and thinking which tends toward fatalism.

What has been said above is meant merely to show how today's ministry of the word ought to direct its activity toward this world: "...it is demanded from the Church that she inject the perennial, vital, divine power of the Gospel into the human society of today" (John XXIII, Apost. Const. *Humanae salutis, AAS*, 1962, p. 6).

The Situation in Regard to Religious Feeling

5   That form of civilization which is called scientific, technical, industrial, and urban not infrequently diverts the attention of men from matters divine and makes their inner concerns with regard to religion more difficult. Many feel that God is less present, and less needed, and God seems to them less able to explain things in both personal and social life. Hence a religious crisis can easily arise (cf. GS, 5, 7).

The Christian faith, as are the other religious confessions, is experiencing a crisis of this sort among its followers. It has an urgent duty, therefore, to manifest its true nature, by virtue of which it transcends every advancement of culture, and to show forth its newness in cultures which have been secularized and desacralized.

It is a function of the ministry of the word to uncover, purify, and develop the authentic values which are found in the spiritual heritage of those human cultures wherein a religious sense remains alive and operative and is all-pervasive in human life.

In times past, faulty opinions and errors about the faith and the Christian way of life generally reached a comparatively small number of people, and were to a greater extent than is so today confined within groups of intellectuals. Now, however, human progress and the instruments of social communication are having this effect: faulty opinions are being spread abroad with greater speed and are exerting an ever-wider influence among the faithful, young adults especially, who suffer grave crises and are not infrequently driven to adopt ways of acting and thinking that are hostile to religion. This situation calls for pastoral remedies that are truly adapted to the circumstances.

THE CHURCH

The particular characteristics of the spiritual condition of the world are also found in the life of the Church herself.

"Traditional" Faith

6 The faith of many Christians is strained to a critical point in those places where religion was seeming to favor the prerogatives of certain social classes to an excessive degree, or where it was depending too much on ancestral customs and on regional unanimity in religious profession.

Great numbers are drifting little by little into religious indifferentism, or are continuing in danger of keeping the faith without the dynamism that is necessary, a faith without effective influence on their actual lives. The question now is not one of merely preserving traditional religious customs, but rather one of also fostering an appropriate re-evangelization of men, obtaining their reconversion, and giving them a deeper and more mature education in the faith.

By no means, however, is the above to be interpreted in such a way that it results in neglect of the genuine faith which is preserved within groups in a culture that is traditionally Christian, or in a low estimation of the popular religious sense. Despite the growth of secularization, a religious sense continues to flourish in the various parts of the Church. No one can fail to note it, for it is expressed in ordinary life by a very large number of people, and for the most part in a sincere and authentic way. In fact, the popular religious sense provides an opportunity or starting point for proclaiming the faith. The question is, as is clear, only one of purifying it and of correctly appraising its valid elements, so that no one will be content with forms of pastoral action which today have become unequal to the task, altogether unsuitable, and perhaps even irrelevant.

Religious Indifferentism and Atheism

7 Many baptized persons have withdrawn so far from their religion that they profess a form of indifferentism or something close to atheism. "Still, many of our contemporaries recognize in no way this intimate and vital link with God, or else they explicitly reject it. Thus atheism must be accounted among the most serious problems of this age, and must be subjected to closer examination" (GS, 19).

The Second Vatican Council gave the matter careful consideration (cf. GS, 19-20) and dealt expressly with remedies to be applied: "The remedy which must be applied to atheism, however, is to be sought in a proper presentation of the Church's teaching as well as in the integral life of the Church and her members. For it is a function of the Church to make God the Father and his incarnate Son present and in a sense visible by ceaselessly renewing and purifying herself under the guidance of the Holy Spirit. This result is achieved chiefly by the witness of a living and mature faith, namely, one trained to see difficulties clearly and to master them" (GS, 21).

There are also cases in which the Christian faith is found contaminated with a new form of paganism, even though some religious sense and some faith in a Supreme Being persist. A religious disposition can exist far from the influence of the word of God and from the practice of the sacraments, but be nourished by the practice of superstition and magic; moral life can fall back into pre-Christian ethics. Sometimes elements of nature worship, animism, and divination are introduced into the Christian religion, and thus in some places a lapse into syncretism can occur. Moreover, religious sects are being propagated which mingle together the Christian mysteries and elements of fables from antiquity.

In these cases, there is the greatest possible need for the ministry of the word, especially evangelization and catechesis, to be renewed in accord with the *Decree on the Missionary Activity of the Church*, nn. 13, 14, 21, 22.

Faith and Various Cultures

8 There are some members of the faithful who have had an excellent Christian education who are having difficulty with regard to the way of expressing the faith. They think it is bound up too much with ancient and obsolete formulations and too much tied to Western culture. They are, therefore, seeking a new way of expressing the truths of religion, one which conforms to the present human condition, allows the faith to illumine the realities pressing upon men today, and makes it possible for the Gospel to be brought over to other cultures. The Church certainly has a duty to give all possible consideration to this aspiration of men.

What is declared in the *Decree on the Missionary Activity of the Church* for recently established churches is also valid for all who labor in the ministry of the word: "From the customs and traditions of their people, from their wisdom and their learning, from their arts and sciences, these churches borrow all those things which can contribute to the glory of their Creator, the revelation of the Savior's grace, and the proper arrangement of Christian life" (AG, 22; cf. AG, 21; Paul VI, Alloc., August 6, 1969).

Consequently, "by presenting the Gospel message to men in a renewed way, the ministry of the word should show clearly the unity of the divine plan of salvation. Avoiding confusions and simplistic identifications, the message should always show clearly the deep and intimate harmony that exists between God's salvific plan, fulfilled in Christ the Lord, and human aspirations, between the history of salvation and human history, between the Church, the People of God, and human communities, between God's revelatory action and man's experience, between supernatural gifts and charisms and human values" (Comm. 5-s/comm. 2 General Conference of Bishops of Latin America, 1968).

The Work of Renewal

9 In this new state of affairs, it is possible for one to suppose that the apostolic fervor which the Church is now striving to promote is being impeded. Certainly neither the shepherds nor the faithful should be faulted on zeal, which they in fact have in large measure. The impediments seem rather to result either from a widespread failure to prepare suitably for the new and difficult tasks, or from a kind of thinking, as yet not fully developed, which is at times expressed in theories that hinder rather than help evangelization.

Having duly considered these things, the Sacred Synod of Vatican II time and again urged renewal of the ministry of the word in the Church. This renewal seems today to be entering a period of crisis, being led there especially by:

—*those who are unable to understand the depth of the proposed renewal*, as though the issue here were merely one of eliminating ignorance of the doctrine which must be taught. According to the thinking of those people, the remedy would be more frequent catechetical instruction. Once the matter has been considered that way, that remedy is immediately seen to be altogether unequal to the needs. In fact, the catechetical plan is to be thoroughly renewed, and this renewal has to do with a continuing education in the faith, not only for children but also for adults.

—those who are inclined to reduce the Gospel message to the consequences it has in men's temporal existence.

The Gospel and its law of love do, of course, demand that Christians, each according to his strength, work together—fulfilling their secular duties and responsibilities—to restore justice and brotherhood among men more and more. That, however, does not in any way satisfy the need to give due witness to Jesus Christ, God's Son and our Savior, whose mystery, which revealed God's ineffable love (cf. 1 John 4, 9), must be proclaimed openly and in its entirety to those being evangelized, and must be examined by them.

The teaching of the *Pastoral Constitution on the Church in the Modern World* and the *Declaration on Religious Freedom* countenance no "minimalism" in explaining the service of the faith directed through the ministry of the word. Both these documents show concern for providing a remedy for the state of affairs described above. Renewal in the ministry of the word, especially in catechesis, can in no way be separated from general pastoral renewal.

Steps which are effective and indeed of the greatest importance for good results must be taken: promoting the growth of the customary forms of the ministry of the word and stimulating new ones; evangelizing and catechizing men of lower cultural levels; reaching the educated classes and taking care of their needs; improving the traditional forms of the Christian presence and finding new ways; gathering together all the practical aids of the Church and at the same time avoiding forms which are not in accord with the Gospel.

In carrying out this task, the Church places her hope in all members of the People of God. Everyone—bishops, priests, men and women religious, lay people—should by all means fulfill his mission, each according to his responsibilities. And indeed each should fulfill his mission with attention to the state of the world which profoundly affects the life of faith.

So that effective help may be given these workers in the service of the Gospel, the catechetical renewal ought to use the help which can be given by the sacred sciences, theology, bible studies, pastoral thought, and the human sciences, and also the instruments by which ideas and opinions are spread, especially the social communications media.

Part Two
The Ministry of the Word

CHAPTER ONE

The Ministry of The Word and Revelation

Revelation: God's Gift

10   In the *Dogmatic Constitution on Divine Revelation*, the General Council looked at revelation as the act by which God communicates himself in a personal way: "In his goodness and wisdom, God chose to reveal himself and to make known the hidden purpose of his will...so that he may invite and take men into fellowship with himself" (DV, 2). God appears there as one who wishes to communicate himself, carrying out a plan which proceeds from love.

Catechesis, then, ought to take its beginning from this gift of divine love. Faith is the acceptance and coming to fruit of the divine gift in us. This characteristic, by which faith is to be considered as a gift, has a direct bearing on the whole subject-matter of the ministry of the word.

Revelation: Deeds and Words

11 So that men may come to a knowledge of his plan, God works in this way, namely, through events in the history of salvation and through the divinely inspired words which accompany these events and clarify them: "This plan of revelation is realized by deeds and words having an inner unity: the deeds wrought by God in the history of salvation manifest and confirm the teaching and realities signified by the words, while the words proclaim the deeds and clarify the mystery contained in them" (DV, 2).

Revelation, therefore, consists of deeds and words, the ones illuminating, and being illuminated by, the others. The ministry of the word should proclaim these deeds and words in such a way that the loftiest mysteries contained in them are further explained and communicated by it. In this way the ministry of the word not only recalls the revelation of God's wonders which was made in time and brought to perfection in Christ, but at the same time, in the light of this revelation, interprets human life in our age, the signs of the times, and the things of this world, for the plan of God works in these for the salvation of men.

Jesus Christ: Mediator and Fullness of All Revelation

12 "By this revelation, then, the deepest truth...is made clear to us in Christ, who is the Mediator and at the same time the fullness of all revelation" (DV, 2).

Christ is not only the greatest of prophets, who by his teaching fulfilled those things which had been said and done by God in earlier times. He himself is the eternal Son of God, made man, and thus the last event to which all events in the history of salvation look and which fulfills and manifests the final plans of God. "For this reason he...perfected revelation by fulfilling it..." (DV, 4; cf. LG, 9).

The ministry of the word ought to direct attention to this wonderful characteristic peculiar to the economy of revelation. The Son of God inserts himself into the history of men, takes to himself the life and death of a man, and in this history fulfills his plan of the Covenant.

In the same way as does the Evangelist Luke, the ministry of the word ought first to recall the event of Jesus for believers, by manifesting its meaning and by searching more and more into this unique and irreversible fact: "Many have undertaken to compile a narrative of the events which have been fulfilled in our midst. ...I too have carefully traced the whole sequence of events from the beginning, and have decided to set it in writing for you" (Luke 1, 1-3).

Therefore, the ministry of the word should be based on the divinely inspired exposition regarding the redemptive incarnation, the exposition which has been given us by Jesus himself and by the first disciples and especially the apostles, who were witnesses of the events. "It is common knowledge that among all [the Scriptures]...the Gospels have a special pre-eminence, and rightly so, for they are the principal witness of the life and teaching of the incarnate Word, our Savior" (DV, 18).

Moreover, it is to be recalled that Jesus, the Messiah and Lord, is through his Spirit always present to his Church (cf. John 14, 26; 15, 26; 16, 13; Apoc. 2, 7). Accordingly, the ministry of the word presents Christ not only as its object but also as the one who opens the hearts of hearers to receive and understand the divine proclamation (cf. Acts 16, 14).

Ministry of the Word or Preaching of the Word of God: Act of Living Tradition

13 "Now what was handed on by the apostles includes everything which contributes to the holiness of life and the increase in faith of the People of God; and so the Church, in her teaching, life, and worship, perpetuates and hands on to all generations all that she herself is, all that she believes" (DV, 8).

This tradition is bound up with things that have been said. In scope and depth, however, it is more than these sayings. It is a living tradition, since through it God continues his conversation. "And thus God, who spoke of old, uninterruptedly converses with the Bride of his beloved Son; and the Holy Spirit, through whom the living voice of the Gospel resounds in the Church, and through her, in the world..." (DV, 8).

This is why the ministry of the word can be considered as that which gives voice to this living tradition, within the totality of tradition. "This tradition which comes from the apostles develops in the Church with the help of the Holy Spirit. For there is a growth in the understanding of the realities and the words which have been handed down. This happens through the contemplation and study made by believers, who treasure these things in their hearts, through the intimate understanding of spiritual things they experience, and through the preaching of those who have received through episcopal succession the sure gift of truth" (DV, 8).

On the one hand, the divine revelation which constitutes the object of the Catholic faith and which was completed at the time of the apostles, must be clearly distinguished from the grace of the Holy Spirit, without whose inspiration and illumination no one can believe. On the other hand, God, who formerly spoke to the human race by revealing himself through divine deeds together with the message of the prophets, of Christ, and of the apostles, even now still secretly directs, through the Holy Spirit, in sacred tradition, by the light and sense of the faith, the Church, his bride, and he speaks with her, so that the People of God, under the leadership of the Magisterium, may attain a fuller understanding of revelation.

The Church's shepherds not only proclaim and explain directly to the People of God the deposit of faith which has been committed to them, but moreover they make authentic judgments regarding expressions of that deposit and the explanations which the faithful seek and offer. They do this in such a way that "in holding to, practicing, and professing the heritage of the faith, there results on the part of the bishops and faithful a remarkable common effort" (DV, 10).

From this it follows that it is necessary for the ministry of the word to set forth the divine revelation such as it is taught by the Magisterium and such as it expresses itself, under the watchfulness of the Magisterium, in the living awareness and faith of the People of God. In this way the ministry of the word is not a mere repetition of ancient doctrine, but rather it is a faithful reproduction of it, with adaptation to new problems and with a growing understanding of it.

Sacred Scripture

14 Under special inspiration of the Holy Spirit, divine revelation has also been expressed in writings, that is, in the sacred books of the Old and New Testaments, books which contain and present divinely revealed truth (cf. DV, 11).

The Church, guardian and interpreter of the Sacred Scriptures, learns from them, by constantly meditating on and penetrating more and more into their teaching. Remaining faithful in tradition, the ministry of the word finds its nourishment and its norm in Sacred Scripture (cf. DV, 21, 24, 25). For in the sacred books the Father, who is in heaven, very lovingly meets with his children and speaks with them (cf. DV, 21).

But if it takes its norm for thinking from Sacred Scripture, the Church, inspired by the Spirit, interprets that same Scripture: "and the sacred writings themselves are more profoundly understood and unceasingly made active in her" (DV, 8).

The ministry of the word, therefore, takes its beginning from Holy Writ and from the preaching of the apostles, as these are understood, explained, and applied in concrete situations by the Church.

Faith: Response to the Word of God

15 By faith man accepts revelation, and through it he consciously becomes a sharer in the gift of God.

The obedience of faith must be offered to the God who reveals. By this, man, with full homage of his mind and will, freely assents to the Gospel of the grace of God (cf. Acts, 20, 24). Instructed by faith, man, through the gift of the Spirit, comes to contemplate and savor the God of love, the God who has made known the riches of his glory in Christ (cf. Col. 1, 26). Indeed, a living faith is the beginning in us of eternal life in which the mysteries of God (cf. 1 Cor. 2, 10) will at last be seen unveiled. Informed of God's plan of salvation, faith leads man to full discernment of the divine will towards us in this world, and to cooperation with his grace. "For faith throws a new light on everything, manifests God's design for man's total vocation, and thus directs the mind to solutions which are fully human" (GS, 11).

Function of the Ministry of the Word

16 To put the whole matter in a few words, the minister of the word should be honestly aware of the mission assigned to him. It is to stir up a lively faith which turns the mind to God, impels conformance with his action, leads to a living knowledge of the expressions of tradition, and speaks and manifests the true significance of the world and human existence.

The ministry of the word is the communication of the message of salvation: it brings the Gospel to men. The mystery which has been announced and handed down deeply influences that will to have life, that innermost desire for attaining fulfillment, and that expectation of future happiness which God has implanted in the heart of every man and which by his grace he raises to the supernatural order.

The truths to be believed include God's love. He created all things for the sake of Christ and restored us to life in Christ Jesus. The various aspects of the mystery are to be explained in such a way that the central fact, Jesus, as he is God's greatest gift to men, holds first place, and that from him the other truths of Catholic teaching derive their order and hierarchy from the educational point of view (cf. nn. 43, 49).

CHAPTER TWO

Catechesis in the Pastoral Mission of the Church (Nature, Purpose, Efficacy)

Ministry of the Word in the Church

17 The ministry of the word takes many forms, including catechesis, according to the different conditions under which it is practiced and the ends which it strives to achieve.

There is the form called evangelization, or missionary preaching. This has as its purpose the arousing of the beginnings of faith (cf. CD, 11, 13; AG, 6, 13, 14), so that men will adhere to the word of God.

Then there is the catechetical form, "which is intended to make men's faith become living, conscious, and active, through the light of instruction" (CD, 14).

And then there is the liturgical form, within the setting of a liturgical celebration, especially that of the Eucharist (e.g., the homily) (cf SC, 33, 52; *Inter Oecum.* 54).

Finally, there is the theological form, that is, the systematic treatment and the scientific investigation of the truths of faith.

For our purpose it is important to keep these forms distinct, since they are governed by their own laws. Nevertheless, in the concrete reality of the pastoral ministry, they are closely bound together.

Accordingly, all that has so far been said about the ministry of the word in general is to be applied also to catechesis.

Catechesis and Evangelization

18 Catechesis proper presupposes a global adherence to Christ's Gospel as presented by the Church. Often, however, it is directed to men who, though they belong to the Church, have in fact never given a true personal adherence to the message of revelation.

This shows that, according to circumstances, evangelization can precede or accompany the work of catechesis proper. In every case, however, one must keep in mind that the element of conversion is always present in the dynamism of faith, and for that reason any form of catechesis must also perform the role of evangelization.

Forms of Catechesis

19 Because of varied circumstances and multiple needs, catechetical activity necessarily takes various forms.

In regions which have been Christian from of old, catechesis often takes the form of religious instruction given to children and adolescents in schools or outside a school atmosphere. Also found in those regions are various catechetical programs for adults. There are also various catechumenate programs for those who are preparing themselves for the reception of baptism, or for those who have been baptized but lack a proper Christian initiation. Very often the actual condition of large numbers of the faithful necessarily demands that some form of evangelization of the baptized precede catechesis.

In churches that have been established recently, special importance is placed on the work of evangelizing in the strict sense. Accordingly, they have the well-known form of the catechumenate for those who are being initiated in the faith so that they may prepare themselves for receiving baptism (cf. AG, 4).

In a word, catechetical activity can take on forms and structures that are quite varied, that is to say, it can be systematic or occasional, for individuals or for communities, organized or spontaneous, and so on.

20 Shepherds of souls should always keep in mind the obligation they have of safeguarding and promoting the enlightenment of Christian existence through the word of God for people of all ages and in all historical circumstances (cf. CD, 14), so that it may be possible to have contact with every individual and community in the spiritual state in which each one is.

They should also remember that catechesis for adults, since it deals with persons who are capable of an adherence that is fully responsible, must be considered the chief form of catechesis. All the other forms, which are indeed always necessary, are in some way oriented to it. In obedience to the norms of the Second Vatican Council, shepherds of souls should also strive "to reestablish or better adapt the instruction of adult catechumens" (CD, 14; cf. AG, 14).

Functions of Catechesis

21 Within the scope of pastoral activity, catechesis is the term to be used for that form of ecclesial action which leads both communities and individual members of the faithful to maturity of faith.

With the aid of catechesis, communities of Christians acquire for themselves a more profound living knowledge of God and of his plan of salvation, which has its center in Christ, the incarnate Word of God. They build themselves up by striving to make their faith mature and enlightened, and to share this mature faith with men who desire to possess it.

For every man whose mind is open to the message of the Gospel, catechesis is a particularly apt means for him to understand God's plan in his own life and to examine the highest meaning of existence and history so that the life of individual men and of society may be illumined by the light of the kingdom of God and be conformed to its demands, and the mystery of the Church as the community of those who believe in the Gospel may be able to be recognized.

All these things determine the functions proper to catechesis.

Catechesis and the Grace of Faith

22 Faith is a gift of God which calls men to conversion. "For this faith to be given, the grace of God and the interior help of the Holy Spirit must precede and assist, moving the heart and turning it to God, opening the eyes of the mind and giving joy and ease to everyone in assenting to the truth and believing it" (DV, 5).

The Christian community, listening to the word of God religiously, lives in a mature faith, constantly strives for conversion and renewal, and gives diligent ear to what the Spirit says to the Church.

Catechesis performs the function of disposing men to receive the action of the Holy Spirit and to deepen their conversion. It does this through the word, to which are joined the witness of life and prayer.

Catechesis and Performance of the Duties of the Faith

23   A person mature in the faith fully accepts the Gospel invitation by which he is impelled to communion with God and with his brothers; he takes on in his life the duties that are connected with this invitation (cf. AG, 12).

Catechesis performs the functions of helping men make this communion with God a reality, and of presenting the Christian message in such a way that it is clear that the highest value of human life is safeguarded by it. All this requires that catechesis keep in mind the legitimate aspirations of men, as also the progress and success of the values contained in these aspirations.

Communion with God and adherence to him entail the carrying out of human responsibilities and the duty of solidarity, since all these things are in keeping with the will of God the Savior (cf. GS, 4).

Catechesis, therefore, must foster and illumine the increase of theological charity in individual members of the faithful as well as in ecclesial communities, and also the manifestations of that same virtue in connection with the duties that pertain to individuals and to the community.

Catechesis and Knowledge of the Faith

24   A person mature in the faith knows the mystery of salvation revealed in Christ, and the divine signs and works which are witnesses to the fact that this mystery is being carried out in human history. It is, therefore, not sufficient for catechesis merely to stimulate a religious experience, even if it is a true one; rather, catechesis should contribute to the gradual grasping of the whole truth about the divine plan by preparing the faithful for the reading of Sacred Scripture and the learning of tradition.

Catechesis and the Life of Liturgical and Private Prayer

25 "Every liturgical celebration, because it is an action of Christ the priest and of his Body the Church, is a sacred action surpassing all others. No other action of the Church can match its claim to efficacy, nor equal the degree of it" (SC, 7). And the more mature a Christian community becomes in faith, the more it lives its worship in spirit and in truth (cf. John 4, 23) in its liturgical celebrations, especially at the Eucharist.

Therefore, catechesis must promote an active, conscious, genuine participation in the liturgy of the Church, not merely by explaining the meaning of the ceremonies, but also by forming the minds of the faithful for prayer, for thanksgiving, for repentance, for praying with confidence, for a community spirit, and for understanding correctly the meaning of the creeds. All these things are necessary for a true liturgical life.

"The spiritual life, however, is not confined to participation in the liturgy. The Christian is assuredly called to pray with his brethren, but he must also enter into his chamber to pray to the Father in secret (cf. Matt. 6, 6), indeed, according to the teaching of the Apostle Paul (cf. 1 Thess. 5, 17), he should pray without ceasing" (SC, 12).

Therefore, catechesis must also train the faithful to meditate on the word of God and to engage in private prayer.

Catechesis and Christian Light on Human Existence

26 A person mature in the faith is able to recognize in various circumstances and encounters with his fellowman the invitation of God whereby he is called to work toward the fulfillment of the divine plan of salvation.

Catechesis has the task, then, of emphasizing this function by teaching the faithful to give a Christian interpretation to human events, especially to the signs of the times, so that all "will be able to test and interpret all things in a wholly Christian spirit" (GS, 62).

Catechesis and Unity of Christians

27 Communities of the faithful should, according to the circumstances in which they live, take part in ecumenical dialogue and the other undertakings for the restoring of Christian unity (cf. UR, 5).

Catechesis should, therefore, assist in this cause (cf. UR, 6) by clearly explaining the Church's doctrine in its entirety (cf. UR, 11) and by fostering a suitable knowledge of other confessions, both in matters where they agree with the Catholic faith, and also in matters where they differ. In doing this, it should avoid words and methods of explaining doctrine that could "lead separated brethren or anyone else into error regarding the true doctrine of the Church" (LG, 67). The order or hierarchy of the truths of Catholic teaching should be kept (cf. UR, 11; AG, 15; *Ad Ecclesiam totam*, May 14, 1967, *AAS*, 1967, pp. 574-592). However, the case for Catholic doctrine should be presented with charity as well as with due firmness.

Catechesis and the Mission of the Church in the World

28 The Church is in Christ like a sacrament or sign and an instrument of the salvation and of the unity of the whole human race (cf. LG, 1). It will be more noted as such, however, the more mature in faith the individual communities of the faithful become.

Catechesis should help these communities to spread the light of the Gospel and to establish a fruitful dialogue with men and cultures that are not Christian, preserving here religious freedom correctly understood (cf. DH; AG, 22).

Catechesis and Eschatological Hope

29   A person mature in the faith directs his thoughts and desires to the full consummation of the kingdom in eternal life.

Catechesis, therefore, performs the function of directing the hope of men in the first place to the future goods which are in the heavenly Jerusalem. At the same time, it calls men to be willing to cooperate in the undertakings of their neighbors and of the human race for the improvement of human society (cf. GS, 39, 40-43).

Catechesis and Development of the Life of Faith

30   Among the faithful the one faith is found to be more or less intense according to the grace that is given to each one by the Holy Spirit, grace which must constantly be asked for in prayer (cf. Mark, 9, 23), and according to the response that each one gives to this grace. Moreover, the life of faith passes through various stages, just as does man's existence while he is attaining maturity and taking on the duties of his life. Consequently, the life of faith admits of various degrees, both in the global acceptance of the total word of God and in the explanation of that word and the application of it to the different duties of human life, according to the maturity of each and the differences of individuals (cf. n. 38). Certainly, the acceptance of this faith and its explanation and application to the life of man are different according to whether there is question of the very young, children, adolescents, young adults, or adults. Catechesis has the function of lending aid for the beginning and the progress of this life of faith throughout the entire course of a man's existence, all the way to the full explanation of revealed truth and the application of it to man's life.

Richness of Catechetical Work

31   Catechesis is concerned with the community, but it does not neglect the individual believer. It is linked with the other pastoral functions of the Church, but it does not lose its own specific character. At one and the same time it performs the functions of initiation, education, and formation.

It is very important that catechesis retain the richness of these various aspects in such a way that one aspect is not separated from the rest to the detriment of the others.

Efficacy of the Word of God in Catechesis

32 This sentence from Sacred Scripture is pertinent also to catechesis: "Indeed, God's word is living and effective" (Heb. 4, 12).

The divine word becomes present in catechesis through the human word. So that it may bear fruit in man and generate inner movements which expel indifference or uncertainty and lead him to embrace the faith, catechesis ought to express the word of God faithfully and present it suitably. Furthermore, the witness given by the life of both the catechist and the ecclesial community contributes very much to the efficacy of catechesis (cf. n. 35).

Catechesis, therefore, should convey the word of God, as it is presented by the Church, in the language of the men to whom it is directed (cf. DV, 13; OT, 16). When God revealed himself to the human race, he made the human word the sign of his word, expressing his word in a language that belonged to a particular culture (cf. DV, 12). The Church, to whom Christ entrusted the deposit of revelation, strives until the consummation of the world to transmit, explain, and interpret this word in a lively manner for the peoples of every culture and for men of every condition.

Pedagogy of God in Revealing and of the Church in Catechizing

33 In the history of revelation God used pedagogy in such a way that he announced his plan of salvation in the Old Covenant prophetically and by means of figures, and thus prepared the coming of his Son, the author of the New Covenant and the perfecter of the faith (cf. Heb. 12, 2).

Now, however, after the consummation of revelation, the Church has the obligation of sharing the entire mystery of our salvation in Christ with the people to be instructed. Mindful of the pedagogy used by God, she too uses a pedagogy, a new one, however, one that corresponds to the new demands of his message. The

Church sees to it, of course, that this message, when it has been presented without adulteration or mutilation, is accommodated to the ability of the people to be taught.

On the one hand, in order to take account of the limited ability of some, the Church explains matters rather simply and briefly, using even suitable summary formulas, which may be explained further later. On the other hand, she tries to satisfy the requirements of the more lively and capable minds by using more profound explanations.

Preserving Fidelity to God and Having Concern for Men

34 The Church performs this kind of function chiefly by means of catechesis (cf. DV, 24). By drawing the truth from the word of God and faithfully adhering to the secure expression of this word, catechesis strives to teach this word of God with complete fidelity. The function of catechesis, however, cannot be restricted to repetition of traditional formulas; in fact, it demands that these formulas be understood, and be faithfully expressed in language adapted to the intelligence of the hearers, using even new methods when necessary. The language will be different for different age levels, social conditions of men, human cultures, and forms of civil life (cf. DV, 8; CD, 14).

The Necessity of Ecclesial Witness

35 Catechesis, finally, demands the witness of faith, both from the catechists and from the ecclesial community, a witness that is joined to an authentic example of Christian life and to a readiness for sacrifice (cf. LG, 12, 17; NA, 2).

Man encounters Christ not only through the sacred ministry, but also through individual members of the faithful and their communities (cf. LG, 35), and these accordingly have a duty to give witness. If such witness is lacking, there arises in the listeners an obstacle to the acceptance of God's word.

Catechesis must be supported by the witness of the ecclesial community. It speaks more effectively about those things which in fact exist in the community's external life as well. The catechist is in a certain way the interpreter of the Church among those who are to be instructed. He reads the signs of faith and he teaches others how to read them. The chief of these signs is the Church herself (cf. First Vatican Council, Dogm. Const. *Dei Filius*, Dz.-Sch. 3014).

Hence it is clear how necessary it is that the ecclesial community, according to the mind of the Church and under the guidance of her bishops, remove or correct things that mar the appearance of the Church and constitute an obstacle for men to embrace the faith (cf. GS, 19).

Catechists, therefore, have the duty not only to impart catechesis directly, but also to offer their help in making the ecclesial community come alive, so that it will be able to give a witness that is authentically Christian.

Catechetical action, therefore, fits into that general pastoral action in which all elements of ecclesial life are properly ordered and bound together (cf. GS, 4, 7, 43).

Part Three
The Christian Message

Significance and Purpose of This Part

36 Faith, the maturing of which is to be promoted by catechesis (cf. n. 21), can be considered in two ways, either as the total adherence given by man under the influence of grace to God revealing himself (the faith *by which* one believes), or as the content of revelation and of the Christian message (the faith *which* one believes). These two aspects are by their very nature inseparable, and a normal maturing of the faith assumes progress of both together. The two can, however, be distinguished for reasons of methodology.

The subject of this third part is the content of the faith, and it is treated in the way indicated here. The first chapter points out the norms or criteria which catechesis must observe in the discovery and exposition of its content. The second chapter will deal with that content itself. This second chapter is by no means intended to set forth each and every one of the Christian truths which constitute the object of faith and of catechesis. Nor is it desired here to present an enumeration of the chief errors of our age, or of the truths of the faith which today are being more sharply denied or neglected. The ordinary or extraordinary Magisterium of the Church provides for this point authoritatively by its public pronouncements.

Much less is there an attempt in that second chapter to show a suitable way for ordering the truths of faith according to an organic plan in a kind of synthesis which would take just account of their objective hierarchy, or of the needs more intensely felt by the men of our age, whether men are considered in the context of their age or in the perspective of their social and cultural formation. This is the task of sacred theology and of the various other kinds of exposition of Christian doctrine.

Rather, it has seemed opportune to expound in that chapter—by means of those broad formulations which encompass fuller explanations—some of the more outstanding elements contained in the saving message, elements which certainly are organically interrelated, especially in those particular features which must be brought out more clearly in a new, adapted catechesis which pursues its goal faithfully.

CHAPTER ONE

Norms or Criteria

The Content of Catechesis in Relation to the Various Forms of Ecclesial Life, in Relation to Differing Cultures, and in Relation to Different Languages of Men

37 Revelation is the manifestation of the mystery of God and of his saving action in history. It takes place through a personal communication from God to man. The content of this communication constitutes the message of salvation which is to be preached to all men.

It is, consequently, the supreme and absolutely necessary function of the Church's prophetic ministry to make the content of this message intelligible to men of all times, in order that they may be converted to God through Christ, that they may interpret their whole life in the light of faith, having considered the special conditions of events and times in which that life develops, and that they may lead a life in keeping with the dignity which the message of salvation has brought them and that faith has revealed to them.

To achieve this end, catechesis, as a most excellent opportunity for the prophetic ministry of the Church, must not only foster a strong and continuous contact with the various forms of life in the ecclesial community, but it must strive to promote a greater accord between the possible formulations of the divine message and the various cultures and diverse languages of peoples.

The Goal of Catechesis Is To Present the Entire Content

38 The content of the message of salvation is made up of parts that are closely interrelated, even though its revelation was given by God gradually, in times past through the prophets, last of all in his Son (cf. Heb. 1, 1). Since the purpose of catechesis, as was said, consists in leading individual Christians and communities to a mature faith, it must take diligent care faithfully to present the entire treasure of the Christian message. This must surely be done according to the example of the divine pedagogy (cf. n. 33), but with the full store of revelation that has been divinely communicated being taken into account, so that the People of God may be nourished by it and live from it.

Catechesis begins, therefore, with a rather simple presentation of the entire structure of the Christian message (using also summary or global formulas), and it presents this in a way appropriate to the various cultural and spiritual conditions of those to be taught. By no means, however, can it stop with this first presentation, but it must be interested in presenting the content in an always more detailed and developed manner, so that individuals among the faithful and the Christian community may arrive at an always more profound and vital acceptance of the Christian message, and may judge the concrete conditions and practices of Christian life by the light of revelation.

This task of catechesis, not an easy one, must be carried out under the guidance of the Magisterium of the Church, whose duty it is to safeguard the truth of the divine message, and to watch that the ministry of the word uses appropriate forms of speaking, and prudently considers the help which theological research and the human sciences can give.

The Content of Catechesis Forms a Certain Organic and Living Body

39 The object of faith embraces a content which of its very nature is complex, namely, God in his own mystery and in his saving intervention in history. All these things are known through what God himself has revealed about himself and about his works. Christ has central importance both in the salvific intervention of God and in the manifestation of him to men. Catechesis, therefore, has as object God's mystery and works, namely, the works that God has done, is doing, and will do for us men and for our salvation.

A catechesis that neglects this interrelation and harmony of its content can become entirely useless for achieving its proper end.

Christocentrism of Catechesis

40   Christ Jesus, the incarnate Word of God, since he is the supreme reason why God intervenes in the world and manifests himself to men, is the center of the Gospel message within salvation history.

He is "the image of the invisible God, the firstborn of all creation. In him everything...was created" (Col. 1, 15). For he stands out as the one mighty mediator through whom God draws near to man and man is led to God (cf. 1 Tim. 2, 5). In him the Church has its foundation. In him all things are brought together (cf. Eph. 1, 10). For this reason, created things and the conscience of men and the genuine values which are found in other religions and the diverse signs of the times are all to be thought of, though not univocally, as paths and steps by which it is possible to draw near to God, under the influence of grace and with an ordering to the Church of Christ (cf. LG, 16).

Hence catechesis must necessarily be Christocentric.

Trinitarian Theocentrism of Catechesis

41   Just as Christ is the center of the history of salvation, so the mystery of God is the center from which this history takes its origin and to which it is ordered as to its last end. The crucified and risen Christ leads men to the Father by sending the Holy Spirit upon the People of God. For this reason the structure of the whole content of catechesis must be theocentric and trinitarian: through Christ, to the Father, in the Spirit.

Through Christ: The entire economy of salvation receives its meaning from the incarnate Word. It prepared his coming; it manifests and extends his kingdom on earth from the time of his death and resurrection up to his second glorious coming, which will complete the work of God. So it is that the mystery of Christ illumines the whole content of catechesis. The diverse elements —biblical, evangelical, ecclesial, human, and even cosmic—which catechetical education must take up and expound are all to be referred to the incarnate Son of God.

To the Father: The supreme purpose of the incarnation of the Word and of the whole economy of salvation consists in this: that all men be led to the Father. Catechesis, therefore, since it must help to an ever-deeper understanding of this plan of love of the heavenly Father, must take care to show that the supreme meaning of human life is this: to acknowledge God and to glorify him by doing his will, as Christ taught us by his words and the example of his life, and thus to come to eternal life.

In the Spirit: The knowledge of the mystery of Christ and the way to the Father are realized in the Holy Spirit. Therefore, catechesis, when expounding the content of the Christian message, must always put in clear light this presence of the Holy Spirit, by which men are continually moved to have communion with God and men and to fulfill their duties.

If catechesis lacks these three elements or neglects their close relationship, the Christian message can certainly lose its proper character.

For Us Men and for Our Salvation

42 The theocentric-trinitarian purpose of the economy of salvation cannot be separated from its objective, which is this: that men, set free from sin and its consequences, should be made as much like Christ as possible (cf. LG, 39). As the incarnation of the Word, so every revealed truth is for us men and for our salvation. To view the diverse Christian truths in their relation to the ultimate end of man is one of the conditions needed for a most fruitful understanding of them (cf. First Vatican Council, Dogm. Const. *Dei Filius*, Dz.-Sch., 3016).

Catechesis must, then, show clearly the very close connection of the mystery of God and Christ with man's existence and his ultimate end. This method in no way implies any contempt for the earthly goals which men are divinely called to pursue by individual or common efforts; it does, however, clearly teach that man's ultimate end is not confined to these temporal goals, but rather surpasses them beyond all expectation, to a degree that only God's love for men could make possible.

Hierarchy of Truths To Be Observed in Catechesis

43 In the message of salvation there is a certain hierarchy of truths (cf. UR, 11), which the Church has always recognized when it composed creeds or summaries of the truths of faith. This hierarchy does not mean that some truths pertain to faith itself less than others, but rather that some truths are based on others as of a higher priority, and are illumined by them.

On all levels catechesis should take account of this hierarchy of the truths of faith.

These truths may be grouped under four basic heads: the mystery of God the Father, the Son, and the Holy Spirit, Creator of all things; the mystery of Christ the incarnate Word, who was born of the Virgin Mary, and who suffered, died, and rose for our salvation; the mystery of the Holy Spirit, who is present in the Church, sanctifying it and guiding it until the glorious coming of Christ, our Savior and Judge; and the mystery of the Church, which is Christ's Mystical Body, in which the Virgin Mary holds the preeminent place.

Historical Character of the Mystery of Salvation

44 The economy of salvation is being worked out in time: in time past it began, made progress, and in Christ reached its highest point; in the present time it displays its force and awaits its consummation in the future. Hence in the exposition of the content of catechesis, memory of the past, awareness of the present, and hope of the future life ought to be evident by all means.

Therefore, catechesis recalls the supreme event of the whole history of salvation, the event with which Christians are united by faith, namely, the incarnation, passion, death, and resurrection of Christ.

Moreover, catechesis enables the faithful to recognize how the saving mystery of Christ works today and throughout the ages through the Holy Spirit and the ministry of the Church, and leads them to understand their duties toward God, themselves, and their neighbors.

Finally, catechesis rightly disposes hearts to hope in the future life that is the consummation of the whole history of salvation.

Towards this goal Christians ought to tend with filial confidence, but not without a holy fear of divine judgment. Through this hope the Christian community is deeply filled with an inner eschatological expectation which enables it to think correctly about human and earthly goods by keeping them in proper perspective, while not despising them as worthless.

These three main viewpoints are to be kept in mind continuously and practically in the exposition of the content of catechesis.

Sources of Catechesis

45 The content of catechesis is found in God's word, written or handed down; it is more deeply understood and developed by the people exercising their faith under the guidance of the Magisterium, which alone teaches authentically; it is celebrated in the liturgy; it shines forth in the life of the Church, especially in the just and in the saints; and in some way it is known too from those genuine moral values which, by divine providence, are found in human society.

Catechesis has all these as its sources. These sources are either principal or subsidiary, and so they are by no means all to be taken as sources in exactly the same sense. In using them, the catechist must first and always look to the unquestionable preeminence of revelation, written or handed down, and to the authority of the Magisterium of the Church in matters connected with faith.

Moreover, in regard to any particular part of the content of faith that is to be explained, the catechist should carefully note how the mystery of Christ is the center of that part; how the Church interprets and defines that part, and how she celebrates it and puts it into practice, sharing it in her liturgy and in the practice of the Christian life. Finally, the catechist must consider how, with the aid of the Holy Spirit, the plan of God can be fulfilled in the present era.

General Principles of Catechetical Methodology

46 The norms pointed out above, about the exposition of the content of catechesis, must be applied in the various forms of catechesis, that is to say, in biblical and liturgical catechesis, in doctrinal summaries, in the interpretation of the conditions of human existence, and so on.

It is not possible, however, to deduce from those norms an order which must be followed in the exposition of the content. It is right to begin with God and proceed to Christ, or to do the reverse; similarly, it is permissible to begin with man and proceed to God, or to do the reverse; and so on. In selecting a pedagogical method, one ought to take into account the circumstances in which the ecclesial community or the individuals among the faithful to whom catechesis is directed live. From this there arises the need to use great diligence in looking into and finding ways and methods which better respond to the various circumstances.

The Conferences of Bishops have the task of giving more specific norms in this matter and of applying them by means of catechetical directories, of catechisms for various age levels and cultural conditions, and of the other helps that seem appropriate for the task (cf. below, Part Six).

CHAPTER TWO

The More Outstanding Elements of The Christian Message

The Mystery of the One God: Father, Son, Holy Spirit

47   The history of salvation is identical with the history of the way and the plan by which God, true and one, the Father, the Son, the Holy Spirit, reveals himself to men, and reconciles and unites with himself those turned away from sin.

The Old Testament, while clearly affirming the unity of God in a polytheistic world, already gives some foreshadowings of the mystery of the Trinity. These are completely explicitated, however, in the person, the works, and the words of Jesus Christ. Indeed, when he reveals himself as the Son of God, he at the same time reveals the Father and the Holy Spirit. An intimate knowledge of the true God imbues the whole mind of the Divine Teacher, and he shares it with his disciples, calling them to become sons of God, through the Gift of his filial Spirit, which he bestows on them (cf. John 1, 12; Rom. 8, 15).

In catechesis, therefore, the meeting with the Triune God occurs first and foremost when the Father, the Son, and the Spirit are acknowledged as the authors of the plan of salvation that has its culmination in the death and resurrection of Jesus (cf. Irenaeus, *Proof of the Apostolic Preaching*, n. 6, *Sources chretiennes*, 62, pp. 39 ff.). In this way the growing awareness of the faithful responds to the revelation of the mystery transmitted by the Church; for the faithful understand through faith that their life, beginning at baptism, consists in acquiring a more intimate familiarity with the three divine Persons, inasmuch as the faithful are called to share in their divine nature. Finally, Christians, through the gift of the Holy

Spirit, can already now contemplate with eyes of faith and cherish with filial love the Most Holy Trinity of Persons, as it is from eternity in God's intimate life.

Genuine Worship of God in a Secularized World

48 "The God and Father of our Lord Jesus Christ" (Eph. 1, 3) is "the living God" (Matt. 16, 16). He is a holy, just, and merciful God; He is God the author of the covenant with men; God who sees, frees, and saves; God who loves as a father, as a spouse. Catechesis joyfully proclaims this God who is the source of our every hope (cf. 1 Pet. 1, 3-4).

Catechesis, however, cannot ignore the fact that not a few men of our era strongly sense a remoteness and even absence of God. This fact, which is part of the process of secularization, surely constitutes a danger for the faith; but it also impels us to have a purer faith and to become more humble in the presence of the mystery of God, as we ought: "Truly you are a hidden God, the God of Israel, the Savior" (Isa. 45, 15). With this perspective, it is possible also to understand more easily the true nature of the worship which God demands and which glorifies him, a worship, that is, which includes a resolve to fulfill his will in every field of activity, and faithfully to increase in charity the talents given by the Lord (cf. Matt. 25, 14 ff.). In the sacred liturgy the faithful bring the fruits of every kind of act of charity, of justice, of peace, in order to make a humble offering of them to God, and to receive in return the words of life and the graces they need to enable them in the world to profess the truth in love (cf. Eph. 4, 15) in communion with Christ, who offers his Body and Blood for men.

Knowledge of God and the Witness of Charity

49 The greatest way the faithful can help the atheistic world for coming to God is by the witness of a life which agrees with the message of Christ's love and of a living and mature faith that is manifested by works of justice and charity (cf. GS, 21).

However, the right use of human reason may not be neglected; for, as the Church holds and teaches, from created things this reason can come to a knowledge of God as the beginning and the end of all things (cf. First Vatican Council, Dogm. Const. *Dei Filius,* Dz.-Sch., 3004-3005, 3026). This knowledge of God not only does no harm to human dignity, but rather gives it a basis and strength.

Though the eternal salvation of men is the objective of the Church, nevertheless faith in the living God carries with it the urgent duty of collaborating in the solution of human questions (cf. 1 John 4, 20-21). In this area the faithful must give witness by their works to the value of the Lord's message.

Jesus Christ, Son of God, the Firstborn of All Creation and Savior

50 The greatest of God's works is the incarnation of his Son, Jesus Christ. Being the Firstborn of all creation, he is before all and all things hold together in him (cf. Col. 1, 15-17). All things have been created in him, through him, and for him (cf. Col. 1, 15 ff.).

Having become obedient unto death, he was exalted as Lord of all things, and was manifested to us through his resurrection as God's Son in power (cf. Rom. 1, 4). Being the Firstborn of the dead, he gives life to all (cf. 1 Cor. 15, 22): in him we were created new men (cf. Eph. 2, 10); through him all creatures will be liberated from the slavery of corruption (cf. Rom. 8, 19-21). "There is no salvation in anyone else" (Acts 4, 12).

Creation, the Beginning of the Economy of Salvation

51 The entire world created out of nothing is the world in which salvation and redemption are in fact accomplished through Jesus Christ.

Already in the Old Testament the truth of God's creative action is not presented as an abstract philosophical principle; rather, it enters the minds of the Israelites, with the help of a notion of the oneness of God, as a message declaring the power and victory of Yahweh, as the basis for showing that the Lord remains always with his people (cf. Isa. 40, 27-28; 51, 9-13). The omnipotence of God the Creator is also manifested in a splendid way in Christ's resurrection, wherein is revealed "the immeasurable scope of his power" (Eph. 1, 19).

For this reason the truth of creation is not to be presented simply as a truth standing by itself, torn from the rest, but as something which is in fact ordered to the salvation wrought by Jesus Christ. The creation of visible and invisible things, of the world and of angels, is the beginning of the mystery of salvation (cf. DV, 3); the creation of man (cf. Pius XII, Encycl. *Humani generis, AAS*, 1950, p. 575; GS, 12, 14) is to be regarded as the first gift and the first call that leads to glorification in Christ (cf. Rom. 8, 29-30). When a Christian hears the explanation of the doctrine about creation, besides thinking about the first act whereby God "created the heavens and the earth" (Gen. 1, 1), he should turn his mind to all the salvific undertakings of God. These things are always present in the history of man and of the world; they also shine forth especially in the history of Israel; they lead to the supreme event of Christ's resurrection; and, finally, they will be brought to completion at the end of the world, when there will be "new heavens and a new earth" (cf. 2 Pet. 3, 13).

Jesus Christ, the Center of the Entire Economy of Salvation

52 A Christian recognizes that in Jesus Christ he is linked with all of history and is in communion with all men. The history of salvation is being accomplished in the midst of the history of the world. By this history of salvation God fulfills his plan, and thus the People of God, that is, "the whole Christ," is being perfected in time. The Christian acknowledges with simplicity and sincerity that he has a role in such work, which through the power of Jesus the Savior is aimed at having creation give the greatest possible glory to God (cf. 1 Cor. 15, 28).

Jesus Christ, True Man and True God in the Unity of the Divine Person

53 This great mystery, namely, Christ as Head and Lord of the universe, "has been manifested in the flesh" (1 Tim. 3, 16) to men.

The man, Jesus Christ, who dwelt among men—the one who as man worked with his hands, thought with a human mind, acted with a human will, loved with a human heart—he is truly the Word and the Son of God, who through the incarnation in a certain way joined himself with every single man (cf. GS, 22).

Catechesis must proclaim Jesus in his concrete existence and in his message, that is, it must open the way for men to the wonderful perfection of his humanity in such a way that they will be able to acknowledge the mystery of his divinity. Christ Jesus, for a fact, who was united with the Father in a constant and unique practice of prayer, always lived in close communion with men. By his goodness he embraced all men, the just and the sinners, the poor and the rich, fellow-citizens and foreigners. If he loved some more particularly than others, this predilection was showered on the sick, the poor, the lowly. For the human person he had a reverence and a solicitude such as no one before him had ever manifested.

Catechesis ought daily to defend and strengthen belief in the divinity of Jesus Christ, in order that he may be accepted not merely for his admirable human life, but that men might recognize him through his words and signs as God's only-begotten Son (cf. John 1, 18), "God from God, light from light, true God from true God, begotten not made, consubstantial with the Father" (Dz.-Sch. 150). The correct explanation of the mystery of the Incarnation developed in Christian tradition: through a diligent understanding of the faith, the Fathers and the Councils made efforts to determine more precisely the concepts, to explain more profoundly the peculiar nature of Christ's mystery, to investigate the hidden connections that bind him to his heavenly Father and to men. Besides, there was the witness of the Christian life about this truth—a witness that the Church presented throughout the centuries: that God's communion with men, which is had in Christ, is the source of joy and inexhaustible hope. In Christ there is all fullness of divinity; through him God's love for men is shown forth.

St. Ignatius wrote to the Ephesians: "There is only one physician, both in body and in spirit, born and unborn, God become man, true life in death; sprung both from Mary and from God, first incapable of suffering and then capable of it, Jesus Christ our Lord *(Enchiridion patristicum,* 39).

Jesus Christ, Savior and Redeemer of the World

54 The mystery of Christ appears in the history of men and of the world—a history subject to sin—not only as the mystery of the incarnation but also as the mystery of salvation and redemption.

God so loved sinners that he gave his Son, reconciling the world to himself (cf. 2 Cor. 5, 19). Jesus therefore as the Firstborn among many brethren (cf. Rom. 8, 29), holy, innocent, undefiled (cf. Heb. 7, 26), being obedient to his Father freely and out of filial love (cf. Phil. 2, 8), on behalf of his brethren, sinners that they were, and as their Mediator, accepted the death which is for them the wages of sin (cf. Rom. 6, 23; GS, 18). By this his most holy death he redeemed mankind from the slavery of sin and of the devil, and he poured out on it the spirit of adoption, thus creating in himself a new humanity.

The Sacraments, Actions of Christ in the Church, the Primordial Sacrament

55 The mystery of Christ is continued in the Church, which always enjoys his presence and ministers to him. This is done in a specific way through the signs that Christ instituted, which signify the gift of grace and produce it, and are properly called sacraments (cf. Council of Trent, *Decree on the Sacraments*, Dz.-Sch., 1601).

The Church herself, however, is in some way to be considered the primordial sacrament, since she is not only the People of God but also in Christ a kind of "sign and instrument of the intimate union with God, and of the unity of the entire human race" (LG, 1).

Sacraments are the principal and fundamental actions whereby Jesus Christ unceasingly bestows his Spirit on the faithful, thus making them the holy people which offers itself, in him and with him, as an oblation acceptable to the Father. The sacraments are surely to be considered inestimable blessings of the Church. To her, then, belongs the power of administering them; and yet they are always to be referred to Christ, from whom they receive their efficacy. In reality, it is Christ who baptizes. It is not so much a man who celebrates the Eucharist as Christ himself; for he it is who offers himself in the sacrifice of the Mass by the ministry of the priests (cf. Council of Trent, *Decree on the Sacrifice of the Mass*,

Dz.-Sch., 1743). The sacramental action is, in the first place, the action of Christ, and the ministers of the Church are as his instruments.

Full Meaning of the Sacraments

56 Catechesis will have the duty of presenting the seven sacraments according to their full meaning.

First, they must be presented as sacraments of faith. Of themselves they certainly express the efficacious will of Christ the Savior; but men, on their part, must show a sincere will to respond to God's love and mercy. Hence, catechesis must concern itself with the acquisition of the proper dispositions, with the stimulation of sincerity and generosity for a worthy reception of the sacraments.

Second, the sacraments must be presented, each according to its own nature and end, not only as remedies for sin and its consequences, but especially as sources of grace in individuals and in communities, so that the entire dispensation of grace in the life of the faithful may be related in some way to the sacramental economy.

Catechesis on the Sacraments

57 Baptism cleanses man from original sin and from all personal sins, gives him rebirth as a child of God, incorporates him into the Church, sanctifies him with the gifts of the Holy Spirit, and, impressing on his soul an indelible character, initiates him in Christ's priestly, prophetic, and kingly roles (cf. 1 Pet. 2, 9; LG, 31).

Confirmation binds the Christian more perfectly to the Church and enriches him with a special strength of the Holy Spirit, that he may live in the world as a witness of Christ.

Since the life of Christians, which on earth is a warfare, is liable to temptations and sins, the way of the sacrament of Penance is open for them, so that they may obtain pardon from the merciful God and reconcile themselves with the Church.

Holy Orders in a special way conforms certain members of the People of God to Christ the Mediator by conferring on them a sacred power, that they may shepherd the Church, nourish the faithful with the word of God, and make them holy, and, in the first place, that they, representing Christ's person, may offer the Sacrifice of the Mass and preside at the Eucharistic banquet.

"By the sacred anointing of the sick and the prayer of her priests, the whole Church commends those who are ill to the suffering and glorified Lord, that He may lighten their sufferings and save them" (LG, 11; cf. James 5, 14-16).

In catechesis on the sacraments, much importance should be placed on the explanation of the signs. Catechesis should lead the faithful through the visible signs to ponder God's invisible mysteries of salvation.

The Eucharist, Center of the Entire Sacramental Life

58 The primacy of the Eucharist over all the other sacraments is unquestionable, as is also its supreme efficacy in building up the Church (cf. LG, 11, 17; Instruction, *Eucharisticum mysterium*, nn. 5-15).

For in the Eucharist, when the words of consecration have been pronounced, the profound (not the phenomenal) reality of bread and wine is changed into the body and blood of Christ, and this wonderful change has in the Church come to be called "transubstantiation." Accordingly, under the appearances (that is, the phenomenal reality) of the bread and wine, the humanity of Christ, not only by its power but by itself (that is, substantially), united with his divine Person, lies hidden in an altogether mysterious way (cf. Paul VI, Encycl. *Mysterium fidei, AAS*, 1965, p. 766).

This sacrifice is not merely a rite commemorating a past sacrifice. For in it Christ by the ministry of the priests perpetuates the sacrifice of the Cross in an unbloody manner through the course of the centuries (cf. SC, 47). In it too he nourishes the faithful with himself, the Bread of Life, in order that, filled with love of God and neighbor, they may become more and more a people acceptable to God.

Having been nourished with the Victim of the sacrifice of the Cross, the faithful should by a genuine and active love remove the prejudices because of which they are at times accused of a sterile worship that keeps them from being brotherly and from cooperating with other people. By its nature the Eucharistic banquet is meant to help the faithful to unite their hearts with God more each day in frequent prayer, and thence to acknowledge and love other men as brothers of Christ and sons of God the Father.

The Sacrament of Matrimony

59 In our days, with the pre-eminence that the Christian message ascribes to consecrated virginity being preserved (cf. 1 Cor. 7, 38; Council of Trent, *Canons on the Sacrament of Matrimony,* Dz.-Sch. 1810), a special importance must be assigned to religious education on matrimony, which the Creator himself instituted and endowed with various blessings, purposes, and laws (cf. GS, 48).

Supported by the words of faith and by the natural law, under the guidance of the Magisterium of the Church, which is responsible for authoritative interpretation of both the moral and the natural law (cf. Paul VI, Encycl. *Humanae vitae,* n. 4, *AAS,* 1968, p. 483), and at the same time taking due account of contemporary advances in the anthropological sciences, catechesis must make matrimony the foundation of family life, with regard to its values and its divine law of unity and indissolubility, and with regard to its duties of love, which by its natural character has been ordered towards the procreation and education of offspring. In regulating procreation, conjugal chastity must be preserved in accord with the teaching of the Church (cf. Encycl. *Humanae vitae,* n. 14, *AAS,* 1968, p. 490).

Since Christ elevated matrimony to the dignity of a sacrament for the baptized, the spouses, who are the ministers of the sacrament when they give personal and irrevocable consent, living in Christ's grace imitate and in a certain way represent the love of Christ himself for his Church (cf. Eph. 5, 25). Christian spouses are strengthened and as it were consecrated by this special sacrament for fulfilling the duties of their state and for upholding its dignity (cf. GS, 48).

Finally, it is part of the family's vocation to become a community, one which is also open to the Church and to the world.

The New Man

60 When man accepts the Spirit of Christ, he establishes a way of life that is totally new and gratuitous.

The Holy Spirit, present in the soul of the Christian, makes him a partaker of the divine nature and intimately unites him to the Father and Christ in a communion of life which not even death can break (cf. John 14, 23). The Holy Spirit heals man of his spiritual weaknesses and infirmities, frees him from the slavery of his passions and of immoderate self-love, by giving him power to keep the divine law, strengthens him with hope and fortitude, enlightens him in the pursuit of the good, and infuses in him the fruits of charity, joy, peace, patience, kindness, goodness, longanimity, humility, fidelity, modesty, continence, and chastity (cf. Gal. 5, 22-23). This is why the Holy Spirit is invoked as the guest of the soul.

Justification from sin and God's indwelling in the soul are a grace. When we say a sinner is justified by God, is given life by the Holy Spirit, possesses in himself Christ's life, or has grace, we are using expressions which in different words mean one and the same thing, namely, dying to sin, becoming partakers of the divinity of the Son through the Spirit of adoption, and entering into an intimate communion with the Most Holy Trinity.

The man belonging to the history of salvation is the man ordered to the grace of filial adoption and to eternal life. Christian anthropology finds its own proper character in the grace of Christ the Savior.

Human and Christian Freedom

61 The divine call of man requires him to give a free response in Jesus Christ.

It is not possible for man to be unfree. It is also very much part of his dignity and duty, since he has dominion over his actions, to keep the moral law in the order of nature and in the order of grace, and thus to adhere closely to God who revealed himself in Christ. The freedom of fallen man has been so weakened that he would be unable for long to observe even the duties of the natural law without the help of God's grace; but, when he has received grace, his freedom is so elevated and strengthened that the life he lives in the flesh, he is able to live holily in the faith of Jesus Christ (cf. (Gal. 2, 20).

The Church has a duty to defend and promote a true sense of freedom and its right use against every kind of unjust force. She also protects freedom against those who deny it, who think man's activity is wholly dependent on psychological determinism and on economic, social, cultural, and such other conditions.

The Church is by no means unaware that freedom, even when assisted by divine grace, is liable to grave psychological difficulties and to the influence of external conditions in which each one lives, with the result that human responsibility is not rarely diminished, and indeed in some cases is barely preserved, and in some cases it is not preserved at all. The Church likewise takes note of the researches and modern progress in the anthropological sciences concerning the use and limits of human freedom. For this reason she is solicitous both to educate for and to foster genuine freedom, and also to bring about suitable conditions in the psychological, social, economic, political, and religious fields, so that freedom will be able to be truly and justly exercised. Christians, therefore, must work sedulously and sincerely in the temporal sphere, so that as far as possible the best conditions may be established for the right exercise of freedom. They have this duty, of course, in common with all men of good will; yet Christians know they are bound to the same duty because of a more important and more urgent reason. For here it is question not only of promoting a good that belongs to this life on earth, but also of a duty which ultimately serves the acquisition of the inestimable good of grace and of eternal salvation.

Sin of Man

62   Nevertheless, the conditions of history and of life are not to be considered the main impediment to human freedom. When man freely applies himself to the work of salvation, he finds sin the greatest obstacle.

"Although he was made by God in a state of holiness, from the very dawn of history man abused his liberty, at the urging of the Evil One. Man set himself against God and sought to find fulfillment apart from God" (GS, 13). "Through one man sin entered the world, and with sin death, death thus coming to all men inasmuch as all sinned" (Rom. 5, 12). "It is human nature so fallen, stripped of the grace that clothed it, injured in its own natural powers and subjected to the dominion of death, that is transmitted to all men, and it is in this sense that every man is born in sin" (Paul VI, *Professio fidei*, n. 16, *AAS*, 1968, p. 439). The multitude of sins, then, has become a sorrowful experience for mankind, and it is also the cause of manifold sorrows and ruin. One must not neglect the teaching on the nature and effects of personal sins, whereby man, acting knowingly and deliberately, by his act violates the moral law, and in a serious matter also seriously offends God.

The history of salvation is also the history of liberation from sin. Every intervention of God both in the Old and in the New Testament was to give guidance to men in the struggle against the forces of sin. The role entrusted to Christ in the history of salvation relates to the destruction of sin, and is fulfilled through the mystery of the cross. The profound reflections found in St. Paul (cf. Rom. 5) concerning the reality of sin and Christ's consequent "work of justice" must be numbered among the principal points of the Christian faith, and it is not right to pass over them in silence in catechesis.

But the salvation brought by Jesus Christ involves much more than redemption from sin. For it fulfills the plan begun by God that he would communicate himself in Jesus with such fullness that it utterly transcends human understanding. The plan in question does not come to an end because of men's transgressions, but it confers a grace that is superabundant compared to the death which sin brought (cf. Rom. 5, 15-17). This plan, which has proceeded from love, by virtue of which men are called by the Holy Spirit to share in divine life itself, is always in force and belongs to all times. Even though man is a sinner, he always remains in the one order which God willed, namely, in the order in which God mercifully shares himself with us in Jesus Christ, and man can, therefore, under the impulse of grace, attain salvation through repentance.

Moral Life of Christians

63 Christ commissioned his apostles to teach the observance of everything that he had commanded (cf. Matt. 28, 20). Catechesis, therefore, must include not only those things which are to be believed, but also those things which are to be done.

The moral life of Christians, which is a way of acting that is worthy of a man and an adopted son of God, is a response to the duty of living and growing, under the guidance of the Holy Spirit, in the new life communicated through Jesus Christ.

The moral life of Christians is guided by the grace and gifts of the Holy Spirit. "The love of God has been poured out in our hearts through the Holy Spirit who has been given to us" (Rom. 5, 5).

The docility with which the Holy Spirit must be obeyed entails a faithful observance of the commandments of God, the laws of the Church, and just civil laws.

Christian freedom still needs to be ruled and directed in the concrete circumstances of human life. Accordingly, the conscience of the faithful, even when informed by the virtue of prudence, must be subject to the Magisterium of the Church, whose duty it is to explain the whole moral law authoritatively, in order that it may rightly and correctly express the objective moral order.

Further, the conscience itself of Christians must be taught that there are norms which are absolute, that is, which bind in every case and on all people. That is why the saints confessed Christ through the practice of heroic virtues; indeed, the martyrs suffered even torture and death rather than deny Christ.

The Perfection of Charity

64 The action of the Spirit of Christ is made clear when the peculiar characteristic of Christian moral teaching is brought to light; all precepts and counsels of this moral teaching are summarized in faith working through charity (cf. Gal. 5, 6), and this is as it were its soul.

Man is called to adhere freely to the will of God in all things; this is "the obedience of faith by which man entrusts his whole self freely to God" (DV, 5). However, since God is love, and his plan calls for communicating his love in Jesus Christ and for uniting men in mutual love, it follows that adhering freely and perfectly to God and to his will is the same as following a way of life in which love reigns in the keeping of the commandments; in other words, it is identical with embracing and putting into practice the precept of charity as a new precept.

Man, therefore, is called to embrace, in faith, a life of charity toward God and other men; in this lies his greatest responsibility and his exalted moral dignity. The holiness of a man, whatever his vocation or state of life may be, is nothing other than the perfection of charity (cf. LG, 39-42).

The Church, People of God and Saving Institution

65 The Church, instituted by Christ, had its origin in his death and resurrection. She is the new People of God, prepared for in the course of the history of Israel; a people to which Christ gives life and growth through the outpouring of the Spirit, and which he perpetually renews and directs by his hierarchical and charismatic gifts; "a people made one with the unity of the Father and the Son and the Holy Spirit" (LG, 4).

The Church, therefore, inasmuch as she is the People of God, the society of the faithful, and the communion of men in Christ, is the work of God's saving love in Christ.

And the principles which give birth to Christians, form them, and establish them as a community (namely, the deposit of faith, the sacraments, and the apostolic ministries) are found in the Catholic Church. To her they have been entrusted, and from them spring the ecclesial activities. In other words, in the Church there are all the means necessary for assembling herself and guiding herself to maturity as the communion of men in Christ. This work is the fruit not only of the action of a transcendent God, and of the invisible working of Christ and of his Spirit, but also of the institutions, offices, and saving actions of the Church. The Church, therefore, besides being a society of the faithful, is also mother of the faithful because of her ministerial and salutary work.

The Church is the holy People of God which shares in the prophetic office of Christ (cf. LG, 12). Assembled by the word of God, it accepts it and gives witness to it throughout the world. She is a priestly people: "Christ the Lord, High Priest taken from among men, 'made a kingdom and priests to God his Father' (Apoc. 1, 6) out of this new people. The baptized, by regeneration and the anointing of the Holy Spirit, are consecrated into a spiritual house and a holy priesthood. Thus through all those works befitting Christian men they can offer spiritual sacrifices and proclaim the power of him who has called them out of darkness into his marvelous light" (LG, 10). The Church, however, is essentially a hierarchical society; it is a people guided by its Shepherds, who are in union with the Supreme Pontiff, the Vicar of Christ, and who are under his direction (cf. LG, 22). To them the faithful look with filial love and obedient homage. The Church is a people on pilgrimage toward fullness of the mystery of Christ.

The Holy Spirit's presence in the Church, on the one hand, safeguards in her, in an indefectible manner, the objective conditions required for her sanctifying meeting with Christ; on the other hand, the Holy Spirit's presence brings it about that the Church strives for continual purification and renewal in her members, and for the sake of her members, and in her changeable structures.

The Church as Communion

66   The Church is a communion. She herself acquired a fuller awareness of that truth in the Second Vatican Council.

The Church is a people assembled by God and united by close spiritual bonds. Her structure needs a diversity of gifts and offices; and yet the distinctions within her, though they can be not only of degree but also of essence, as is the case between the ministerial priesthood and the common priesthood of the people, by no means takes away the basic and essential quality of persons. "The chosen People of God is one: 'one Lord, one faith, one baptism' (Eph. 4, 5). As members, they share a common dignity from their rebirth in Christ. They have the same filial grace and the same vocation to perfection. They possess in common one salvation, one hope, and one undivided charity.... And if by the will of Christ some are made teachers, dispensers of mysteries, and shepherds on behalf of others, yet all share a true equality with regard to the dignity and the activity common to all the faithful for the building up of the Body of Christ" (LG, 32).

In the Church, therefore, every vocation is worthy of honor and is a call to the fullness of love, that is, to holiness; every person is endowed with his own supernatural excellence, and must be given respect. All gifts and charisms, even though some are objectively more excellent than others (cf. 1 Cor. 12, 31; 7, 38), work together for the good of all members by means of the provident multiplicity of forms, which the apostolic office must discover and coordinate (cf. LG, 12). This holds also for all particular churches individually; for in each one, though it be small and poor or living in dispersion, "Christ is present, and by his power the one, holy, catholic, and apostolic Church is gathered together" (LG, 26).

The Catholic faithful ought to be solicitous for the separated Christians who do not live in full communion with the Catholic Church, by praying for them, communicating with them about Church matters, and taking the first steps toward them. First of all, however, each one according to his condition, should weigh sincerely and attentively the things in the Catholic family itself which ought to be renewed and achieved, in order that its life might bear a more faithful and clear witness to the doctrine and institutions handed down by Christ through the apostles (cf. UR, 4, 5).

The Church as Saving Institution

67   The Church is not only a communion among brothers, whose head is Christ, but she manifests herself also as an institution to whom the universal saving mission has been entrusted. The People of God, established by Christ "as a communion of life, of charity, and of truth, is also used by him as an instrument for the redemption of all, and is sent forth into the whole world as the light of the world and the salt of the earth" (LG, 9).

For this reason the Church is shown by the Second Vatican Council as a reality that embraces all history, accepts all its different cultures and directs them to God; and by virtue of the action of Christ's spirit is constituted "the universal sacrament of salvation." Likewise, she is shown as the Church that is engaged in dialogue with the world. Taking note of the signs of the times, she discovers what men are considering important and on what things she is in agreement with them. Moreover, she takes pains to be understood and recognized by the world, striving to divest herself of those external forms which seem less Gospel-like, and in which traces of eras already ended appear all too clearly.

The Church, of course, is not of this world, she is "inspired by no earthly ambition" (GS, 3) and she will be perfect only in heaven, on which she has her eyes fixed and toward which she is journeying. And yet she is connected with the world and its history. However, "the deep solicitude of the Church, the Spouse of Christ, for the needs of men, for their joys and hopes, their griefs and efforts, is nothing other than her great desire to be present to them, in order to illuminate them with the light of Christ and to gather them all in him, their only Savior. This solicitude can never mean that the Church conform herself to the things of this world, or that she lessen the ardor of her expectation of her Lord and of the eternal Kingdom" (Paul VI, *Professio fidei*, n. 27, *AAS*, 1968, p. 444).

Mary, Mother of God, Mother and Model of the Church

68 Mary is united in an ineffable manner with the Lord, being his Ever-Virgin Mother, who "occupies in the Holy Church the place which is highest after Christ and yet very close to us" (LG, 54).

The gift of Christ's Spirit is manifested in her in an altogether singular manner, because Mary is "full of grace" (Luke 1, 28), and is "a model of the Church" (LG, 63). In her, who was preserved from all stain of original sin, who was freely and fully faithful to the Lord, and who was assumed body and soul into heavenly glory, the Holy Spirit has fully manifested his gift. For she was completely conformed "to her Son, the Lord of lords, and the Conqueror of sin and death" (LG, 59). Because she is the Mother of God and "mother to us in the order of grace" (LG, 61), the type of the virginity and motherhood of the total Church (cf. LG, 63-65), and the sign of a secure hope and solace for the pilgrim People of God (cf. LG, 69), Mary "in a certain way unites and mirrors within herself the central truths of the faith," and she "summons the believers to her Son and to his sacrifice, and to love for the Father" (LG, 65). Therefore, the Church who honors the faithful and the saints who are already with the Lord and are interceding for us (LG, 49, 50), venerates in a most special way Christ's Mother, who is also her mother.

Final Communion with God

69 In Christ Jesus and through his mystery, the faithful already in this earthly life hopefully await "our Lord Jesus Christ, who will give a new form to this lowly body of ours and remake it according to the pattern of his glorified body" (Phil. 3, 21; cf. 1 Cor. 15). The very last realities, however, will become manifest and perfect when and only when Christ comes with power, as Judge of the living and the dead, to bring history to its end and to hand over his people to the Father, so that "God may be all in all" (1 Cor. 15, 24-28). Until "the Lord comes in his majesty, and all the angels with him, and until death is destroyed and all things are subject to him, some of his disciples are pilgrims on earth, some have finished this life and are being purified, and others are in glory, beholding clearly God himself three and one, as he is" (LG, 49).

On the day of the Lord's coming, the entire Church will reach her perfection and enter into the fullness of God. This is the very foundation of the hope and prayer of Christians ("Thy kingdom come"). Catechesis on the subject of the last things should, on the one hand, be taught under the aspect of consolation, of hope, and of salutary fear (cf. 1 Thess. 4, 18), of which modern men have such great need; on the other hand, it should be imparted in such a way that the whole truth can be seen. It is not right to minimize the grave responsibility which every one has regarding his future destiny. Catechesis can not pass over in silence the judgment after death of each man, or the expiatory punishments of Purgatory, or the sad and lamentable reality of eternal death, or the final judgment. On that day each man will fully arrive at his destiny, because all of us will be revealed "before the tribunal of Christ, so that each one may receive the recompense, good or bad, according to his life in the body" (2 Cor. 5, 10), and "those who have done right shall rise to live; the evildoers shall rise to be damned" (John 5, 29; cf. LG, 48).

Part Four
Elements of Methodology

Nature and Purpose of This Part

70 Within our present century, catechists have thoroughly investigated questions raised by the psychological, educational, and pedagogical sciences. Indeed, studies have been undertaken with regard to the method to be used in the catechism lesson; the role of activity methods in the teaching of catechesis has been pointed out; the act of catechesis has been investigated in all its parts according to the principles which govern the art of teaching (experience, imagination, memory, intelligence); and finally, a differential methodology has been worked out, that is, a methodology which varies according to the age, social conditions, and degree of psychological maturity of those who are to be taught.

Not all problems of this sort are considered here; rather, here are set forth only certain points to which great importance is being attributed today. Attacking these problems in an appropriate and specific way in individual countries will be the task of the various directories and the other tools.

Function of the Catechist

71 No method, not even one much proved in use, frees the catechist from the personal task of assimilating and passing judgment on the concrete circumstances, and from some adjustment to them. For outstanding human and Christian qualities in the catechists will be able to do more to produce successes than will the methods selected.

The work of the catechist must be considered of greater importance than the selection of texts and other tools (cf. AG, 17).

The importance and magnitude of the work to be done by catechists does not prevent the necessary establishing of boundaries around the role of catechists. They are responsible for choosing and creating suitable conditions which are necessary for the Christian message to be sought, accepted, and more profoundly investigated. This is the point to which the action of catechists extends—and there it stops. For adherence on the part of those to be taught is a fruit of grace and freedom, and does not ultimately depend on the catechist; and catechetical action, therefore, should be accompanied by prayer. That remark is self-evident, but it is nevertheless useful to recall it in present-day conditions, because today much is being demanded of the talent and of the genuine Christian spirit of the catechist, while at the same time he is being urged to have the greatest possible regard for the freedom and "creativity" of those to be taught.

Inductive and Deductive Methods

72 The method called inductive offers great advantages.

It serves in the presentation of facts (such as biblical events, liturgical actions, the life of the Church, and daily life) and in the consideration and examination of those facts in order that in them may be recognized the meaning they have in the Christian mystery. This method is in harmony with the economy of revelation and with one of the fundamental processes of the human spirit, one that comes to grasp intelligible realities through visible things, and also with the particular characteristic of knowledge of the faith, that is, a knowing through signs.

The inductive method does not exclude the deductive, but rather even requires it. The deductive method is used in interpreting and explaining the facts by proceeding from their causes. The deductive synthesis usually manifests its full force, however, when the inductive process has already been carried out.

Formulations

73 The advantages of the inductive method, chief among which are the active exercise of the spiritual faculties and the constant reference to concrete things in the explanation of intellectual concepts, must in no way lead to a forgetting of the need for and the usefulness of formulas.

Formulas permit the thoughts of the mind to be expressed accurately, are appropriate for a correct exposition of the faith, and, when committed to memory, help toward the firm possession of truth. Finally, they make it possible for a uniform way of speaking to be used among the faithful.

Formulas are generally presented and explained when the lesson or inquiry has reached the point of synthesis.

To be selected in preference to the others are those formulas which, while expressing faithfully the truth of the faith, are adapted to the capacity of the listeners. It must not be forgotten that dogmatic formulas are a true profession of Catholic doctrine, and are accordingly to be accepted as such by the faithful in the sense in which the Church has understood and does understand them (cf. First Vatican Dogm. Const. *Dei Filius*, Dz.-Sch., n. 3020, 3043). The traditional formulas for professing the faith and for praying, such as the Apostles' Creed, the Lord's Prayer, the Hail Mary, and the like, are to be taught with special care.

Experience

74 *a)* Experience begets concerns and questionings, hopes and anxieties, reflections and judgments; these merge and there results a certain desire to steer the human way of life.

Therefore, catechesis should be concerned with making men attentive to their more significant experiences, both personal and social; it also has the duty of placing under the light of the Gospel the questions which arise from those experiences, so that there may be stimulated within men a right desire to transform their ways of life.

In this fashion, experience also makes men respond in an active way to the gift of God.

b) Experience can also help make the Christian message more intelligible.

Christ himself preached the kingdom of God by illustrating its nature with parables drawn from the experience of human life. He recalled to mind certain human situations (the merchant who carries on a good business, the servants who to a greater or lesser extent increase the talents given to them, and so forth) in order to explain eschatological and transcendent realities, and then to teach the way of life which these realities demand of us.

Thus it is that experience serves in the examination and acceptance of the truths which are contained in the deposit of revelation.

c) Experience, considered in itself, must be illumined by the light of revelation. By recalling to mind the action of God who works our salvation, catechesis should help men to explore, interpret, and judge their own experiences, and also to ascribe a Christian meaning to their own existence.

In this aspect, experience is as it were an object to be interpreted and illumined by the catechist. This task, even though it is not without its difficulties, must not be overlooked.

Stimulating the Activity or Creativity of Those Catechized

75 All human education and all real communication require first of all that interior activity be made possible and be stimulated in the one to whom they are directed. In catechesis, therefore, one must stir up the activity of faith (of hope, too, and of charity); for correctness and vigor of judgment, which are to be stimulated by an active style of instruction, here help to bring about acceptance of the word of God. But the confidence which inspires active education should never lead one to forget that the act of faith necessarily involves a conversion of the one making it.

From what has been said it is evident that this active way of catechizing is in complete harmony with the economy of revelation and salvation. The pedagogical art which promotes an active response on the part of those to be catechized is in harmony with the general condition of the Christian life in which the faithful actively respond to God's gifts through prayers, through participation in the sacraments and the sacred liturgy, through acceptance of responsibilities in the Church and in social life, and through the practice of charity.

Those to be taught, especially if they are adults, can contribute in an active way to the progress of the catechesis. Thus, they should be asked how they understand the Christian message and how they can explain it in their own words. Then a comparison should be made between the results of that questioning and what is taught by the Magisterium of the Church, and only those things which are in agreement with the faith should be approved. In this way powerful aids can be found to hand on effectively the one true Christian message.

Groups

76 In catechesis, the importance of the group is becoming greater and greater.

In the catechesis of children, the group helps to further their education for social life, both in the case of children who attend catechism classes together, and in the case of those brought together in a small number to engage in some activities.

For adolescents and young adults, the group must be considered a vital necessity. In a group, the adolescent or the young adult comes to know himself and finds support and stimulation.

In the case of adults, the group can today be considered a requisite for catechesis which aims at fostering a sense of Christian co-responsibility.

In groups which include adolescents or adults, catechesis takes on the character of a joint study.

Such joint study aims at exploring the mutual relationships and ties between the content of the Christian message, which is always the norm for believing and acting, and the experiences of the group.

The catechist should take part in the joint study, but in such a way as to maintain his particular place in the group. For in the name of the Church he acts as a witness of the Christian message, one who ministers to others, shares with them the fruits of his own mature faith, and wisely orders the joint study toward the accomplishment of its purpose.

This function of the witness of the message does not necessarily mean that the catechist must be set over the group as its director.

A group which has achieved a high degree of perfection in carrying out its task will be able to give its members not only an occasion for religious education, but also an excellent experience of ecclesial life.

Catechesis performed in this way will be able to show the young that the Church is not at all something unrelated to their own existence, but is rather a great reality for which all, each in keeping with his own calling and service, have some responsibility.

Part Five

Catechesis According to Age Levels

Nature and Purpose of This Part

77 There are many methods and plans by which the Christian message is made to meet the various needs of men.

If missionary activity is considered, there is the method of evangelization, and of the initiation of catechumens and neophytes.

If the physical and spiritual development of those who are to be taught is considered, there is catechesis according to age levels.

If the sociological and cultural conditions in which men live are considered, there is catechesis suited to various mental outlooks (catechesis for workers, for technicians, and so on).

Finally, if the various stances which those who have been baptized can take towards the faith are considered, there is catechesis for believers who desire to obtain a fuller and more profound knowledge of the faith, and there is a catechesis for those who still lack the very basics of the faith.

Each of these methods, which are interconnected and interdependent, obviously has its own value and importance.

National or regional catechetical directories will have the task of providing specific and definite norms in this whole area, in accord with concrete local conditions and needs.

Here, for the sake of an example, are presented only some general principles of a catechesis adapted to various age levels, to show the force and importance of such a catechesis.

Infancy and Its Importance

78   The first roots of religious and moral life appear at the very beginning of human life. In the families of believers the first months and years of life, which are of the greatest importance for a man's balance in the years to come, can already provide the right conditions for developing a Christian personality. The baptism of infants takes on its full meaning when the Christian life of the parents, of the mother especially but not exclusively, makes it possible for the baptismal grace to produce its fruits. For the infant absorbs into himself, as though through an "osmosis" process, the manner of acting and the attitudes of the members of his family. And so it is that the immense number of his experiences will be, as it were, pressed together within him to form a foundation of that life of faith which will then gradually develop and manifest itself.

The right orientation of a trusting spirit depends at first on a good relationship between the infant and his mother, and then also on one between him and his father; it is nourished by sharing their joyfulness and by experiencing their loving authority. The theological virtues depend in part upon the growth of that healthy orientation for their own unimpeded development, and at the same time they tend to strengthen that orientation. At this time, too, there arises the affirmation of personality, or autonomy; this is needed for the acquisition of the moral virtues and for leading a life in community. It itself demands a balance between firmness and acceptance. Next, the capacity for spontaneous action can gradually develop; this will be most necessary for beginning social life as well as for promoting and strengthening the service of God and of the Church.

An education in prayer must accompany all these acquisitions, so that the little child may learn to call upon the God who loves us and protects us, and upon Jesus, the Son of God and our brother, who leads us to the Father, and upon the Holy Spirit, who dwells within our hearts; and so that this child may also direct confident prayers to Mary, the Mother of Jesus and our mother.

If these foundations are lacking, catechesis must determine whether there are any insufficiencies as a result, what they may be, and how they may be compensated. Suitable assistance on the part of Christian parents must be supported by giving the parents an adequate formation. This formation must be given to them by competent educators, even though it is to be simple and adapted to the cultural level of the parents. This task of pastors is not supererogatory; for when parents are helped to perform their duties rightly, the Church is being built up. This also provides a splendid occasion for catechizing adults.

Childhood and Its Importance

79 When the child goes to school he enters a society wider than that of his family, and he is initiated into the society of adults in an intensive way that absorbs a great part of his resources and concerns. He gets his first experience of working in school (cf. GE, 5).

Before this point, the family served a mediating role between the child and the People of God. But now the child is ready to begin sharing directly in the life of the Church, and can be admitted to the sacraments.

The child's intelligence develops gradually. Catechesis must be adapted to this mental development. The child seeks to understand the religious life of adults. Accordingly, the genuine Christian life of the adult community helps very much toward giving the children a solid formation, and it does this in a truly instructive way when it explains the religious life of adults and the activities of the People of God suitably in the light of salvation history.

The initial experience of working should not be thought unrelated to the aim of catechesis. The joy of doing things and doing them well, cooperation with others, discipline arising out of this as something easy to understand and reasonable—in all this one finds many experiences which are useful not only for sharing in social life but also for active participation in the life of the Church.

With these things in mind, catechetical pedagogy, whatever method it follows, should stimulate activity on the part of the children. If it should fail to do so, catechesis could not satisfy its obligation to teach the believer to give an ever more personal response to the word and the gift of God. This active pedagogy should not be satisfied with external expressions only, however useful they may be, but it should strive to bring forth a response from the heart and a taste for prayer. This interior education is indeed rendered more difficult, but also more necessary, because of the character of contemporary civilization which tends to disperse spiritual energies.

Cooperation between catechists and parents (sharing with one another their opinions about programs, about methods, and about difficulties which arise) is necessary if the education of the children is to proceed in a suitable and harmonious way. This kind of cooperation is useful for both the catechists and the parents and helps them in carrying out their own specific duties.

Children Who Do Not Attend School

80 There are also regions, even very large and sometimes heavily populated areas, in which there are not enough schools. Where this is so, earnest pastoral action should be directed to the families themselves, and, to the extent that it is possible, various associations should be set up to take care of the children. These associations should be set up in such a way that they can take account of the local circumstances and meet the spiritual needs of the children.

Children Who Grow Up in Families Affected by Religious Indifference

81 The difficulty of giving catechesis to children living in families who do not practice their religion at all or do so in an entirely inadequate way is becoming more and more marked. Sometimes questions are raised about the very possibility and appropriateness of giving them a catechesis.

Catechesis is certainly not to be omitted for such children; rather, it is to be planned and carried out in a way that fits in with actual circumstances and conditions. In these cases there is need to establish contact with the families and to study their mental attitudes and styles of life, so that some means can be found to open a dialogue with them. It is also necessary that catechesis present its material in a way that really responds to the concrete possibilities of these children.

Adolescence and Early Adulthood, and Their Importance

82 The period of adolescence and, in a larger sense, the so-called "phenomenon of youth" have very great importance (cf. AA, 12). In pre-industrial societies which have only a smaller number of schools, the transition from childhood to the adult community takes place as it were directly. In our time the custom is spreading more and more of extending the time of education in schools for adolescents. This custom creates in society a generation which is not immediately occupied with gainful labor, and which, though it already enjoys physical and intellectual vitality, is engaged in no activity other than study and preparation for a future profession. This social class has a great impact on adult society; and this creates no small problem.

This problem is also found in the Church, and although it takes different forms here, it is just as serious. Adolescents and young adults are less exposed to the danger of violently opposing the Church than they are to the temptation of leaving it. The fact that it is often difficult for adults to acknowledge that adolescents and young adults can contribute anything worthwhile is a further reason why this is a very serious problem in catechesis.

But the young will be less distrustful, the more the catechists show an ability to understand their roles and to accept them.

Pre-Adolescence, Adolescence, and Early Adulthood, and Their Importance

83 National directories should distinguish pre-adolescence, adolescence, and early adulthood.

Here it can only be pointed out that in sophisticated regions where the point is raised, the special difficulties of pre-adolescence are in practice not sufficiently nor always recognized. The educator can be tempted to treat pre-adolescents in the same way as children, and thus it is to be feared that he will not win their attention; or he can treat them as adolescents, and in that case give them themes and methods of working which presuppose a maturity of personality and of experience that they have not yet attained.

The age of pre-adolescence has as its peculiar note the troublesome beginning of concern with one's self. Hence it is important not to continue at this age the simple and objective kind of instruction which is appropriate for children; at the same time, however, one must be careful not to propose problems and themes that belong properly to adolescence.

A concrete type of instruction which would explain the lives and works of the Saints and of other outstanding persons, together with reflections on the actual life of the Church, could provide catechetical students of this age with wholesome nourishment.

The time of young adulthood, taken strictly, which follows adolescence, is also a period of life which has not yet been sufficiently studied and investigated, and its special characteristics are not yet sufficiently known.

Some think that theological instruction should begin at this age. Others believe that human and social questions should be presented for study, together with simple theological explanations and with certain encouragements to Christian behavior. The method that seems most desirable is that of treating fundamental problems and problems of most concern to this age with the serious, scholarly apparatus of the theological and human sciences, using at the same time a suitable group-discussion method.

Searching into the Meaning of Life

84 The adolescent notices profound physical and psychological changes within himself. He is looking for his place in society. Although he is no longer content with the religious forms of his childhood, he has not yet reached the maturity of faith proper to an adult; and therefore he seeks a basic orientation by which he can unify his life anew. But this searching often leads to a religious crisis.

The principal task of catechesis in adolescence will be to further a genuinely Christian understanding of life. It must shed the light of the Christian message on the realities which have greater impact on the adolescent, such as the meaning of bodily existence, love and the family, the standards to be followed in life, work and leisure, justice and peace, and so on.

Focusing Attention on Genuine Values

85 The adolescent makes an effort to direct the vision of his life and the course of his existence according to certain principal and primary values. Today, however, the adolescent feels himself immersed in "values" that are opposed to one another. This fact sharpens the conflict within the adolescent among the various values which he is in search of, and he persuades himself to reject those values which he does not find expressed in the way adults live.

Catechesis must help him more and more to discover genuine values and to put them in order.

Personal Autonomy

86 In order to attain the autonomy which he very much desires, the adolescent often exaggerates his self-expression and at times finds fault with the pattern of life which he has received from adults.

Adults must realize that adolescents hold fast to the faith and strengthen themselves in it, not because of any identification with adults, but because of their own convictions as these are gradually explored.

From this kind of autonomy there arises what can be called a "temptation to naturalism," which makes adolescents tend to perform their actions and to seek their salvation by their own powers. The bolder the personality, the stronger will be an inclination of this sort.

It is, therefore, the task of catechesis to bring the adolescent to that personal maturity which will allow him to overcome subjectivism and to discover a new hope in the strength and the wisdom of God.

Groups of Adolescents

87 In order to maintain their autonomy adolescents seek to form associations among themselves, so that they may be able to follow out more easily their own ideas and talents, and so that by means of groups they may protect their own autonomy from adult groups. Again within the orbit of these groups the adolescent is urged on by various life values and is moved to live in accordance with them. In daily life practice adolescents communicate more easily with young people of their own age than with adults.

Catechesis has the task of working with these youth groups, which can serve to mediate between young people and the whole community of the Church (cf. AA, 12).

Youth groups do not always have positive values. For this reason there is an urgent need to promote relationships between them and Christian communities, so that the human and Christian values of the latter may be duly recognized and appreciated by the adolescents (cf. AA, 12).

Intellectual Demands

88 The adolescent possesses essentially the "formal" use of reason. He is learning how the intellect is to be used rightly, and is discovering that the culture set before him demands reflection and must be actively applied in his own life.

If catechesis is to be able to awaken an experience of the life of faith, it simply cannot neglect the formation of a religious way of thinking which will show the connection of the mysteries with one another and with man's final end (cf. First Vatican Council, Dogm. Const. *Dei Filius*, c. IV, Dz.-Sch., 3015-3020). To make firm the inner coherence of this kind of religious thinking, witnessing is not enough. Today scientific strictness is demanded everywhere; hence catechesis must also provide the rational foundations for faith with the greatest care.

The intellectual building up of the faith of adolescents must by no means be considered as merely a kind of addition, but rather it should be counted as an essential need for the life of faith. The manner of teaching is of special importance. The catechist, in dialogue with the adolescent, must stimulate the mind of the adolescent.

Action

89 Action is necessary for the development of the adolescent's personality. Freedom from egocentrism and subjectivism demands dealing with reality itself, whether with success or with failure.

Catechesis, which should encourage personal experience of faith and at the same time well-ordered reflection on religious matters, is brought to perfection when it leads to the fulfillment of religious duties. Christian catechesis should educate adolescents to assume the responsibilities of faith and gradually make them capable of upholding their Christian profession before all men.

Adolescents Who Do Not Attend School

90 An immense number of young people who are engaged in the manual or professional skills are drawn into an accelerated development of their personality. This accelerated development of personality may turn out to be favorable or unfavorable, complete or incomplete.

It follows, then, that it is necessary to establish a special catechesis for such adolescents. This will have to consider the immediate problems of everyday life, support the young as they begin working and help them, in accordance with their individual capacities, to carry on their activity by working together with Catholic associations.

Moreover, since the special characteristics and needs of adolescents remain present in the young worker, it will be the task of catechesis not only to shed light on his concrete activity, but also to lead him to embrace the whole of God's plan.

Children and Adolescents Not Adjusted to the Conditions of Life

91 The duty here cannot be considered one that is secondary or one that is taken care of elsewhere. Maladjusted children and adolescents make up no small part of the citizenry. The conditions of society today not infrequently make it difficult for young people to have a harmonious life development and to have a suitable adjustment to society.

Catechesis must provide for these young people the possibility of living a life of faith in accordance with their own state. This is an eminently evangelical task and witness of great value, which the Church has carried out in every age.

The education of these young people in the faith has a pastoral value, and indeed one of great importance, also because it offers the possibility of reaching very many families.

Finally, the peculiar difficulty in performing this task and the necessity of imparting to such young people only the essential elements can give catechesis in general the benefit of employing the methods and ways which pedagogical research discovers and makes available for the sake of these young people.

Adulthood

92 This *General Directory* earnestly affirms the need of catechesis for adults, for these reasons:

a) The undertaking of tasks in social life, and the responsibilities of family, professional, civic, and political life demand of adults that they complete their Christian formation according to the norm of the word of God in a special and suitable way (cf. AA, 29-32). Cooperation should be promoted between those who catechize adults and those who take part in the various forms of the apostolate of the laity.

b) Aptitudes and capacities which reach their full development in adult life, such as the experience of life, maturity of personality, and so on, must be cultivated and illumined by the word of God.

c) The adult, moreover, must successfully pass through certain periods of life which are full of crises. Although these crises are less obvious than those experienced by adolescents, they are not to be considered less dangerous or less profound; in these times the adult's faith must be constantly illumined, developed, and fortified.

Dynamic Notes of Adulthood—Fellowship and Loneliness

93 When a person arrives at adult age, he ordinarily becomes more capable of having fellowship with others and of establishing mutual relationships with them.

This capacity and the need for fellowship come into play within the framework of family duties and within the relationships of social life; and all these things serve at times to promote this fellowship and at times to hinder it.

As a matter of fact, people, especially in contemporary society, often experience too much loneliness.

Catechesis ought to show that God, who is love, is really the author of the community of faith, which is the Church, and at the same time it should enkindle a desire for entering into fellowship with every man. It reminds married couples that their intimate union is, in virtue of the sacrament of matrimony, a sign of the mystery of unity and fruitful love between Christ and the Church, and that it shares in that mystery (cf. Eph. 5, 32).

Within the frame of small groups of the faithful, catechesis will help adults to live Christian charity to the full. Indeed, this charity, as the sign of a certain common experience, makes them be of assistance to one another in the faith.

Full Development of the Personality

94 Adult age is distinguished chiefly by the awareness of having achieved a fully developed personality.

The man who has successfully passed through each stage of his development and who has been able to enter into fellowship with others and to exercise creative ability, tries, when he has reached adult age, to reduce to a unified whole all the experiences of his personal, social, and spiritual life. A danger lies in the fact that the adult, especially if he belongs to an industrial society, may think that he can obtain this unity merely by conforming himself to the society in which he lives. But the perfect attainment of personality does not consist in a merely exterior balance between personal life and its social context, but it looks especially toward the attainment of Christian wisdom.

For this reason catechesis must strive to lead man to observe the order of priority among ends, that is, to perceive more fully the meaning of life and death, in the light of the death and resurrection of Christ.

Old Age

95 The importance of old age is still not sufficiently recognized in the pastoral ministry.

In our times the number of the aged is increasing more and more. The aged are often neglected by contemporary society, however, and this fact must be carefully noted for its relevance to pastoral activity.

As a matter of fact, the aged can contribute no small benefit to the community both by their work, which is not always justly appreciated, and by the witness that flows from their experience.

Moreover, there is a duty in justice to help the aged by a catechesis that has reference to death, which biologically is near at hand, and socially is to some extent already present, since almost nothing is expected any more from their activity.

Catechesis should teach the aged to have supernatural hope, by virtue of which death is considered a crossing over to true life and as a meeting with the divine Savior. In this way old age can become a sign of the presence of God, of immortal life, and of the future resurrection. This will, indeed, be an eschatological witness that the aged can bear by their patience toward themselves and toward others, by their benevolence, by their prayers poured out in praise of God, by their spirit of poverty and the trust that they put in God.

Unquestionably, it would be a serious loss to the Church if the great number of the aged who have been baptized were not to show that their faith shines with a brighter light when death approaches.

Special Forms of Catechesis for Adults

96 There are conditions and circumstances that demand special forms of catechesis.

a) There is the catechesis of Christian initiation or the catechumenate for adults.

b) There is the catechesis for those who are involved in the lay apostolate in a special way. Clearly catechesis must provide for a deeper study of the Christian message in these cases.

c) There is a catechesis which is to be given on the occasion of the principal events of life, such as marriage, the baptism of one's children, first communion and confirmation, the more difficult periods of the children's education, one's illness, and so forth. These are times when people are moved more strongly than ever to seek the true meaning of life.

d) There is a catechesis which is to be given on the occasion of some change in the circumstances of one's life, as for example on the occasion of starting work, on entering military life, when migrating, or when changing one's profession or social status. These changes can indeed increase one's spiritual goods, but they can also disturb the spirit and snatch away hope. The Christian community has a duty to supply those who experience them with necessary helps in fraternal love. The word of God, which in these circumstances is sometimes more readily accepted, ought to be a light and an aid to them.

e) There is the catechesis which is concerned with a Christian use of leisure, and that·which is to be given on the occasion of recreational traveling (cf. *Directorium Generale pro ministerio pastorali quoad "turismum,"* n. 19, 25).

f) There is the catechesis which is to be given on the occasion of special events touching the life of the Church or of society.

These special forms of catechesis in no way lessen the need for establishing catechetical cycles which are devoted to a systematic study of the entire Christian message. This organic and well-organized formation is certainly not to be reduced to a simple series of conferences or sermons.

The Special Functions of Catechesis for Adults

97   So that it will always be able to respond to the more urgent demands of our time, a catechesis for adults should:

a) *Teach them to evaluate correctly, in the light of faith, the sociological and cultural changes in contemporary society.* The Christian people are becoming more and more aware of the necessity of examining where the contemporary development of society may be leading and of distinguishing between true blessings and the dangers of our present human civilization. They desire help in evaluating the changes which are constantly taking place, and they want to be enlightened about the styles of behavior which they can and should make their own.

b) *Explain contemporary questions in religious and moral matters.* Catechesis must make its own the new questions which men of this age are asking themselves. For example, today great importance is attached to questions that deal with social relations. Man wishes to imprint a new form on the society in which he lives. Such attempts at renewal, in which the responsibilities and also the limits of man are clearly evident (cf Encycl. *Populorum progressio, AAS,* 1967, pp. 257-299), simply cannot escape the interest of catechesis.

c) *Shed light on the relations between temporal action and ecclesial action.* Catechesis should educate Christians to perceive the mutual relations between temporal duties and ecclesial duties. Catechesis should make it clear that the performance of temporal duties can have a useful influence on the ecclesial community itself, when it makes it more aware of its transcendent goal and of its mission in the world, and that the performance of ecclesial duties serves in turn to benefit human society (cf. GS, 40-45).

d) *Develop the rational foundations of the faith.* The Church has always guarded the rational foundations of the faith against fideism. Catechesis must develop more and more a correct understanding of the faith, and thereby show that the act of faith and the truths which are to be believed are in conformity with the demands of human reason. Catechesis must show that the Gospel is always contemporary and always relevant. For this reason pastoral action must be promoted in the area of Christian doctrine and Christian culture.

Part Six
Pastoral Activity in the Ministry of the Word

Pastoral Action

98   Those things which have been explained about the catechetical act and the content of catechesis provide the basis for a plan of pastoral action, the main points of which are treated in this part.

This pastoral action requires appropriate organs on the national level, to be set up by the Conferences of Bishops, for the purpose of planning or research and for administration. Generally these organs include: *(a)* an episcopal commission for catechesis on which work selected *ex officio* members and experts; and *(b)* a permanent executive structure (office, center, and so on).

So that with the aid of these organs the pastoral action in the ministry of the word can be carried out in an efficient and coordinated way, it is necessary that:

1) a report be prepared about the actual state of affairs and the place, and about what it is possible to achieve through the ministry of the word under those conditions;

2) a program of the action to be carried out be published;

3) attention be given to the formation and instruction of those who have responsibility in this matter;

4) appropriate aids for the work be rightly planned and made available;

5) organizational structures suitable for catechesis be promoted;

6) pastoral action in catechesis be coordinated with the other fields of pastoral work;

7) provision be made for research; and

8) international cooperation be encouraged.

The guides and suggestions presented in this part cannot be implemented always and all at the same time in all parts of the Church. In the case of countries or regions where catechetical action is not yet sufficiently advanced, the purpose of these suggestions and guides is to point out goals which are to be accomplished gradually.

CHAPTER ONE

Analysis of the Situation

Purpose

99 It is necessary that there be within a Conference a clear knowledge of the situation in which the ministry of the word is exercised.

The analysis aims at bringing out to what extent the Church's evangelical activity is attaining the goals that have been set for it. Careful study must be made of the way in which the ministry of the word is being practiced and of the results—to the extent that these can be ascertained by human knowledge—which have been obtained by catechesis or by other ways of presenting the Christian message. To be subjected to examination are the undertakings of the Church and how they have been received, where and by what persons, with what results, and so on.

Object

100 The object of this investigation is multiple. Included are examination of pastoral action and analysis of the religious situation as well as of the sociological, cultural, and economic conditions, to the extent that these facts of collective life can greatly influence the success of evangelization.

Methods

101 Since this work is rather arduous, it is necessary that two dangers be avoided, that is to say, one must guard against:

a) considering principles and indications which have not been sufficiently tested and proved as though they were certain;

b) demanding a degree of scientific accuracy so high that it cannot be attained.

It must also be rightly noted that technical research carried out by means of questionnaires or interviews is of little value unless preceded by diligent consideration of the various forms of pastoral action that can be chosen. It seems necessary, then, for the Conferences of Bishops to have a complete picture of the situation. This can be obtained by consulting experts truly skilled in examining the evidence available and by drawing conclusions from pastoral action which has already been started. Monographs can be of very useful help in this regard.

The entire Christian community should share in the study of the situation, so that the people may be made aware of the questions and be disposed to action.

Effects

102 An investigation of this sort is not its own end. Rather, it should bring to light the more effective activities and pave the way for the undertaking of them, both by intensifying the works and undertakings that have already been proved effective and by promoting others. For it deals with foreseeing and preparing for those things that will necessarily have to be done in the future.

An investigation of this sort should also convince those who work in the ministry of the word that, so far as pastoral action is concerned, human situations are ambivalent. Therefore, workers in the service of the Gospel should learn to note the many possibilities that are opening up for their action in new and diverse circumstances. There is a danger that knowledge of difficulties might lead one to conclude that pastoral action is impossible. On the contrary, everyone should be convinced that cultural realities are not inert, immutable, univocal principles which have the effect of reducing grace and pastoral action to impotence as it were in their regard. For always possible is a process of change which can make clear the way to the faith.

CHAPTER TWO

Program of Action

Program of Action

103 After the situation has been carefully examined, it is necessary to proceed to the publishing of a program of action, especially by means of a catechetical directory. This program determines the objectives, the tools for pastoral catechetical action, and the guiding norms for that same action, and these are determined in such a way that they are altogether in harmony with the objectives and norms of the universal Church and at the same time they fully respond to the local needs.

In proposing a program of action, one should carefully bear in mind the functions of strictly ecclesial institutions, such as parishes, special communities of the faithful, and societies devoted to the apostolate; of the institution of the family; of educational institutions, such as schools, both Christian and neutral; and of all other forms of social and cultural groups.

The goals to be attained and the means to be used should be considered the cardinal points of any program of action.

Goals To Be Attained

104 The goals to be attained in the field of pastoral action may differ in degree and style according to differences of place and of needs. Nevertheless, all must pertain to the growth of faith and morality among Christians and to a strengthening of their relationships with God and neighbor. They should, for example, have the objectives that adults achieve a mature faith, that Christian teaching reach scientific and technical groups, that the family be able to carry out its Christian duties, that the Christian presence exert an influence on the work of social transformation.

Since the goals are generally numerous, it is altogether advisable that they be determined in due time and according to an order of priority for the objectives to be accomplished.

It is also helpful for the pastoral goals established in one region to be opportunely compared with those established by the Conferences of Bishops that are closest to it geographically or culturally.

Means To Be Used

105 The chief means to be used are: catechetical institutes, which are to be promoted or supported; programs; texts (cf. Chapter 5 of this part); working tools; instructions on methods (cf. Part Four). The area of research on means can hardly be defined. Yet this is always to be carefully borne in mind: the means proposed should always respond appropriately to the spiritual objectives that are to be attained.

Norms

106 The norms that can be given with regard to catechesis are many and they vary with the ends to be attained. In comparison with the others, the norms for preparing the faithful for the sacraments have a special importance. These include, for example, norms for the catechumenate of adults, for the sacramental initiation of children, and for the preparation of families for the baptism of their children.

To be effective, all such norms should be few in number, simple in character, and set external rather than internal criteria.

As is obvious, no particular norm can derogate from the Church's general laws and common practice without the approval of the Apostolic See.

Distribution and Promotion of Responsibilities

107 First of all, attention must be given to a clear and effective distribution of tasks and responsibilities. It is very important, for example, to clarify and put in their proper light the responsibilities of Christian families, of associations of the faithful, of the clergy, and of catechists. Nevertheless, it is not enough to rest content with the distribution of forces already existing; it is also necessary that effort on the part of all Christians be more and more stimulated and promoted. Care must be taken to make the Christian community every day conscious of its duty, which is to be a sign of the wisdom and love of God that was revealed to us in Christ. For this, it is expedient that the entire community and each of its members as far as possible always be informed at the proper time about what things are to be done, and also that all be invited to take an active part in the undertaking of projects, in the making of decisions, and in the carrying out of what has been decided.

In preparing programs of catechetical activity, one must consider well the fact that various undertakings can at times give rise to inconveniences and disputes. For example, difficulties can arise from the changes in terminology and from the new opinions on the relationship between education and the apostolate. In these cases, every effort should be made to avoid all those things which can unduly disturb people.

Finally, it is necessary that all catechetical activities be provided with suitable financial support.

CHAPTER THREE

Catechetical Formation

Catechetical Formation

108 Any pastoral activity for the carrying out of which there are not at hand persons with the right formation and preparation will necessarily come to nothing. The working tools themselves cannot be effective unless used by catechists who have been rightly formed. Hence, the suitable formation of catechists must come before reform in texts and strengthening of the organization for handling catechesis.

First of all, it is necessary that attention be given to the formation of those who carry out catechetical activities on the national level. The duty here belongs to the Conferences of Bishops. Nevertheless, the formation of those who direct catechetical activities on a national level should be joined, as it were with an extension and completion of itself, with the formation of the catechists who carry out this activity on regional and diocesan levels. Responsibility for this latter formation belongs to the regional Conferences of Bishops, where such exist, and to the individual bishops.

Higher Institutes and Catechetical Schools

109 Higher institutes for training in pastoral catechetics should be promoted or founded, so that catechists capable of directing catechesis at the diocesan level, or within the area of activities to which religious congregations are dedicated, may be prepared. These higher institutes can be national or even international. They ought to function as a university so far as curriculum, length of courses, and requisites for admission are concerned.

Schools of religious education should also be founded within individual dioceses, or at least within the area of regional Conferences, in order that, through a curriculum that is less advanced but still effective, full-time catechetical personnel may be prepared.

Continuing Formation

110 Continuing formation includes diverse methods and grade levels. It is necessary that this formation be continued over the entire time that the catechists remain committed to their functions. Thus this pertains to directors of catechesis as well as to ordinary catechists.

Continuing formation cannot be entrusted to the central offices alone. Rather, Christian communities on lower levels must also give attention to it, also for the reason that the conditions and needs for catechesis can vary from place to place. The clergy and all who have responsibilities for supervising and directing catechesis have a duty to see to the continuing formation of all their co-workers in catechesis.

Objective of Catechetical Formation

111 The summit and center of catechetical formation lies in an aptitude and ability to communicate the Gospel message. This formation requires, therefore, an accurate formation in theological doctrine, in anthropology, and in methodology, geared to the level of knowledge that is to be attained. The formation does not end, however, with the acquisition of doctrinal knowledge. The formation is complete when the catechist becomes competent to select the most suitable method for communicating the Gospel message to groups and individuals who live in circumstances always different and singular.

Theological-Doctrinal, Anthropological, and Methodological Formation

112 a) *Doctrine.* That a strong doctrinal heritage must be acquired is self-evident. This must always include adequate knowledge of Catholic doctrine, together with a degree of scientific theology obtained at higher catechetical institutes. Sacred Scripture should be as it were the soul of this entire formation.

In any case, the doctrine ought to be mastered in such a way that the catechist will be able not only to communicate the Gospel message accurately, but also to make those being taught capable of receiving it actively and of discerning what in their spiritual journey agrees with the faith.

b) *Human sciences.* Our era is marked and distinguished by a very great growth in the sciences about man. These sciences are no longer reserved for the learned and the specialists. They penetrate the awareness that modern man has of himself. They influence social relationships and shape a cultural pattern, as it were, for humanity today, even that not very sophisticated.

In the teaching of human sciences, given their very great number and diversity, there are difficult problems in regard to choosing from among them and in regard to the method of teaching them. Since the question here is one of training catechists, not experts in psychology, the norm to be followed is this: determine and choose that which can directly help them to acquire facility in communication.

c) *Methodological formation.* Methodology is by its very nature nothing other than careful consideration of means that have stood the test of experience. Therefore, more importance is to be attributed to practical exercises than to theoretical instruction on pedagogy. Still, theoretical instruction is necessary for helping the catechist to meet various situations appropriately, for avoiding an empirical form of teaching catechesis, for grasping the changes found in educational reports, and for directing future work correctly.

Careful attention should be given to the fact that, when it is a question of training ordinary catechists (that is, those who teach the primary elements of catechesis), the principles we have considered above can be acquired better if they are taught at the same time the work is being performed (for example, during sessions in which lessons of catechesis are being prepared and tested).

Learning the Art of Catechesis

113 The preparation of the catechist must be such that he will be able accurately to interpret the reactions of each person or group, and thus be able to discern their spiritual capacities and choose the means by which the Gospel message can be received fruitfully and effectively. Many methods for this can be given: practical exercises, working in groups, analysis of cases, and so on. The whole question here turns on weighing well and understanding the communicative power of the Christian message. Catechesis, which is the Church's practice, is not learned in a merely theoretical way. The art of teaching catechesis is acquired from experience, from the guidance of skilled teachers, and from actually performing the function. An aptitude for apostolic action and knowledge of the faith, of men, and of the laws that govern the development both of individual men and of communities, contribute to the acquisition of skill in this art.

Spiritual Life of Catechists

114 The function entrusted to the catechist demands of him a fervent sacramental and spiritual life, a practice of prayer, and a deep feeling for the excellence of the Christian message and for the power it has to transform one's life; it also demands of him the pursuit of the charity, humility, and prudence which allow the Holy Spirit to complete his fruitful work in those being taught.

Formation of Catechists

115 It is necessary that ecclesiastical authorities regard the formation of catechists as a task of the greatest importance.

This formation is meant for all catechists (cf. AG, 17, 26), both lay and religious, and also for Christian parents, who will be able to receive therefrom effective help for taking care of the initial and occasional catechesis for which they are responsible. This formation is meant for deacons, and especially for priests, for "by the power of the sacrament of Orders, and in the image of the Eternal High Priest (cf. Heb. 5, 1-10; 7, 24; 9, 11-28), they are consecrated to preach the Gospel, shepherd the faithful, and celebrate divine worship as true priests of the New Testament" (LG, 28). Indeed, in individual parishes the preaching of the word of God is committed chiefly to the priests, who are obliged to open the riches of Sacred Scripture to the faithful, and to explain the mysteries of the faith and the norms of Christian living in homilies throughout the course of the liturgical year (cf. SC, 51, 52). Hence it is of great importance that a thorough catechetical preparation be given students in seminaries and scholasticates, which should be completed afterwards by the continuing formation mentioned above (cf. n. 110).

Finally, the formation is meant for teachers of religion in public schools, whether these belong to the Church or to the state. To carry out a task of such great importance, only persons should be selected who are distinguished for talent, doctrine, and spiritual life (cf. GS, 5).

It is highly desirable that in this area of formation there be genuine cooperation between the various apostolic activities and catechesis, because they are performing, although under different aspects, a common task, that of communicating the Christian message.

CHAPTER FOUR

Catechetical Aids

Aids

116 Of the chief working tools for catechesis, the following are considered here:
—directories of the Conferences of Bishops;
—programs;
—catechisms;
—textbooks;
—audiovisual aids.

Catechetical Directories

117 Directories are concerned with promoting and coordinating catechetical action in the territory of a region or nation, or even of several nations of the same sociocultural condition. Before they are promulgated, every local Ordinary should be heard, and they should be submitted to the Apostolic See for approval (cf. n. 134).

Programs

118 Programs set up the educational goals to be attained according to ages or places or set times, the methodological criteria to be used, and the content to be taught in catechesis. By all means care must be taken that the mysteries of faith to be believed by adults are already indicated in the programs for children's and adolescents' catechisms in a way adapted to their age (cf. n. 134).

Catechisms

119   The greatest importance must be attached to catechisms published by ecclesiastical authority. Their purpose is to provide, under a form that is condensed and practical, the witnesses of revelation and of Christian tradition as well as the chief principles which ought to be useful for catechetical activity, that is, for personal education in faith. The witnesses of tradition should be held in due esteem, and very great care must be taken to avoid presenting as doctrines of the faith special interpretations which are only private opinions or the views of some theological school. The doctrine of the Church must be presented faithfully. Here the norms set forth in Chapter I of Part Three are to be followed.

In view of the great difficulties in putting these works together and the great importance of these witnesses, it is most expedient that:

a) there be collaboration by a number of experts in catechetics and in theology;

b) there be consultation with specialists in other religious and human disciplines, and also with the other pastoral organizations;

c) individual local Ordinaries be consulted and their opinions be carefully considered;

d) limited experiments be tried before definitive publication; and

e) these texts be duly reviewed after a certain period of time.

Before promulgation, these catechisms must be submitted to the Apostolic See for review and approval (cf. n. 134).

Textbooks

120   Textbooks are aids offered to the Christian community that is engaged in catechesis. No text can take the place of a live communication of the Christian message; nevertheless, the texts do have great value in that they make it possible to present a fuller exposition of the witnesses of Christian tradition and of principles that foster catechetical activity. The putting together of these texts requires a cooperative effort by a number of catechetical experts, and also consultation with other experts.

Manuals for Catechists

121 These books should contain:

—an explanation of the message of salvation (constant reference must be made to the sources, and a clear distinction must be kept between those things which pertain to the faith and to the doctrine that must be held, and those things which are mere opinions of theologians);

—psychological and pedagogical advice;

—suggestions about methods.

Books and other printed materials intended for study and activity by those being taught should also be provided. These printed materials can be made part of the books for the use of those being taught, or they can be published as separate booklets.

Finally, care should be taken to publish books for the use of parents, if the question is one of giving catechesis to children.

Audiovisual Aids

122 Audiovisual aids are used especially:

a) as resources for enriching catechetical instruction with objective elements; for this use, they should excel in truthfulness, careful selection of ideas, and pedagogical clarity; and

b) as images for properly cultivating the powers of the senses and the imagination; for this use they should have real beauty and be effective in moving people.

In regard to these aids, the following are necessary functions:

—fostering studies concerning the criteria which should guide the production and selection of these aids in keeping with the particular aspects of the Christian message that are to be presented and the particular groups of people for whom they are intended; and

—instructing catechists in a right use of these aids (it often happens that catechists are ignorant of the proper nature of visual language; it happens more often that audiovisual aids used improperly lead to passive rather than active behavior; and so on).

Mass Media

123   The mass media have the effect, among other things, of giving an aura of reality and actuality to the events, undertakings, and ideas about which they speak, and, contrariwise, of diminishing in popular estimation the importance of the things they are silent about.

The message of salvation, therefore, must have a place among the media of social communication (cf. IM, 3). It is not enough to perfect the media that the Church already possesses in this field, but rather it is necessary to promote cooperation among the producers, writers, and actors who offer their services for this purpose. Such cooperation requires that on the national and international levels there be set up groups of experts who can give genuine assistance if consulted about programs of activities that pertain to religion.

Also, it is the function of catechesis to educate the faithful to discern the nature and value of things presented through the mass media. This, as is obvious, demands a technical knowledge of the language proper to these media.

Programmed Instruction

124   Catechesis can and should use audiovisual aids so that it will be better able to achieve its goal. In this area there is a new method which is gaining ground more and more today and which in the educational field is called "programmed instruction." It ought not to be ignored.

In this matter, however, one must consider the difficulties which arise, either from the truths to be taught, or from the purpose of catechesis itself. Unprepared explanations are to be avoided. Rather, both for preparing the programs, as well as for expressing truths with the help of pictures, one should call upon the joint effort of experts in sacred theology, in catechetics, and in the art of audiovisual teaching.

CHAPTER FIVE

Organization for Catechesis

Organization for Catechesis

125 The organization for catechesis within the area of every Conference of Bishops consists chiefly of diocesan, regional and national structures.

The principal purposes of these structures are:

a) to promote catechetical activities; and

b) to cooperate with other apostolic undertakings and works (for example, with the liturgical commission, with associations for the lay apostolate, with the ecumenical commission, and so on), because all these activities of the Church have a part, even though in different ways, in the ministry of the word.

Diocesan Structures

126 The Decree *Provido sane* (cf. *AAS*, 1935, pp. 151 ff.) established the Diocesan Catechetical Office, the function of which is to supervise the entire catechetical organization. This diocesan office should have a staff of persons who have special competence. The extent and diversity of the problems which must be handled demand that the responsibilities be divided among a number of truly skilled people.

It is also the task of the diocesan office to promote and direct the work of those organizations (such as the parish catechetical center, the Confraternity of Christian Doctrine, and so on) which are as it were the basic cells of catechetical action.

Permanent centers for training catechists should be set up by local communities. It will thus become clear among Christian people that the work of evangelization and the teaching of the message of salvation pertain to all.

The Catechetical Office, therefore, which is part of the diocesan curia, is the means which the bishop as head of the community and teacher of doctrine utilizes to direct and moderate all the catechetical activities of the diocese.

No diocese can be without its own Catechetical Office.

Regional Structures

127 It is useful for a number of dioceses to combine their actions, bringing together for common benefit their experiences and undertakings, their offices and equipment; for the dioceses that are better provided for to give help to the others; and for a common action program to be prepared for the region as a whole.

National Structures

128 It is by all means necessary that the Conferences of Bishops, and more directly, the Bishops' Catechetical Commission, be equipped with a permanent structure.

This National Catechetical Office or Center has a twofold task:

—to serve the catechetical needs of the country as a whole. The effort here would extend to publications of national importance, national congresses, relations with the mass media, and generally all those works and projects which are beyond the powers of individual dioceses and regions;

—to serve dioceses and regions by publicizing catechetical ideas and undertakings, by coordinating action, and by giving assistance to those dioceses that are less advanced in catechetical matters.

Another function of the National Office or Center is to coordinate its own work with the action of the rest of the national pastoral undertakings, and also to cooperate with the international catechetical movement.

CHAPTER SIX

Coordination of Pastoral Catechetics with all Pastoral Work

Catechesis and Pastoral Action

129 Since every important act in the Church participates in the ministry of the word, and since catechesis always has a relation to the universal life of the Church, it follows that catechetical action must necessarily be coordinated with the overall pastoral action. The aim of this cooperation is to have the Christian community grow and develop in a harmonious and orderly fashion; for, surely, although it has distinct aspects because of the various functions, it nevertheless strives toward a single basic goal.

It is necessary, therefore, that catechesis be associated with other pastoral activities (cf. *Motu proprio, Ecclesiae sanctae*, n. 17), that is, with the biblical, liturgical, and ecumenical movements, with the lay apostolate and social action, and so on. Besides, it must be kept in mind that this cooperation is necessary from the very outset, that is, from the time that studies and plans for the organization of pastoral work are started.

Catechumenate for Adults

130 The catechumenate for adults, which at one and the same time includes catechesis, liturgical participation, and community living, is an excellent example of an institute that springs from the cooperation of diverse pastoral functions. Its purpose is to direct the spiritual journey of persons who are preparing themselves for the reception of baptism, and to give direction to their habits of thought and changes in moral living. It is a preparatory school in Christian living, an introduction to the religious, liturgical, charitable, and apostolic life of the People of God (cf. AG, 13-14; SC, 65; CD, 14). Not only the priests and catechists, but the entire Christian community, through sponsors who act in its name, is engaged in this work.

CHAPTER SEVEN

Necessity of Promoting Scientific Study

Scientific Study

131 Because of the rapid development in present-day culture, the catechetical movement will in no way be able to advance without scientific study.

Hence it is necessary that the national organs of the Conferences of Bishops promote joint research projects. Clearly it is necessary that a program of questions to be researched be determined, that there be awareness of the questions already under study and occasional consultation with the experts who are working on them, and that a study be undertaken of questions that have not yet been researched, the necessary financial support for this having been provided.

There can be subjects for research that have universal importance: for example, the relations between catechesis and modern exegesis, between catechesis and anthropology, between catechesis and the mass media, and so on. Because of the nature and difficulties of such kinds of research, international cooperation is often advisable.

CHAPTER EIGHT

International Cooperation and Relations with the Apostolic See

International Cooperation

132 The Apostolic College performs its function in a closely cooperative way (cf. LG, 22-23; AG, 38; CD, 2, 4). Consequences of this solidarity which affect catechesis have been considered a number of times in this part of the *Directory* (for example, Chapter II: comparing pastoral goals among neighboring countries; Chapter III: establishing higher institutes; Chapter IV: working out common aids; Chapter VII: doing scientific research).

International cooperation is also required in the ministry of the word for immigrants.

The task to be accomplished is twofold. On the one hand, the word of God must be brought to the immigrants. Because of the differences in language, culture and customs, this requires an exchange both of information and of persons between the churches of the countries from which the immigrants come and the churches of the countries which accept them. On the other hand, it is necessary that this ministry of the word make the Christians of the host countries aware of the pressing problems of the immigrants, and ready to welcome them out of brotherly love.

International cooperation is also required for the catechesis of tourists. It is clear that "tourism," as it is called, is spreading more and more among all nations (cf. *Directorium Generale pro ministerio pastorali quoad "turismum,"* passim).

International cooperation must show regard for the tasks and conditions of the local churches. Hence, those countries that have made greater advances in personnel, in economic goods, and in scientific research, should assist the other countries that have not progressed that far, but should not impose their own styles of thinking and acting, nor their own methods.

Holy See

133 Just as Peter was made the head of the Apostolic College and the foundation upon which the Church is built, so the Successor to Peter, namely, the Roman Pontiff (cf. LG, 22), is the visible head of the College of Bishops and of the entire People of God. He fulfills his universal office of teaching and of ruling as Vicar of Christ and Shepherd of the whole Church (cf. LG, 22), always for the welfare and spiritual development of the People of God. He can, however, freely carry out this office according to the needs of the Church, either in a personal way, or in a strictly collegial way, that is, together with the bishops of the entire Church. The personal way he exercises either by his own acts or through acts of his ministers, principally by acts of the Offices of the Roman Curia.

Sacred Congregation for the Clergy

134 The central responsibility for catechesis in territories of so-called common law has been entrusted to the Sacred Congregation for the Clergy (Second Office). This Congregation has the task of working out, of coordinating, and of moderating matters that have to do with promoting the preaching of the word of God and the works of the apostolate; it also has the task of publishing information, and of promoting, as much as possible, collaboration among the various countries.

This Office assists the development of and gives guidance to offices that are in charge of catechesis.

It reviews and approves catechetical directories, catechisms, and programs for preaching the word of God produced by Conferences of Bishops. It encourages national catechetical congresses, or it approves or calls international ones (cf. Const. Apost., *Regimini Ecclesiae universae*, n. 69; Letter of the Secretariat of State, August 20, 1969, N. 143741).

ADDENDUM

The First Reception of the Sacraments of Penance and the Eucharist

Among the tasks of catechesis, the preparation of children for the sacraments of Penance and the Eucharist is of great importance. With regard to this, it is held opportune to recall certain principles and to make some observations about certain experiments that have been taking place very recently in some regions or places of the Church.

The Age of Discretion

1 The suitable age for the first reception of these sacraments is deemed to be that which in documents of the Church is called the age of reason or of discretion. This age "both for Confession and for Communion is that at which the child begins to reason, that is, about the seventh year, more or less. From that time on the obligation of fulfilling the precepts of Confession and Communion begins" (Decree *Quam singulari*, I, *AAS*, 1910, p. 582). It is praiseworthy to study by research in pastoral psychology and to describe this age which develops gradually, is subject to various conditions, and which presents a peculiar nature in every child. One should, however, be on guard not to extend beyond the above-mentioned limits, which are not rigid, the time at which the precept of Confession and Communion begins to oblige *per se*.

Formation and Growth of the Moral Conscience of Children

2 While the capacity to reason is evolving gradually in a child, his moral conscience too is being trained, that is, the faculty of judging his acts in relation to a norm of morality. A number of varying elements and circumstances come together in forming this moral conscience of a child: the character and discipline of his family, which is one of the most important educative factors during the first years of a child's life, his associations with others, and the activities and the witness of the ecclesial community. Catechesis, while carrying out its task of instructing and forming in the Christian faith, puts order into these various factors of education, promotes them, and works in conjunction with them. Only in this way will catechesis be able to give to the child timely direction toward the heavenly Father and correct any goings astray or incorrect orientations of life that can occur. Without doubt children at this age should be told in the simplest possible way about God as our Lord and Father, about his love for us, about Jesus, the Son of God, who was made man for us, and who died and rose again. By thinking about the love of God, the child will be able gradually to perceive the malice of sin, which always offends God the Father and Jesus, and which is opposed to the charity with which we must love our neighbor and ourselves.

Importance of Explaining the Sacrament of Penance to Children

3 When a child begins to offend God by sin, he also begins to have the desire of receiving pardon, not only from parents or relatives, but also from God. Catechesis helps him by nourishing this desire wholesomely, and it instills a holy aversion to sin, an awareness of the need for amendment, and especially love for God. The special task of catechesis here is to explain in a suitable way that sacramental Confession is a means offered children of the Church to obtain pardon for sin, and furthermore that it is even necessary *per se* if one has fallen into serious sin. To be sure, Christian parents and religious educators ought to teach the child in such a way that above all he will strive to advance to a more intimate love of the Lord Jesus and to genuine love of neighbor. The doctrine on the sacrament of Penance is to be presented in a broad framework of attaining purification and spiritual growth with great confidence in the mercy and love of God. In this way, children not only can little by little acquire a delicate understanding of conscience, but do not lose heart when they fall into some lesser fault.

The Eucharist is the summit and center of the entire Christian life. In addition to the required state of grace, great purity of soul is clearly fitting for the reception of Communion. One must be very careful, however, that the children do not get the impression that Confession is necessary before receiving the Eucharist even when one sincerely loves God and has not departed from the path of God's commandments in a serious way.

Certain New Experiments

4 In very recent times in certain regions of the Church experiments relative to the first reception of the sacraments of Penance and of the Eucharist have been made. These have given rise to doubt and confusion.

So that the Communion of children may be appropriately received early, and so that psychological disturbances in the future Christian life which can result from a too early use of Confession may be avoided, and so that better education for the spirit of penance and a more valid catechetical preparation for Confession itself may be fostered, it has seemed to some that children should be admitted to first Communion without first receiving the sacrament of Penance.

In fact, however, going to the sacrament of Penance from the beginning of the use of reason does not in itself harm the minds of the children, provided it is preceded, as it should be, by a kind and prudent catechetical preparation. The spirit of penance can be developed more fully by continuing catechetical instruction after first Communion; likewise, there can be growth in knowledge and appreciation of the great gift that Christ has given to sinful men in the sacrament of the pardon they will receive and of reconciliation with the Church (cf. LG, 11).

These things have not prevented the introduction in certain places of a practice in which some years regularly elapse between first Communion and first Confession. In other places, however, the innovations made have been more cautious, either because first Confession was not so much delayed, or because consideration is given the judgment of the parents who prefer to have their children go to the sacrament of Penance before first Communion.

The Common Practice in Force Must Be Highly Esteemed

5 The Supreme Pontiff, Pius X, declared, "The custom of not admitting children to Confession or of never giving them absolution, when they have arrived at the use of reason, must be wholly condemned" (Decree *Quam singulari*, VII, *AAS*, 1910, p. 583). One can scarcely have regard for the right that baptized children have of confessing their sins, if at the beginning of the age of discretion they are not prepared and gently led to the sacrament of Penance.

One should also keep in mind the usefulness of Confession, which retains its efficacy even when only venial sins are in question, and which gives an increase of grace and of charity, increases the child's good dispositions for receiving the Eucharist, and also helps to perfect the Christian life. Hence, it appears the usefulness of Confession cannot be dismissed in favor of those forms of penance or those ministries of the word, by which the virtue of penance is aptly fostered in children, and which can be fruitfully practiced together with the sacrament of Penance, when a suitable catechetical preparation has been made. The pastoral experience of the Church, which is illustrated by many examples even in our day, teaches her how much the so-called age of discretion is suited for effecting that the children's baptismal grace, by means of a well-prepared reception of the sacraments of Penance and of the

Eucharist, shows forth its first fruits, which are certainly to be augmented afterwards by means of a continued catechesis.

Having weighed all these points, and keeping in mind the common and general practice which *per se* cannot be derogated without the approval of the Apostolic See, and also having heard the Conferences of Bishops, the Holy See judges it fitting that the practice now in force in the Church of putting Confession ahead of first Communion should be retained. This in no way prevents this custom from being carried out in various ways, as, for instance, by having a communal penitential celebration precede or follow the reception of the sacrament of Penance.

The Holy See is not unmindful of the special conditions that exist in various countries, but it exhorts the bishops in this important matter not to depart from the practice in force without having first entered into communication with the Holy See in a spirit of hierarchical communion. Nor should they in any way allow the pastors or educators or religious institutes to begin or to continue to abandon the practice in force.

In regions, however, where new practices have already been introduced which depart notably from the pristine practice, the Conferences of Bishops will wish to submit these experiments to a new examination. If after that they wish to continue these experiments for a longer time, they should not do so unless they have first communicated with the Holy See, which will willingly hear them, and they are at one mind with the Holy See.

The Supreme Pontiff, PAUL VI, by a letter of his Secretariat of State, n. 177335, dated March 18, 1971, approved this General Directory together with the Addendum, confirmed it by his authority and ordered it to be published.

Rome, April 11, 1971, Feast of the Resurrection of Our Lord.

JOHN J. CARDINAL WRIGHT, *Prefect*
✠ PIETRO PALAZZINI, *Secretary*

POPE PAUL VI

Evangelii Nuntiandi, 1975

Evangelization in the Modern World

Apostolic Exhortation to the Episcopate,
to the Clergy, and to all the Faithful of the Entire World

Venerable brothers and dear sons and daughters: health and the apostolic blessing.

Special Commitment to Evangelization

1 There is no doubt that the effort to proclaim the Gospel to the people of today, who are buoyed up by hope but at the same time often oppressed by fear and distress, is a service rendered to the Christian community and also to the whole of humanity.

For this reason the duty of confirming the brethren—a duty which with the office of being the Successor of Peter[1] we have

---

1. Cf. Lk. 22:32.

received from the Lord, and which is for us a "daily preoccupation,"[2] a program of life and action, and a fundamental commitment of our Pontificate—seems to us all the more noble and necessary when it is a matter of encouraging our brethren in their mission as evangelizers, in order that, in this time of uncertainty and confusion, they may accomplish this task with ever increasing love, zeal and joy.

On the Occasion of Three Events

2 This is precisely what we wish to do here, at the end of this Holy Year during which the Church, "striving to proclaim the Gospel to all people,"[3] has had the single aim of fulfilling her duty of being the messenger of the Good News of Jesus Christ—the Good News proclaimed through two fundamental commands: "Put on the new self"[4] and "Be reconciled to God."[5]

We wish to do so on this tenth anniversary of the closing of the Second Vatican Council, the objectives of which are definitively summed up in this single one: to make the Church of the twentieth century ever better fitted for proclaiming the Gospel to the people of the twentieth century.

We wish to do so one year after the Third General Assembly of the Synod of Bishops, which as is well known, was devoted to evangelization; and we do so all the more willingly because it has been asked of us by the Synod Fathers themselves. In fact, at the end of that memorable assembly, the Fathers decided to remit to the Pastor of the universal Church, with great trust and simplicity, the fruits of all their labors, stating that they awaited from him a fresh forward impulse, capable of creating within a Church still more firmly rooted in the undying power and strength of Pentecost a new period of evangelization.[6]

---

2. 2 Cor. 11:28.
3. Cf. Second Vatican Ecumenical Council, Decree on the Church's Missionary Activity *Ad gentes*, 1: *AAS* 58 (1966), p. 947.
4. Cf. Eph. 4:24. 2:15; Col. 3:10; Gal. 3:27; Rom. 13:14; 2 Cor. 5:17.
5. 2 Cor. 5:20.
6. Cf. Paul VI, Address for the closing of the Third General Assembly of the Synod of Bishops (October 26, 1974): *AAS* 66 (1974), pp. 634-635, 637.

Theme Frequently Emphasized in the Course of Our Pontificate

3 We have stressed the importance of this theme of evangelization on many occasions, well before the Synod took place. On June 22, 1973, we said to the Sacred College of Cardinals: "The conditions of the society in which we live oblige all of us therefore to revise methods, to seek by every means to study how we can bring the Christian message to modern man. For it is only in the Christian message that modern man can find the answer to his questions and the energy for his commitment of human solidarity."[7] And we added that in order to give a valid answer to the demands of the Council which call for our attention, it is absolutely necessary for us to take into account a heritage of faith that the Church has the duty of preserving in its untouchable purity, and of presenting it to the people of our time, in a way that is as understandable and persuasive as possible.

In the Line of the 1974 Synod

4 This fidelity both to a message whose servants we are and to the people to whom we must transmit it living and intact is the central axis of evangelization. It poses three burning questions, which the 1974 Synod kept constantly in mind:

—In our day, what has happened to that hidden energy of the Good News, which is able to have a powerful effect on man's conscience?

—To what extent and in what way is that evangelical force capable of really transforming the people of this century?

—What methods should be followed in order that the power of the Gospel may have its effect?

Basically, these inquiries make explicit the fundamental question that the Church is asking herself today and which may be expressed in the following terms: after the Council and thanks to the Council, which was a time given her by God, at this turning-point of history, does the Church or does she not find herself better

---

7. Paul VI, Address to the College of Cardinals (June 22, 1973): *AAS* 65 (1973), p. 383.

equipped to proclaim the Gospel and to put it into people's hearts with conviction, freedom of spirit and effectiveness?

Invitation to Meditation

5   We can all see the urgency of giving a loyal, humble and courageous answer to this question, and of acting accordingly.

In our "anxiety for all the Churches,"[8] we would like to help our brethren and sons and daughters to reply to these inquiries. Our words come from the wealth of the Synod and are meant to be a meditation on evangelization. May they succeed in inviting the whole People of God assembled in the Church to make the same meditation; and may they give a fresh impulse to everyone, especially those "who are assiduous in preaching and teaching,"[9] so that each one of them may follow "a straight course in the message of the truth,"[10] and may work as a preacher of the Gospel and acquit himself perfectly of his ministry.

Such an exhortation seems to us to be of capital importance, for the presentation of the Gospel message is not an optional contribution for the Church. It is the duty incumbent on her by the command of the Lord Jesus, so that people can believe and be saved. This message is indeed necessary. It is unique. It cannot be replaced. It does not permit either indifference, syncretism or accommodation. It is a question of people's salvation. It is the beauty of the Revelation that it represents. It brings with it a wisdom that is not of this world. It is able to stir up by itself faith—faith that rests on the power of God.[11] It is truth. It merits having the apostle consecrate to it all his time and all his energies, and to sacrifice for it, if necessary, his own life.

---

8. 2 Cor. 11:28.
9. 1 Tm. 5:17.
10. 2 Tm. 2:15.
11. Cf. 1 Cor. 2:5.

I

FROM CHRIST THE EVANGELIZER TO THE EVANGELIZING CHURCH

Witness and Mission of Jesus

6 The witness that the Lord gives of Himself and that Saint Luke gathered together in his Gospel—"I must proclaim the Good News of the kingdom of God"[12]—without doubt has enormous consequences, for it sums up the whole mission of Jesus: "That is what I was sent to do."[13] These words take on their full significance if one links them with the previous verses, in which Christ has just applied to Himself the words of the prophet Isaiah: "The Spirit of the Lord has been given to me, for he has anointed me. He has sent me to bring the good news to the poor."[14]

Going from town to town, preaching to the poorest—and frequently the most receptive—the joyful news of the fulfillment of the promises and of the Covenant offered by God is the mission for which Jesus declares that He is sent by the Father. And all the aspects of His mystery—the Incarnation itself, His miracles, His teaching, the gathering together of the disciples, the sending out of the Twelve, the cross and the resurrection, the permanence of His presence in the midst of His own—were components of His evangelizing activity.

Jesus, the First Evangelizer

7 During the Synod, the bishops very frequently referred to this truth: Jesus Himself, the Good News of God,[15] was the very first and the greatest evangelizer; He was so through and through: to perfection and to the point of the sacrifice of His earthly life.

To evangelize: what meaning did this imperative have for Christ? It is certainly not easy to express in a complete synthesis the

---

12. Lk. 4:43.
13. *Ibid*.
14. Lk. 4:18; cf. Is. 61:1.
15. Cf. Mk. 1:1; Rom. 1:1-3.

meaning, the content and the modes of evangelization as Jesus conceived it and put it into practice. In any case the attempt to make such a synthesis will never end. Let it suffice for us to recall a few essential aspects.

Proclamation of the Kingdom of God

8 As an evangelizer, Christ first of all proclaims a kingdom, the kingdom of God; and this is so important that, by comparison, everything else becomes "the rest," which is "given in addition."[16] Only the kingdom therefore is absolute, and it makes everything else relative. The Lord will delight in describing in many ways the happiness of belonging to this kingdom (a paradoxical happiness which is made up of things that the world rejects),[17] the demands of the kingdom and its Magna Carta,[18] the heralds of the kingdom,[19] its mysteries,[20] its children,[21] the vigilance and fidelity demanded of whoever awaits its definitive coming.[22]

Proclamation of Liberating Salvation

9 As the kernel and center of His Good News, Christ proclaims salvation, this great gift of God which is liberation from everything that oppresses man but which is above all liberation from sin and the Evil One, in the joy of knowing God and being known by Him, of seeing Him, and of being given over to Him. All of this is begun during the life of Christ and definitively accomplished by His death and resurrection. But it must be patiently carried on during the course of history, in order to be realized fully on the day of the final coming of Christ, whose date is known to no one except the Father.[23]

---

16. Cf. Mt. 6:33.
17. Cf. Mt. 5:3-12.
18. Cf. Mt. 5-7.
19. Cf. Mt. 10.
20. Cf. Mt. 13.
21. Mt. 18.
22. Cf. Mt. 24-25.
23. Cf. Mt. 24:36; Acts 1:7; 1 Thes. 5:1-2.

At the Price of Crucifying Effort

10 This kingdom and this salvation, which are the key words of Jesus Christ's evangelization, are available to every human being as grace and mercy, and yet at the same time each individual must gain them by force—they belong to the violent, says the Lord,[24] through toil and suffering, through a life lived according to the Gospel, through abnegation and the cross, through the spirit of the beatitudes. But above all each individual gains them through a total interior renewal which the Gospel calls *metanoia*; it is a radical conversion, a profound change of mind and heart.[25]

Tireless Preaching

11 Christ accomplished this proclamation of the kingdom of God through the untiring preaching of a word which, it will be said, has no equal elsewhere: "Here is a teaching that is new, and with authority behind it."[26] "And he won the approval of all, and they were astonished by the gracious words that came from his lips."[27] "There has never been anybody who has spoken like him."[28] His words reveal the secret of God, His plan and His promise, and thereby change the heart of man and his destiny.

With Evangelical Signs

12 But Christ also carries out this proclamation by innumerable signs, which amaze the crowds and at the same time draw them to Him in order to see Him, listen to Him and allow themselves to be transformed by Him: the sick are cured, water is changed into wine, bread is multiplied, the dead come back to life. And among all these signs there is the one to which He attaches great importance: the humble and the poor are evangelized, become His disciples and gather together "in His name" in the

---

24. Cf. Mt. 11:12; Lk. 16:16.
25. Cf. Mt. 4:17.
26. Mk. 1:27.
27. Lk. 4:22.
28. Jn. 7:46.

great community of those who believe in Him. For this Jesus who declared, "I must preach the Good News of the kingdom of God"[29] is the same Jesus of whom John the Evangelist said that He had come and was to die "to gather together in unity the scattered children of God."[30] Thus He accomplishes His revelation, completing it and confirming it by the entire revelation that He makes of Himself, by words and deeds, by signs and miracles, and more especially by His death, by His resurrection and by the sending of the Spirit of Truth.[31]

For an Evangelized and Evangelizing Community

13 Those who sincerely accept the Good News, through the power of this acceptance and of shared faith, therefore gather together in Jesus' name in order to seek together the kingdom, build it up and live it. They make up a community which is in its turn evangelizing. The command to the Twelve to go out and proclaim the Good News is also valid for all Christians, though in a different way. It is precisely for this reason that Peter calls Christians "a people set apart to sing the praises of God,"[32] those marvelous things that each one was able to hear in his own language.[33] Moreover, the Good News of the kingdom which is coming and which has begun is meant for all people of all times. Those who have received the Good News and who have been gathered by it into the community of salvation can and must communicate and spread it.

Evangelization: Vocation Proper to the Church

14 The Church knows this. She has a vivid awareness of the fact that the Savior's words, "I must proclaim the Good News of the kingdom of God,"[34] apply in all truth to herself. She willingly

---

29. Lk. 4:43.
30. Jn. 11:52.
31. Cf. Second Vatican Ecumenical Council, Dogmatic Constitution on Divine Revelation *Dei Verbum*, 4: *AAS* 58 (1966), pp. 818-819.
32. 1 Pt. 2:9.
33. Cf. Acts 2:11.
34. Lk. 4:43.

adds with St. Paul: "Not that I boast of preaching the gospel, since it is a duty that has been laid on me; I should be punished if I did not preach it!"[35] It is with joy and consolation that at the end of the great Assembly of 1974 we heard these illuminating words: "We wish to confirm once more that the task of evangelizing all people constitutes the essential mission of the Church."[36] It is a task and mission which the vast and profound changes of present-day society make all the more urgent. Evangelizing is in fact the grace and vocation proper to the Church, her deepest identity. She exists in order to evangelize, that is to say, in order to preach and teach, to be the channel of the gift of grace, to reconcile sinners with God, and to perpetuate Christ's sacrifice in the Mass, which is the memorial of His death and glorious resurrection.

Reciprocal Links Between the Church and Evangelization

15   Anyone who rereads in the New Testament the origins of the Church, follows her history step by step and watches her live and act, sees that she is linked to evangelization in her most intimate being:

—The Church is born of the evangelizing activity of Jesus and the Twelve. She is the normal, desired, most immediate and most visible fruit of this activity: "Go, therefore, make disciples of all the nations."[37] Now, "they accepted what he said and were baptized. That very day about three thousand were added to their number.... Day by day the Lord added to their community those destined to be saved."[38]

—Having been born consequently out of being sent, the Church in her turn is sent by Jesus. The Church remains in the world when the Lord of glory returns to the Father. She remains as a sign—simultaneously obscure and luminous—of a new presence of Jesus, of His departure and of His permanent presence. She pro-

---

35. 1 Cor. 9:16.
36. "Declaration of the Synod Fathers," 4: *L'Osservatore Romano* (October 27, 1974), p. 6.
37. Mt. 28:19.
38. Acts 2:41, 47.

longs and continues Him. And it is above all His mission and His condition of being an evangelizer that she is called upon to continue.[39] For the Christian community is never closed in upon itself. The intimate life of this community—the life of listening to the Word and the Apostles' teaching, charity lived in a fraternal way, the sharing of bread[40]—this intimate life only acquires its full meaning when it becomes a witness, when it evokes admiration and conversion, and when it becomes the preaching and proclamation of the Good News. Thus it is the whole Church that receives the mission to evangelize, and the work of each individual member is important for the whole.

—The Church is an evangelizer, but she begins by being evangelized herself. She is the community of believers, the community of hope lived and communicated, the community of brotherly love; and she needs to listen unceasingly to what she must believe, to her reasons for hoping, to the new commandment of love. She is the People of God immersed in the world, and often tempted by idols, and she always needs to hear the proclamation of the "mighty works of God"[41] which converted her to the Lord; she always needs to be called together afresh by Him and reunited. In brief, this means that she has a constant need of being evangelized, if she wishes to retain freshness, vigor and strength in order to proclaim the Gospel. The Second Vatican Council recalled[42] and the 1974 Synod vigorously took up again this theme of the Church which is evangelized by constant conversion and renewal, in order to evangelize the world with credibility.

—The Church is the depositary of the Good News to be proclaimed. The promises of the New Alliance in Jesus Christ, the teaching of the Lord and the Apostles, the Word of life, the sources of grace and of God's loving kindness, the path of salvation—all these things have been entrusted to her. It is the content of the

---

39. Cf. Second Vatican Ecumenical Council, Dogmatic Constitution on the Church *Lumen gentium*, 8: *AAS* 57 (1965), p. 11; Decree on the Church's Missionary Activity *Ad gentes*, 5: *AAS* 58 (1966), pp. 951-952.

40. Cf. Acts 2:42-46; 4:32-35; 5:12-16.

41. Cf. Acts 2:11; 1 Pt. 2:9.

42. Cf. Decree on the Church's Missionary Activity *Ad gentes*, 5, 11-12: *AAS* 58 (1966), pp. 951-952, 959-961.

Gospel, and therefore of evangelization, that she preserves as a precious living heritage, not in order to keep it hidden but to communicate it.

—Having been sent and evangelized, the Church herself sends out evangelizers. She puts on their lips the saving Word, she explains to them the message of which she herself is the depositary, she gives them the mandate which she herself has received and she sends them out to preach. To preach not their own selves or their personal ideas,[43] but a Gospel of which neither she nor they are the absolute masters and owners, to dispose of it as they wish, but a Gospel of which they are the ministers, in order to pass it on with complete fidelity.

The Church, Inseparable from Christ

16 There is thus a profound link between Christ, the Church and evangelization. During the period of the Church that we are living in, it is she who has the task of evangelizing. This mandate is not accomplished without her, and still less against her.

It is certainly fitting to recall this fact at a moment like the present one when it happens that not without sorrow we can hear people—whom we wish to believe are well-intentioned but who are certainly misguided in their attitude—continually claiming to love Christ but without the Church, to listen to Christ but not the Church, to belong to Christ but outside the Church. The absurdity of this dichotomy is clearly evident in this phrase of the Gospel: "Anyone who rejects you rejects me."[44] And how can one wish to love Christ without loving the Church, if the finest witness to Christ is that of St. Paul: "Christ loved the Church and sacrificed himself for her"?[45]

---

43. Cf. 2 Cor. 4:5; St. Augustine, *Sermo XLVI, De Pastoribus: CCL XLI,* pp. 529-530.

44. Lk. 10:16; cf. St. Cyprian, *De Unitate Ecclesiae,* 14: *PL* 4, 527; St. Augustine, *Enarrat.* 88, *Sermo,* 2, 14: *PL* 37, 1140; St. John Chrysostom, *Hom. de capto Eutropio,* 6: *PG* 52, 462.

45. Eph. 5:25.

II

WHAT IS EVANGELIZATION?

Complexity of Evangelizing Action

17 In the Church's evangelizing activity there are of course certain elements and aspects to be specially insisted on. Some of them are so important that there will be a tendency simply to identify them with evangelization. Thus it has been possible to define evangelization in terms of proclaiming Christ to those who do not know Him, of preaching, of catechesis, of conferring Baptism and the other sacraments.

Any partial and fragmentary definition which attempts to render the reality of evangelization in all its richness, complexity and dynamism does so only at the risk of impoverishing it and even of distorting it. It is impossible to grasp the concept of evangelization unless one tries to keep in view all its essential elements.

These elements were strongly emphasized at the last Synod, and are still the subject of frequent study, as a result of the Synod's work. We rejoice in the fact that these elements basically follow the lines of those transmitted to us by the Second Vatican Council, especially in *Lumen gentium, Gaudium et spes* and *Ad gentes*.

Renewal of Humanity

18 For the Church, evangelizing means bringing the Good News into all the strata of humanity, and through its influence transforming humanity from within and making it new: "Now I am making the whole of creation new."[46] But there is no new humanity if there are not first of all new persons renewed by Baptism[47] and by lives lived according to the Gospel.[48] The purpose of evangelization is therefore precisely this interior change, and if it had to be expressed in one sentence the best way of stating it would be to say

---

46. Rev. 21:5; cf. 2 Cor. 5:17; Gal. 6:15.
47. Cf. Rom. 6:4.
48. Cf. Eph. 4:23-24; Col. 3:9-10.

that the Church evangelizes when she seeks to convert,[49] solely through the divine power of the message she proclaims, both the personal and collective consciences of people, the activities in which they engage, and the lives and concrete milieu which are theirs.

And of the Strata of Humanity

19   Strata of humanity which are transformed: for the Church it is a question not only of preaching the Gospel in ever wider geographic areas or to ever greater numbers of people, but also of affecting and as it were upsetting, through the power of the Gospel, mankind's criteria of judgment, determining values, points of interest, lines of thought, sources of inspiration and models of life, which are in contrast with the Word of God and the plan of salvation.

Evangelization of Cultures

20   All this could be expressed in the following words: what matters is to evangelize man's culture and cultures (not in a purely decorative way, as it were, by applying a thin veneer, but in a vital way, in depth and right to their very roots), in the wide and rich sense which these terms have in *Gaudium et spes*,[50] always taking the person as one's starting-point and always coming back to the relationships of people among themselves and with God.

The Gospel, and therefore evangelization, are certainly not identical with culture, and they are independent in regard to all cultures. Nevertheless, the kingdom which the Gospel proclaims is lived by men who are profoundly linked to a culture, and the building up of the kingdom cannot avoid borrowing the elements of human culture or cultures. Though independent of cultures, the Gospel and evangelization are not necessarily incompatible with them; rather they are capable of permeating them all without becoming subject to any one of them.

---

49. Cf. Rom. 1:16; 1 Cor. 1:18, 2:4.
50. Cf. 53: *AAS* 58 (1966), p. 1075.

The split between the Gospel and culture is without a doubt the drama of our time, just as it was of other times. Therefore every effort must be made to ensure a full evangelization of culture, or more correctly of cultures. They have to be regenerated by an encounter with the Gospel. But this encounter will not take place if the Gospel is not proclaimed.

Primary Importance of Witness of Life

21 Above all the Gospel must be proclaimed by witness. Take a Christian or a handful of Christians who, in the midst of their own community, show their capacity for understanding and acceptance, their sharing of life and destiny with other people, their solidarity with the efforts of all for whatever is noble and good. Let us suppose that, in addition, they radiate in an altogether simple and unaffected way their faith in values that go beyond current values, and their hope in something that is not seen and that one would not dare to imagine. Through this wordless witness these Christians stir up irresistible questions in the hearts of those who see how they live: Why are they like this? Why do they live in this way? What or who is it that inspires them? Why are they in our midst? Such a witness is already a silent proclamation of the Good News and a very powerful and effective one. Here we have an initial act of evangelization. The above questions will ask, whether they are people to whom Christ has never been proclaimed, or baptized people who do not practice, or people who live as nominal Christians but according to principles that are in no way Christian, or people who are seeking, and not without suffering, something or someone whom they sense but cannot name. Other questions will arise, deeper and more demanding ones, questions evoked by this witness which involves presence, sharing, solidarity, and which is an essential element, and generally the first one, in evangelization.[51]

All Christians are called to this witness, and in this way they can be real evangelizers. We are thinking especially of the responsibility incumbent on immigrants in the country that receives them.

---

51. Cf. Tertullian *Apologeticum*, 39: *CCL*, I, pp. 150-153; Minucius Felix, *Octavius* 9 and 31: *CSLP*, Turin 1963², pp. 11-13, 47-48.

Need of Explicit Proclamation

22 Nevertheless this always remains insufficient, because even the finest witness will prove ineffective in the long run if it is not explained, justified—what Peter called always having "your answer ready for people who ask you the reason for the hope you all have"[52]—and made explicit by a clear and unequivocal proclamation of the Lord Jesus. The Good News proclaimed by the witness of life sooner or later has to be proclaimed by the word of life. There is no true evangelization if the name, the teaching, the life, the promises, the kingdom and the mystery of Jesus of Nazareth, the Son of God, are not proclaimed. The history of the Church, from the discourse of Peter on the morning of Pentecost onwards, has been intermingled and identified with the history of this proclamation. At every new phase of human history, the Church, constantly gripped by the desire to evangelize, has but one preoccupation: whom to send to proclaim the mystery of Jesus? In what way is this mystery to be proclaimed? How can one ensure that it will resound and reach all those who should hear it? This proclamation—kerygma, preaching or catechesis—occupies such an important place in evangelization that it has often become synonymous with it; and yet it is only one aspect of evangelization.

For a Vital and Community Acceptance

23 In fact the proclamation only reaches full development when it is listened to, accepted and assimilated, and when it arouses a genuine adherence in the one who has thus received it. An adherence to the truths which the Lord in His mercy has revealed; still more, an adherence to a program of life—a life henceforth transformed—which He proposes. In a word, adherence to the kingdom, that is to say, to the "new world," to the new state of things, to the new manner of being, of living, of living in community, which the Gospel inaugurates. Such an adherence, which cannot remain abstract and unincarnated, reveals itself concretely by a visible entry into a community of believers. Thus those whose life has been transformed enter a community which is itself a sign of

---

52. 1 Pt. 3:15.

transformation, a sign of newness of life: it is the Church, the visible sacrament of salvation.[53] Our entry into the ecclesial community will in its turn be expressed through many other signs which prolong and unfold the sign of the Church. In the dynamism of evangelization, a person who accepts the Church as the Word which saves[54] normally translates it into the following sacramental acts: adherence to the Church, and acceptance of the sacraments, which manifest and support this adherence through the grace which they confer.

Involving a New Apostolate

24 Finally, the person who has been evangelized goes on to evangelize others. Here lies the test of truth, the touchstone of evangelization: it is unthinkable that a person should accept the Word and give himself to the kingdom without becoming a person who bears witness to it and proclaims it in his turn.

To complete these considerations on the meaning of evangelization, a final observation must be made, one which we consider will help to clarify the reflections that follow.

Evangelization, as we have said, is a complex process made up of varied elements: the renewal of humanity, witness, explicit proclamation, inner adherence, entry into the community, acceptance of signs, apostolic initiative. These elements may appear to be contradictory, indeed mutually exclusive. In fact they are complementary and mutually enriching. Each one must always be seen in relationship with the others. The value of the last Synod was to have constantly invited us to relate these elements rather than to place them in opposition one to the other, in order to reach a full understanding of the Church's evangelizing activity.

It is this global vision which we now wish to outline, by examining the content of evangelization and the methods of evangelizing

---

53. Cf. Second Vatican Ecumenical Council, Dogmatic Constitution on the Church *Lumen gentium*, 1, 9, 48; *AAS* 57 (1965), pp. 5, 12-14, 53-54; Pastoral Constitution on the Church in the Modern World *Gaudium et spes*, 42, 45, *AAS* 58 (1966), pp. 1060-1061, 1065-1066; Decree on the Church's Missionary Activity *Ad gentes*, 1, 5: *AAS* 58 (1966); pp. 947, 951-952.

54. Cf. Rom. 1:16; 1 Cor. 1:18.

and by clarifying to whom the Gospel message is addressed and who today is responsible for it.

III

THE CONTENT OF EVANGELIZATION

Essential Content and Secondary Elements

25 In the message which the Church proclaims there are certainly many secondary elements. Their presentation depends greatly on changing circumstances. They themselves also change. But there is the essential content, the living substance, which cannot be modified or ignored without seriously diluting the nature of evangelization itself.

Witness Given to the Father's Love

26 It is not superfluous to recall the following points: to evangelize is first of all to bear witness, in a simple and direct way, to God revealed by Jesus Christ, in the Holy Spirit; to bear witness that in His Son God has loved the world—that in His Incarnate Word He has given being to all things and has called men to eternal life. Perhaps this attestation of God will be for many people the unknown God[55] whom they adore without giving Him a name, or whom they seek by a secret call of the heart when they experience the emptiness of all idols. But it is fully evangelizing in manifesting the fact that for man the Creator is not an anonymous and remote power; He is the Father: "...that we should be called children of God; and so we are."[56] And thus we are one another's brothers and sisters in God.

At the Center of the Message: Salvation in Jesus Christ

27 Evangelization will also always contain—as the foundation, center, and at the same time, summit of its dynamism—a clear

---

55. Cf. Acts 17:22-23.
56. 1 Jn. 3:1; cf. Rom. 8:14-17.

proclamation that, in Jesus Christ, the Son of God made man, who died and rose from the dead, salvation is offered to all men, as a gift of God's grace and mercy.[57] And not an immanent salvation, meeting material or even spiritual needs, restricted to the framework of temporal existence and completely identified with temporal desires, hopes, affairs and struggles, but a salvation which exceeds all these limits in order to reach fulfillment in a communion with the one and only divine Absolute: a transcendent and eschatological salvation, which indeed has its beginning in this life but which is fulfilled in eternity.

Under the Sign of Hope

28 Consequently evangelization cannot but include the prophetic proclamation of a hereafter, man's profound and definitive calling, in both continuity and discontinuity with the present situation: beyond time and history, beyond the transient reality of this world, and beyond the things of this world, of which a hidden dimension will one day be revealed—beyond man himself, whose true destiny is not restricted to his temporal aspect but will be revealed in the future life.[58] Evangelization therefore also includes the preaching of hope in the promises made by God in the new Covenant in Jesus Christ; the preaching of God's love for us and of our love for God; the preaching of brotherly love for all men—the capacity of giving and forgiving, of self-denial, of helping one's brother and sister—which, springing from the love of God, is the kernel of the Gospel; the preaching of the mystery of evil and of the active search for good. The preaching likewise—and this is always urgent—of the search for God Himself through prayer which is principally that of adoration and thanksgiving, but also through communion with the visible sign of the encounter with God which is the Church of Jesus Christ; and this communion in its turn is

---

57. Cf. Eph. 2:8; Rom. 1:16. Cf. Sacred Congregation for the Doctrine of the Faith, *Declaratio ad fidem tuendam in mysteria Incarnationis et SS. Trinitatis e quibusdam recentibus erroribus* (February 21, 1972): *AAS* 64 (1972), pp. 237-241.

58. Cf. 1 Jn. 3:2; Rom. 8:29; Phil. 3:20-21. Cf. Second Vatican Ecumenical Council, Dogmatic Constitution on the Church *Lumen gentium*, 48-51: *AAS* 57 (1965), pp. 53-58.

expressed by the application of those other signs of Christ living and acting in the Church which are the sacraments. To live the sacraments in this way, bringing their celebration to a true fullness, is not, as some would claim, to impede or to accept a distortion of evangelization: it is rather to complete it. For in its totality, evangelization—over and above the preaching of a message—consists in the implantation of the Church, which does not exist without the driving force which is the sacramental life culminating in the Eucharist.[59]

Message Touching Life as a Whole

29 But evangelization would not be complete if it did not take account of the unceasing interplay of the Gospel and of man's concrete life, both personal and social. This is why evangelization involves an explicit message, adapted to the different situations constantly being realized, about the rights and duties of every human being, about family life without which personal growth and development is hardly possible,[60] about life and society, about international life, peace, justice and development—a message especially energetic today about liberation.

A Message of Liberation

30 It is well known in what terms numerous bishops from all the continents spoke of this at the last Synod, especially the bishops from the Third World, with a pastoral accent resonant with the voice of the millions of sons and daughters of the Church who make up those peoples. Peoples, as we know, engaged with all their energy in the effort and struggle to overcome everything which condemns them to remain on the margin of life: famine, chronic

---

59. Cf. Sacred Congregation for the Doctrine of the Faith, *Declaratio circa Catholicam Doctrinam de Ecclesia contra nonnullos errores hodiernos tuendam* (June 24, 1973): *AAS* 65 (1973), pp. 396-408.
60. Cf. Second Vatican Ecumenical Council, Pastoral Constitution on the Church in the Modern World *Gaudium et spes*, 47-52: *AAS* 58 (1966), pp. 1067-1074; Paul VI, Encyclical Letter *Humanae vitae*: *AAS* 60 (1968), pp. 481-503.

disease, illiteracy, poverty, injustices in international relations and especially in commercial exchanges, situations of economic and cultural neo-colonialism sometimes as cruel as the old political colonialism. The Church, as the bishops repeated, has the duty to proclaim the liberation of millions of human beings, many of whom are her own children—the duty of assisting the birth of this liberation, of giving witness to it, of ensuring that it is complete. This is not foreign to evangelization.

Necessarily Linked to Human Advancement

31 Between evangelization and human advancement—development and liberation—there are in fact profound links. These include links of an anthropological order, because the man who is to be evangelized is not an abstract being but is subject to social and economic questions. They also include links in the theological order, since one cannot dissociate the plan of creation from the plan of redemption. The latter plan touches the very concrete situations of injustice to be combated and of justice to be restored. They include links of the eminently evangelical order, which is that of charity: how in fact can one proclaim the new commandment without promoting in justice and in peace the true, authentic advancement of man? We ourself have taken care to point this out, by recalling that it is impossible to accept "that in evangelization one could or should ignore the importance of the problems so much discussed today, concerning justice, liberation, development and peace in the world. This would be to forget the lesson which comes to us from the Gospel concerning love of our neighbor who is suffering and in need."[61]

The same voices which during the Synod touched on this burning theme with zeal, intelligence and courage have, to our great joy, furnished the enlightening principles for a proper understanding of the importance and profound meaning of liberation, such as it was proclaimed and achieved by Jesus of Nazareth and such as it is preached by the Church.

---

61. Paul VI, Address for the opening of the Third General Assembly of the Synod of Bishops (September 27, 1974): *AAS* 66 (1974), p. 562.

Without Reduction or Ambiguity

32 We must not ignore the fact that many, even generous Christians who are sensitive to the dramatic questions involved in the problem of liberation, in their wish to commit the Church to the liberation effort, are frequently tempted to reduce her mission to the dimensions of a simply temporal project. They would reduce her aims to a man-centered goal; the salvation of which she is the messenger would be reduced to material well-being. Her activity, forgetful of all spiritual and religious preoccupation, would become initiatives of the political or social order. But if this were so, the Church would lose her fundamental meaning. Her message of liberation would no longer have any originality and would easily be open to monopolization and manipulation by ideological systems and political parties. She would have no more authority to proclaim freedom as in the name of God. This is why we have wished to emphasize, in the same address at the opening of the Synod, "the need to restate clearly the specifically religious finality of evangelization. This latter would lose its reason for existence if it were to diverge from the religious axis that guides it: the kingdom of God, before anything else, in its fully theological meaning...."[62]

Evangelical Liberation

33 With regard to the liberation which evangelization proclaims and strives to put into practice one should rather say this:

—it cannot be contained in the simple and restricted dimension of economics, politics, social or cultural life; it must envisage the whole man, in all his aspects, right up to and including his openness to the absolute, even the divine Absolute;

—it is therefore attached to a view of man which it can never sacrifice to the needs of any strategy, practice or short-term efficiency.

Centered on the Kingdom of God

34 Hence, when preaching liberation and associating herself with those who are working and suffering for it, the Church is cer-

---

62. *Ibid.*

tainly not willing to restrict her mission only to the religious field and dissociate herself from man's temporal problems. Nevertheless she reaffirms the primacy of her spiritual vocation and refuses to replace the proclamation of the kingdom by the proclamation of forms of human liberation; she even states that her contribution to liberation is incomplete if she neglects to proclaim salvation in Jesus Christ.

On an Evangelical Concept of Man

35   The Church links human liberation and salvation in Jesus Christ, but she never identifies them, because she knows through revelation, historical experience and the reflection of faith that not every notion of liberation is necessarily consistent and compatible with an evangelical vision of man, of things and of events; she knows too that in order that God's kingdom should come it is not enough to establish liberation and to create well-being and development.

And what is more, the Church has the firm conviction that all temporal liberation, all political liberation—even if it endeavors to find its justification in such or such a page of the Old or New Testament, even if it claims for its ideological postulates and its norms of action theological data and conclusions, even if it pretends to be today's theology—carries within itself the germ of its own negation and fails to reach the ideal that it proposes for itself whenever its profound motives are not those of justice in charity, whenever its zeal lacks a truly spiritual dimension and whenever its final goal is not salvation and happiness in God.

Involving a Necessary Conversion

36   The Church considers it to be undoubtedly important to build up structures which are more human, more just, more respectful of the rights of the person and less oppressive and less enslaving, but she is conscious that the best structures and the most idealized systems soon become inhuman if the inhuman inclinations of the human heart are not made wholesome, if those who live in these structures or who rule them do not undergo a conversion of heart and of outlook.

Excluding Violence

37 The Church cannot accept violence, especially the force of arms—which is uncontrollable once it is let loose—and indiscriminate death as the path to liberation, because she knows that violence always provokes violence and irresistibly engenders new forms of oppression and enslavement which are often harder to bear than those from which they claimed to bring freedom. We said this clearly during our journey in Colombia: "We exhort you not to place your trust in violence and revolution: That is contrary to the Christian spirit, and it can also delay instead of advancing that social uplifting to which you lawfully aspire."[63] "We must say and reaffirm that violence is not in accord with the Gospel, that it is not Christian; and that sudden or violent changes of structures would be deceitful, ineffective of themselves, and certainly not in conformity with the dignity of the people."[64]

Specific Contribution of the Church

38 Having said this, we rejoice that the Church is becoming ever more conscious of the proper manner and strictly evangelical means that she possesses in order to collaborate in the liberation of many. And what is she doing? She is trying more and more to encourage large numbers of Christians to devote themselves to the liberation of men. She is providing these Christian "liberators" with the inspiration of faith, the motivation of fraternal love, a social teaching which the true Christian cannot ignore and which he must make the foundation of his wisdom and of his experience in order to translate it concretely into forms of action, participation and commitment. All this must characterize the spirit of a committed Christian, without confusion with tactical attitudes or with the service of a political system. The Church strives always to insert the Christian struggle for liberation into the universal plan of salvation which she herself proclaims.

---

63. Paul VI, Address to the *Campesinos* of Colombia (August 23, 1968): *AAS* 60 (1968), p. 623.

64. Paul VI, Address for the *"Day of Development"* at Bogota (August 23, 1968): *AAS* 60 (1968), p. 627; cf. St. Augustine, *Epistola* 229, 2: *PL* 33, 1020.

What we have just recalled comes out more than once in the Synod debates. In fact we devoted to this theme a few clarifying words in our address to the Fathers at the end of the assembly.[65]

It is to be hoped that all these considerations will help to remove the ambiguity which the word "liberation" very often takes on in ideologies, political systems or groups. The liberation which evangelization proclaims and prepares is the one which Christ Himself announced and gave to man by His sacrifice.

Religious Liberty

39 The necessity of ensuring fundamental human rights cannot be separated from this just liberation which is bound up with evangelization and which endeavors to secure structures safeguarding human freedoms. Among these fundamental human rights, religious liberty occupies a place of primary importance. We recently spoke of the relevance of this matter, emphasizing "how many Christians still today, because they are Christians, because they are Catholics, live oppressed by systematic persecution! The drama of fidelity to Christ and of the freedom of religion continues, even if it is disguised by categorical declarations in favor of the rights of the person and of life in society!"[66]

IV

THE METHODS OF EVANGELIZATION

Search for Suitable Means

40 The obvious importance of the content of evangelization must not overshadow the importance of the ways and means.

This question of "how to evangelize" is permanently relevant, because the methods of evangelizing vary according to the

---

65. Paul VI, Address for the closing of the Third General Assembly of the Synod of Bishops (October 26, 1974): *AAS* 66 (1974), p. 637.

66. Address given on October 15, 1975: *L'Osservatore Romano* (October 17, 1975).

different circumstances of time, place and culture, and because they thereby present a certain challenge to our capacity for discovery and adaptation.

On us particularly, the pastors of the Church, rests the responsibility for reshaping with boldness and wisdom, but in complete fidelity to the content of evangelization, the means that are most suitable and effective for communicating the Gospel message to the men and women of our times.

Let it suffice, in this meditation, to mention a number of methods which, for one reason or another, have a fundamental importance.

The Witness of Life

41   Without repeating everything that we have already mentioned, it is appropriate first of all to emphasize the following point: for the Church, the first means of evangelization is the witness of an authentically Christian life, given over to God in a communion that nothing should destroy and at the same time given to one's neighbor with limitless zeal. As we said recently to a group of lay people, "Modern man listens more willingly to witnesses than to teachers, and if he does listen to teachers, it is because they are witnesses."[67] St. Peter expressed this well when he held up the example of a reverent and chaste life that wins over even without a word those who refuse to obey the word.[68] It is therefore primarily by her conduct and by her life that the Church will evangelize the world, in other words, by her living witness of fidelity to the Lord Jesus—the witness of poverty and detachment, of freedom in the face of the powers of this world, in short, the witness of sanctity.

A Living Preaching

42   Secondly, it is not superfluous to emphasize the importance and necessity of preaching. "And how are they to believe

---

67. Pope Paul VI, Address to the Members of the *Consilium de Laicis* (October 2, 1974): *AAS* 66 (1974), p. 568.
68. Cf. 1 Pt. 3:1.

in him of whom they have never heard? And how are they to hear without a preacher?... So faith comes from what is heard and what is heard comes by the preaching of Christ."[69] This law once laid down by the Apostle Paul maintains its full force today.

Preaching, the verbal proclamation of a message, is indeed always indispensable. We are well aware that modern man is sated by talk; he is obviously often tired of listening and, what is worse, impervious to words. We are also aware that many psychologists and sociologists express the view that modern man has passed beyond the civilization of the word, which is now ineffective and useless, and that today he lives in the civilization of the image. These facts should certainly impel us to employ, for the purpose of transmitting the Gospel message, the modern means which this civilization has produced. Very positive efforts have in fact already been made in this sphere. We cannot but praise them and encourage their further development. The fatigue produced these days by so much empty talk and the relevance of many other forms of communication must not, however, diminish the permanent power of the word, or cause a loss of confidence in it. The word remains ever relevant, especially when it is the bearer of the power of God.[70] This is why St. Paul's axiom, "Faith comes from what is heard,"[71] also retains its relevance: It is the Word that is heard which leads to belief.

Liturgy of the Word

43 This evangelizing preaching takes on many forms, and zeal will inspire the reshaping of them almost indefinitely. In fact, there are innumerable events in life and human situations which offer the opportunity for a discreet but incisive statement of what the Lord has to say in this or that particular circumstance. It suffices to have true spiritual sensitivity for reading God's message in events. But at a time when the liturgy renewed by the Council has given greatly

---

69. Rom. 10:14, 17.
70. Cf. 1 Cor. 2:1-5.
71. Rom. 10:17.

increased value to the Liturgy of the Word, it would be a mistake not to see in the homily an important and very adaptable instrument of evangelization. Of course it is necessary to know and put to good use the exigencies and the possibilities of the homily, so that it can acquire all its pastoral effectiveness. But above all it is necessary to be convinced of this and to devote oneself to it with love. This preaching, inserted in a unique way into the Eucharistic Celebration, from which it receives special force and vigor, certainly has a particular role in evangelization, to the extent that it expresses the profound faith of the sacred minister and is impregnated with love. The faithful assembled as a Paschal Church, celebrating the feast of the Lord present in their midst, expect much from this preaching and will greatly benefit from it provided that it is simple, clear, direct, well-adapted, profoundly dependent on Gospel teaching and faithful to the Magisterium, animated by a balanced apostolic ardor coming from its own characteristic nature, full of hope, fostering belief, and productive of peace and unity. Many parochial or other communities live and are held together thanks to the Sunday homily, when it possesses these qualities.

Let us add that, thanks to the same liturgical renewal, the Eucharistic Celebration is not the only appropriate moment for the homily. The homily has a place and must not be neglected in the celebration of all the sacraments, at paraliturgies, and in assemblies of the faithful. It will always be a privileged occasion for communicating the Word of the Lord.

Catechetics

44 A means of evangelization that must not be neglected is that of catechetical instruction. The intelligence, especially that of children and young people, needs to learn through systematic religious instruction the fundamental teachings, the living content of the truth which God has wished to convey to us and which the Church has sought to express in an ever richer fashion during the course of her long history. No one will deny that this instruction must be given to form patterns of Christian living and not to remain only notional. Truly the effort for evangelization will profit greatly—at the level of catechetical instruction given at church, in the schools, where this is possible, and in every case in Christian homes—if those giving catechetical instruction have suitable texts, updated with wisdom and competence, under the authority of the bishops. The methods must be adapted to the age, culture and aptitude of the persons concerned; they must seek always to fix in the memory, intelligence and heart the essential truths that must impregnate all of life. It is necessary above all to prepare good instructors—parochial catechists, teachers, parents—who are desirous of perfecting themselves in this superior art, which is indispensable and requires religious instruction. Moreover, without neglecting in any way the training of children, one sees that present conditions render ever more urgent catechetical instruction, under the form of the catechumenate, for innumerable young people and adults who, touched by grace, discover little by little the face of Christ and feel the need of giving themselves to Him.

Utilization of the Mass Media

45 Our century is characterized by the mass media or means of social communication, and the first proclamation, catechesis or the further deepening of faith cannot do without these means, as we have already emphasized.

When they are put at the service of the Gospel, they are capable of increasing almost indefinitely the area in which the Word of God is heard; they enable the Good News to reach millions of people. The Church would feel guilty before the Lord if she did not utilize these powerful means that human skill is daily rendering more perfect. It is through them that she proclaims "from the housetops"[72] the message of which she is the depositary. In them she finds a modern and effective version of the pulpit. Thanks to them she succeeds in speaking to the multitudes.

Nevertheless, the use of the means of social communication for evangelization presents a challenge: Through them the evangelical message should reach vast numbers of people, but with the capacity of piercing the conscience of each individual, of implanting itself in his heart as though he were the only person being addressed,

---

72. Cf. Mt. 10:27; Lk. 12:3.

with all his most individual and personal qualities, and evoke an entirely personal adherence and commitment.

Indispensable Personal Contact

46 For this reason, side by side with the collective proclamation of the Gospel, the other form of transmission, the person-to-person one, remains valid and important. The Lord often used it (for example, with Nicodemus, Zacchaeus, the Samaritan woman, Simon the Pharisee), and so did the Apostles. In the long run, is there any other way of handing on the Gospel than by transmitting to another person one's personal experience of faith? It must not happen that the pressing need to proclaim the Good News to the multitudes should cause us to forget this form of proclamation whereby an individual's personal conscience is reached and touched by an entirely unique world that he receives from someone else. We can never sufficiently praise those priests who through the sacrament of Penance or through pastoral dialogue show their readiness to guide people in the ways of the Gospel, to support them in their efforts, to raise them up if they have fallen, and always to assist them with discernment and availability.

Role of the Sacraments

47 Yet, one can never sufficiently stress the fact that evangelization does not consist only of the preaching and teaching of a doctrine. For evangelization must touch life: the natural life to which it gives a new meaning, thanks to the evangelical perspectives that it reveals; and the supernatural life, which is not the negation but the purification and elevation of the natural life.

This supernatural life finds its living expression in the seven sacraments and in the admirable radiation of grace and holiness which they possess.

Evangelization thus exercises its full capacity when it achieves the most intimate relationship, or better still, a permanent and unbroken intercommunication, between the Word and the sacraments. In a certain sense it is a mistake to make a contrast between evangelization and sacramentalization, as is sometimes done. It is indeed true that a certain way of administering the sacraments, without the solid support of catechesis regarding these same sacraments and a global catechesis, could end up by depriving them of their effectiveness to a great extent. The role of evangelization is precisely to educate people in the faith in such a way as to lead each individual Christian to live the sacraments as true sacraments of faith—and not to receive them passively or reluctantly.

Popular Piety

48 Here we touch upon an aspect of evangelization which cannot leave us insensitive. We wish to speak about what today is often called popular religiosity.

One finds among the people particular expressions of the search for God and for faith, both in the regions where the Church has been established for centuries and where she is in the course of becoming established. These expressions were for a long time regarded as less pure and were sometimes despised, but today they are almost everywhere being rediscovered. During the last Synod the bishops studied their significance with remarkable pastoral realism and zeal.

Popular religiosity, of course, certainly has its limits. It is often subject to penetration by many distortions of religion and even superstitions. It frequently remains at the level of forms of worship not involving a true acceptance by faith. It can even lead to the creation of sects and endanger the true ecclesial community.

But if it is well oriented, above all by a pedagogy of evangelization, it is rich in values. It manifests a thirst for God which only the simple and poor can know. It makes people capable of generosity and sacrifice even to the point of heroism, when it is a question of manifesting belief. It involves an acute awareness of profound attributes of God: fatherhood, providence, loving and constant presence. It engenders interior attitudes rarely observed to the same degree elsewhere: patience, the sense of the cross in daily life, detachment, openness to others, devotion. By reason of these aspects, we readily call it "popular piety," that is, religion of the people, rather than religiosity.

Pastoral charity must dictate to all those whom the Lord has placed as leaders of the ecclesial communities the proper attitude in regard to this reality, which is at the same time so rich and so vulnerable. Above all one must be sensitive to it, know how to perceive its interior dimensions and undeniable values, be ready to help it to overcome its risks of deviation. When it is well oriented, this popular religiosity can be more and more for multitudes of our people a true encounter with God in Jesus Christ.

V

THE BENEFICIARIES OF EVANGELIZATION

Addressed to Everyone

49 Jesus' last words in St. Mark's Gospel confer on the evangelization which the Lord entrusts to His Apostles a limitless universality: "Go out to the whole world; proclaim the Good News to all creation."[73]

The Twelve and the first generation of Christians understood well the lesson of this text and other similar ones; they made them into a program of action. Even persecution, by scattering the Apostles, helped to spread the Word and to establish the Church in ever more distant regions. The admission of Paul to the rank of the Apostles and his charism as the preacher to the pagans (the non-Jews) of Jesus' Coming underlined this universality still more.

Despite All the Obstacles

50 In the course of twenty centuries of history, the generations of Christians have periodically faced various obstacles to this universal mission. On the one hand, on the part of the evangelizers themselves, there has been the temptation for various reasons to narrow down the field of their missionary activity. On the other hand, there has been the often humanly insurmountable resistance of the people being addressed by the evangelizer. Furthermore, we must note with sadness that the evangelizing work of the Church is strongly opposed, if not prevented, by certain public powers. Even

---

73. Mk. 16:15.

in our own day it happens that preachers of God's Word are deprived of their rights, persecuted, threatened or eliminated solely for preaching Jesus Christ and His Gospel. But we are confident that despite these painful trials the activity of these apostles will never meet final failure in any part of the world.

Despite such adversities, the Church constantly renews her deepest inspiration, that which comes to her directly from the Lord: To the whole world! To all creation! Right to the ends of the earth! She did this once more at the last Synod, as an appeal not to imprison the proclamation of the Gospel by limiting it to one sector of mankind or to one class of people or to a single type of civilization. Some examples are revealing.

First Proclamation to Those Who Are Far Off

51 To reveal Jesus Christ and His Gospel to those who do not know them has been, ever since the morning of Pentecost, the fundamental program which the Church has taken on as received from her Founder. The whole of the New Testament, and in a special way the Acts of the Apostles, bears witness to a privileged and in a sense exemplary moment of this missionary effort which will subsequently leave its mark on the whole history of the Church.

She carries out this first proclamation of Jesus Christ by a complex and diversified activity which is sometimes termed "pre-evangelization" but which is already evangelization in a true sense, although at its initial and still incomplete stage. An almost indefinite range of means can be used for this purpose: explicit preaching, of course, but also art, the scientific approach, philosophical research and legitimate recourse to the sentiments of the human heart.

Renewed Proclamation to a Dechristianized World

52 This first proclamation is addressed especially to those who have never heard the Good News of Jesus, or to children. But, as a result of the frequent situations of dechristianization in our day, it also proves equally necessary for innumerable people who have been baptized but who live quite outside Christian life, for simple people who have a certain faith but an imperfect knowledge of the foundations of that faith, for intellectuals who feel the need to know Jesus Christ in a light different from the instruction they received as children, and for many others.

Non-Christian Religions

53 This first proclamation is also addressed to the immense sections of mankind who practice non-Christian religions. The Church respects and esteems these non-Christian religions because they are the living expression of the soul of vast groups of people. They carry within them the echo of thousands of years of searching for God, a quest which is incomplete but often made with great sincerity and righteousness of heart. They possess an impressive patrimony of deeply religious texts. They have taught generations of people how to pray. They are all impregnated with innumerable "seeds of the Word"[74] and can constitute a true "preparation for the Gospel,"[75] to quote a felicitous term used by the Second Vatican Council and borrowed from Eusebius of Caesarea.

Such a situation certainly raises complex and delicate questions that must be studied in the light of Christian Tradition and the Church's Magisterium, in order to offer to the missionaries of today and of tomorrow new horizons in their contacts with non-Christian religions. We wish to point out, above all today, that neither respect and esteem for these religions nor the complexity of the questions raised is an invitation to the Church to withhold from these non-Christians the proclamation of Jesus Christ. On the contrary the Church holds that these multitudes have the right to know the riches of the mystery of Christ[76]—riches in which we believe

---

74. Cf. St. Justin, *I Apol.* 46, 1-4: *PG* 6, II *Apol.* 7 (8) 1-4; 10, 1-3; 13, 3-4; *Florilegium Patristicum* II, Bonn 1911², pp. 81, 125, 129, 133; Clement of Alexandria, *Stromata* I, 19, 91; 94; *S. Ch.* pp. 117-118; 119-110; Second Vatican Ecumenical Council, Decree on the Church's Missionary Activity *Ad gentes*, 11: *AAS* 58 (1966), p. 960; cf. Dogmatic Constitution on the Church *Lumen gentium*, 17: *AAS* 57 (1965), p. 21.

75. Eusebius of Caesarea, *Praeparatio Evangelica*, I, 1: *PG* 21, 26-28; cf. Second Vatican Ecumenical Council, Dogmatic Constitution on the Church *Lumen gentium*, 16: *AAS* 57 (1965), p. 20.

76. Cf. Eph. 3:8.

that the whole of humanity can find, in unsuspected fullness, everything that it is gropingly searching for concerning God, man and his destiny, life and death, and truth. Even in the face of natural religious expressions most worthy of esteem, the Church finds support in the fact that the religion of Jesus, which she proclaims through evangelization, objectively places man in relation with the plan of God, with His living presence and with His action; she thus causes an encounter with the mystery of divine paternity that bends over towards humanity. In other words, our religion effectively establishes with God an authentic and living relationship which the other religions do not succeed in doing, even though they have, as it were, their arms stretched out towards heaven.

This is why the Church keeps her missionary spirit alive, and even wishes to intensify it in the moment of history in which we are living. She feels responsible before entire peoples. She has no rest so long as she has not done her best to proclaim the Good News of Jesus the Savior. She is always preparing new generations of apostles. Let us state this fact with joy at a time when there are not lacking those who think and even say that ardor and the apostolic spirit are exhausted, and that the time of the missions is now past. The Synod has replied that the missionary proclamation never ceases and that the Church will always be striving for the fulfillment of this proclamation.

Support for the Faith of Believers

54 Nevertheless the Church does not feel dispensed from paying unflagging attention also to those who have received the Faith and who have been in contact with the Gospel often for generations. Thus she seeks to deepen, consolidate, nourish and make ever more mature the faith of those who are already called the faithful or believers, in order that they may be so still more.

This faith is nearly always today exposed to secularism, even to militant atheism. It is a faith exposed to trials and threats, and even more, a faith besieged and actively opposed. It runs the risk of perishing from suffocation or starvation if it is not fed and sustained each day. To evangelize must therefore very often be to give this necessary food and sustenance to the faith of believers, especially through a catechesis full of Gospel vitality and in a language suited to people and circumstances.

The Church also has a lively solicitude for the Christians who are not in full communion with her. While preparing with them the unity willed by Christ, and precisely in order to realize unity in truth, she has the consciousness that she would be gravely lacking in her duty if she did not give witness before them of the fullness of the revelation whose deposit she guards.

Non-Believers

55 Also significant is the preoccupation of the last Synod in regard to two spheres which are very different from one another but which at the same time are very close by reason of the challenge which they make to evangelization, each in its own way.

The first sphere is the one which can be called the increase of unbelief in the modern world. The Synod endeavored to describe this modern world: How many currents of thought, values and countervalues, latent aspirations or seeds of destruction, old convictions which disappear and new convictions which arise are covered by this generic name!

From the spiritual point of view, the modern world seems to be forever immersed in what a modern author has termed "the drama of atheistic humanism."[77]

On the one hand one is forced to note in the very heart of this contemporary world the phenomenon which is becoming almost its most striking characteristic: secularism. We are not speaking of secularization, which is the effort, in itself just and legitimate and in no way incompatible with faith or religion, to discover in creation, in each thing or each happening in the universe, the laws which regulate them with a certain autonomy, but with the inner conviction that the Creator has placed these laws there. The last Council has in this sense affirmed the legitimate autonomy of culture and particularly of the sciences.[78] Here we are thinking of a true secularism: a concept of the world according to which the latter is

---

77. Cf. Henri de Lubac, *Le drame de l'humanisme athee*, ed. Spes, Paris, 1945.
78. Cf. Pastoral Constitution on the Church in the Modern World *Gaudium et spes*, 59: *AAS* 58 (1966), p. 1080.

self-explanatory, without any need for recourse to God, who thus becomes superfluous and an encumbrance. This sort of secularism, in order to recognize the power of man, therefore ends up by doing without God and even by denying Him.

New forms of atheism seem to flow from it: a man-centered atheism, no longer abstract and metaphysical but pragmatic, systematic and militant. Hand in hand with this atheistic secularism, we are daily faced, under the most diverse forms, with a consumer society, the pursuit of pleasure set up as the supreme value, a desire for power and domination, and discrimination of every kind: the inhuman tendencies of this "humanism."

In this same modern world, on the other hand, and this is a paradox, one cannot deny the existence of real stepping-stones to Christianity, and of evangelical values at least in the form of a sense of emptiness or nostalgia. It would not be an exaggeration to say that there exists a powerful and tragic appeal to be evangelized.

The Non-Practicing

56 The second sphere is that of those who do not practice. Today there is a very large number of baptized people who for the most part have not formally renounced their Baptism but who are entirely indifferent to it and not living in accordance with it. The phenomenon of the non-practicing is a very ancient one in the history of Christianity; it is the result of a natural weakness, a profound inconsistency which we unfortunately bear deep within us. Today, however, it shows certain new characteristics. It is often the result of the uprooting typical of our time. It also springs from the fact that Christians live in close proximity with non-believers and constantly experience the effects of unbelief. Furthermore, the non-practicing Christians of today, more so than those of previous periods, seek to explain and justify their position in the name of an interior religion, of personal independence or authenticity.

Thus we have atheists and unbelievers on the one side and those who do not practice on the other, and both groups put up a considerable resistance to evangelization. The resistance of the former takes the form of a certain refusal and an inability to grasp the new order of things, the new meaning of the world, of life and of history; such is not possible if one does not start from a divine absolute. The resistance of the second group takes the form of inertia and the slightly hostile attitude of the person who feels that he is one of the family, who claims to know it all and to have tried it all and who no longer believes it.

Atheistic secularism and the absence of religious practice are found among adults and among the young, among the leaders of society and among the ordinary people, at all levels of education, and in both the old Churches and the young ones. The Church's evangelizing action cannot ignore these two worlds, nor must it come to a standstill when faced with them; it must constantly seek the proper means and language for presenting, or re-presenting, to them God's revelation and faith in Jesus Christ.

Proclamation to the Multitudes

57 Like Christ during the time of His preaching, like the Twelve on the morning of Pentecost, the Church too sees before her an immense multitude of people who need the Gospel and have a right to it, for God "wants everyone to be saved and reach full knowledge of the truth."[79]

The Church is deeply aware of her duty to preach salvation to all. Knowing that the Gospel message is not reserved to a small group of the initiated, the privileged or the elect, but is destined for everyone, she shares Christ's anguish at the sight of the wandering and exhausted crowds, "like sheep without a shepherd," and she often repeats His words: "I feel sorry for all these people."[80] But the Church is also conscious of the fact that, if the preaching of the Gospel is to be effective, she must address her message to the heart of the multitudes, to communities of the faithful whose action can and must reach others.

Ecclesial "Communautés de Base"

58 The last Synod devoted considerable attention to these "small communities," or *communautés de base*, because they are

---

79. 1 Tm. 2:4.
80. Mt. 9:36; 15:32.

often talked about in the Church today. What are they, and why should they be the special beneficiaries of evangelization and at the same time evangelizers themselves?

According to the various statements heard in the Synod, such communities flourish more or less throughout the Church. They differ greatly among themselves both within the same region and even more so from one region to another.

In some regions they appear and develop, almost without exception, within the Church, having solidarity with her life, being nourished by her teaching and united with her pastors. In these cases, they spring from the need to live the Church's life more intensely, or from the desire and quest for a more human dimension such as larger ecclesial communities can only offer with difficulty, especially in the big modern cities which lend themselves both to life in the mass and to anonymity. Such communities can quite simply be in their own way an extension on the spiritual and religious level—worship, deepening of faith, fraternal charity, prayer, contact with pastors—of the small sociological community such as the village, etc. Or again their aim may be to bring together, for the purpose of listening to and meditating on the Word, for the sacraments and the bond of the *agape,* groups of people who are linked by age, culture, civil state or social situation: married couples, young people, professional people, etc.; people who already happen to be united in the struggle for justice, brotherly aid to the poor, human advancement. In still other cases, they bring Christians together in places where the shortage of priests does not favor the normal life of a parish community. This is all presupposed within communities constituted by the Church, especially individual Churches and parishes.

In other regions, on the other hand, *communautés de base* come together in a spirit of bitter criticism of the Church, which they are quick to stigmatize as "institutional" and to which they set themselves up in opposition as charismatic communities, free from structures and inspired only by the Gospel. Thus their obvious characteristic is an attitude of fault-finding and of rejection with regard to the Church's outward manifestations: her hierarchy, her signs. They are radically opposed to the Church. By following these lines their main inspiration very quickly becomes ideological, and it rarely happens that they do not quickly fall victim to some political option or current of thought, and then to a system, even a party, with all the attendant risks of becoming its instrument.

The difference is already notable: The communities which by their spirit of opposition cut themselves off from the Church, and whose unity they wound, can well be called *communautés de base*, but in this case it is a strictly sociological name. They could not, without a misuse of terms, be called ecclesial *communautés de base*, even if, while being hostile to the hierarchy, they claim to remain within the unity of the Church. This name belongs to the other groups, those which come together within the Church in order to unite themselves to the Church and to cause the Church to grow.

These latter communities will be a place of evangelization, for the benefit of the bigger communities, especially the individual Churches. And, as we said at the end of the last Synod, they will be a hope for the universal Church to the extent:

—that they seek their nourishment in the Word of God and do not allow themselves to be ensnared by political polarization or fashionable ideologies, which are ready to exploit their immense human potential;

—that they avoid the ever present temptation of systematic protest and a hypercritical attitude, under the pretext of authenticity and a spirit of collaboration;

—that they remain firmly attached to the local Church in which they are inserted, and to the universal Church, thus avoiding the very real danger of becoming isolated within themselves, then of believing themselves to be the only authentic Church of Christ, and hence of condemning the other ecclesial communities;

—that they maintain a sincere communion with the pastors whom the Lord gives to His Church, and with the Magisterium which the Spirit of Christ has entrusted to these pastors;

—that they never look on themselves as the sole beneficiaries or sole agents of evangelization—or even the only depositaries of the Gospel—but, being aware that the Church is much more vast and diversified, accept the fact that this Church becomes incarnate in other ways than through themselves;

—that they constantly grow in missionary consciousness, fervor, commitment and zeal;

—that they show themselves to be universal in all things and never sectarian.

On these conditions, which are certainly demanding but also uplifting, the ecclesial *communautés de base* will correspond to their most fundamental vocation: As hearers of the Gospel which is proclaimed to them and privileged beneficiaries of evangelization, they will soon become proclaimers of the Gospel themselves.

VI

THE WORKERS FOR EVANGELIZATION

The Church: Missionary in Her Entirety

59 If people proclaim in the world the Gospel of salvation, they do so by the command of, in the name of and with the grace of Christ the Savior. "They will never have a preacher unless one is sent,"[81] wrote he who was without doubt one of the greatest evangelizers. No one can do it without having been sent.

But who then has the mission of evangelizing?

The Second Vatican Council gave a clear reply to this question: It is upon the Church that "there rests, by divine mandate, the duty of going out into the whole world and preaching the Gospel to every creature."[82] And in another text: "...the whole Church is missionary, and the work of evangelization is a basic duty of the People of God."[83]

We have already mentioned this intimate connection between the Church and evangelization. While the Church is proclaiming the kingdom of God and building it up, she is establishing herself in the midst of the world as the sign and instrument of this kingdom which is and which is to come. The Council repeats the following

---

81. Rom. 10:15.

82. Declaration on Religious Liberty *Dignitatis humanae*, 13: *AAS* 58 (1966), p. 939; cf. Dogmatic Constitution on the Church *Lumen gentium*, 5: *AAS* 57 (1965), pp. 7-8; Decree on the Church's Missionary Activity *Ad gentes*, 1: *AAS* 58 (1966), p. 947.

83. Decree on the Church's Missionary Activity *Ad gentes*, 35: *AAS* 58 (1966), p. 983.

expression of St. Augustine on the missionary activity of the Twelve: "They preached the word of truth and brought forth Churches."[84]

An Ecclesial Act

60   The observation that the Church has been sent out and given a mandate to evangelize the world should awaken in us two convictions.

The first is this: Evangelization is for no one an individual and isolated act; it is one that is deeply ecclesial. When the most obscure preacher, catechist or pastor in the most distant land preaches the Gospel, gathers his little community together or administers a sacrament, even alone, he is carrying out an ecclesial act, and his action is certainly attached to the evangelizing activity of the whole Church by institutional relationships, but also by profound invisible links in the order of grace. This presupposes that he acts not in virtue of a mission which he attributes to himself or by a personal inspiration, but in union with the mission of the Church and in her name.

From this flows the second conviction: If each individual evangelizes in the name of the Church, who herself does so by virtue of a mandate from the Lord, no evangelizer is the absolute master of his evangelizing action, with a discretionary power to carry it out in accordance with individualistic criteria and perspectives; he acts in communion with the Church and her pastors.

We have remarked that the Church is entirely and completely evangelizing. This means that, in the whole world and in each part of the world where she is present, the Church feels responsible for the task of spreading the Gospel.

The Perspective of the Universal Church

61   Brothers and sons and daughters, at this stage of our reflection, we wish to pause with you at a question which is particularly

---

84. St. Augustine, *Enarratio in Ps.* 44:23: *CCL* XXXVIII, p. 510; cf. Decree on the Church's Missionary Activity *Ad gentes*, 1: *AAS* 58 (1966), p. 947.

important at the present time. In the celebration of the liturgy, in their witness before judges and executioners and in their apologetical texts, the first Christians readily expressed their deep faith in the Church by describing her as being spread throughout the universe. They were fully conscious of belonging to a large community which neither space nor time can limit: From the just Abel right to the last of the elect,[85] "indeed to the ends of the earth,"[86] "to the end of time."[87]

This is how the Lord wanted His Church to be: universal, a great tree whose branches shelter the birds of the air,[88] a net which catches fish of every kind[89] or which Peter drew in filled with one hundred and fifty-three big fish,[90] a flock which a single shepherd pastures.[91] A universal Church without boundaries or frontiers except, alas, those of the heart and mind of sinful man.

The Perspective of the Individual Church

62 Nevertheless this universal Church is in practice incarnate in the individual Churches made up of such or such an actual part of mankind, speaking such and such a language, heirs of a cultural patrimony, of a vision of the world, of an historical past, of a particular human substratum. Receptivity to the wealth of the individual Church corresponds to a special sensitivity of modern man.

Let us be very careful not to conceive of the universal Church as the sum, or, if one can say so, the more or less anomalous federation of essentially different individual Churches. In the mind of the Lord the Church is universal by vocation and mission, but when she puts down her roots in a variety of cultural, social and human terrains, she takes on different external expressions and appearances in each part of the world.

Thus each individual Church that would voluntarily cut itself off from the universal Church would lose its relationship to God's

---

85. St. Gregory the Great, *Homil. in Evangelia* 19, 1: *PL* 76, 1154.
86. Acts 1:8; cf. *Didache* 9, 1: Funk, *Patres Apostolici*, 1, 22.
87. Mt. 28:20.
88. Cf. Mt. 13:32.
89. Cf. Mt. 13:47.
90. Cf. Jn. 21:11.
91. Cf. Jn. 10:1-16.

plan and would be impoverished in its ecclesial dimension. But, at the same time, a Church *toto orbe diffusa* would become an abstraction if she did not take body and life precisely through the individual Churches. Only continual attention to these two poles of the Church will enable us to perceive the richness of this relationship between the universal Church and the individual Churches.

Adaptation and Fidelity in Expression

63 The individual Churches, intimately built up not only of people but also of aspirations, of riches and limitations, of ways of praying, of loving, of looking at life and the world, which distinguish this or that human gathering, have the task of assimilating the essense of the Gospel message and of transposing it, without the slightest betrayal of its essential truth, into the language that these particular people understand, then of proclaiming it in this language.

The transposition has to be done with the discernment, seriousness, respect and competence which the matter calls for in the field of liturgical expression,[92] and in the areas of catechesis, theological formulation, secondary ecclesial structures, and ministries. And the word "language" should be understood here less in the semantic or literary sense than in the sense which one may call anthropological and cultural.

The question is undoubtedly a delicate one. Evangelization loses much of its force and effectiveness if it does not take into consideration the actual people to whom it is addressed, if it does not use their language, their signs and symbols, if it does not answer the questions they ask, and if it does not have an impact on their concrete life. But on the other hand, evangelization risks losing its power and disappearing altogether if one empties or adulterates its content under the pretext of translating it; if, in other words, one sacrifices this reality and destroys the unity without which there is no universality, out of a wish to adapt a universal reality to a local

---

92. Cf. Second Vatican Ecumenical Council, Constitution on the Sacred Liturgy *Sacrosanctum Concilium*, 37-38: *AAS* 56 (1964), p. 110; cf. also the liturgical books and other documents subsequently issued by the Holy See for the putting into practice of the liturgical reform desired by the same Council.

situation. Now, only a Church which preserves the awareness of her universality and shows that she is in fact universal is capable of having a message which can be heard by all, regardless of regional frontiers.

Legitimate attention to individual Churches cannot fail to enrich the Church. Such attention is indispensable and urgent. It responds to the very deep aspirations of peoples and human communities to find their own identity ever more clearly.

Openness to the Universal Church

64 But this enrichment requires that the individual Churches should keep their profound openness towards the universal Church. It is quite remarkable, moreover, that the most simple Christians, the ones who are most faithful to the Gospel and most open to the true meaning of the Church, have a completely spontaneous sensitivity to this universal dimension. They instinctively and very strongly feel the need for it, they easily recognize themselves in such a dimension. They feel with it and suffer very deeply within themselves when, in the name of theories which they do not understand, they are forced to accept a Church deprived of this universality, a regionalist Church, with no horizon.

As history in fact shows, whenever an individual Church has cut itself off from the universal Church and from its living and visible center—sometimes with the best of intentions, with theological, sociological, political or pastoral arguments, or even in the desire for a certain freedom of movement or action—it has escaped only with great difficulty (if indeed it has escaped) from two equally serious dangers. The first danger is that of a withering isolationism, and then, before long, of a crumbling away, with each of its cells breaking away from it just as it itself has broken away from the central nucleus. The second danger is that of losing its freedom when, being cut off from the center and from the other Churches which gave it strength and energy, it finds itself all alone and a prey to the most varied forces of slavery and exploitation.

The more an individual Church is attached to the universal Church by solid bonds of communion, in charity and loyalty, in receptiveness to the Magisterium of Peter, in the unity of the *lex orandi* which is also the *lex credendi*, in the desire for unity with all the other Churches which make up the whole—the more such a Church will be capable of translating the treasure of faith into the legitimate variety of expressions of the profession of faith, of prayer and worship, of Christian life and conduct and of the spiritual influence on the people among which it dwells. The more will it also be truly evangelizing, that is to say, capable of drawing upon the universal patrimony in order to enable its own people to profit from it, and capable too of communicating to the universal Church the experience and the life of this people, for the benefit of all.

The Unchangeable Deposit of Faith

65 It was precisely in this sense that at the end of the last Synod we spoke clear words full of paternal affection, insisting on the role of Peter's Successor as a visible, living and dynamic principle of the unity between the Churches and thus of the universality of the one Church.[93] We also insisted on the grave responsibility incumbent upon us, but which we share with our brothers in the episcopate, of preserving unaltered the content of the Catholic Faith which the Lord entrusted to the Apostles. While being translated into all expressions, this content must be neither impaired nor mutilated. While being clothed with the outward forms proper to each people, and made explicit by theological expression which takes account of differing cultural, social and even racial milieu, it must remain the content of the Catholic Faith just exactly as the ecclesial Magisterium has received it and transmits it.

Differing Tasks

66 The whole Church, therefore, is called upon to evangelize, and yet within her we have different evangelizing tasks to accomplish. This diversity of services in the unity of the same mission makes up the richness and beauty of evangelization. We shall briefly recall these tasks.

First, we would point out in the pages of the Gospel the insistence with which the Lord entrusted to the Apostles the task of pro-

---

93. Paul VI, Address for the closing of the Third General Assembly of the Synod of Bishops (October 26, 1974): *AAS* 66 (1974), p. 636.

claiming the Word. He chose them,[94] trained them during several years of intimate company,[95] constituted[96] and sent them out[97] as authorized witnesses and teachers of the message of salvation. And the Twelve in their turn sent out their successors who, in the apostolic line, continue to preach the Good News.

The Successor of Peter

67 The Successor of Peter is thus, by the will of Christ, entrusted with the preeminent ministry of teaching the revealed truth. The New Testament often shows Peter "filled with the Holy Spirit" speaking in the name of all.[98] It is precisely for this reason that St. Leo the Great describes him as he who has merited the primacy of the apostolate.[99] This is also why the voice of the Church shows the Pope "at the highest point—*in apice, in specula*—of the apostolate."[100] The Second Vatican Council wished to reaffirm this when it declared that "Christ's mandate to preach the Gospel to every creature (cf. Mk. 16:15) primarily and immediately concerns the bishops with Peter and under Peter."[101]

The full, supreme and universal power[102] which Christ gives to His Vicar for the pastoral government of His Church is thus especially exercised by the Pope in the activity of preaching and causing to be preached the Good News of salvation.

---

94. Cf. Jn. 15:16; Mk. 3:13-19; Lk. 6:13-16.
95. Cf. Acts 1:21-22.
96. Cf. Mk. 3:14.
97. Cf. Mk. 3:14-15; Lk. 9:2.
98. Acts 4:8; cf. 2:14, 3:12.
99. Cf. St. Leo the Great, *Sermo* 69, 3; *Sermo* 70, 1-3; *Sermo* 94, 3; *Sermo* 95, 2; *S.C.* 200, pp. 50-52; 58-66; 258-260; 268.
100. Cf. First Ecumenical Council of Lyons, Constitution *Ad apostolicae dignitatis: Conciliorum oecumenicorum decreta*, ed. *Istituto per le Scienze Religiose*, Bologna 1973¹, p. 278; Ecumenical Council of Vienne, Constitution *Ad providam Christi, ed. cit.*, p. 343; Fifth Lateran Ecumenical Council, Constitution *In apostolici culminis, ed. cit.*, p. 608; Constitution *Postquam ad universalis, ed. cit.*, p. 609; Constitution *Supernae dispositionis, ed. cit.*, p. 614; Constitution *Divina disponente clementia, ed. cit.*, p. 638.
101. Decree on the Church's Missionary Activity *Ad gentes*, 38: *AAS* 58 (1966), p. 985.
102. Cf. Second Vatican Ecumenical Council, Dogmatic Constitution on the Church *Lumen gentium*, 22: *AAS* 57 (1965), p. 26.

Bishops and Priests

68 In union with the Successor of Peter, the bishops, who are successors of the Apostles, receive through the power of their episcopal ordination the authority to teach the revealed truth in the Church. They are teachers of the faith.

Associated with the bishops in the ministry of evangelization and responsible by a special title are those who through priestly ordination "act in the person of Christ."[103] They are educators of the People of God in the faith and preachers, while at the same time being ministers of the Eucharist and of the other sacraments.

We pastors are therefore invited to take note of this duty, more than any other members of the Church. What identifies our priestly service, gives a profound unity to the thousand and one tasks which claim our attention day by day and throughout our lives, and confers a distinct character on our activities, is this aim, ever present in all our action: to proclaim the Gospel of God.[104]

A mark of our identity which no doubts ought to encroach upon and no objection eclipse is this: as pastors, we have been chosen by the mercy of the Supreme Pastor,[105] in spite of our inadequacy, to proclaim with authority the Word of God, to assemble the scattered People of God, to feed this People with the signs of the action of Christ which are the sacraments, to set this People on the road to salvation, to maintain it in that unity of which we are, at different levels, active and living instruments, and unceasingly to keep this community gathered around Christ faithful to its deepest vocation. And when we do all these things, within our human limits and by the grace of God, it is a work of evangelization that we are carrying out. This includes ourself as Pastor of the universal Church, our brother bishops at the head of the individual Churches, priests and deacons united with their bishops and whose assistants they are, by a communion which has its source in the sacrament of Orders and in the charity of the Church.

---

103. Cf. Second Vatican Ecumenical Council, Dogmatic Constitution on the Church *Lumen gentium*, 10, 37; *AAS* 57 (1965), pp. 14, 43; Decree on the Church's Missionary Activity *Ad gentes*, 39; *AAS* 58 (1966), p. 986; Decree on the Ministry and Life of Priests *Presbyterorum ordinis*, 2, 12, 13: *AAS* 58 (1966), pp. 992, 1010, 1011.

104. Cf. 1 Thes. 2:9.

105. Cf. 1 Pt. 5:4.

Religious

69 Religious, for their part, find in their consecrated life a privileged means of effective evangelization. At the deepest level of their being they are caught up in the dynamism of the Church's life, which is thirsty for the divine Absolute and called to holiness. It is to this holiness that they bear witness. They embody the Church in her desire to give herself completely to the radical demands of the beatitudes. By their lives they are a sign of total availability to God, the Church and the brethren.

As such they have a special importance in the context of the witness which, as we have said, is of prime importance in evangelization. At the same time as being a challenge to the world and to the Church herself, this silent witness of poverty and abnegation, of purity and sincerity, of self-sacrifice in obedience, can become an eloquent witness capable of touching also non-Christians who have good will and are sensitive to certain values.

In this perspective one perceives the role played in evangelization by religious men and women consecrated to prayer, silence, penance and sacrifice. Other religious, in great numbers, give themselves directly to the proclamation of Christ. Their missionary activity depends clearly on the hierarchy and must be coordinated with the pastoral plan which the latter adopts. But who does not see the immense contribution that these religious have brought and continue to bring to evangelization? Thanks to their consecration they are eminently willing and free to leave everything and to go and proclaim the Gospel even to the ends of the earth. They are enterprising and their apostolate is often marked by an originality, by a genius that demands admiration. They are generous: Often they are found at the outposts of the mission, and they take the greatest of risks for their health and their very lives. Truly the Church owes them much.

The Laity

70 Lay people, whose particular vocation places them in the midst of the world and in charge of the most varied temporal tasks, must for this very reason exercise a very special form of evangelization.

Their primary and immediate task is not to establish and develop the ecclesial community—this is the specific role of the pastors—but to put to use every Christian and evangelical possibility latent but already present and active in the affairs of the world. Their own field of evangelizing activity is the vast and complicated world of politics, society and economics, but also the world of culture, of the sciences and the arts, of international life, of the mass media. It also includes other realities which are open to evangelization, such as human love, the family, the education of children and adolescents, professional work, suffering. The more Gospel-inspired lay people there are engaged in these realities, clearly involved in them, competent to promote them and conscious that they must exercise to the full their Christian powers which are often buried and suffocated, the more these realities will be at the service of the kingdom of God and therefore of salvation in Jesus Christ, without in any way losing or sacrificing their human content but rather pointing to a transcendent dimension which is often disregarded.

The Family

71 One cannot fail to stress the evangelizing action of the family in the evangelizing apostolate of the laity.

At different moments in the Church's history and also in the Second Vatican Council, the family has well deserved the beautiful name of "domestic Church."[106] This means that there should be found in every Christian family the various aspects of the entire Church. Furthermore, the family, like the Church, ought to be a place where the Gospel is transmitted and from which the Gospel radiates.

In a family which is conscious of this mission, all the members evangelize and are evangelized. The parents not only communicate the Gospel to their children, but from their children they can themselves receive the same Gospel as deeply lived by them.

---

106. Dogmatic Constitution on the Church *Lumen gentium*, 11: *AAS* 57 (1965), p. 16; Decree on the Apostolate of the Laity *Apostolicam actuositatem*, 11: *AAS* 58 (1966), p. 846; St. John Chrysostom, *In Genesim Serm.* VI, 2; VII, 1: *PG* 54, 607-68.

And such a family becomes the evangelizer of many other families, and of the neighborhood of which it forms part. Families resulting from a mixed marriage also have the duty of proclaiming Christ to the children in the fullness of the consequences of a common Baptism; they have moreover the difficult task of becoming builders of unity.

Young People

72 Circumstances invite us to make special mention of the young. Their increasing number and growing presence in society and likewise the problems assailing them should awaken in every one the desire to offer them with zeal and intelligence the Gospel ideal as something to be known and lived. And on the other hand, young people who are well trained in faith and prayer must become more and more the apostles of youth. The Church counts greatly on their contribution, and we ourself have often manifested our full confidence in them.

Diversified Ministries

73 Hence the active presence of the laity in the temporal realities takes on all its importance. One cannot, however, neglect or forget the other dimension: The laity can also feel themselves called, or be called, to work with their pastors in the service of the ecclesial community, for its growth and life, by exercising a great variety of ministries according to the grace and charisms which the Lord is pleased to give them.

We cannot but experience a great inner joy when we see so many pastors, religious and lay people, fired with their mission to evangelize, seeking ever more suitable ways of proclaiming the Gospel effectively. We encourage the openness which the Church is showing today in this direction and with this solicitude. It is an openness to meditation first of all, and then to ecclesial ministries capable of renewing and strengthening the evangelizing vigor of the Church.

It is certain that, side by side with the ordained ministries, whereby certain people are appointed pastors and consecrate themselves in a special way to the service of the community, the Church recognizes the place of non-ordained ministries which are able to offer a particular service to the Church.

A glance at the origins of the Church is very illuminating, and gives the benefit of an early experience in the matter of ministries. It was an experience which was all the more valuable in that it enabled the Church to consolidate herself and to grow and spread. Attention to the sources however has to be complemented by attention to the present needs of mankind and of the Church. To drink at these ever inspiring sources without sacrificing anything of their values, and at the same time to know how to adapt oneself to the demands and needs of today—these are the criteria which will make it possible to seek wisely and to discover the ministries which the Church needs and which many of her members will gladly embrace for the sake of ensuring greater vitality in the ecclesial community. These ministries will have a real pastoral value to the extent that they are established with absolute respect for unity and adhering to the directives of the pastors, who are the ones who are responsible for the Church's unity and the builders thereof.

These ministries, apparently new but closely tied up with the Church's living experience down the centuries—such as catechists, directors of prayer and chant, Christians devoted to the service of God's Word or to assisting their brethren in need, the heads of small communities, or other persons charged with the responsibility of apostolic movements—these ministries are valuable for the establishment, life, and growth of the Church, and for her capacity to influence her surroundings and to reach those who are remote from her. We owe also our special esteem to all the lay people who accept to consecrate a part of their time, their energies, and sometimes their entire lives, to the service of the missions.

A serious preparation is needed for all workers for evangelization. Such preparation is all the more necessary for those who devote themselves to the ministry of the Word. Being animated by the conviction, ceaselessly deepened, of the greatness and riches of the Word of God, those who have the mission of transmitting it must give the maximum attention to the dignity, precision and adaptation of their language. Everyone knows that the art of speaking takes on today a very great importance. How would preachers and catechists be able to neglect this?

We earnestly desire that in each individual Church the bishops should be vigilant concerning the adequate formation of all the ministers of the Word. This serious preparation will increase in them the indispensable assurance and also the enthusiasm to proclaim today Jesus Christ.

VII

THE SPIRIT OF EVANGELIZATION

Pressing Appeal

74 We would not wish to end this encounter with our beloved brethren and sons and daughters without a pressing appeal concerning the interior attitudes which must animate those who work for evangelization.

In the name of the Lord Jesus Christ, and in the name of the Apostles Peter and Paul, we wish to exhort all those who, thanks to the charisms of the Holy Spirit and to the mandate of the Church, are true evangelizers to be worthy of this vocation, to exercise it without the reticence of doubt or fear, and not to neglect the conditions that will make this evangelization not only possible but also active and fruitful. These, among many others, are the fundamental conditions which we consider it important to emphasize.

Under the Action of the Holy Spirit

75 Evangelization will never be possible without the action of the Holy Spirit. The Spirit descends on Jesus of Nazareth at the moment of His baptism when the voice of the Father—"This is my beloved Son with whom I am well pleased"[107]—manifests in an external way the election of Jesus and His mission. Jesus is "led by the Spirit" to experience in the desert the decisive combat and the supreme test before beginning this mission.[108] It is "in the power of the Spirit"[109] that He returns to Galilee and begins His preaching at

---

107. Mt. 3:17.
108. Mt. 4:1.
109. Lk. 4:14.

Nazareth, applying to Himself the passage of Isaiah: "The Spirit of the Lord is upon me." And He proclaims: "Today this Scripture has been fulfilled."[110] To the disciples whom He was about to send forth He says, breathing on them, "Receive the Holy Spirit."[111]

In fact, it is only after the coming of the Holy Spirit on the day of Pentecost that the Apostles depart to all the ends of the earth in order to begin the great work of the Church's evangelization. Peter explains this event as the fulfillment of the prophecy of Joel: "I will pour out my spirit."[112] Peter is filled with the Holy Spirit so that he can speak to the people about Jesus, the Son of God.[113] Paul too is filled with the Holy Spirit[114] before dedicating himself to his apostolic ministry, as is Stephen when he is chosen for the ministry of service and later on for the witness of blood.[115] The Spirit, who causes Peter, Paul and the Twelve to speak, and who inspires the words that they are to utter, also comes down "on those who heard the word."[116]

It is in the "consolation of the Holy Spirit" that the Church increases.[117] The Holy Spirit is the soul of the Church. It is He who explains to the faithful the deep meaning of the teaching of Jesus and of His mystery. It is the Holy Spirit who, today just as at the beginning of the Church, acts in every evangelizer who allows himself to be possessed and led by Him. The Holy Spirit places on his lips the words which he could not find by himself, and at the same time the Holy Spirit predisposes the soul of the hearer to be open and receptive to the Good News and to the kingdom being proclaimed.

Techniques of evangelization are good, but even the most advanced ones could not replace the gentle action of the Spirit. The most perfect preparation of the evangelizer has no effect without the Holy Spirit. Without the Holy Spirit the most convincing dialectic has no power over the heart of man. Without Him the

---

110. Lk. 4:18, 21; cf. Is. 61:1.
111. Jn. 20:22.
112. Acts 2:17.
113. Cf. Acts 4:8.
114. Cf. Acts 9:17.
115. Cf. Acts 6:5, 10; 7:55.
116. Acts 10:44.
117. Acts 9:31.

most highly developed schemas resting on a sociological or psychological basis are quickly seen to be quite valueless.

We live in the Church at a privileged moment of the Spirit. Everywhere people are trying to know Him better, as the Scripture reveals Him. They are happy to place themselves under His inspiration. They are gathering about Him; they want to let themselves be led by Him. Now if the Spirit of God has a preeminent place in the whole life of the Church, it is in her evangelizing mission that He is most active. It is not by chance that the great inauguration of evangelization took place on the morning of Pentecost, under the inspiration of the Spirit.

It must be said that the Holy Spirit is the principal agent of evangelization: It is He who impels each individual to proclaim the Gospel, and it is He who in the depths of consciences causes the word of salvation to be accepted and understood.[118] But it can equally be said that He is the goal of evangelization: He alone stirs up the new creation, the new humanity of which evangelization is to be the result, with that unity in variety which evangelization wishes to achieve within the Christian community. Through the Holy Spirit the Gospel penetrates to the heart of the world, for it is He who causes people to discern the signs of the times—signs willed by God—which evangelization reveals and puts to use within history.

The Bishops' Synod of 1974, which insisted strongly on the place of the Holy Spirit in evangelization, also expressed the desire that pastors and theologians—and we would also say the faithful marked by the seal of the Spirit by Baptism—should study more thoroughly the nature and manner of the Holy Spirit's action in evangelization today. This is our desire too, and we exhort all evangelizers, whoever they may be, to pray without ceasing to the Holy Spirit with faith and fervor and to let themselves prudently be guided by Him as the decisive inspirer of their plans, their initiatives and their evangelizing activity.

---

118. Cf. Second Vatican Ecumenical Council, Decree on the Church's Missionary Activity *Ad gentes*, 4: *AAS* 58 (1966), pp. 950-951.

Authentic Witness of Life

76 Let us now consider the very persons of the evangelizers.

It is often said nowadays that the present century thirsts for authenticity. Especially in regard to young people it is said that they have a horror of the artificial or false and that they are searching above all for truth and honesty.

These "signs of the times" should find us vigilant. Either tacitly or aloud—but always forcefully—we are being asked: Do you really believe what you are proclaiming? Do you live what you believe? Do you really preach what you live? The witness of life has become more than ever an essential condition for real effectiveness in preaching. Precisely because of this we are, to a certain extent, responsible for the progress of the Gospel that we proclaim.

"What is the state of the Church ten years after the Council?" we asked at the beginning of this meditation. Is she firmly established in the midst of the world and yet free and independent enough to call for the world's attention? Does she testify to solidarity with people and at the same time to the divine Absolute? Is she more ardent in contemplation and adoration and more zealous in missionary, charitable and liberating action? Is she ever more committed to the effort to search for the restoration of the complete unity of Christians, a unity that makes more effective the common witness, "so that the world may believe"?[119] We are all responsible for the answers that could be given to these questions.

We therefore address our exhortation to our brethren in the episcopate, placed by the Holy Spirit to govern the Church.[120] We exhort the priests and deacons, the bishops' collaborators in assembling the People of God and in animating spiritually the local communities. We exhort the religious, witnesses of a Church called to holiness and hence themselves invited to a life that bears testimony to the beatitudes of the Gospel. We exhort the laity: Christian families, youth, adults, all those who exercise a trade or profession, leaders, without forgetting the poor who are often rich in faith and hope—all lay people who are conscious of their evangelizing role in the service of their Church or in the midst of

---

119. Jn. 17:21.
120. Cf. Acts 20:28.

society and the world. We say to all of them: Our evangelizing zeal must spring from true holiness of life, and, as the Second Vatican Council suggests, preaching must in its turn make the preacher grow in holiness, which is nourished by prayer and above all by love for the Eucharist.[121]

The world which, paradoxically, despite innumerable signs of the denial of God, is nevertheless searching for Him in unexpected ways and painfully experiencing the need of Him—the world is calling for evangelizers to speak to it of a God whom the evangelists themselves should know and be familiar with as if they could see the invisible.[122] The world calls for and expects from us simplicity of life, the spirit of prayer, charity towards all, especially towards the lowly and the poor, obedience and humility, detachment and self-sacrifice. Without this mark of holiness, our word will have difficulty in touching the heart of modern man. It risks being vain and sterile.

The Search for Unity

77 The power of evangelization will find itself considerably diminished if those who proclaim the Gospel are divided among themselves in all sorts of ways. Is this not perhaps one of the great sicknesses of evangelization today? Indeed, if the Gospel that we proclaim is seen to be rent by doctrinal disputes, ideological polarizations or mutual condemnations among Christians, at the mercy of the latter's differing views on Christ and the Church and even because of their different concepts of society and human institutions, how can those to whom we address our preaching fail to be disturbed, disoriented, even scandalized?

The Lord's spiritual testament tells us that unity among His followers is not only the proof that we are His but also the proof that He is sent by the Father. It is the test of the credibility of Christians and of Christ Himself. As evangelizers, we must offer Christ's faithful not the image of people divided and separated by unedifying quarrels, but the image of people who are mature in faith and

---

121. Cf. Decree on the Ministry and Life of Priests *Presbyterorum ordinis*, 13: *AAS* 58 (1966), p. 1011.
122. Cf. Heb. 11:27.

capable of finding a meeting-point beyond the real tensions, thanks to a shared, sincere and disinterested search for truth. Yes, the destiny of evangelization is certainly bound up with the witness of unity given by the Church. This is a source of responsibility and also of comfort.

At this point we wish to emphasize the sign of unity among all Christians as the way and instrument of evangelization. The division among Christians is a serious reality which impedes the very work of Christ. The Second Vatican Council states clearly and emphatically that this division "damages the most holy cause of preaching the Gospel to all men, and it impedes many from embracing the faith."[123] For this reason, in proclaiming the Holy Year we considered it necessary to recall to all the faithful of the Catholic world that "before all men can be brought together and restored to the grace of God our Father, communion must be re-established between those who by faith have acknowledged and accepted Jesus Christ as the Lord of mercy who sets men free and unites them in the Spirit of love and truth."[124]

And it is with a strong feeling of Christian hope that we look to the efforts being made in the Christian world for this restoration of the full unity willed by Christ. St. Paul assures us that "hope does not disappoint us."[125] While we still work to obtain full unity from the Lord, we wish to see prayer intensified. Moreover we make our own the desire of the Fathers of the Third General Assembly of the Synod of Bishops, for a collaboration marked by greater commitment with the Christian brethren with whom we are not yet united in perfect unity, taking as a basis the foundation of Baptism and the patrimony of faith which is common to us. By doing this we can already give a greater common witness to Christ before the world in the very work of evangelization. Christ's command urges us to do this; the duty of preaching and of giving witness to the Gospel requires this.

---

123. Decree on the Church's Missionary Activity *Ad gentes*, 6: *AAS* 58 (1966), pp. 954-955; cf. Decree on Ecumenism *Unitatis redintegratio*, 1: *AAS* 57 (1965), pp. 90-91.
124. Bull *Apostolorum Limina*, VII: *AAS* 66 (1974), p. 305.
125. Rom. 5:5.

Servants of the Truth

78 The Gospel entrusted to us is also the word of truth. A truth which liberates[126] and which alone gives peace of heart is what people are looking for when we proclaim the Good News to them. The truth about God, about man and his mysterious destiny, about the world; the difficult truth that we seek in the Word of God and of which, we repeat, we are neither the masters nor the owners, but the depositaries, the heralds and the servants.

Every evangelizer is expected to have a reverence for truth, especially since the truth that he studies and communicates is none other than revealed truth and hence, more than any other, a sharing in the first truth which is God Himself. The preacher of the Gospel will therefore be a person who even at the price of personal renunciation and suffering always seeks the truth that he must transmit to others. He never betrays or hides truth out of a desire to please men, in order to astonish or to shock, nor for the sake of originality or a desire to make an impression. He does not refuse truth. He does not obscure revealed truth by being too idle to search for it, or for the sake of his own comfort, or out of fear. He does not neglect to study it. He serves it generously, without making it serve him.

We are the pastors of the faithful people, and our pastoral service impels us to preserve, defend, and to communicate the truth regardless of the sacrifices that this involves. So many eminent and holy pastors have left us the example of this love of truth. In many cases it was an heroic love. The God of truth expects us to be the vigilant defenders and devoted preachers of truth.

Men of learning—whether you be theologians, exegetes or historians—the work of evangelization needs your tireless work of research, and also care and tact in transmitting the truth to which your studies lead you but which is always greater than the heart of man, being the very truth of God.

Parents and teachers, your task—and the many conflicts of the present day do not make it an easy one—is to help your children and your students to discover truth, including religious and spiritual truth.

---

126. Cf. Jn. 8:32.

Animated by Love

79 The work of evangelization presupposes in the evangelizer an ever-increasing love for those whom he is evangelizing. That model evangelizer, the Apostle Paul, wrote these words to the Thessalonians, and they are a program for us all: "With such yearning love we chose to impart to you not only the gospel of God but our very selves, so dear had you become to us."[127] What is this love? It is much more than that of a teacher; it is the love of a father; and again, it is the love of a mother.[128] It is this love that the Lord expects from every preacher of the Gospel, from every builder of the Church. A sign of love will be the concern to give the truth and to bring people into unity. Another sign of love will be a devotion to the proclamation of Jesus Christ, without reservation or turning back. Let us add some other signs of this love.

The first is respect for the religious and spiritual situation of those being evangelized. Respect for their tempo and pace; no one has the right to force them excessively. Respect for their conscience and convictions, which are not to be treated in a harsh manner.

Another sign of this love is concern not to wound the other person, especially if he or she is weak in faith,[129] with statements that may be clear for those who are already initiated but which for the faithful can be a source of bewilderment and scandal, like a wound in the soul.

Yet another sign of love will be the effort to transmit to Christians not doubts and uncertainties born of an erudition poorly assimilated but certainties that are solid because they are anchored in the Word of God. The faithful need these certainties for their Christian life; they have a right to them, as children of God who abandon themselves entirely into His arms and to the exigencies of love.

With the Fervor of the Saints

80 Our appeal here is inspired by the fervor of the greatest preachers and evangelizers, whose lives were devoted to the apos-

---

127. 1 Thes. 2:8; cf. Phil. 1:8.
128. Cf. 1 Thes. 2:7-11; 1 Cor. 4:15; Gal. 4:19.
129. Cf. 1 Cor. 8:9-13; Rom. 14:15.

tolate. Among these we are glad to point out those whom we have proposed to the veneration of the faithful during the course of the Holy Year. They have known how to overcome many obstacles to evangelization.

Such obstacles are also present today, and we shall limit ourself to mentioning the lack of fervor. It is all the more serious because it comes from within. It is manifested in fatigue, disenchantment, compromise, lack of interest and, above all, lack of joy and hope. We exhort all those who have the task of evangelizing, by whatever title and at whatever level, always to nourish spiritual fervor.[130]

This fervor demands first of all that we should know how to put aside the excuses which would impede evangelization. The most insidious of these excuses are certainly the ones which people claim to find support for in such and such a teaching of the Council.

Thus one too frequently hears it said, in various terms, that to impose a truth, be it that of the Gospel, or to impose a way, be it that of salvation, cannot but be a violation of religious liberty. Besides, it is added, why proclaim the Gospel when the whole world is saved by uprightness of heart? We know likewise that the world and history are filled with "seeds of the Word"; is it not therefore an illusion to claim to bring the Gospel where it already exists in the seeds that the Lord Himself has sown?

Anyone who takes the trouble to study in the Council's documents the questions upon which these excuses draw too superficially will find quite a different view.

It would certainly be an error to impose something on the consciences of our brethren. But to propose to their consciences the truth of the Gospel and salvation in Jesus Christ, with complete clarity and with a total respect for the free options which it presents —"without coercion, or dishonorable or unworthy pressure"[131]— far from being an attack on religious liberty is fully to respect that liberty, which is offered the choice of a way that even non-believers consider noble and uplifting. Is it then a crime against others'

---

130. Cf. Rom. 12:11.
131. Cf. Second Vatican Ecumenical Council, Declaration on Religious Liberty *Dignitatis humanae*, 4: *AAS* 58 (1966), p. 933.

freedom to proclaim with joy a Good News which one has come to know through the Lord's mercy?[132] And why should only falsehood and error, debasement and pornography have the right to be put before people and often unfortunately imposed on them by the destructive propaganda of the mass media, by the tolerance of legislation, the timidity of the good and the impudence of the wicked? The respectful presentation of Christ and His kingdom is more than the evangelizer's right; it is his duty. It is likewise the right of his fellow men to receive from him the proclamation of the Good News of salvation. God can accomplish this salvation in whomsoever He wishes by ways which He alone knows.[133] And yet, if His Son came, it was precisely in order to reveal to us, by His word and by His life, the ordinary paths of salvation. And He has commanded us to transmit this revelation to others with His own authority. It would be useful if every Christian and every evangelizer were to pray about the following thought: men can gain salvation also in other ways, by God's mercy, even though we do not preach the Gospel to them; but as for us, can we gain salvation if through negligence or fear or shame—what St. Paul called "blushing for the Gospel"[134]—or as a result of false ideas we fail to preach it? For that would be to betray the call of God, who wishes the seed to bear fruit through the voice of the ministers of the Gospel; and it will depend on us whether this grows into trees and produces its full fruit.

Let us therefore preserve our fervor of spirit. Let us preserve the delightful and comforting joy of evangelizing, even when it is in tears that we must sow. May it mean for us—as it did for John the Baptist, for Peter and Paul, for the other Apostles and for a multitude of splendid evangelizers all through the Church's history—an interior enthusiasm that nobody and nothing can quench. May it be the great joy of our consecrated lives. And may the world of our time, which is searching, sometimes with anguish, sometimes with hope, be enabled to receive the Good News not from evangelizers who are dejected, discouraged, impatient or anxious, but

---

132. Cf. *Ibid.*, 9-14: *loc. cit.*, pp. 935-940.

133. Cf. Second Vatican Ecumenical Council, Decree on the Church's Missionary Activity *Ad gentes*, 7: *AAS* 58 (1966), p. 955.

134. Cf. Rom. 1:16.

from ministers of the Gospel whose lives glow with fervor, who have first received the joy of Christ, and who are willing to risk their lives so that the kingdom may be proclaimed and the Church established in the midst of the world.

CONCLUSION

Heritage of the Holy Year

81 This then, brothers and sons and daughters, is our heartfelt plea. It echoes the voice of our brethren assembled for the Third General Assembly of the Synod of Bishops. This is the task we have wished to give you at the close of a Holy Year which has enabled us to see better than ever the needs and the appeals of a multitude of brethren, both Christians and non-Christians, who await from the Church the Word of salvation.

May the light of the Holy Year, which has shone in the local Churches and in Rome for millions of consciences reconciled with God, continue to shine in the same way after the Jubilee through a program of pastoral action with evangelization as its basic feature, for these years which mark the eve of a new century, the eve also of the third millennium of Christianity.

Mary, Star of Evangelization

82 This is the desire that we rejoice to entrust to the hands and the heart of the Immaculate Blessed Virgin Mary, on this day which is especially consecrated to her and which is also the tenth anniversary of the close of the Second Vatican Council. On the morning of Pentecost she watched over with her prayer the beginning of evangelization prompted by the Holy Spirit: may she be the Star of the evangelization ever renewed which the Church, docile to her Lord's command, must promote and accomplish, especially in these times which are difficult but full of hope!

In the name of Christ we bless you, your communities, your families, all those who are dear to you, in the words which Paul addressed to the Philippians: "I give thanks to my God every time I think of you—which is constantly, in every prayer I utter—rejoicing, as I plead on your behalf, at the way you have all continually helped to promote the gospel.... I hold all of you dear—you who...are sharers of my gracious lot...to defend the solid grounds on which the gospel rests. God himself can testify how much I long for each of you with the affection of Christ Jesus!"[135]

Given in Rome, at St. Peter's, on the Solemnity of the Immaculate Conception of the Blessed Virgin Mary, December 8, 1975, the thirteenth year of our Pontificate.

Pope Paul VI

---

135. Phil. 1:3-4, 7-8.

POPE JOHN PAUL II

Catechesi tradendae, 1979

On Catechesis in Our Time

INTRODUCTION

Christ's Final Command

1 The Church has always considered catechesis one of her primary tasks, for, before Christ ascended to His Father after His resurrection, He gave the Apostles a final command—to make disciples of all nations and to teach them to observe all that He had commanded.[1] He thus entrusted them with the mission and power to proclaim to humanity what they had heard, what they had seen with their eyes, what they had looked upon and touched with their hands, concerning the Word of Life.[2] He also entrusted them with the mission and power to explain with authority what He had taught them, His words and actions, His signs and commandments. And He gave them the Spirit to fulfill this mission.

Very soon the name of catechesis was given to the whole of the efforts within the Church to make disciples, to help people to believe that Jesus is the Son of God, so that believing they might

---

1. Cf. Mt. 28:19-20.
2. Cf. 1 Jn. 1:1.

have life in His name,³ and to educate and instruct them in this life and thus build up the Body of Christ. The Church has not ceased to devote her energy to this task.

Paul VI's Solicitude

2 The most recent Popes gave catechesis a place of eminence in their pastoral solicitude. Through his gestures, his preaching, his authoritative interpretation of the Second Vatican Council (considered by him the great catechism of modern times), and through the whole of his life, my venerated Predecessor Paul VI served the Church's catechesis in a particularly exemplary fashion. On March 18, 1971, he approved the General Catechetical Directory prepared by the Sacred Congregation for the Clergy, a directory that is still the basic document for encouraging and guiding catechetical renewal throughout the Church. He set up the International Council for Catechesis in 1975. He defined in masterly fashion the role and significance of catechesis in the life and mission of the Church when he addressed the participants in the first International Catechetical Congress on September 25, 1971,⁴ and he returned explicitly to the subject in his apostolic exhortation *Evangelii nuntiandi*.⁵ He decided that catechesis, especially that meant for children and young people, should be the theme of the Fourth General Assembly of the Synod of Bishops,⁶ which was held in October 1977 and which I myself had the joy of taking part in.

A Fruitful Synod

3 At the end of that Synod the Fathers presented the Pope with a very rich documentation, consisting of the various interventions

---

3. Cf. Jn. 20:31.
4. Cf. *AAS* 63 (1971), pp. 758-764.
5. Cf. 44; cf. also 45-48 and 54: *AAS* 68 (1976), pp. 34-35; 35-38; 43.
6. According to the Motu Proprio *Apostolica Sollicitudo* of Sept. 15, 1965, the Synod of Bishops can come together in general assembly, in extraordinary assembly or in special assembly. In the present apostolic exhortation the words "Synod," "Synod Fathers" and "Synod hall" always refer, unless otherwise indicated, to the Fourth General Assembly of the Synod of Bishops on catechesis, held in Rome in October 1977.

during the assembly, the conclusions of the working groups, the message that they had with his consent sent to the People of God,[7] and especially the imposing list of "propositions" in which they expressed their views on a very large number of aspects of present-day catechesis.

The Synod worked in an exceptional atmosphere of thanksgiving and hope. It saw in catechetical renewal a precious gift from the Holy Spirit to the Church of today, a gift to which the Christian communities at all levels throughout the world are responding with a generosity and inventive dedication that win admiration. The requisite discernment could then be brought to bear on a reality that is very much alive and it could benefit from great openness among the People of God to the grace of the Lord and the directives of the Magisterium.

Purpose of This Exhortation

4 It is in the same climate of faith and hope that I am today addressing this apostolic exhortation to you, venerable brothers and dear sons and daughters. The theme is extremely vast and the exhortation will keep to only a few of the most topical and decisive aspects of it, as an affirmation of the happy results of the Synod. In essence, the exhortation takes up again the reflections that were prepared by Pope Paul VI, making abundant use of the documents left by the Synod. Pope John Paul I, whose zeal and gifts as a catechist amazed us all, had taken them in hand and was preparing to publish them when he was suddenly called to God. To all of us he gave an example of catechesis at once popular and concentrated on the essential, one made up of simple words and actions that were able to touch the heart. I am therefore taking up the inheritance of these two Popes in response to the request which was expressly formulated by the bishops at the end of the Fourth General Assembly of the Synod and which was welcomed by Pope Paul VI in his closing speech.[8] I am also doing so in order to fulfill

---

7. Cf. *Synodus Episcoporum, De catechesi hoc nostro tempore tradenda praesertim pueris atque iuvenibus, Ad Populum Dei Nuntius,* e Civitate Vaticana, 28-X-1977; cf. *L'Osservatore Romano,* Oct. 30, 1977, pp. 3-4.

8. Cf. *AAS* 69 (1977), p. 633.

one of the chief duties of my apostolic charge. Catechesis has always been a central care in my ministry as a priest and as a bishop.

I ardently desire that this apostolic exhortation to the whole Church should strengthen the solidity of the faith and of Christian living, should give fresh vigor to the initiatives in hand, should stimulate creativity—with the required vigilance—and should help to spread among the communities the joy of bringing the mystery of Christ to the world.

I

WE HAVE BUT ONE TEACHER, JESUS CHRIST

Putting Into Communion With the Person of Christ

5 The Fourth General Assembly of the Synod of Bishops often stressed the Christocentricity of all authentic catechesis. We can here use the word "Christocentricity" in both its meanings, which are not opposed to each other or mutually exclusive, but each of which rather demands and completes the other.

In the first place, it is intended to stress that at the heart of catechesis we find, in essence, a Person, the Person of Jesus of Nazareth, "the only Son from the Father...full of grace and truth,"[9] who suffered and died for us and who now, after rising, is living with us forever. It is Jesus who is "the way, and the truth, and the life,"[10] and Christian living consists in following Christ, the *sequela Christi*.

The primary and essential object of catechesis is, to use an expression dear to St. Paul and also to contemporary theology, "the mystery of Christ." Catechizing is in a way to lead a person to study this mystery in all its dimensions: "to make all men see what is the plan of the mystery...comprehend with all the saints what is

---

9. Jn. 1:14.
10. Jn. 14:6.

the breadth and length and height and depth...know the love of Christ which surpasses knowledge...(and be filled) with all the fullness of God."[11] It is therefore to reveal in the Person of Christ the whole of God's eternal design reaching fulfillment in that Person. It is to seek to understand the meaning of Christ's actions and words and of the signs worked by Him, for they simultaneously hide and reveal His mystery. Accordingly, the definitive aim of catechesis is to put people not only in touch but in communion, in intimacy, with Jesus Christ: Only He can lead us to the love of the Father in the Spirit and make us share in the life of the Holy Trinity.

Transmitting Christ's Teaching

6 Christocentricity in catechesis also means the intention to transmit not one's own teaching or that of some other master, but the teaching of Jesus Christ, the Truth that He communicates or, to put it more precisely, the Truth that He is.[12] We must therefore say that in catechesis it is Christ, the Incarnate Word and Son of God, who is taught—everything else is taught with reference to Him—and it is Christ alone who teaches—anyone else teaches to the extent that he is Christ's spokesman, enabling Christ to teach with his lips. Whatever be the level of his responsibility in the Church, every catechist must constantly endeavor to transmit by his teaching and behavior the teaching and life of Jesus. He will not seek to keep directed towards himself and his personal opinions and attitudes the attention and the consent of the mind and heart of the person he is catechizing. Above all, he will not try to inculcate his personal opinions and options as if they expressed Christ's teaching and the lessons of His life. Every catechist should be able to apply to himself the mysterious words of Jesus: "My teaching is not mine, but his who sent me."[13] St. Paul did this when he was dealing with a question of prime importance: "I received from the

---

11. Eph. 3:9, 18-19.
12. Cf. Jn. 14:6.
13. Jn. 7:16. This is a theme dear to the fourth Gospel: cf. Jn. 3:34; 8:28; 12:49-50; 14:24; 17:8, 14.

Lord what I also delivered to you."[14] What assiduous study of the Word of God transmitted by the Church's Magisterium, what profound familiarity with Christ and with the Father, what a spirit of prayer, what detachment from self must a catechist have in order that he can say: "My teaching is not mine!"

Christ the Teacher

7 This teaching is not a body of abstract truths. It is the communication of the living mystery of God. The Person teaching it in the Gospel is altogether superior in exellence to the "masters" in Israel, and the nature of His doctrine surpasses theirs in every way because of the unique link between what He says, what He does and what He is. Nevertheless, the Gospels clearly relate occasions when Jesus "taught." "Jesus began to do and teach"[15]—with these two verbs, placed at the beginning of the Book of the Acts, St. Luke links and at the same time distinguishes two poles in Christ's mission.

Jesus taught. It is the witness that He gives of Himself: "Day after day I sat in the temple teaching."[16] It is the admiring observation of the evangelists, surprised to see Him teaching everywhere and at all times, teaching in a manner and with an authority previously unknown: "Crowds gathered to him again; and again, as his custom was, he taught them"[17]; "and they were astonished at his teaching, for he taught them as one who had authority."[18] It is also what His enemies note for the purpose of drawing from it grounds for accusation and condemnation: "He stirs up the people, teaching throughout all Judaea, from Galilee even to this place."[19]

---

14. 1 Cor. 11:23: The word "deliver" employed here by St. Paul was frequently repeated in the Apostolic Exhortation *Evangelii nuntiandi* to describe the evangelizing activity of the Church, for example 4, 15, 78, 79.

15. Acts. 1:1.

16. Mt. 26:55; cf. Jn. 18:20.

17. Mk. 10:1.

18. Mk. 1:22; cf. Mt. 5:2; 11:1; 13:54; 22:16; Mk. 2:13; 4:1; 6:2, 6; Lk. 5:3, 17; Jn. 7:14; 8:2, etc.

19. Lk. 23:5.

The One "Teacher"

8 One who teaches in this way has a unique title to the name of "teacher." Throughout the New Testament, especially in the Gospels, how many times is He given this title of teacher![20] Of course the Twelve, the other disciples, and the crowds of listeners call Him "Teacher" in tones of admiration, trust and tenderness.[21] Even the Pharisees and the Sadducees, the doctors of the law, and the Jews in general do not refuse Him the title: "Teacher, we wish to see a sign from you"[22]; "Teacher, what shall I do to inherit eternal life?"[23] But above all, Jesus Himself at particularly solemn and highly significant moments calls Himself Teacher: "You call me teacher and Lord; and you are right, for so I am"[24]; and He proclaims the singularity, the uniqueness of His character as teacher: "You have one teacher,"[25] the Christ. One can understand why people of every kind, race and nation have for 2,000 years in all the languages of the earth given Him this title with veneration, repeating in their own ways the exclamation of Nicodemus: "We know that you are a teacher come from God."[26]

This image of Christ the Teacher is at once majestic and familiar, impressive and reassuring. It comes from the pen of the evangelists and it has often been evoked subsequently in iconography since earliest Christian times,[27] so captivating is it. And I am pleased to evoke it in my turn at the beginning of these considerations on catechesis in the modern world.

---

20. In nearly 50 places in the four Gospels, this title, inherited from the whole Jewish tradition but here given a new meaning that Christ Himself often seeks to emphasize, is attributed to Jesus.

21. Cf., among others, Mt. 8:19; Mk. 4:38; 9:38; 10:35; 13:1; Jn. 11:28.

22. Mt. 12:38.

23. Lk. 10:25; cf. Mt. 22:16.

24. Jn. 13:13-14; cf. also Mt. 10:25; 26:18 and parallel passages.

25. Mt. 23:8. St. Ignatius of Antioch takes up this affirmation and comments as follows: "We have received the faith; this is why we hold fast, in order to be recognized as disciples of Jesus Christ, our only Teacher" *(Epistola ad Magnesios,* IX, 2, Funk 1, 198).

26. Jn. 3:2.

27. The portrayal of Christ as teacher goes back as far as the Roman catacombs. It is frequently used in the mosaics of Romano-Byzantium art of the third and fourth centuries. It was to form a predominant artistic motif in the sculptures of the great Romanesque and Gothic cathedrals of the Middle Ages.

Teaching Through His Life as a Whole

9   In doing so, I am not forgetful that the majesty of Christ the Teacher and the unique consistency and persuasiveness of His teaching can only be explained by the fact that His words, His parables and His arguments are never separable from His life and His very being. Accordingly, the whole of Christ's life was a continual teaching: His silences, His miracles, His gestures, His prayer, His love for people, His special affection for the little and the poor, His acceptance of the total sacrifice on the cross for the redemption of the world, and His resurrection are the actualization of His word and the fulfillment of revelation. Hence for Christians the crucifix is one of the most sublime and popular images of Christ the Teacher.

These considerations follow in the wake of the great traditions of the Church and they all strengthen our fervor with regard to Christ, the Teacher who reveals God to man and man to himself, the Teacher who saves, sanctifies and guides, who lives, who speaks, rouses, moves, redresses, judges, forgives, and goes with us day by day on the path of history, the Teacher who comes and will come in glory.

Only in deep communion with Him will catechists find light and strength for an authentic, desirable renewal of catechesis.

II

AN EXPERIENCE AS OLD AS THE CHURCH

The Mission of the Apostles

10   The image of Christ the Teacher was stamped on the spirit of the Twelve and of the first disciples, and the command "Go... and make disciples of all nations"[28] set the course for the whole of their lives. St. John bears witness to this in his Gospel when he reports the words of Jesus: "No longer do I call you servants, for the servant does not know what his master is doing; but I have

---

28. Mt. 28:19.

called you friends, for all that I have heard from my Father I have made known to you."[29] It was not they who chose to follow Jesus; it was Jesus who chose them, kept them with Him, and appointed them even before His Passover, that they should go and bear fruit and that their fruit should remain.[30] For this reason He formally conferred on them after the resurrection the mission of making disciples of all nations.

The whole of the book of the Acts of the Apostles is a witness that they were faithful to their vocation and to the mission they had received. The members of the first Christian community are seen in it as "devoted to the apostles' teaching and fellowship, to the breaking of bread and the prayers."[31] Without any doubt we find in that a lasting image of the Church being born of and continually nourished by the Word of the Lord, thanks to the teaching of the Apostles, celebrating that Word in the Eucharistic Sacrifice and bearing witness to it before the world in the sign of charity.

When those who opposed the Apostles took offense at their activity, it was because they were "annoyed because (the apostles) were teaching the people"[32] and the order they gave them was not to teach at all in the name of Jesus.[33] But we know that the Apostles considered it right to listen to God rather than to men on this very matter.[34]

Catechesis in the Apostolic Age

11 The Apostles were not slow to share with others the ministry of apostleship.[35] They transmitted to their successors the task of teaching. They entrusted it also to the deacons from the moment of their institution: Stephen, "full of grace and power," taught unceasingly, moved by the wisdom of the Spirit.[36] The

---

29. Jn. 15:15.
30. Cf. Jn. 15:16.
31. Acts 2:42.
32. Acts 4:2.
33. Cf. Acts 4:18; 5:28.
34. Cf. Acts 4:19.
35. Cf. Acts 1:25.
36. Cf. Acts 6:8ff.; cf. also Philip catechizing the minister of the queen of the Ethiopians: Acts 8:26ff.

Apostles associated "many others" with themselves in the task of teaching,[37] and even simple Christians scattered by persecution "went about preaching the word."[38] St. Paul was in a pre-eminent way the herald of this preaching, from Antioch to Rome, where the last picture of him that we have in Acts is that of a person "teaching about the Lord Jesus Christ quite openly."[39] His numerous letters continue and give greater depth to his teaching. The letters of Peter, John, James and Jude are also, in every case, evidence of catechesis in the apostolic age.

Before being written down, the Gospels were the expression of an oral teaching passed on to the Christian communities, and they display with varying degrees of clarity a catechetical structure. St. Matthew's account has indeed been called the catechist's Gospel, and St. Mark's the catechumen's Gospel.

The Fathers of the Church

12 This mission of teaching that belonged to the apostles and their first fellow workers was continued by the Church. Making herself day after day a disciple of the Lord, she earned the title of "Mother and Teacher."[40] From Clement of Rome to Origen,[41] the post-apostolic age saw the birth of remarkable works. Next we see a striking fact: Some of the most impressive bishops and pastors, especially in the third and fourth centuries, considered it an important part of their episcopal ministry to deliver catechetical instructions and write treatises. It was the age of Cyril of Jerusalem and John Chrysostom, of Ambrose and Augustine, the age that saw the

---

37. Cf. Acts 15:35.
38. Acts 8:4.
39. Acts 28:31.
40. Cf. Pope John XXIII, Encyclical *Mater et Magistra* (*AAS* 53 [1961], p. 401): the Church is "mother" because by baptism she unceasingly begets new children and increases God's family; she is "teacher" because she makes her children grow in the grace of their baptism by nourishing their *sensus fidei* through instruction in the truths of faith.

41. Cf. for example the letter of Clement of Rome to the Church of Corinth, the *Didache*, the *Epistola Apostolorum*, the writings of Irenaeus of Lyons (*Demonstratio Apostolicae Praedicationis* and *Adversus Haereses*), of Tertullian (*De Baptismo*), of Clement of Alexandria (*Paedagogus*), of Cyprian (*Testimonia ad Quirinum*), of Origen (*Contra Celsum*), etc.

flowering, from the pen of numerous Fathers of the Church, of works that are still models for us.

It would be impossible here to recall, even very briefly, the catechesis that gave support to the spread and advance of the Church in the various periods of history, in every continent, and in the widest variety of social and cultural contexts. There was indeed no lack of difficulties. But the Word of the Lord completed its course down the centuries; it sped on and triumphed, to use the words of the Apostle Paul.[42]

Councils and Missionary Activity

13 The ministry of catechesis draws ever fresh energy from the councils. The Council of Trent is a noteworthy example of this. It gave catechesis priority in its constitutions and decrees. It lies at the origin of the Roman catechism, which is also known by the name of that council and which is a work of the first rank as a summary of Christian teaching and traditional theology for use by priests. It gave rise to a remarkable organization of catechesis in the Church. It aroused the clergy to their duty of giving catechetical instruction. Thanks to the work of holy theologians such as Saint Charles Borromeo, St. Robert Bellarmine and St. Peter Canisius, it involved the publication of catechisms that were real models for that period. May the Second Vatican Council stir up in our time a like enthusiasm and similar activity.

The missions are also a special area for the application of catechesis. The People of God have thus continued for almost 2,000 years to educate themselves in the Faith in ways adapted to the various situations of believers and the many different circumstances in which the Church finds herself.

Catechesis is intimately bound up with the whole of the Church's life. Not only her geographical extension and numerical increase, but even more, her inner growth and correspondence with God's plan depend essentially on catechesis. It is worthwhile pointing out some of the many lessons to be drawn from the experiences in Church history that we have just recalled.

---

42. Cf. 2 Thes. 3:1.

Catechesis as the Church's Right and Duty

14 To begin with, it is clear that the Church has always looked on catechesis as a sacred duty and an inalienable right. On the one hand, it is certainly a duty springing from a command given by the Lord and resting above all on those who in the new covenant receive the call to the ministry of being pastors. On the other hand, one can likewise speak of a right: From the theological point of view every baptized person, precisely by reason of being baptized, has the right to receive from the Church instruction and education enabling him or her to enter on a truly Christian life; and from the viewpoint of human rights, every human being has the right to seek religious truth and adhere to it freely, that is to say, "without coercion on the part of individuals or of social groups and any human power," in such a way that in this matter of religion, "no one is to be forced to act against his or her conscience or prevented from acting in conformity to it."[43]

That is why catechetical activity should be able to be carried out in favorable circumstances of time and place, and should have access to the mass media and suitable equipment, without discrimination against parents, those receiving catechesis or those imparting it. At present this right is admittedly being given growing recognition, at least on the level of its main principles, as is shown by international declarations and conventions in which, whatever their limitations, one can recognize the desires of the consciences of many people today.[44] But the right is being violated by many States, even to the point that imparting catechesis, having it imparted, and receiving it become punishable offenses. I vigorously raise my voice in union with the Synod Fathers against all discrimination in the field of catechesis, and at the same time I again make a pressing appeal to those in authority to put a complete end to these constraints on human freedom in general and on religious freedom in particular.

---

43. Second Vatican Council, Declaration on Religious Liberty, *Dignitatis humanae*, 2: *AAS* 58 (1966), p. 930.

44. Cf. The Universal Declaration of Human Rights (UNO), December 10, 1948, Art. 18; The International Pact on Civil and Political Rights (UNO), December 16, 1966, Art. 4; Final Act of the Conference on European Security and Cooperation, Para. VII.

Priority of This Task

15   The second lesson concerns the place of catechesis in the Church's pastoral programs. The more the Church, whether on the local or the universal level, gives catechesis priority over other works and undertakings the results of which would be more spectacular, the more she finds in catechesis a strengthening of her internal life as a community of believers and of her external activity as a missionary Church. As the 20th century draws to a close, the Church is bidden by God and by events—each of them a call from Him—to renew her trust in catechetical activity as a prime aspect of her mission. She is bidden to offer catechesis her best resources in people and energy, without sparing effort, toil or material means, in order to organize it better and to train qualified personnel. This is no mere human calculation; it is an attitude of faith. And an attitude of faith always has reference to the faithfulness of God, who never fails to respond.

Shared But Differentiated Responsibility

16   The third lesson is that catechesis always has been and always will be a work for which the whole Church must feel responsible and must wish to be responsible. But the Church's members have different responsibilities, derived from each one's mission. Because of their charge, pastors have, at differing levels, the chief responsibility for fostering, guiding and coordinating catechesis. For his part, the Pope has a lively awareness of the primary responsibility that rests on him in this field: In this he finds reasons for pastoral concern but principally a source of joy and hope. Priests and religious have in catechesis a pre-eminent field for their apostolate. On another level, parents have a unique responsibility. Teachers, the various ministers of the Church, catechists, and also organizers of social communications, all have in various degrees very precise responsibilities in this education of the believing conscience, an education that is important for the life of the Church and affects the life of society as such. It would be one of the best results of the general assembly of the Synod that was entirely devoted to catechesis if it stirred up in the Church as a whole and in each sector of the Church a lively and active awareness of this differentiated but shared responsibility.

Continual Balanced Renewal

17   Finally, catechesis needs to be continually renewed by a certain broadening of its concept, by the revision of its methods, by the search for suitable language, and by the utilization of new means of transmitting the message. Renewal is sometimes unequal in value; the Synod Fathers realistically recognized not only an undeniable advance in the vitality of catechetical activity and promising initiatives, but also the limitations or even "deficiencies" in what has been achieved to date.[45] These limitations are particularly serious when they endanger integrity of content. The message to the People of God rightly stressed that "routine, with its refusal to accept any change, and improvisation, with its readiness for any venture, are equally dangerous" for catechesis.[46] Routine leads to stagnation, lethargy and eventual paralysis. Improvisation begets confusion on the part of those being given catechesis and, when these are children, on the part of their parents; it also begets all kinds of deviations, and the fracturing and eventually the complete destruction of unity. It is important for the Church to give proof today, as she has done at other periods of her history, of evangelical wisdom, courage and fidelity in seeking out and putting into operation new methods and new prospects for catechetical instruction.

III

CATECHESIS IN THE CHURCH'S PASTORAL AND MISSIONARY ACTIVITY

Catechesis as a Stage in Evangelization

18   Catechesis cannot be dissociated from the Church's pastoral and missionary activity as a whole. Nevertheless it has a specific character which was repeatedly the object of inquiry during

---

45. Cf. *Synodus Episcoporum, De catechesi hoc nostro tempore tradenda praesertim pueris atque iuvenibus, Ad Populum Dei Nuntius,* 1: *loc. cit.,* pp. 3-4; cf. *L'Osservatore Romano,* October 30, 1977, p. 3.

46. *Ibid.,* 6; *loc. cit.,* pp. 7-8.

the preparatory work and throughout the course of the Fourth General Assembly of the Synod of Bishops. The question also interests the public both within and outside the Church.

This is not the place for giving a rigorous formal definition of catechesis, which has been sufficiently explained in the General Catechetical Directory.[47] It is for specialists to clarify more and more its concept and divisions.

In view of uncertainties in practice, let us simply recall the essential landmarks—they are already solidly established in Church documents—that are essential for an exact understanding of catechesis and without which there is a risk of failing to grasp its full meaning and import.

All in all, it can be taken here that catechesis is an education of children, young people and adults in the Faith, which includes especially the teaching of Christian doctrine imparted, generally speaking, in an organic and systematic way, with a view to initiating the hearers into the fullness of Christian life. Accordingly, while not being formally identified with them, catechesis is built on a certain number of elements of the Church's pastoral mission that have a catechetical aspect, that prepare for catechesis, or that spring from it. These elements are: the initial proclamation of the Gospel or missionary preaching through the *kerygma* to arouse faith, apologetics or examination of the reasons for belief, experience of Christian living, celebration of the sacraments, integration into the ecclesial community, and apostolic and missionary witness.

Let us first of all recall that there is no separation or opposition between catechesis and evangelization. Nor can the two be simply identified with each other. Instead, they have close links whereby they integrate and complement each other.

The Apostolic Exhortation *Evangelii nuntiandi* of December 8, 1975, on evangelization in the modern world, rightly stressed that evangelization—which has the aim of bringing the Good News to the whole of humanity, so that all may live by it—is a rich, complex and dynamic reality, made up of elements, or one could say moments, that are essential and different from each other, and that

---

47. Sacred Congregation for the Clergy, *Directorium Catechisticum Generale*, 17-35; *AAS* 64 (1972), pp. 110-118.

must all be kept in view simultaneously.[48] Catechesis is one of these moments—a very remarkable one—in the whole process of evangelization.

Catechesis and the Initial Proclamation of the Gospel

19 The specific character of catechesis, as distinct from the initial conversion-bringing proclamation of the Gospel, has the two-fold objective of maturing the initial faith and of educating the true disciple of Christ by means of a deeper and more systematic knowledge of the Person and the message of our Lord Jesus Christ.[49]

But in catechetical practice, this model order must allow for the fact that the initial evangelization has often not taken place. A certain number of children baptized in infancy come for catechesis in the parish without receiving any other initiation into the Faith and still without any explicit personal attachment to Jesus Christ; they only have the capacity to believe placed within them by Baptism and the presence of the Holy Spirit; and opposition is quickly created by the prejudices of their non-Christian family background or of the positivist spirit of their education. In addition, there are other children who have not been baptized and whose parents agree only at a later date to religious education: For practical reasons, the catechumenal stage of these children will often be carried out largely in the course of the ordinary catechesis. Again, many pre-adolescents and adolescents who have been baptized and been given a systematic catechesis and the sacraments still remain hesitant for a long time about committing their whole lives to Jesus Christ—if, moreover, they do not attempt to avoid religious education in the name of their freedom. Finally, even adults are not safe from temptations to doubt or to abandon their Faith, especially as a result of their unbelieving surroundings. This means that "catechesis" must often concern itself not only with nourishing and teaching the Faith, but also with arousing it unceasingly with the

---

48. Cf. 17-24: *AAS* 68 (1976), pp. 17-22.
49. Cf. *Synodus Episcoporum, De catechesi hoc nostro tempore tradenda praesertim pueris atque iuvenibus, Ad Populum Dei Nuntius,* 1: *loc. cit.*, pp. 3-4; cf. *L'Osservatore Romano,* October 30, 1977, p. 3.

help of grace, with opening the heart, with converting, and with preparing total adherence to Jesus Christ on the part of those who are still on the threshold of faith. This concern will in part decide the tone, the language and the method of catechesis.

Specific Aim of Catechesis

20 Nevertheless, the specific aim of catechesis is to develop, with God's help, an as yet initial faith, and to advance in fullness and to nourish day by day the Christian life of the faithful, young and old. It is in fact a matter of giving growth, at the level of knowledge and in life, to the seed of faith sown by the Holy Spirit with the initial proclamation and effectively transmitted by Baptism.

Catechesis aims, therefore, at developing understanding of the mystery of Christ in the light of God's Word, so that the whole of a person's humanity is impregnated by that Word. Changed by the working of grace into a new creature, the Christian thus sets himself to follow Christ and learns more and more within the Church to think like Him, to judge like Him, to act in conformity with His commandments, and to hope as He invites us to.

To put it more precisely: Within the whole process of evangelization, the aim of catechesis is to be the teaching and maturation stage, that is to say, the period in which the Christian, having accepted by faith the Person of Jesus Christ as the one Lord and having given Him complete adherence by sincere conversion of heart, endeavors to know better this Jesus to whom he has entrusted himself: to know His "mystery," the kingdom of God proclaimed by Him, the requirements and promises contained in His Gospel message, and the paths that He has laid down for anyone who wishes to follow Him.

It is true that being a Christian means saying "yes" to Jesus Christ, but let us remember that this "yes" has two levels: It consists in surrendering to the Word of God and relying on it, but it also means, at a later stage, endeavoring to know better and better the profound meaning of this Word.

Need for Systematic Catechesis

21 In his closing speech at the Fourth General Assembly of the Synod, Pope Paul VI rejoiced "to see how everyone drew attention to the absolute need for systematic catechesis, precisely because it is this reflective study of the Christian mystery that fundamentally distinguishes catechesis from all other ways of presenting the Word of God."[50]

In view of practical difficulties, attention must be drawn to some of the characteristics of this instruction:

—It must be systematic, not improvised but programmed to reach a precise goal;

—It must deal with essentials, without any claim to tackle all disputed questions or to transform itself into theological research or scientific exegesis;

—It must nevertheless be sufficiently complete, not stopping short at the initial proclamation of the Christian mystery such as we have in the *kerygma;*

—It must be an integral Christian initiation, open to all the other factors of Christian life.

I am not forgetting the interest of the many different occasions for catechesis connected with personal, family, social and ecclesial life—these occasions must be utilized, and I shall return to them in Chapter VI—but I am stressing the need for organic and systematic Christian instruction, because of the tendency in various quarters to minimize its importance.

Catechesis and Life Experience

22 It is useless to play off orthopraxis against orthodoxy: Christianity is inseparably both. Firm and well-thought-out convictions lead to courageous and upright action; the endeavor to educate the faithful to live as disciples of Christ today calls for and facilitates a discovery in depth of the mystery of Christ in the history of salvation.

---

50. Concluding Address to the Synod, October 29, 1977: *AAS* 69 (1977), p. 634.

It is also quite useless to campaign for the abandonment of serious and orderly study of the message of Christ in the name of a method concentrating on life experience. "No one can arrive at the whole truth on the basis solely of some simple private experience, that is to say, without an adequate explanation of the message of Christ, who is 'the way, and the truth, and the life' (Jn. 14:6)."[51]

Nor is any opposition to be set up between a catechesis taking life as its point of departure and a traditional doctrinal and systematic catechesis.[52] Authentic catechesis is always an orderly and systematic initiation into the revelation that God has given of Himself to humanity in Christ Jesus, a revelation stored in the depths of the Church's memory and in Sacred Scripture, and constantly communicated from one generation to the next by a living, active *traditio*. This revelation is not, however, isolated from life or artificially juxtaposed to it. It is concerned with the ultimate meaning of life, and it illumines the whole of life with the light of the Gospel, to inspire it or to question it.

That is why we can apply to catechists an expression used by the Second Vatican Council with special reference to priests: "Instructors (of the human being and his life) in the faith."[53]

Catechesis and Sacraments

23 Catechesis is intrinsically linked with the whole of liturgical and sacramental activity, for it is in the sacraments, especially in the Eucharist, that Christ Jesus works in fullness for the transformation of human beings.

In the early Church, the catechumenate and preparation for the sacraments of Baptism and the Eucharist were the same thing. Although in the countries that have long been Christian the Church has changed her practice in this field, the catechumenate has never been abolished; on the contrary, it is experiencing a renewal in

---

51. *Ibid.*
52. *Directorium Catechisticum Generale*, 40 and 46: *AAS* 64 (1972), pp. 121 and 124-125.
53. Cf. Decree on the Ministry and Life of Priests, *Presbyterorum ordinis*, 6: *AAS* 58 (1966), p. 999.

those countries[54] and is abundantly practiced in the young missionary Churches. In any case, catechesis always has reference to the sacraments. On the one hand, the catechesis that prepares for the sacraments is an eminent kind, and every form of catechesis necessarily leads to the sacraments of faith. On the other hand, authentic practice of the sacraments is bound to have a catechetical aspect. In other words, sacramental life is impoverished and very soon turns into hollow ritualism if it is not based on serious knowledge of the meaning of the sacraments, and catechesis becomes intellectualized if it fails to come alive in the sacramental practice.

Catechesis and Ecclesial Community

24 Finally, catechesis is closely linked with the responsible activity of the Church and of Christians in the world. A person who has given adherence to Jesus Christ by faith and is endeavoring to consolidate that faith by catechesis needs to live in communion with those who have taken the same step. Catechesis runs the risk of becoming barren if no community of faith and Christian life takes the catechumen in at a certain stage of his catechesis. That is why the ecclesial community at all levels has a twofold responsibility with regard to catechesis: It has the responsibility of providing for the training of its members, but it also has the responsibility of welcoming them into an environment where they can live as fully as possible what they have learned.

Catechesis is likewise open to missionary dynamism. If catechesis is done well, Christians will be eager to bear witness to their Faith, to hand it on to their children, to make it known to others, and to serve the human community in every way.

Catechesis in the Wide Sense Necessary for Maturity and Strength of Faith

25 Thus through catechesis the Gospel *kerygma* (the initial ardent proclamation by which a person is one day overwhelmed and brought to the decision to entrust himself to Jesus Christ by

---

54. Cf. *Ordo Initiationis Christianae Adultorum.*

faith) is gradually deepened, developed in its implicit consequences, explained in language that includes an appeal to reason, and channelled towards Christian practice in the Church and the world. All this is no less evangelical than the *kerygma*, in spite of what is said by certain people who consider that catechesis necessarily rationalizes, dries up and eventually kills all that is living, spontaneous and vibrant in the *kerygma*. The truths studied in catechesis are the same truths that touched the person's heart when he heard them for the first time. Far from blunting or exhausting them, the fact of knowing them better should make them even more challenging and decisive for one's life.

In the understanding expounded here, catechesis keeps the entirely pastoral perspective with which the Synod viewed it. This broad meaning of catechesis in no way contradicts but rather includes and goes beyond a narrow meaning which was once commonly given to catechesis in didactic expositions, namely, the simple teaching of the formulas that express faith.

In the final analysis, catechesis is necessary both for the maturation of the faith of Christians and for their witness in the world: It is aimed at bringing Christians to "attain to the unity of the faith and of the knowledge of the Son of God, to mature manhood, to the measure of the stature of the fullness of Christ"[55]; it is also aimed at making them prepared to make a defense to anyone who calls them to account for the hope that is in them.[56]

IV

THE WHOLE OF THE GOOD NEWS DRAWN FROM ITS SOURCE

Content of the Message

26   Since catechesis is a moment or aspect of evangelization, its content cannot be anything else but the content of evangelization as a whole. The one message—the Good News of salvation—that has been heard once or hundreds of times and has been accepted with the heart is in catechesis probed unceasingly by

---

55. Eph. 4:13.
56. Cf. 1 Pt. 3:15.

reflection and systematic study, by awareness of its repercussions on one's personal life—an awareness calling for ever greater commitment—and by inserting it into an organic and harmonious whole, namely, Christian living in society and the world.

The Source

27 Catechesis will always draw its content from the living source of the Word of God transmitted in Tradition and the Scriptures, for "sacred Tradition and Sacred Scripture make up a single sacred deposit of the Word of God, which is entrusted to the Church," as was recalled by the Second Vatican Council, which desired that "the ministry of the word—pastoral preaching, catechetics and all forms of Christian instruction...—(should be) healthily nourished and (should) thrive in holiness through the word of Scripture."[57]

To speak of Tradition and Scripture as the source of catechesis is to draw attention to the fact that catechesis must be impregnated and penetrated by the thought, the spirit and the outlook of the Bible and the Gospels through assiduous contact with the texts themselves; but it is also a reminder that catechesis will be all the richer and more effective for reading the texts with the intelligence and the heart of the Church and for drawing inspiration from the 2,000 years of the Church's reflection and life.

The Church's teaching, liturgy and life spring from this source and lead back to it, under the guidance of the pastors and, in particular, of the doctrinal Magisterium entrusted to them by the Lord.

The Creed, an Exceptionally Important Expression of Doctrine

28 An exceptionally important expression of the living heritage placed in the custody of the pastors is found in the Creed or, to put it more concretely, in the Creeds that at crucial moments

---

57. Dogmatic Constitution on Divine Revelation *Dei Verbum*, 10 and 24: *AAS* 58 (1966), pp. 822 and 828-829; cf. also Sacred Congregation for the Clergy, *Directorium Catechisticum Generale*, 45 (*AAS* 64 [1972], p. 124), where the principal and complementary sources of catechesis are well set out.

have summed up the Church's Faith in felicitous syntheses. In the course of the centuries an important element of catechesis was constituted by the *traditio Symboli* (transmission of the summary of the Faith), followed by the transmission of the Lord's Prayer. This expressive rite has in our time been reintroduced into the initiation of catechumens.[58] Should not greater use be made of an adapted form of it to mark that most important stage at which a new disciple of Jesus Christ accepts with full awareness and courage the content of what will from then on be the object of his earnest study?

In the Creed of the People of God, proclaimed at the close of the 19th centenary of the martyrdom of the Apostles Peter and Paul, my Predecessor Paul VI decided to bring together the essential elements of the Catholic Faith, especially those that presented greater difficulty or risked being ignored.[59] This is a sure point of reference for the content of catechesis.

Factors That Must Not Be Neglected

29   In the third chapter of his Apostolic Exhortation *Evangelii nuntiandi*, the same Pope recalled "the essential content, the living substance" of evangelization.[60] Catechesis, too, must keep in mind each of these factors and also the living synthesis of which they are part.[61]

---

58. Cf. *Ordo Initiationis Christianae Adultorum*, 25-26; 183-187.

59. Cf. *AAS* 60 (1968), pp. 436-445. Besides these great professions of faith of the Magisterium, note also the popular professions of faith, rooted in the traditional Christian culture of certain countries; cf. what I said to the young people at Gniezno, June 3, 1979, regarding the *Bogurodzica* song-message: "This is not only a song: It is also a profession of faith, a symbol of the Polish Credo; it is a catechesis and also a document of Christian education. The principal truths of Faith and the principles of morality are contained here. This is not only a historical object. It is a document of life. (It has even been called 'the Polish catechism' " [*AAS* 71, 1979], p. 754.)

60. 25: *AAS* 68 (1976), p. 23.

61. *Ibid.*, especially 26-39; *loc. cit.*, pp. 23-25; the "principal elements of the Christian message" are presented in a more systematic fashion in the *Directorium Catechisticum Generale*, 47-69 *(AAS* 64 [1972], pp. 125-141), where one also finds the norm for the essential doctrinal content of catechesis.

I shall therefore limit myself here simply to recalling one or two points.[62] Anyone can see, for instance, how important it is to make the child, the adolescent, the person advancing in faith understand "what can be known about God"[63]; to be able in a way to tell them: "What you worship as unknown, this I proclaim to you"[64]; to set forth briefly for them[65] the mystery of the Word of God become Man and accomplishing man's salvation by His Passover, that is to say, through His death and resurrection, but also by His preaching, by the signs worked by Him, and by the sacraments of His permanent presence in our midst. The Synod Fathers were indeed inspired when they asked that care should be taken not to reduce Christ to His humanity alone or His message to a no more than earthly dimension, but that He should be recognized as the Son of God, the Mediator giving us in the Spirit free access to the Father.[66]

It is important to display before the eyes of the intelligence and of the heart, in the light of faith, the sacrament of Christ's presence constituted by the mystery of the Church, which is an assembly of human beings who are sinners and yet have at the same time been sanctified and who make up the family of God gathered together by the Lord under the guidance of those whom "the Holy Spirit has made...guardians, to feed the Church of God."[67]

It is important to explain that the history of the human race, marked as it is by grace and sin, greatness and misery, is taken up by God in His Son Jesus, "foreshadowing in some way the age which is to come."[68]

Finally, it is important to reveal frankly the demands —demands that involve self-denial but also joy—made by what the Apostle Paul liked to call "newness of life,"[69] "a new creation,"[70]

---

62. Consult also on this point the *Directorium Catechisticum Generale*, 37-46 (*loc. cit.*, pp. 120-125).
63. Rom. 1:19.
64. Acts 17:23.
65. Cf. Eph. 3:3.
66. Cf. Eph. 2:18.
67. Acts 20:28.
68. Second Vatican Council, Pastoral Constitution on the Church in the Modern World *Gaudium et spes*, 39: *AAS* 58 (1966), pp. 1056-1057.
69. Rom. 6:4.
70. 2 Cor. 5:17.

being in Christ,[71] and "eternal life in Christ Jesus,"[72] which is the same thing as life in the world but lived in accordance with the beatitudes and called to an extension and transfiguration hereafter.

Hence the importance in catechesis of personal moral commitments in keeping with the Gospel and of Christian attitudes, whether heroic or very simple, to life and the world—what we call the Christian or evangelical virtues. Hence also, in its endeavor to educate faith, the concern of catechesis not to omit but to clarify properly realities such as man's activity for his integral liberation,[73] the search for a society with greater solidarity and fraternity, the fight for justice and the building of peace.

Besides, it is not to be thought that this dimension of catechesis is altogether new. As early as the patristic age, St. Ambrose and St. John Chrysostom—to quote only them—gave prominence to the social consequences of the demands made by the Gospel. Close to our own time, the catechism of St. Pius X explicitly listed oppressing the poor and depriving workers of their just wages among the sins that cry to God for vengeance.[74] Since *Rerum novarum* especially, social concern has been actively present in the catechetical teaching of the Popes and the bishops. Many Synod Fathers rightly insisted that the rich heritage of the Church's social teaching should, in appropriate forms, find a place in the general catechetical education of the faithful.

Integrity of Content

30   With regard to the content of catechesis, three important points deserve special attention today.

The first point concerns the integrity of the content. In order that the sacrificial offering of his or her faith[75] should be perfect, the person who becomes a disciple of Christ has the right to receive "the word of faith"[76] not in mutilated, falsified or diminished form

---

71. Cf. *ibid.*
72. Rom. 6:23.
73. Cf. Pope Paul VI, Apostolic Exhortation, *Evangelii nuntiandi*, 30-38: *AAS* 68 (1976), pp. 25-30.
74. Cf. *Catechismo Maggiore*, Fifth Part, Chap. 6. 965-966.
75. Cf. Phil. 2:17.
76. Rom. 10:8.

but whole and entire, in all its rigor and vigor. Unfaithfulness on some point to the integrity of the message means a dangerous weakening of catechesis and putting at risk the results that Christ and the ecclesial community have a right to expect from it. It is certainly not by chance that the final command of Jesus in Matthew's Gospel bears the mark of a certain entireness: "All authority...has been given to me...make disciples of all nations...teaching them to observe all...I am with you always." This is why, when a person first becomes aware of "the surpassing worth of knowing Christ Jesus,"[77] whom he has encountered by faith, and has the perhaps unconscious desire to know Him more extensively and better, "hearing about Him and being taught in Him, as the truth is in Jesus,"[78] there is no valid pretext for refusing him any part whatever of that knowledge. What kind of catechesis would it be that failed to give their full place to man's creation and sin; to God's plan of redemption and its long, loving preparation and realization; to the incarnation of the Son of God; to Mary, the Immaculate One, the Mother of God, ever Virgin, raised body and soul to the glory of heaven, and to her role in the mystery of salvation; to the mystery of lawlessness at work in our lives[79] and the power of God freeing us from it; to the need for penance and asceticism; to the sacramental and liturgical actions; to the reality of the Eucharistic Presence; to participation in divine life here and hereafter, and so on? Thus, no true catechist can lawfully, on his own initiative, make a selection of what he considers important in the deposit of faith as opposed to what he considers unimportant, so as to teach the one and reject the other.

By Means of Suitable Pedagogical Methods

31   This gives rise to a second remark. It can happen that in the present situation of catechesis reasons of method or pedagogy suggest that the communication of the riches of the content of catechesis should be organized in one way rather than another. Besides, integrity does not dispense from balance and from the

---

77. Phil. 3:8.
78. Cf. Eph. 4:20-21.
79. Cf. 2 Thes. 2:7.

organic hierarchical character through which the truths to be taught, the norms to be transmitted, and the ways of Christian life to be indicated will be given the proper importance due to each. It can also happen that a particular sort of language proves preferable for transmitting this content to a particular individual or group. The choice made will be a valid one to the extent that, far from being dictated by more or less subjective theories or prejudices stamped with a certain ideology, it is inspired by the humble concern to stay closer to a content that must remain intact. The method and language used must truly be means for communicating the whole and not just a part of "the words of eternal life"[80] and the "ways of life."[81]

Ecumenical Dimension of Catechesis

32 The great movement, one certainly inspired by the Spirit of Jesus, that has for some years been causing the Catholic Church to seek with other Christian Churches or confessions the restoration of the perfect unity willed by the Lord, brings me to the question of the ecumenical character of catechesis. This movement reached its full prominence in the Second Vatican Council[82] and since then has taken on a new extension within the Church, as is shown concretely by the impressive series of events and initiatives with which everyone is now familiar.

Catechesis cannot remain aloof from this ecumenical dimension, since all the faithful are called to share, according to their capacity and place in the Church, in the movement towards unity.[83]

Catechesis will have an ecumenical dimension if, while not ceasing to teach that the fullness of the revealed truths and of the means of salvation instituted by Christ is found in the Catholic

---

80. Jn. 6:69; cf. Acts 5:20; 7:38.

81. Acts 2:28, quoting Ps. 16:11.

82. Cf. the entire Decree on Ecumenism *Unitatis redintegratio: AAS* 57 (1965), pp. 90-112.

83. Cf. *ibid.*, 5: *loc. cit.*, p. 96; cf. also Second Vatican Council, Decree on the Missionary Activity of the Church *Ad gentes*, 15: *AAS* 58 (1966), pp. 963-965; Sacred Congregation for the Clergy, *Directorium Catechisticum Generale* 27: *AAS* 64 (1972), p. 115.

Church,[84] it does so with sincere respect, in words and in deeds, for the ecclesial communities that are not in perfect communion with this Church.

In this context, it is extremely important to give a correct and fair presentation of the other Churches and ecclesial communities that the Spirit of Christ does not refrain from using as means of salvation; "moreover, some, even very many, of the outstanding elements and endowments which together go to build up and give life to the Church herself, can exist outside the visible boundaries of the Catholic Church."[85] Among other things this presentation will help Catholics to have both a deeper understanding of their own Faith and a better acquaintance with and esteem for their other Christian brethren, thus facilitating the shared search for the way towards full unity in the whole truth. It should also help non-Catholics to have a better knowledge and appreciation of the Catholic Church and her conviction of being the "universal help toward salvation."

Catechesis will have an ecumenical dimension if, in addition, it creates and fosters a true desire for unity. This will be true all the more if it inspires serious efforts—including the effort of self-purification in the humility and the fervor of the Spirit in order to clear the ways—with a view not to facile irenics made up of omissions and concessions on the level of doctrine, but to perfect unity, when and by what means the Lord will wish.

Finally, catechesis will have an ecumenical dimension if it tries to prepare Catholic children and young people, as well as adults, for living in contact with non-Catholics, affirming their Catholic identity while respecting the faith of others.

Ecumenical Collaboration in the Field of Catechesis

33 In situations of religious plurality, the bishops can consider it opportune or even necessary to have certain experiences of collaboration in the field of catechesis between Catholics and other Christians, complementing the normal catechesis that must in any

---

84. Cf. Second Vatican Council, Decree on Ecumenism *Unitatis redintegratio*, 3-4: *AAS* 57 (1965), pp. 92-96.

85. *Ibid.*, 3: *loc. cit.*, p. 93.

case be given to Catholics. Such experiences have a theological foundation in the elements shared by all Christians.[86] But the communion of faith between Catholics and other Christians is not complete and perfect; in certain cases there are even profound divergences. Consequently, this ecumenical collaboration is by its very nature limited: It must never mean a "reduction" to a common minimum. Furthermore, catechesis does not consist merely in the teaching of doctrine: It also means initiating into the whole of Christian life, bringing full participation in the sacraments of the Church. Therefore, where there is an experience of ecumenical collaboration in the field of catechesis, care must be taken that the education of Catholics in the Catholic Church should be well ensured in matters of doctrine and of Christian living.

During the Synod, a certain number of bishops drew attention to what they referred to as the increasingly frequent cases in which the civil authority or other circumstances impose on the schools in some countries a common instruction in the Christian religion, with common textbooks, class periods, etc., for Catholics and non-Catholics alike. Needless to say, this is not true catechesis. But this teaching also has ecumenical importance when it presents Christian doctrine fairly and honestly. In cases where circumstances impose it, it is important that in addition a specifically Catholic catechesis should be ensured with all the greater care.

The Question of Textbooks Dealing with the Various Religions

34 At this point another observation must be made on the same lines but from a different point of view. State schools sometimes provide their pupils with books that for cultural reasons (history, morals or literature) present the various religions, including the Catholic religion. An objective presentation of historical events, of the different religions and of the various Christian confessions can make a contribution here to better mutual understanding. Care will then be taken that every effort is made to ensure that the presentation is truly objective and free from the distorting

---

86. Cf. *ibid.*; cf. also Dogmatic Constitution on the Church *Lumen gentium*, 15: *AAS* 57 (1965), p. 19.

influence of ideological and political systems or of prejudices with claims to be scientific. In any case, such schoolbooks can obviously not be considered catechetical works: They lack both the witness of believers stating their faith to other believers and an understanding of the Christian mysteries and of what is specific about Catholicism, as these are understood within the faith.

V

EVERYBODY NEEDS
TO BE CATECHIZED

The Importance of Children and the Young

35 The theme designated by my Predecessor Paul VI for the Fourth General Assembly of the Synod of Bishops was: "Catechesis in our time, with special reference to the catechesis of children and young people." The increase in the number of young people is without doubt a fact charged with hope and at the same time with anxiety for a large part of the contemporary world. In certain countries, especially those of the Third World, more than half of the population is under 25 or 30 years of age. This means millions and millions of children and young people preparing for their adult future. And there is more than just the factor of numbers: Recent events, as well as the daily news, tell us that, although this countless multitude of young people is here and there dominated by uncertainty and fear, seduced by the escapism of indifference or drugs, or tempted by nihilism and violence, nevertheless it constitutes in its major part the great force that amid many hazards is set on building the civilization of the future.

In our pastoral care we ask ourselves: How are we to reveal Jesus Christ, God made Man, to this multitude of children and young people, reveal Him not just in the fascination of a first fleeting encounter but through an acquaintance, growing deeper and clearer daily, with Him, His message, the plan of God that He has revealed, the call He addresses to each person, and the kingdom that He wishes to establish in this world with the "little flock"[87] of

---

87. Lk. 12:32.

those who believe in Him, a kingdom that will be complete only in eternity? How are we to enable them to know the meaning, the import, the fundamental requirements, the law of love, the promises and the hopes of this kingdom?

There are many observations that could be made about the special characteristics that catechesis assumes at the different stages of life.

Infants

36 One moment that is often decisive is the one at which the very young child receives the first elements of catechesis from its parents and the family surroundings. These elements will perhaps be no more than a simple revelation of a good and provident Father in heaven to whom the child learns to turn its heart. The very short prayers that the child learns to lisp will be the start of a loving dialogue with this hidden God whose word it will then begin to hear. I cannot insist too strongly on this early initiation by Christian parents in which the child's faculties are integrated into a living relationship with God. It is a work of prime importance. It demands great love and profound respect for the child who has a right to a simple and true presentation of the Christian faith.

Children

37 For the child there comes soon, at school and in Church, in institutions connected with the parish or with the spiritual care of the Catholic or state school not only an introduction into a wider social circle, but also the moment for a catechesis aimed at inserting him or her organically into the life of the Church, a moment that includes an immediate preparation for the celebration of the sacraments. This catechesis is didactic in character, but is directed towards the giving of witness in the faith. It is an initial catechesis but not a fragmentary one, since it will have to reveal, although in an elementary way, all the principal mysteries of faith and their effects on the child's moral and religious life, it is a catechesis that gives meaning to the sacraments, but at the same time it receives from the experience of the sacraments a living dimension that keeps it from remaining merely doctrinal, and it communicates to the child the joy of being a witness to Christ in ordinary life.

Adolescents

38 Next comes puberty and adolescence, with all the greatness and dangers which that age brings. It is the time of discovering oneself and one's own inner world, the time of generous plans, the time when the feeling of love awakens, with the biological impulses of sexuality, the time of the desire to be together, the time of a particularly intense joy connected with the exhilarating discovery of life. But often it is also the age of deeper questioning, of anguished or even frustrating searching, of a certain mistrust of others and dangerous introspection, and the age sometimes of the first experiences of setbacks and of disappointments. Catechesis cannot ignore these changeable aspects of this delicate period of life. A catechesis capable of leading the adolescent to re-examine his or her life and to engage in dialogue, a catechesis that does not ignore the adolescent's great questions—self-giving, belief, love and the means of expressing it constituted by sexuality—such a catechesis can be decisive. The revelation of Jesus Christ as a Friend, Guide and Model, capable of being admired but also imitated; the revelation of this message which provides an answer to the fundamental questions; the revelation of the loving plan of Christ the Savior as the Incarnation of the only authentic love and as the possibility of uniting the human race—all this can provide the basis for genuine education in faith. Above all, the mysteries of the passion and death of Jesus, through which, according to St. Paul, He merited His glorious resurrection, can speak eloquently to the adolescent's conscience and heart and cast light on his first sufferings and on the suffering of the world that he is discovering.

The Young

39 With youth comes the moment of the first great decisions. Although the young may enjoy the support of the members of their family and their friends, they have to rely on themselves and their own conscience and must ever more frequently and decisively assume responsibility for their destiny. Good and evil, grace and sin, life and death will more and more confront one another within them, not just as moral categories but chiefly as fundamental options which they must accept or reject lucidly, conscious of their own responsibility. It is obvious that a catechesis which denounces selfishness in the name of generosity, and which without any illusory over-simplification presents the Christian meaning of work, of the common good, of justice and charity, a catechesis on international peace and on the advancement of human dignity, on development, and on liberation, as these are presented in recent documents of the Church,[88] fittingly completes in the minds of the young the good catechesis on strictly religious realities which is never to be neglected. Catechesis then takes on considerable importance, since it is the time when the Gospel can be presented, understood and accepted as capable of giving meaning to life and thus of inspiring attitudes that would have no other explanation, such as self-sacrifice, detachment, forbearance, justice, commitment, reconciliation, a sense of the Absolute and the unseen. All these are traits that distinguish a young person from his or her companions as a disciple of Jesus Christ.

Catechesis thus prepares for the important Christian commitments of adult life. For example, it is certain that many vocations to the priesthood and religious life have their origin during a well-imparted catechesis in infancy and adolescence.

From infancy until the threshold of maturity, catechesis is thus a permanent school of the faith and follows the major stages of life, like a beacon lighting the path of the child, the adolescent and the young person.

The Adaptation of Catechesis for Young People

40 It is reassuring to note that, during the Fourth General Assembly of the Synod and the following years, the Church has widely shared in concern about how to impart catechesis to children and young people. God grant that the attention thus

---

88. Cf., for example, Second Vatican Council, Pastoral Constitution on the Church in the Modern World *Gaudium et spes, AAS* 58 (1966), pp. 1025-1120; Pope Paul VI, Encyclical *Populorum progressio: AAS* 59 (1967), pp. 257-299; Apostolic Letter *Octogesima adveniens: AAS* 63 (1971), pp. 401-441; Apostolic Exhortation *Evangelii nuntiandi: AAS* 68 (1976), pp. 5-76.

aroused will long endure in the Church's consciousness. In this way the Synod has been valuable for the whole Church by seeking to trace with the greatest possible precision the complex characteristics of present-day youth; by showing that these young persons speak a language into which the message of Jesus must be translated with patience and wisdom and without betrayal; by demonstrating that, in spite of appearances, these young people have within them, even though often in a confused way, not just a readiness or openness, but rather a real desire to know "Jesus...who is called Christ"[89]; and by indicating that if the work of catechesis is to be carried out rigorously and seriously, it is today more difficult and tiring than ever before, because of the obstacles and difficulties of all kinds that it meets; but it is also more consoling, because of the depth of the response it receives from children and young people. This is a treasure which the Church can and should count on in the years ahead.

The Handicapped

41 Children and young people who are physically or mentally handicapped come first to mind. They have a right, like others of their age, to know "the mystery of faith." The greater difficulties that they encounter give greater merit to their efforts and to those of their teachers. It is pleasant to see that Catholic organizations especially dedicated to young handicapped people contributed to the Synod a renewed desire to deal better with this important problem. They deserve to be given warm encouragement in this endeavor.

Young People Without Religious Support

42 My thoughts turn next to the ever-increasing number of children and young people born and brought up in a non-Christian or at least non-practicing home but who wish to know the Christian faith. They must be ensured a catechesis attuned to them, so

---

89. Mt. 1:16.

that they will be able to grow in faith and live by it more and more, in spite of the lack of support or even the opposition they meet in their surroundings.

Adults

43 To continue the series of receivers of catechesis, I cannot fail to emphasize now one of the most constant concerns of the Synod Fathers, a concern imposed with vigor and urgency by present experiences throughout the world: I am referring to the central problem of the catechesis of adults. This is the principal form of catechesis, because it is addressed to persons who have the greatest responsibilities and the capacity to live the Christian message in its fully developed form.[90] The Christian community cannot carry out a permanent catechesis without the direct and skilled participation of adults, whether as receivers or as promoters of catechetical activity. The world, in which the young are called to live and to give witness to the faith which catechesis seeks to deepen and strengthen, is governed by adults. The faith of these adults too should continually be enlightened, stimulated and renewed, so that it may pervade the temporal realities in their charge. Thus, for catechesis to be effective, it must be permanent, and it would be quite useless if it stopped short at the threshold of maturity, since catechesis, admittedly under another form, proves no less necessary for adults.

Quasi-Catechumens

44 Among the adults who need catechesis, our pastoral missionary concern is directed to those who were born and reared in areas not yet Christianized, and who have never been able to study deeply the Christian teaching that the circumstances of life have at a certain moment caused them to come across. It is also directed to

---

90. Cf. Second Vatican Council, Decree on the Bishop's Pastoral Office in the Church *Christus Dominus*, 14: *AAS* 58 (1966), p. 679; Decree on the Missionary Activity of the Church *Ad gentes*, 14: *AAS* 58 (1966), pp. 962-963; Sacred Congregation for the Clergy, *Directorium Catechisticum Generale* 20: *AAS* 64 (1972), p. 112; cf. also *Ordo Initiationis Christianae Adultorum*.

those who in childhood received a catechesis suited to their age but who later drifted away from all religious practice and as adults find themselves with religious knowledge of a rather childish kind. It is likewise directed to those who feel the effects of a catechesis received early in life but badly imparted or badly assimilated. It is directed to those who, although they were born in a Christian country or in sociologically Christian surroundings, have never been educated in their Faith and, as adults, are really catechumens.

Diversified and Complementary Forms of Catechesis

45 Catechesis is therefore for adults of every age, including the elderly—persons who deserve particular attention in view of their experience and their problems—no less than for children, adolescents and the young. We should also mention migrants, those who are bypassed by modern developments, those who live in areas of large cities which are often without churches, buildings and suitable organization, and other such groups. It is desirable that initiatives meant to give all these groups a Christian formation, with appropriate means (audiovisual aids, booklets, discussions, lectures), should increase in number, enabling many adults to fill the gap left by an insufficient or deficient catechesis, to complete harmoniously at a higher level their childhood catechesis, or even to prepare themselves enough in this field to be able to help others in a more serious way.

It is important also that the catechesis of children and young people, permanent catechesis, and the catechesis of adults should not be separate, watertight compartments. It is even more important that there should be no break between them. On the contrary, their perfect complementarity must be fostered: Adults have much to give to young people and children in the field of catechesis, but they can also receive much from them for the growth of their own Christian lives.

It must be restated that nobody in the Church of Jesus Christ should feel excused from receiving catechesis. This is true even of young seminarians and young religious, and of all those called to the task of being pastors and catechists. They will fulfill this task all the better if they are humble pupils of the Church, the great giver as well as the great receiver of catechesis.

VI

SOME WAYS AND MEANS OF CATECHESIS

Communications Media

46 From the oral teaching by the Apostles and the letters circulating among the Churches down to the most modern means, catechesis has not ceased to look for the most suitable ways and means for its mission, with the active participation of the communities and at the urging of the pastors. This effort must continue.

I think immediately of the great possibilities offered by the means of social communication and the means of group communication: television, radio, the press, records, tape recordings—the whole series of audiovisual means. The achievements in these spheres are such as to encourage the greatest hope. Experience shows, for example, the effect had by instruction given on radio or television, when it combines a high aesthetic level and rigorous fidelity to the Magisterium. The Church now has many opportunities for considering these questions—as, for instance, on Social Communications Days—and it is not necessary to speak of them at length here, in spite of their prime importance.

Utilization of Various Places, Occasions and Gatherings

47 I am also thinking of various occasions of special value which are exactly suitable for catechesis: for example, diocesan, regional or national pilgrimages, which gain from being centered on some judiciously chosen theme based on the life of Christ, of the Blessed Virgin or of the saints. Then there are the traditional missions, often too hastily dropped but irreplaceable for the periodic and vigorous renewal of Christian life—they should be revived and brought up to date. Again, there are Bible-study groups, which ought to go beyond exegesis and lead their members to live by the Word of God. Yet other instances are the meetings of ecclesial basic communities, insofar as they correspond to the criteria laid down in the Apostolic Exhortation *Evangelii nuntiandi*.[91] I may also mention the youth groups that, under varying names and forms but always with the purpose of making Jesus Christ known and of living by the Gospel, are in some areas multiplying and flourishing in a sort of springtime that is very comforting for the Church. These include Catholic action groups, charitable groups, prayer groups and Christian meditation groups. These groups are a source of great hope for the Church of tomorrow. But, in the name of Jesus, I exhort the young people who belong to them, their leaders, and the priests who devote the best part of their ministry to them: No matter what it costs, do not allow these groups—which are exceptional occasions for meeting others, and which are blessed with such riches of friendship and solidarity among the young, of joy and enthusiasm, of reflection on events and facts—do not allow them to lack serious study of Christian doctrine. If they do, they will be in danger—a danger that has unfortunately proved only too real—of disappointing their members and also the Church.

The catechetical endeavor that is possible in these various surroundings, and in many others besides, will have all the greater chance of being accepted and bearing fruit if it respects their individual nature. By becoming part of them in the right way, it will achieve the diversity and complementarity of approach that will enable it to develop all the riches of its concept, with its three dimensions of word, memorial and witness—doctrine, celebration and commitment in living—which the Synod Message to the People of God emphasized.[92]

The Homily

48 This remark is even more valid for the catechesis given in the setting of the liturgy, especially at the Eucharistic assembly. Respecting the specific nature and proper cadence of this setting, the homily takes up again the journey of faith put forward by catechesis, and brings it to its natural fulfillment. At the same time it

---

91. Cf. 58: *AAS* 68 (1976), pp. 46-49.
92. Cf. *Synodus Episcoporum, De catechesi hoc nostro tempore tradenda praesertim pueris atque iuvenibus, Ad Populum Dei Nuntius*, 7-10: *loc. cit.*, pp. 9-12; cf. *L'Osservatore Romano*, October 30, 1977, p. 3.

encourages the Lord's disciples to begin anew each day their spiritual journey in truth, adoration and thanksgiving. Accordingly, one can say that catechetical teaching too finds its source and its fulfillment in the Eucharist, within the whole circle of the liturgical year. Preaching, centered upon the Bible texts, must then in its own way make it possible to familiarize the faithful with the whole of the mysteries of the Faith and with the norms of Christian living. Much attention must be given to the homily: It should be neither too long nor too short; it should always be carefully prepared, rich in substance and adapted to the hearers, and reserved to ordained ministers. The homily should have its place not only in every Sunday and feastday Eucharist, but also in the celebration of Baptisms, penitential liturgies, marriages and funerals. This is one of the benefits of the liturgical renewal.

Catechetical Literature

49 Among these various ways and means—all the Church's activities have a catechetical dimension—catechetical works, far from losing their essential importance, acquire fresh significance. One of the major features of the renewal of catechetics today is the rewriting and multiplication of catechetical books taking place in many parts of the Church. Numerous very successful works have been produced and are a real treasure in the service of catechetical instruction. But it must be humbly and honestly recognized that this rich flowering has brought with it articles and publications which are ambiguous and harmful to young people and to the life of the Church. In certain places, the desire to find the best forms of expression or to keep up with fashions in pedagogical methods has often enough resulted in certain catechetical works which bewilder the young and even adults, either by deliberately or unconsciously omitting elements essential to the Church's Faith, or by attributing excessive importance to certain themes at the expense of others, or, chiefly, by a rather horizontalist overall view out of keeping with the teaching of the Church's Magisterium.

Therefore, it is not enough to multiply catechetical works. In order that these works may correspond with their aim, several conditions are essential:

a) They must be linked with the real life of the generation to which they are addressed, showing close acquaintance with its anxieties and questionings, struggles and hopes;

b) They must try to speak a language comprehensible to the generation in question;

c) They must make a point of giving the whole message of Christ and His Church, without neglecting or distorting anything, and in expounding it they will follow a line and structure that highlights what is essential;

d) They must really aim to give to those who use them a better knowledge of the mysteries of Christ, aimed at true conversion and a life more in conformity with God's will.

Catechisms

50 All those who take on the heavy task of preparing these catechetical tools, especially catechism texts, can do so only with the approval of the pastors who have the authority to give it, and taking their inspiration as closely as possible from the General Catechetical Directory, which remains the standard of reference.[93]

In this regard, I must warmly encourage the episcopal conferences of the whole world to undertake, patiently but resolutely, the considerable work to be accomplished in agreement with the Apostolic See in order to prepare genuine catechisms which will be faithful to the essential content of revelation and up-to-date in method, and which will be capable of educating the Christian generations of the future to a sturdy faith.

This brief mention of ways and means of modern catechetics does not exhaust the wealth of suggestions worked out by the Synod Fathers. It is comforting to think that at the present time every country is seeing valuable collaboration for a more organic and more secure renewal of these aspects of catechetics. There can be no doubt that the Church will find the experts and the right means for responding, with God's grace, to the complex requirements of communicating with the people of today.

---

93. Cf. Sacred Congregation for the Clergy, *Directorium Catechisticum Generale*, 119-121; 134: *AAS* 64 (1972), pp. 166-167; 172.

VII

HOW TO IMPART CATECHESIS

Diversity of Methods

51   The age and the intellectual development of Christians, their degree of ecclesial and spiritual maturity and many other personal circumstances demand that catechesis should adopt widely differing methods for the attainment of its specific aim: education in the Faith. On a more general level, this variety is also demanded by the social and cultural surrounding in which the Church carries out her catechetical work.

The variety in the methods used is a sign of life and a resource. That is how it was considered by the Fathers of the Fourth General Assembly of the Synod, although they also drew attention to the conditions necessary for that variety to be useful and not harmful to the unity of the teaching of the one Faith.

At the Service of Revelation and Conversion

52   The first question of a general kind that presents itself here concerns the danger and the temptation to mix catechetical teaching unduly with overt or masked ideological views, especially political and social ones, or with personal political options. When such views get the better of the central message to be transmitted, to the point of obscuring it and putting it in second place or even using it to further their own ends, catechesis then becomes radically distorted. The Synod rightly insisted on the need for catechesis to remain above one-sided divergent trends—to avoid "dichotomies" —even in the field of theological interpretation of such questions. It is on the basis of revelation that catechesis will try to set its course, revelation as transmitted by the universal Magisterium of the Church, in its solemn or ordinary form. This revelation tells of a creating and redeeming God, whose Son has come among us in our flesh and enters not only into each individual's personal history but into human history itself, becoming its center. Accordingly, this revelation tells of the radical change of man and the universe, of all that makes up the web of human life under the influence of the Good News of Jesus Christ. If conceived in this way, catechesis goes beyond every form of formalistic moralism, although it will include true Christian moral teaching. Chiefly, it goes beyond any kind of temporal, social or political "messianism." It seeks to arrive at man's innermost being.

The Message Embodied in Cultures

53 Now a second question. As I said recently to the members of the Biblical Commission: "The term 'acculturation' or 'inculturation' may be a neologism, but it expresses very well one factor of the great mystery of the Incarnation."[94] We can say of catechesis, as well as of evangelization in general, that it is called to bring the power of the Gospel into the very heart of culture and cultures. For this purpose, catechesis will seek to know these cultures and their essential components; it will learn their most significant expressions; it will respect their particular values and riches. In this manner it will be able to offer these cultures the knowledge of the hidden mystery[95] and help them to bring forth from their own living tradition original expressions of Christian life, celebration and thought. Two things must however be kept in mind.

On the one hand the Gospel message cannot be purely and simply isolated from the culture in which it was first inserted (the biblical world or, more concretely, the cultural milieu in which Jesus of Nazareth lived), nor, without serious loss, from the cultures in which it has already been expressed down the centuries; it does not spring spontaneously from any cultural soil; it has always been transmitted by means of an apostolic dialogue which inevitably becomes part of a certain dialogue of cultures.

On the other hand, the power of the Gospel everywhere transforms and regenerates. When that power enters into a culture, it is no surprise that it rectifies many of its elements. There would be no catechesis if it were the Gospel that had to change when it came into contact with the cultures.

---

94. Cf. *AAS* (1979), p. 607.
95. Cf. Rom. 16:25; Eph. 3:5.

To forget this would simply amount to what St. Paul very forcefully calls "emptying the cross of Christ of its power."[96]

It is a different matter to take, with wise discernment, certain elements, religious or otherwise, that form part of the cultural heritage of a human group and use them to help its members to understand better the whole of the Christian mystery. Genuine catechists know that catechesis "takes flesh" in the various cultures and milieux: One has only to think of the peoples with their great differences, of modern youth, of the great variety of circumstances in which people find themselves today. But they refuse to accept an impoverishment of catechesis through a renunciation or obscuring of its message, by adaptations, even in language, that would endanger the "precious deposit" of the faith,[97] or by concessions in matters of faith or morals. They are convinced that true catechesis eventually enriches these cultures by helping them to go beyond the defective or even inhuman features in them, and by communicating to their legitimate values the fullness of Christ.[98]

The Contribution of Popular Devotion

54 Another question of method concerns the utilization in catechetical instruction of valid elements in popular piety. I have in mind devotions practiced by the faithful in certain regions with moving fervor and purity of intention, even if the faith underlying them needs to be purified or rectified in many aspects. I have in mind certain easily understood prayers that many simple people are fond of repeating. I have in mind certain acts of piety practiced with a sincere desire to do penance or to please the Lord. Underlying most of these prayers and practices, besides elements that should be discarded, there are other elements which, if they were properly used, could serve very well to help people advance towards knowledge of the mystery of Christ and of His message: the love and mercy of God, the Incarnation of Christ, His redeeming cross and resurrection, the activity of the Spirit in each Christian and in the Church, the mystery of the hereafter, the evangelical

---

96. 1 Cor. 1:17.
97. Cf. 2 Tm. 1:14.
98. Cf. Jn. 1:16; Eph. 1:10.

virtues to be practiced, the presence of the Christian in the world, etc. And why should we appeal to non-Christian or even anti-Christian elements, refusing to build on elements which, even if they need to be revised or improved, have something Christian at their root?

Memorization

55 The final methodological question the importance of which should at least be referred to—one that was debated several times in the Synod—is that of memorization. In the beginnings of Christian catechesis, which coincided with a civilization that was mainly oral, recourse was had very freely to memorization. Catechesis has since then known a long tradition of learning the principal truths by memorizing. We are all aware that this method can present certain disadvantages, not the least of which is that it lends itself to insufficient or at times almost non-existent assimilation, reducing all knowledge to formulas that are repeated without being properly understood. These disadvantages and the different characteristics of our own civilization have in some places led to the almost complete suppression—according to some, alas, the definitive suppression—of memorization in catechesis. And yet certain very authoritative voices made themselves heard on the occasion of the Fourth General Assembly of the Synod, calling for the restoration of a judicious balance between reflection and spontaneity, between dialogue and silence, between written work and memory work. Moreover certain cultures still set great value on memorization.

At a time when, in non-religious teaching in certain countries, more and more complaints are being made about the unfortunate consequences of disregarding the human faculty of memory, should we not attempt to put this faculty back into use in an intelligent and even an original way in catechesis, all the more since the celebration or "memorial" of the great events of the history of salvation require a precise knowledge of them? A certain memorization of the words of Jesus, of important Bible passages, of the ten commandments, of the formulas of profession of the faith, of the liturgical texts, of the essential prayers, of key doctrinal ideas, etc., far from being opposed to the dignity of young Christians, or constituting an obstacle to personal dialogue with the Lord, is a real need, as the Synod Fathers forcefully recalled. We must be realists. The blossoms, if we may call them that, of faith and piety do not grow in the desert places of a memory-less catechesis. What is essential is that the texts that are memorized must at the same time be taken in and gradually understood in depth, in order to become a source of Christian life on the personal level and the community level.

The plurality of methods in contemporary catechesis can be a sign of vitality and ingenuity. In any case, the method chosen must ultimately be referred to a law that is fundamental for the whole of the Church's life: the law of fidelity to God and of fidelity to man in a single loving attitude.

VIII

THE JOY OF FAITH IN A TROUBLED WORLD

Affirming Christian Identity

56 We live in a difficult world in which the anguish of seeing the best creations of man slip away from him and turn against him creates a climate of uncertainty.[99] In this world catechesis should help Christians to be, for their own joy and the service of all, "light" and "salt."[100] Undoubtedly this demands that catechesis should strengthen them in their identity and that it should continually separate itself from the surrounding atmosphere of hesitation, uncertainty and insipidity. Among the many difficulties, each of them a challenge for faith, I shall indicate a few in order to assist catechesis in overcoming them.

In an Indifferent World

57 A few years ago, there was much talk of the secularized world, the post-Christian era. Fashion changes, but a profound reality remains. Christians today must be formed to live in a world

---

99. Cf. Encyclical *Redemptor hominis*, 15-16: *AAS* 71 (1979), pp. 286-295.
100. Cf. Mt. 5:13-16.

which largely ignores God or which, in religious matters, in place of an exacting and fraternal dialogue, stimulating for all, too often flounders in a debasing indifferentism, if it does not remain in a scornful attitude of "suspicion" in the name of the progress it has made in the field of scientific "explanations." To "hold on" in this world, to offer to all a "dialogue of salvation"[101] in which each person feels respected in his or her most basic dignity, the dignity of one who is seeking God, we need a catechesis which trains the young people and adults of our communities to remain clear and consistent in their faith, to affirm serenely their Christian and Catholic identity, to "see him who is invisible"[102] and to adhere so firmly to the absoluteness of God that they can be witnesses to Him in a materialistic civilization that denies Him.

With the Original Pedagogy of the Faith

58 The irreducible originality of Christian identity has for corollary and condition no less original a pedagogy of the Faith. Among the many prestigious sciences of man that are nowadays making immense advances, pedagogy is certainly one of the most important. The attainments of the other sciences—biology, psychology, sociology—are providing it with valuable elements. The science of education and the art of teaching are continually being subjected to review, with a view to making them better adapted or more effective, with varying degrees of success.

There is also a pedagogy of faith, and the good that it can do for catechesis cannot be overstated. In fact, it is natural that techniques perfected and tested for education in general should be adapted for the service of education in the Faith. However, account must always be taken of the absolute originality of faith. Pedagogy of faith is not a question of transmitting human knowledge, even of the highest kind; it is a question of communicating God's revelation in its entirety. Throughout sacred history, especially in the Gospel, God Himself used a pedagogy that must continue to be a model for

---

101. Cf. Pope Paul VI, Encyclical *Ecclesiam Suam*, Part Three, *AAS* 56 (1964), pp. 637-659.
102. Cf. Heb. 11:27.

the pedagogy of faith. A technique is of value in catechesis only to the extent that it serves the faith that is to be transmitted and learned; otherwise it is of no value.

Language Suited to the Service of the Credo

59 A problem very close to the preceding one is that of language. This is obviously a burning question today. It is paradoxical to see that, while modern studies, for instance in the field of communication, semantics and symbology, attribute extraordinary importance to language, nevertheless language is being misused today for ideological mystification, for mass conformity in thought and for reducing man to the level of an object.

All this has extensive influence in the field of catechesis. For catechesis has a pressing obligation to speak a language suited to today's children and young people in general and to many other categories of people—the language of students, intellectuals and scientists; the language of the illiterate or of people of simple culture; the language of the handicapped, and so on. St. Augustine encountered this same problem and contributed to its solution for his own time with his well-known work *De Catechizandis Rudibus.* In catechesis as in theology, there is no doubt that the question of language is of the first order. But there is good reason for recalling here that catechesis cannot admit any language that would result in altering the substance of the content of the Creed, under any pretext whatever, even a pretended scientific one. Deceitful or beguiling language is no better. On the contrary, the supreme rule is that the great advances in the science of language must be capable of being placed at the service of catechesis so as to enable it really to "tell" or "communicate" to the child, the adolescent, the young people and adults of today the whole content of doctrine without distortion.

Research and Certainty of Faith

60 A more subtle challenge occasionally comes from the very way of conceiving faith. Certain contemporary philosophical schools, which seem to be exercising a strong influence on some theological currents and, through them, on pastoral practice, like to emphasize that the fundamental human attitude is that of seeking the infinite, a seeking that never attains its object. In theology, this view of things will state very categorically that faith is not certainty but questioning, not clarity but a leap in the dark.

These currents of thought certainly have the advantage of reminding us that faith concerns things not yet in our possession, since they are hoped for; that as yet we see only "in a mirror dimly"[103]; and that God dwells always in inaccessible light.[104] They help us to make the Christian faith not the attitude of one who has already arrived, but a journey forward as with Abraham. For all the more reason one must avoid presenting as certain things which are not.

However, we must not fall into the opposite extreme, as too often happens. The letter to the Hebrews says that "faith is the assurance of things hoped for, the conviction of things not seen."[105] Although we are not in full possession, we do have an assurance and a conviction. When educating children, adolescents and young people, let us not give them too negative an idea of faith—as if it were absolute non-knowing, a kind of blindness, a world of darkness—but let us show them that the humble yet courageous seeking of the believer, far from having its starting point in nothingness, in plain self-deception, in fallible opinions or in uncertainty, is based on the Word of God who cannot deceive or be deceived, and is unceasingly built on the immovable rock of this Word. It is the search of the Magi under the guidance of a star,[106] the search of which Pascal, taking up a phrase of St. Augustine, wrote so profoundly: "You would not be searching for me, if you had not found me."[107]

It is also one of the aims of catechesis to give young catechumens the simple but solid certainties that will help them to seek to know the Lord more and better.

---

103. 1 Cor. 13:12.
104. Cf. 1 Tm. 6:16.
105. Heb. 11:1.
106. Cf. Mt. 2:1ff.
107. Blaise Pascal, *Le mystère de Jésus: Pensées*, 553.

Catechesis and Theology

61   In this context, it seems important to me that the connection between catechesis and theology should be well understood.

Obviously this connection is profound and vital for those who understand the irreplaceable mission of theology in the service of Faith. Thus it is no surprise that every stirring in the field of theology also has repercussions in that of catechesis. In this period immediately after the Council, the Church is living through an important but hazardous time of theological research. The same must be said of hermeneutics with respect to exegesis.

Synod Fathers from all continents dealt with this question in very frank terms: They spoke of the danger of an "unstable balance" passing from theology to catechesis and they stressed the need to do something about this difficulty. Pope Paul VI himself had dealt with the problem in no less frank terms in the introduction to his Solemn Profession of Faith[108] and in the Apostolic Exhortation marking the fifth anniversary of the close of the Second Vatican Council.[109]

This point must again be insisted on. Aware of the influence that their research and their statements have on catechetical instruction, theologians and exegetes have a duty to take great care that people do not take for a certainty what on the contrary belongs to the area of questions of opinion or of discussion among experts. Catechists for their part must have the wisdom to pick from the field of theological research those points that can provide light for their own reflection and their teaching, drawing, like the theologians, from the true sources, in the light of the Magisterium. They must refuse to trouble the minds of the children and young people, at this stage of their catechesis, with outlandish theories, useless questions and unproductive discussions, things that St. Paul often condemned in his pastoral letters.[110]

The most valuable gift that the Church can offer to the bewildered and restless world of our time is to form within it Chris-

---

108. Pope Paul VI, *Sollemnis Professio Fidei*, 4: *AAS* 60 (1968), p. 434.

109. Pope Paul VI, Apostolic Exhortation *Quinque Iam Anni*: *AAS* 63 (1971), p. 99.

110. Cf. 1 Tm. 1:3ff.; 4:1ff.; 2 Tm. 2:14ff.; 4:1-5; Ti. 1:10-12; cf. also Apostolic Exhortation *Evangelii nuntiandi*, 78: *AAS* 68 (1976), p. 70.

tians who are confirmed in what is essential and who are humbly joyful in their faith. Catechesis will teach this to them, and it will itself be the first to benefit from it: "The man who wishes to understand himself thoroughly—and not just in accordance with immediate, partial, often superficial, and even illusory standards and measures of his being—must come to Christ with his unrest and uncertainty, and even his weakness and sinfulness, his life and death. He must, so to speak, enter into Christ with all his own self, he must 'appropriate' Christ and assimilate the whole of the reality of the Incarnation and redemption in order to find himself."[111]

IX

THE TASK CONCERNS US ALL

Encouragement to All Responsible for Catechesis

62 Now, beloved brothers and sons and daughters, I would like my words, which are intended as a serious and heartfelt exhortation from me in my ministry as pastor of the universal Church, to set your hearts aflame, like the letters of St. Paul to his companions in the Gospel, Titus and Timothy, or like St. Augustine writing for the deacon Deogratias, when the latter lost heart before his task as a catechist, a real little treatise on the joy of catechizing.[112] Yes, I wish to sow courage, hope and enthusiasm abundantly in the hearts of all those many diverse people who are in charge of religious instruction and training for life in keeping with the Gospel.

Bishops

63 To begin with, I turn to my brother bishops: The Second Vatican Council has already explicitly reminded you of your task in the catechetical area,[113] and the Fathers of the Fourth General Assembly of the Synod have also strongly underlined it.

---

111. Encyclical *Redemptor hominis*, 10: *AAS* 71 (1979), p. 274.
112. *De Catechizandis Rudibus*, PL 40, 310-347.
113. Cf. Decree on the Bishop's Pastoral Office in the Church *Christus Dominus*, 14: *AAS* 58 (1966), p. 679.

Dearly beloved brothers, you have here a special mission within your Churches: You are beyond all others the ones primarily responsible for catechesis, the catechists par excellence. Together with the Pope, in the spirit of episcopal collegiality, you too have charge of catechesis throughout the Church. Accept therefore what I say to you from my heart.

I know that your ministry as bishops is growing daily more complex and overwhelming. A thousand duties call you: from the training of new priests to being actively present within the lay communities, from the living, worthy celebration of the sacraments and acts of worship to concern for human advancement and the defense of human rights. But let the concern to foster active and effective catechesis yield to no other care whatever in any way. This concern will lead you to transmit personally to your faithful the doctrine of life. But it should also lead you to take on in your diocese, in accordance with the plans of the episcopal conference to which you belong, the chief management of catechesis, while at the same time surrounding yourselves with competent and trustworthy assistants. Your principal role will be to bring about and maintain in your Churches a real passion for catechesis, a passion embodied in a pertinent and effective organization, putting into operation the necessary personnel, means and equipment, and also financial resources. You can be sure that if catechesis is done well in your local Churches, everything else will be easier to do. And needless to say, although your zeal must sometimes impose upon you the thankless task of denouncing deviations and correcting errors, it will much more often win for you the joy and consolation of seeing your Churches flourishing because catechesis is given in them as the Lord wishes.

Priests

64 For your part, priests, here you have a field in which you are the immediate assistants of your bishops. The Council has called you "instructors in the faith"[114]; there is no better way for

---

114. Decree on the Ministry and Life of Priests, *Presbyterorum ordinis*, 6: *AAS* 58 (1966), p. 999.

you to be such instructors than by devoting your best efforts to the growth of your communities in the faith. Whether you are in charge of a parish, or are chaplains to primary or secondary schools or universities, or have responsibility for pastoral activity at any level, or are leaders of large or small communities, especially youth groups, the Church expects you to neglect nothing with a view to a well-organized and well-oriented catechetical effort. The deacons and other ministers that you may have the good fortune to have with you are your natural assistants in this. All believers have a right to catechesis; all pastors have the duty to provide it. I shall always ask civil leaders to respect the freedom of catechetical teaching; but with all my strength I beg you, ministers of Jesus Christ: Do not, for lack of zeal or because of some unfortunate preconceived idea, leave the faithful without catechesis. Let it not be said that "the children beg for food, but no one gives to them."[115]

Men and Women Religious

65 Many religious institutes for men and women came into being for the purpose of giving Christian education to children and young people, especially the most abandoned. Throughout history, men and women religious have been deeply committed to the Church's catechetical activity, doing particularly apposite and effective work. At a time when it is desired that the links between religious and pastors should be accentuated and consequently the active presence of religious communities and their members in the pastoral projects of the local Churches, I wholeheartedly exhort you, whose religious consecration should make you even more readily available for the Church's service, to prepare as well as possible for the task of catechesis according to the differing vocations of your institutes and the missions entrusted to you, and to carry this concern everywhere. Let the communities dedicate as much as possible of what ability and means they have to the specific work of catechesis.

---

115. Lam. 4:4.

Lay Catechists

66   I am anxious to give thanks in the Church's name to all of you, lay teachers of catechesis in the parishes, the men and the still more numerous women throughout the world, who are devoting yourselves to the religious education of many generations. Your work is often lowly and hidden but it is carried out with ardent and generous zeal, and it is an eminent form of the lay apostolate, a form that is particularly important where for various reasons children and young people do not receive suitable religious training in the home. How many of us have received from people like you our first notions of catechism and our preparation for the sacrament of Penance, for our first Communion and Confirmation! The Fourth General Assembly of the Synod did not forget you. I join with it in encouraging you to continue your collaboration for the life of the Church.

But the term "catechists" belongs above all to the catechists in mission lands. Born of families that are already Christian or converted at some time to Christianity and instructed by missionaries or by another catechist, they then consecrate their lives, year after year, to catechizing children and adults in their own country. Churches that are flourishing today would not have been built up without them. I rejoice at the efforts made by the Sacred Congregation for the Evangelization of Peoples to improve more and more the training of these catechists. I gratefully recall the memory of those whom the Lord has already called to Himself. I beg the intercession of those whom my Predecessors have raised to the glory of the altars. I wholeheartedly encourage those engaged in the work. I express the wish that many others may succeed them and that they may increase in numbers for a task so necessary for the missions.

In the Parish

67   I now wish to speak of the actual setting in which all these catechists normally work. I am returning this time, taking a more overall view, to the "places" for catechesis, some of which have already been mentioned in Chapter VI: the parish, the family, the school, organizations.

It is true that catechesis can be given anywhere, but I wish to stress, in accordance with the desire of very many bishops, that the parish community must continue to be the prime mover and pre-eminent place for catechesis. Admittedly, in many countries the parish has been as it were shaken by the phenomenon of urbanization. Perhaps some have too easily accepted that the parish should be considered old-fashioned, if not doomed to disappear, in favor of more pertinent and effective small communities. Whatever one may think, the parish is still a major point of reference for the Christian people, even for the non-practicing. Accordingly, realism and wisdom demand that we continue along the path aiming to restore to the parish, as needed, more adequate structures and, above all, a new impetus through the increasing integration into it of qualified, responsible and generous members. This being said, and taking into account the necessary diversity of places for catechesis (the parish as such, families taking in children and adolescents, chaplaincies for state schools, Catholic educational establishments, apostolic movements that give periods of catechesis, clubs open to youth in general, spiritual formation weekends, etc.), it is supremely important that all these catechetical channels should really converge on the same confession of faith, on the same membership of the Church, and on commitments in society lived in the same Gospel spirit: "one Lord, one faith, one baptism, one God and Father."[116] That is why every big parish or every group of parishes with small numbers has the serious duty to train people completely dedicated to providing catechetical leadership (priests, men and women religious, and lay people), to provide the equipment needed for catechesis under all aspects, to increase and adapt the places for catechesis to the extent that it is possible and useful to do so, and to be watchful about the quality of the religious formation of the various groups and their integration into the ecclesial community.

In short, without monopolizing or enforcing uniformity, the parish remains, as I have said, the pre-eminent place for catechesis. It must rediscover its vocation, which is to be a fraternal and welcoming family home, where those who have been baptized and confirmed become aware of forming the People of God. In that

---

116. Eph. 4:5-6.

home, the bread of good doctrine and the Eucharistic Bread are broken for them in abundance, in the setting of the one act of worship[117]; from that home they are sent out day by day to their apostolic mission in all the centers of activity of the life of the world.

In the Family

68 The family's catechetical activity has a special character, which is in a sense irreplaceable. This special character has been rightly stressed by the Church, particularly by the Second Vatican Council.[118] Education in the faith by parents, which should begin from the children's tenderest age,[119] is already being given when the members of a family help each other to grow in faith through the witness of their Christian lives, a witness that is often without words but which perseveres throughout a day-to-day life lived in accordance with the Gospel. This catechesis is more incisive when, in the course of family events (such as the reception of the sacraments, the celebration of great liturgical feasts, the birth of a child, a bereavement), care is taken to explain in the home the Christian or religious content of these events. But that is not enough: Christian parents must strive to follow and repeat, within the setting of fam-

---

117. Cf. Second Vatican Council, Constitution on the Sacred Liturgy *Sacrosanctum concilium*, 35, 52: *AAS* 56 (1964), pp. 109, 114; cf. also *Institutio Generalis Missalis Romani*, promulgated by a Decree of the Sacred Congregation of Rites on April 6, 1969, 33, and what has been said above in Chapter VI concerning the homily.

118. Since the High Middle Ages, provincial councils have insisted on the responsibility of parents in regard to education in the Faith: cf. Sixth Council of Arles (813), Canon 19; Council of Mainz (813), Canons 45, 47; Sixth Council of Paris (829), Book 1, Chapter 7: Mansi, *Sacrorum Conciliorum Nova et Amplissima Collectio*, XIV, 62, 74, 542. Among the more recent documents of the Magisterium, note the Encyclical *Divini illius Magistri*, of Pius XI, December 31, 1929: *AAS* 22 (1930), pp. 49-86; the many discourses and messages of Pius XII; and above all the texts of the Second Vatican Council: the Dogmatic Constitution on the Church *Lumen gentium*, 11, 35: *AAS* 57 (1965), pp. 15, 40; the Decree on the Apostolate of the Laity *Apostolicam actuositatem*, 11, 30: *AAS* 58 (1966), pp. 847, 860; the Pastoral Constitution on the Church in the Modern World *Gaudium et spes*, 52: *AAS* 58 (1966), p. 1073; and especially the Declaration on Christian Education *Gravissimum educationis*, 3: *AAS* 58 (1966), p. 731.

119. Cf. Second Vatican Council, Declaration on Christian Education *Gravissimum educationis*, 3: *AAS* 58 (1966), p. 731.

ily life, the more methodical teaching received elsewhere. The fact that these truths about the main questions of faith and Christian living are thus repeated within a family setting impregnated with love and respect will often make it possible to influence the children in a decisive way for life. The parents themselves profit from the effort that this demands of them, for in a catechetical dialogue of this sort each individual both receives and gives.

Family catechesis therefore precedes, accompanies and enriches all other forms of catechesis. Furthermore, in places where anti-religious legislation endeavors even to prevent education in the Faith, and in places where widespread unbelief or invasive secularism makes real religious growth practically impossible, "the church of the home"[120] remains the one place where children and young people can receive an authentic catechesis. Thus there cannot be too great an effort on the part of Christian parents to prepare for this ministry of being their own children's catechists and to carry it out with tireless zeal. Encouragement must also be given to the individuals or institutions that, through person-to-person contacts, through meetings, and through all kinds of pedagogical means, help parents to perform their task: The service they are doing to catechesis is beyond price.

At School

69 Together with and in connection with the family, the school provides catechesis with possibilities that are not to be neglected. In the unfortunately decreasing number of countries in which it is possible to give education in the Faith within the school framework, the Church has the duty to do so as well as possible. This of course concerns first and foremost the Catholic school: It would no longer deserve this title if, no matter how much it shone for its high level of teaching in non-religious matters, there were justification for reproaching it for negligence or deviation in strictly religious education. Let it not be said that such education will always be given implicitly and indirectly. The special character of

---

120. Second Vatican Council, Dogmatic Constitution on the Church *Lumen gentium*, 11: *AAS* 57 (1965), p. 16; cf. Decree on the Apostolate of the Laity *Apostolicam actuositatem*, 11: *AAS* 58 (1966), p. 848.

the Catholic school, the underlying reason for it, the reason why Catholic parents should prefer it, is precisely the quality of the religious instruction integrated into the education of the pupils. While Catholic establishments should respect freedom of conscience, that is to say, avoid burdening consciences from without by exerting physical or moral pressure, especially in the case of the religious activity of adolescents, they still have a grave duty to offer a religious training suited to the often widely varying religious situations of the pupils. They also have a duty to make them understand that, although God's call to serve Him in spirit and truth, in accordance with the commandments of God and the precepts of the Church, does not apply constraint, it is nevertheless binding in conscience.

But I am also thinking of non-confessional and public schools. I express the fervent wish that, in response to a very clear right of the human person and of the family, and out of respect for everyone's religious freedom, all Catholic pupils may be enabled to advance in their spiritual formation with the aid of a religious instruction dependent on the Church, but which, according to the circumstances of different countries, can be offered either by the school or in the setting of the school, or again within the framework of an agreement with the public authorities regarding school timetables, if catechesis takes place only in the parish or in another pastoral center. In fact, even in places where objective difficulties exist, it should be possible to arrange school timetables in such a way as to enable the Catholics to deepen their faith and religious experience, with qualified teachers, whether priests or lay people.

Admittedly, apart from the school, many other elements of life help in influencing the mentality of the young, for instance, recreation, social background and work surroundings. But those who study are bound to bear the stamp of their studies, to be introduced to cultural or moral values within the atmosphere of the establishment in which they are taught, and to be faced with many ideas met with in school. It is important for catechesis to take full account of this effect of the school on the pupils if it is to keep in touch with the other elements of the pupils' knowledge and education; thus the Gospel will impregnate the mentality of the pupils in the field of their learning, and the harmonization of their culture will be achieved in the light of faith. Accordingly, I give encouragement to the priests, religious and lay people who are devoting themselves to sustaining these pupils' faith. This is moreover an occasion for me to reaffirm my firm conviction that to show respect for the Catholic faith of the young to the extent of facilitating its education, its implantation, its consolidation, its free profession and practice would certainly be to the honor of any government, whatever be the system on which it is based or the ideology from which it draws its inspiration.

Within Organizations

70 Lastly, encouragement must be given to the lay associations, movements and groups, whether their aim is the practice of piety, the direct apostolate, charity and relief work, or a Christian presence in temporal matters. They will all accomplish their objectives better, and serve the Church better, if they give an important place in their internal organization and their method of action to the serious religious training of their members. In this way every association of the faithful in the Church has by definition the duty to educate in the Faith.

This makes more evident the role given to the laity in catechesis today, always under the pastoral direction of their bishops, as the propositions left by the Synod stressed several times.

Training Institutes

71 We must be grateful to the Lord for this contribution by the laity, but it is also a challenge to our responsibility as pastors, since these lay catechists must be carefully prepared for what is, if not a formally instituted ministry, at the very least a function of great importance in the Church. Their preparation calls on us to organize special centers and institutes, which are to be given assiduous attention by the bishops. This is a field in which diocesan, interdiocesan or national cooperation proves fertile and fruitful. Here also the material aid provided by the richer Churches to their poor sisters can show the greatest effectiveness, for what better assistance can one Church give to another than to help it to grow as a Church with its own strength?

I would like to recall to all those who are working generously in the service of the Gospel, and to whom I have expressed here my lively encouragement, the instruction given by my venerated Predecessor Paul VI: "As evangelizers, we must offer...the image of people who are mature in faith and capable of finding a meeting-point beyond the real tensions, thanks to a shared, sincere and disinterested search for truth. Yes, the destiny of evangelization is certainly bound up with the witness of unity given by the Church. This is a source of responsibility and also of comfort."[121]

CONCLUSION

The Holy Spirit, the Teacher Within

72 At the end of this apostolic exhortation, the gaze of my heart turns to Him who is the principle inspiring all catechetical work and all who do this work—the Spirit of the Father and of the Son, the Holy Spirit.

In describing the mission that this Spirit would have in the Church, Christ used the significant words: "He will teach you all things, and bring to your remembrance all that I have said to you."[122] And He added: "When the Spirit of truth comes, he will guide you into all the truth...he will declare to you the things that are to come."[123]

The Spirit is thus promised to the Church and to each Christian as a teacher within, who, in the secret of the conscience and the heart, makes one understand what one has heard but was not capable of grasping: "Even now the Holy Spirit teaches the faithful," said St. Augustine in this regard, "in accordance with each one's spiritual capacity. And he sets their hearts aflame with

---

121. Apostolic Exhortation *Evangelii nuntiandi*, 77: *AAS* 68 (1976), p. 69.
122. Jn. 14:26.
123. Jn. 16:13.

greater desire according as each one progresses in the charity that makes him love what he already knows and desire what he has yet to know."[124]

Furthermore, the Spirit's mission is also to transform the disciples into witnesses to Christ: "He will bear witness to me; and you also are witnesses."[125]

But this is not all. For St. Paul, who on this matter synthesizes a theology that is latent throughout the New Testament, it is the whole of one's "being a Christian," the whole of the Christian life, the new life of the children of God, that constitutes a life in accordance with the Spirit.[126] Only the Spirit enables us to say to God: "Abba, Father."[127] Without the Spirit we cannot say: "Jesus is Lord."[128] From the Spirit come all the charisms that build up the Church, the community of Christians.[129]

In keeping with this, St. Paul gives each disciple of Christ the instruction: "Be filled with the Spirit."[130] St. Augustine is very explicit: "Both (our believing and our doing good) are ours because of the choice of our will, and yet both are gifts from the Spirit of faith and charity."[131]

Catechesis, which is growth in faith and the maturing of Christian life towards its fullness, is consequently a work of the Holy Spirit, a work that He alone can initiate and sustain in the Church.

This realization, based on the text quoted above and on many other passages of the New Testament, convinces us of two things.

To begin with, it is clear that, when carrying out her mission of giving catechesis, the Church—and also every individual Christian devoting himself to that mission within the Church and in her name—must be very much aware of acting as a living, pliant instrument of the Holy Spirit. To invoke this Spirit constantly, to

---

124. *In Ioannis Evangelium Tractatus*, 97, 1: *PL* 35, 1877.
125. Jn. 15:26-27.
126. Cf. Rom. 8:14-17; Gal. 4:6.
127. Rom. 8:15.
128. 1 Cor. 12:3.
129. Cf. 1 Cor. 12:4-11.
130. Eph. 5:18.
131. *Retractationum Liber I*, 23, 2: *PL* 32, 621.

be in communion with Him, to endeavor to know His authentic inspirations must be the attitude of the teaching Church and of every catechist.

Secondly, the deep desire to understand better the Spirit's action and to entrust oneself to Him more fully—at a time when "in the Church we are living an exceptionally favorable season of the Spirit," as my Predecessor Paul VI remarked in his Apostolic Exhortation *Evangelii nuntiandi*[132]—must bring about a catechetical awakening. For "renewal in the Spirit" will be authentic and will have real fruitfulness in the Church, not so much according as it gives rise to extraordinary charisms, but according as it leads the greatest possible number of the faithful, as they travel their daily paths, to make a humble, patient and persevering effort to know the mystery of Christ better and better, and to bear witness to it.

I invoke on the catechizing Church this Spirit of the Father and the Son, and I beg Him to renew catechetical dynamism in the Church.

Mary, Mother and Model of the Disciple

73 May the Virgin of Pentecost obtain this for us through her intercession. By a unique vocation, she saw her Son Jesus "increase in wisdom and in stature, and in favor."[133] As He sat on her lap and later as He listened to her throughout the hidden life at Nazareth, this Son, who was "the only Son from the Father," "full of grace and truth," was formed by her in human knowledge of the Scriptures and of the history of God's plan for His people, and in adoration of the Father.[134] She in turn was the first of His disciples. She was the first in time, because even when she found her adolescent Son in the temple she received from Him lessons that she kept in her heart.[135] She was the first disciple above all else because no one has been "taught by God"[136] to such depth. She was "both mother and disciple," as St. Augustine said of her, venturing to add

---
132. 75: *AAS* 68 (1976), p. 66.
133. Cf. Lk. 2:52.
134. Cf. Jn. 1:14; Heb. 10:5; *S. Th.*, III, Q. 12, a. 2; a. 3, ad 3.
135. Cf. Lk. 2:51.
136. Cf. Jn. 6:45.

that her discipleship was more important for her than her motherhood.[137] There are good grounds for the statement made in the synod hall that Mary is "a living catechism" and "the mother and model of catechists."

May the presence of the Holy Spirit, through the prayers of Mary, grant the Church unprecedented enthusiasm in the catechetical work that is essential for her. Thus will she effectively carry out, at this moment of grace, her inalienable and universal mission, the mission given her by her Teacher: "Go therefore and make disciples of all nations."[138]

With my apostolic blessing.

Given in Rome, at St. Peter's, on October 16, 1979, the second year of my pontificate.

POPE JOHN PAUL II

---

137. Cf. *Sermo* 25, 7: *PL* 46, 937-938.
138. Mt. 28:19.

POPE JOHN PAUL II

Dominicae Cenae: Holy Thursday Letters, 1979, 1980

Metanoia: The Mystery and Worship of the Eucharist

HOLY THURSDAY, 1979

To All the Bishops of the Church

Venerable brothers in the episcopate,

The great day is drawing near when we shall share in the liturgy of Holy Thursday together with our brothers in the priesthood and shall meditate together on the priceless gift in which we have become sharers by virtue of the call of Christ the eternal Priest. On that day, before we celebrate the liturgy *In Cena Domini*, we shall gather together in our cathedrals to renew before Him who became for us "obedient unto death"[1] in total self-giving to the Church, His spouse, our giving of ourselves to the exclusive service of Christ in His Church.

On this holy day, the liturgy takes us inside the Upper Room, where, with grateful heart, we set ourselves to listen to the words of the divine Teacher, words full of solicitude for every generation of bishops called, after the Apostles, to take upon themselves care for the Church, for the flock, for the vocation of the whole People of God, for the proclamation of God's Word, for the whole sacra-

---

1. Phil. 2:8.

mental and moral order of Christian living, for priestly and religious vocations, for the fraternal spirit in the community. Christ says: "I will not leave you orphans; I will come back to you."[2] It is precisely this Sacred Triduum of the passion, death and resurrection of the Lord that re-evokes in us, in a vivid way, not only the memory of His departure, but also faith in His return, in His continuous coming. Indeed, what is the meaning of the words: "I am with you always; yes, to the end of time"[3]?

Venerable and dear brothers, in the spirit of this faith, which fills the entire Triduum, it is my desire that, in our vocation and our episcopal ministry, we should feel in a special way this year—the first of my pontificate—that unity which the Twelve shared in when together with our Lord they were assembled for the Last Supper. It was precisely there that they heard those words that were most complimentary and at the same time most binding: "I shall not call you servants any more, because a servant does not know his master's business; I call you friends, because I have made known to you everything I have learned from my Father. You did not choose me, no, I chose you; and I commissioned you to go out and to bear fruit, fruit that will last."[4]

Can anything be added to those words? Should one not rather pause in humility and gratitude before them, given the greatness of the mystery we are about to celebrate? There then takes root even deeper within us our awareness of the gift that we have received from the Lord through our vocation and our episcopal ordination. In fact the gift of the sacramental fullness of the priesthood is greater than all the toils and also all the sufferings involved in our pastoral ministry in the Episcopate.

The Second Vatican Council reminded us and clearly showed us that this ministry, while being a personal duty of each one of us, is nevertheless something that we carry out in the brotherly communion of the whole of the Church's episcopal college or "body." While it is right that we should address every human being, and especially every Christian as "brother," this word takes on an altogether special meaning with regard to us bishops and our

---

2. Jn. 14:18.
3. Mt. 28:20.
4. Jn. 15:15-16.

mutual relationship: in a certain sense it goes back directly to that brotherhood which gathered the Apostles about Christ; it goes back to that friendship with which Christ honored them and through which He united them to one another, as is attested by the words of John's Gospel quoted above.

Therefore, venerable and dear brothers, we must express the wish, today especially, that everything that the Second Vatican Council so wonderfully renewed in our awareness should take on an ever more mature character of collegiality, both as the principle of our collaboration *(collegialitas effectiva)* and as the character of a cordial fraternal bond *(collegialitas affectiva)*, in order to build up the Mystical Body of Christ and to deepen the unity of the whole People of God.

As you gather in your cathedrals, with the diocesan and religious priests who make up the *presbyterium* of your local Churches, your dioceses, you will receive from them—as is provided for—the renewal of the promises that they placed in the hands of you, the bishops, on the day of their priestly ordination. With this in mind, I am sending to the priests another letter that—as I hope—will enable you and them to live even more deeply this unity, this mysterious bond that joins us in the one priesthood of Jesus Christ, brought to completion with the sacrifice of the cross, which merited for Him entrance "into the sanctuary."[5] Venerable brothers, I hope that these words of mine addressed to the priests, at the beginning of my ministry in the See of St. Peter, will also help you to strengthen ever more that communion and unity of the whole *presbyterium*[6] which have their basis in our collegial communion and unity in the Church.

And may there be a renewal of your love for the priests whom the Holy Spirit has given and entrusted to you as the closest collaborators in your pastoral office. Take care of them like beloved sons, brothers and friends. Be mindful of all their needs. Have particular solicitude for their spiritual advancement, for their perseverance in the grace of the sacrament of the priesthood. Since it is into your hands they make—and each year renew—their priestly promises, and especially the commitment to celibacy, do

---

5. Cf. Heb. 9:12.
6. Cf. Dogmatic Constitution *Lumen gentium*, 28.

everything in your power to ensure that they remain faithful to these promises, as is demanded by the holy tradition of the Church, the tradition that sprang from the very spirit of the Gospel.

May this solicitude for our brothers in the priestly ministry also be extended to the seminaries, which constitute, in the Church as a whole and in each of her parts, an eloquent proof of her vitality and spiritual fruitfulness, which are expressed precisely in readiness to give oneself exclusively to the service of God and of souls. Today, every possible effort must again be made to encourage vocations, to form new generations of priests. This must be done in a genuinely evangelical spirit, and at the same time by "reading" properly the signs of the times, to which the Second Vatican Council gave such careful attention. The full reconstitution of the life of the seminaries throughout the Church will be the best proof of the achievement of the renewal to which the Council directed the Church.

Venerable and dear brothers: everything that I am writing to you, as I prepare to live Holy Thursday intensely—the "feast of priests"—I wish to link up closely with the desire that the Apostles heard expressed that day by the lips of their beloved Teacher: "Go out and bear fruit, fruit that will last."[7] We can bear this fruit only if we remain in Him: in the vine.[8] He told us this clearly in His words of farewell on the day before His Passover: "Whoever remains in me, with me in him, bears fruit in plenty; for cut off from me you can do nothing."[9] Beloved brothers, what more could I wish you, what more could we wish one another, than precisely this: to remain in Him, Jesus Christ, and to bear fruit, fruit that will last?

Accept these good wishes. Let us strive to deepen ever more our unity; let us strive to live ever more intensely the sacred Triduum of the Passover of our Lord Jesus Christ.

From the Vatican, April 8, Passion Sunday (Palm Sunday), in the year 1979, the first of the pontificate.

POPE JOHN PAUL II

---

7. Jn. 15:16.
8. Cf. Jn. 15:1-8.
9. Jn. 15:5.

HOLY THURSDAY, 1979

To All the Priests of the Church

Dear Brother Priests,

For You I Am a Bishop, with You I Am a Priest

1 At the beginning of my new ministry in the Church, I feel the deep need to speak to you, to all of you without any exception, priests both diocesan and religious, who are my brothers by virtue of the sacrament of Orders. From the very beginning I wish to express my faith in the vocation that unites you to your bishops, in a special communion of sacrament and ministry, through which the Church, the Mystical Body of Christ, is built up. To all of you therefore, who, by virtue of a special grace and through a singular gift of our Savior, bear "the burden of the day and the heat"[1] in the midst of the many tasks of the priestly and pastoral ministry, I have addressed my thoughts and my heart from the moment when Christ called me to this See, where St. Peter, with his life and his death, had to respond until the end to the question: Do you love me? Do you love me more than these others do?[2]

I think of you all the time, I pray for you, with you *I seek the ways of spiritual union and collaboration*, because by virtue of the sacrament of Orders, which I also received from the hands of my bishop (the Metropolitan of Krakow, Cardinal Adam Stephen Sapieha, of unforgettable memory), you are my brothers. And so, adapting the words of St. Augustine,[3] I want to say to you today: "For you I am a bishop, with you I am a priest." Today, in fact, there is a special circumstance that impels me to confide to you some thoughts that I enclose in this letter: It is the nearness of Holy

---

1. Cf. Mt. 20:12.
2. Cf. Jn. 21:15ff.
3. *Vobis enim sum episcopus, vobiscum sum Christianus: Serm.* 340, 1: *PL* 38, 1483.

Thursday. It is this, the annual feast of our priesthood, that unites the whole presbyterium of each diocese about its bishop in the shared celebration of the Eucharist. It is on this day that all priests are invited to renew, before their own bishop and together with him, the promises they made at their priestly ordination; and this fact enables me, together with all my brothers in the episcopate, to be joined to you in a special unity, and especially to be in the very heart of the mystery of Jesus Christ, the mystery in which we all share.

The Second Vatican Council, which so explicitly highlighted the collegiality of the episcopate in the Church, also gave a new form to the life of the priestly communities, joined together by a special bond of brotherhood, and united to the bishop of the respective local Church. The whole priestly life and ministry serve to deepen and strengthen that bond; and a particular responsibility for the various tasks involved by this life and ministry is taken on by the priests' councils, which, in conformity with the thought of the Council and the Motu Proprio *Ecclesiae sanctae*[4] of Paul VI, should be functioning in every diocese. All this is meant to ensure that each bishop, in union with his presbyterium, can serve ever more effectively the great cause of evangelization. Through this service the Church realizes her mission, indeed her very nature. The importance of the unity of the priests with their own bishop on this point is confirmed by the words of St. Ignatius of Antioch: "Strive to do all things in the harmony of God, with the bishop presiding to represent God, the presbyters representing the council of the apostles, and the deacons, so dear to me, entrusted with the service of Jesus Christ."[5]

Love for Christ and the Church Unites Us

2   It is not my intention to include in this letter everything that makes up the richness of the priestly life and ministry. In this regard I refer to the whole tradition of the Magisterium and of the Church, and in a special way to the doctrine of the Second Vatican

---

4. Cf. I art. 15.
5. *Epistula ad Magnesios*, VI, 1: *Patres Apostolici* I, ed. Funk, p. 235.

Council, contained in the Council's various documents, especially in the Constitution *Lumen gentium* and the Decrees *Presbyterorum ordinis* and *Ad gentes*. I also wish to recall the Encyclical of my Predecessor Paul VI, *Sacerdotalis caelibatus*. Finally, I wish to place great importance upon the Document *De sacerdotio ministeriali*, which Paul VI approved as the fruit of the labors of the 1971 Synod of Bishops, because I find in this document—although the session of the Synod that elaborated it had only a consultative form—a statement of essential importance regarding the specific aspect of the priestly life and ministry in the modern world.

Referring to all these sources, which you are familiar with, I wish in the present letter *only to mention a number of points* which seem to me to be of extreme importance at this moment in the history of the Church and of the world. These are words that are dictated to me by my love for the Church, which will be able to carry out her mission to the world only if—in spite of all human weakness—she maintains her fidelity to Christ. I know that I am addressing those whom only the love of Christ has enabled, by means of a specific vocation, to give themselves to the service of the Church and, in the Church, to the service of man for the solution of the most important problems, and especially those regarding man's eternal salvation.

Although at the beginning of these considerations I refer to many written sources and official documents, nevertheless I wish to refer especially to that living source which is our shared love for Christ and His Church, a love that springs from the grace of the priestly vocation, the love that is the greatest gift of the Holy Spirit.[6]

"Chosen from Among Men... Appointed To Act on Behalf of Men"[7]

3   The Second Vatican Council deepened the idea of the priesthood and presented it, throughout its teaching, as the expres-

---

6. Cf. Rom. 5:5; 1 Cor. 12:31; 13.
7. Heb. 5:1.

sion of the inner forces, those "dynamisms," whereby the mission of the whole People of God in the Church is constituted. Here one should refer especially to the Constitution *Lumen gentium*, and reread carefully the relevant paragraphs. The mission of the People of God is carried out through the sharing in the office and mission of Jesus Christ Himself, which, as we know, has a triple dimension: it is the mission and office of Prophet, Priest and King. If we analyze carefully the conciliar texts, it is obvious that one should speak of a triple dimension of Christ's service and mission, rather than of three different functions. In fact, these functions are closely linked to one another, explain one another, condition one another and clarify one another. Consequently, it is from this threefold unity that our sharing in Christ's mission and office takes its origin. As Christians, members of the People of God, and subsequently, as priests, sharers in the hierarchical order, we take our origin from the combination of the mission and office of our Teacher, who is Prophet, Priest and King, in order to witness to Him in a special way in the Church and before the world.

The priesthood in which we share through the sacrament of Orders, which has been for ever "imprinted" on our souls through a special sign from God, that is to say, the "character," *remains in explicit relationship with the common priesthood of the faithful*, that is to say, the priesthood of all the baptized, but at the same time it differs from that priesthood "essentially and not only in degree."[8] In this way the words of the author of the Letter to the Hebrews about the priest, who has been "chosen from among men...appointed to act on behalf of men,"[9] take on their full meaning.

At this point, it is better to reread once more the whole of this classical conciliar text, which expresses the basic truths on the theme of our vocation in the Church:

> "Christ the Lord, high priest taken from among men (cf. Heb. 5:1), made the new people 'a kingdom of priests to God, his Father' (Rev. 1:6, cf. 5:9-10). The baptized, by regeneration and the anointing of the Holy Spirit, are consecrated to

---

8. Dogmatic Constitution *Lumen gentium*, 10.
9. Heb. 5:1.

be a spiritual house and a holy priesthood, that through all the works of Christian men they may offer spiritual sacrifices and proclaim the perfection of Him who has called them out of darkness into His marvelous light (cf. 1 Pt. 2:4-10). Therefore all the disciples of Christ, persevering in prayer and praising God together (cf. Acts 2:42-47), should present themselves as a sacrifice, living, holy and pleasing to God (cf. Rom. 12:1). They should everywhere on earth bear witness to Christ and give an answer to everyone who asks a reason for the hope of an eternal life which is theirs (cf. 1 Pt. 3:15).

"Though they differ essentially and not only in degree, the common priesthood of the faithful and the ministerial or hierarchical priesthood are nonetheless ordered one to another; each in its own proper way shares in the one priesthood of Christ. The ministerial priest, by the sacred power that he has, forms and rules the priestly people; in the person of Christ he effects the Eucharistic Sacrifice and offers it to God in the name of all the people. The faithful indeed, by virtue of their royal priesthood, participate in the offering of the Eucharist. They exercise that priesthood, too, by the reception of the sacraments, prayer and thanksgiving, the witness of a holy life, abnegation and active charity."[10]

The Priest as a Gift of Christ for the Community

4 We must consider down to the smallest detail not only the theoretical meaning but also the existential meaning of the mutual "relation" that exists between the hierarchical priesthood and the common priesthood of the faithful. The fact that they differ not only in degree but also in essence is a fruit of a particular aspect of the richness of the very priesthood of Christ, which is the one center and the one source both of that participation which belongs to all the baptized and of that other participation which is reached through a distinct sacrament, which is precisely the sacrament of Orders. This sacrament, dear brothers, which is specific for us,

---

10. Dogmatic Constitution *Lumen gentium*, 10.

which is the fruit of the special grace of vocation and the basis of our identity, by virtue of its very nature and of everything that it produces in our life and activity, serves to make the faithful aware of their common priesthood and to activate it:[11] the sacrament reminds them that they are the People of God and enables them "to offer spiritual sacrifices,"[12] through which Christ Himself makes us an everlasting gift to the Father.[13] This takes place, above all, when the priest "by the sacred power that he has...in the person of Christ *(in persona Christi)* effects the Eucharistic Sacrifice and offers it to God in the name of all the people,"[14] as we read in the conciliar text quoted above.

Our sacramental priesthood, therefore, is a "hierarchical" and at the same time "ministerial" priesthood. It constitutes a special *ministerium*, that is to say, "service," in relation to the community of believers. It does not however take its origin from that community, as though it were the community that "called" or "delegated." The sacramental priesthood is truly a gift for this community and comes from Christ Himself, from the fullness of His priesthood. This fullness finds its expression in the fact that Christ, while making everyone capable of offering the spiritual sacrifice, calls some and enables them to be ministers of His own sacramental Sacrifice, the Eucharist—in the offering of which all the faithful share—in which are taken up all the spiritual sacrifices of the People of God.

Conscious of this reality, we understand how our priesthood is "hierarchical," that is to say, connected with the power of forming and governing the priestly people[15] and *precisely for this reason "ministerial."* We carry out this office, through which Christ Himself unceasingly "serves" the Father in the work of our salvation. Our whole priestly existence is and must be deeply imbued with this service, if we wish to effect in an adequate way the Eucharistic Sacrifice *in persona Christi*.

The priesthood calls for a particular integrity of life and service, and precisely such integrity is supremely fitting for our

---

11. Cf. Eph. 4:11-12.
12. Cf. 1 Pt. 2:5.
13. Cf. 1 Pt. 3:18.
14. Dogmatic Constitution *Lumen gentium*, 10.
15. Dogmatic Constitution *Lumen gentium*, 10.

priestly identity. In that identity there are expressed, at the same time, the greatness of our dignity and the "availability" proportionate to it: It is a question of the humble readiness to accept the gifts of the Holy Spirit and to transmit to others the fruits of love and peace, to give them that certainty of faith from which derive the profound understanding of the meaning of human existence and the capacity to introduce the moral order into the life of individuals and of the human setting.

Since the priesthood is given to us so that we can unceasingly serve others, after the example of Christ the Lord, the priesthood cannot be renounced because of the difficulties that we meet and the sacrifices asked of us. Like the apostles, we have left everything to follow Christ[16]; therefore we must persevere beside Him also through the cross.

In the Service of the Good Shepherd

5   As I write, there pass before the eyes of my soul the vast and varied areas of human life, areas into which you are sent, dear brothers, like laborers into the Lord's vineyard.[17] But for you there holds also the parable of the flock,[18] for, thanks to the priestly character, you share in the *pastoral charism*, which is a sign of a special relationship of *likeness to Christ, the Good Shepherd.* You are precisely marked with this quality in a very special way. Although care for the salvation of others is and must be a task of every member of the great community of the People of God, that is to say, also of all our brothers and sisters who make up the laity—as the Second Vatican Council so amply declared[19]—nevertheless you priests are expected to have a care and commitment which are far greater and different from those of any lay person. And this is because your sharing in the priesthood of Jesus Christ differs from their sharing, "essentially and not only in degree."[20]

---

16. Cf. Mt. 19:27.
17. Cf. Mt. 20:1-16.
18. Cf. Jn. 10:1-16.
19. Cf. Dogmatic Constitution *Lumen gentium*, 11.
20. Dogmatic Constitution *Lumen gentium*, 10.

In fact, the priesthood of Jesus Christ is the first source and expression of an unceasing and ever effective care for our salvation, which enables us to look to Him precisely as the Good Shepherd. Do not the words "the good shepherd is one who lays down his life for his sheep"[21] refer to the sacrifice of the cross, to the definitive act of Christ's priesthood? Do they not show all of us that Christ the Lord, through the sacrament of Orders, has made us sharers in His Priesthood, the road that we too must travel? Do these words not tell us that our vocation is a singular *solicitude for the salvation of our neighbor?* that this solicitude is a special *raison d'être* of our priestly life? that it is precisely this solicitude that gives it meaning, and that only through this solicitude can we find the full significance of our own life, perfection and holiness? This theme is taken up, at various places, in the conciliar Decree *Optatam totius*.[22]

However, this matter becomes more comprehensible in the light of the words of our same Teacher, who says: "For anyone who wants to save his life will lose it; but anyone who loses his life for my sake, and for the sake of the gospel, will save it."[23] These are mysterious words, and they seem like a paradox. But they cease to be mysterious if we try to put them into practice. Then the paradox disappears, and the profound simplicity of their meaning is fully revealed. May all of us be granted this grace in our priestly life and zealous service.

"The Supreme Art Is the Direction of Souls"[24]

6 The special care for the salvation of others, for truth, for the love and holiness of the whole People of God, for the spiritual unity of the Church—this care that has been entrusted to us by Christ, together with the priestly power, is exercised in various ways. Of course there is a difference in the ways in which you, dear brothers, fulfill your priestly vocation. Some in the ordinary

---

21. Jn. 10:11.
22. Cf. 8-11; 19-20.
23. Mk. 8:35.
24. St. Gregory the Great, *Regula Pastoralis*, I, 1: PL 77, 14.

pastoral work of parishes; others in mission lands; still others in the field of activities connected with the teaching, training and education of youth, or working in the various spheres and organizations whereby you assist in the development of social and cultural life; yet others near the suffering, the sick, the neglected, and sometimes, you yourselves bedridden and in pain. These ways differ from one another, and it is just impossible to name them all one by one. They are necessarily numerous and different, because of the variety in the structure of human life, in social processes, and in the heritage and historical traditions of the various cultures and civilizations. Nevertheless, within all these differences, *you are always and everywhere the bearers of your particular vocation:* you are bearers of the grace of Christ, the eternal Priest, and bearers of the charism of the Good Shepherd. And this you can never forget; this you can never renounce; this you must put into practice at every moment, in every place and in every way. In this consists that "supreme art" to which Jesus Christ has called you. "The supreme art is the direction of souls," wrote St. Gregory the Great.

I say to you therefore, quoting these words of his: strive to be "artists" of pastoral work. There have been many such in the history of the Church. There speak to each of us, for example, St. Vincent de Paul, St. John of Avila, the holy Curé d'Ars, St. John Bosco, Blessed Maximilian Kolbe, and many, many others. Each of them was different from the others, was himself, was the son of his own time and was "up-to-date" with respect to his own time. But this "bringing up-to-date" of each of them was an original response to the Gospel, a response needed precisely for those times; it was the response of holiness and zeal. There is no other rule apart from this for "bringing ourselves up-to-date," in our priestly life and activity, with our time and with the world as it is today. Without any doubt, the various attempts and projects aimed at the "secularization" of the priestly life cannot be considered an adequate "bringing up-to-date."

Steward and Witness

7   The priestly life is built upon the foundation of the sacrament of Orders, which imprints on our soul the mark of an indelible character. This mark, impressed in the depths of our being, has its "personalistic" dynamism. *The priestly personality* must be *for others* a clear and plain *sign and indication*. This is the first condition for our pastoral service. The people from among whom we have been chosen and for whom we have been appointed[25] want above all to see in us such a sign and indication, and to this they have a right. It may sometimes seem to us that they do not want this, or that they wish us to be in every way "like them"; at times it even seems that they demand this of us. And here one very much needs a profound "sense of faith" and "the gift of discernment." In fact, it is very easy to let oneself be guided by appearances and fall victim to a fundamental illusion in what is essential. Those who call for the secularization of priestly life and applaud its various manifestations will undoubtedly abandon us when we succumb to temptation. We shall then cease to be necessary and popular. Our time is characterized by different forms of "manipulation" and "exploitation" of man, but we cannot give in to any of these.[26] In practical terms, the only priest who will always prove necessary to people is the priest who is conscious of the full meaning of his priesthood: the priest who believes profoundly, who professes his faith with courage, who prays fervently, who teaches with deep conviction, who serves, who puts into practice in his own life the program of the beatitudes, who knows how to love disinterestedly, who is close to everyone, and especially to those who are most in need.

Our pastoral activity demands that we should be close to people and all their problems, whether these problems be personal, family or social ones, but it also demands that we should be close to all these problems "in a priestly way." Only then, in the sphere of all those problems, do we remain ourselves. Therefore, if we are really of assistance in those human problems, and they are sometimes very difficult ones, then we keep our identity and are really faithful to our vocation. With great perspicacity we must seek, together with all men, truth and justice, the true and definitive

---

25. Cf. Heb. 5:1.

26. "Let us not deceive ourselves in thinking we serve the Gospel, if we try 'to dilute' our priestly charism...": Pope John Paul II, *Discourse to the Clergy of Rome* (November 9, 1978), no. 3: *L'Osservatore Romano* (November 10, 1978), p. 2.

dimension of which we can only find in the Gospel, or rather in Christ Himself. Our task is to serve *truth and justice* in the dimensions of human "temporality," but *always in a perspective* that is the perspective *of eternal salvation.* This salvation takes into account the temporal achievements of the human spirit in the spheres of knowledge and morality, as the Second Vatican Council wonderfully recalled,[27] but it is not identical with them, and in fact it goes higher than them: "The things that no eye has seen and no ear has heard...all that God has prepared for those who love him."[28] Our brethren in the faith, and unbelievers too, expect us always to be able to show them this perspective, to become real witnesses to it, to be dispensers of grace, to be servants of the Word of God. They expect us to be men of prayer.

Among us there are also those who have united their priestly vocation in a special way with an intense life of prayer and penance in the strictly contemplative form of their religious orders. Let them remember that their priestly ministry also in this form is—in a special way—"ordered" to the great solicitude of the Good Shepherd—solicitude for the salvation of every human being.

And this we must all remember: that it is not lawful for any of us to deserve the name of "hireling," that is to say, the name of one "to whom the sheep do not belong," one who, "since he is not the shepherd and the sheep do not belong to him, abandons the sheep and runs away as soon as he sees the wolf coming, and then the wolf attacks and scatters the sheep; this is because he is only a hired man and has no concern for the sheep."[29] The solicitude of every good shepherd is that all people "may have life and have it to the full,"[30] so that none of them may be lost,[31] but should have eternal life. Let us endeavor to make this solicitude penetrate deeply into our souls; let us strive to live it. May it characterize our personality, and be at the foundation of our priestly identity.

---

27. Cf. Pastoral Constitution *Gaudium et spes*, 38-39, 42.
28. 1 Cor. 2:9.
29. Jn. 10:12-13.
30. Jn. 10:10.
31. Cf. Jn. 17:12.

Meaning of Celibacy

8   Allow me at this point to touch upon the question of priestly celibacy. I shall deal with it summarily, because it has already been considered in a profound and complete way during the Council, and subsequently in the Encyclical *Sacerdotalis caelibatus*, and again at the ordinary session of the 1971 Synod of Bishops. This reflection has shown itself to be necessary both in order to present the matter in a still more mature way, and also in order to explain even more deeply the meaning of the decision that the Latin Church took so many centuries ago and to which she has sought to be faithful, and desires to maintain this fidelity also in the future. The importance of the question under consideration is so great, and its link with the language of the Gospel itself so close, that in this case we cannot reason with categories different from those used by the Council, the Synod of Bishops and the great Pope Paul VI himself. We can only seek to understand this question more deeply and to respond to it more maturely, freeing ourselves from the various objections that have always—as happens today too—been raised against priestly celibacy, and also freeing ourselves from the different interpretations that appeal to criteria alien to the Gospel, to Tradition and to the Church's Magisterium—criteria, we would add, whose "anthropological" correctness and basis in fact are seen to be very dubious and of relative value.

Nor must we be too surprised at all the objections and criticisms which have intensified during the postconciliar period, even though today in some places they seem to be growing less. Did not Jesus Christ, after He had presented the disciples with the question of the renunciation of marriage "for the sake of the kingdom of heaven," add these significant words: "Let anyone accept this who can"[32]? The Latin Church has wished, and continues to wish, referring to the example of Christ the Lord Himself, to the apostolic teaching and to the whole Tradition that is proper to her, that *all those who receive the sacrament of Orders should embrace this renunciation "for the sake of the kingdom of heaven."* This tradition, however, is linked with respect for different traditions of other Churches. In fact, this tradition constitutes a characteristic, a

---

32. Mt. 19:12.

peculiarity and a heritage of the Latin Catholic Church, a tradition to which she owes much and in which she is resolved to persevere, in spite of all the difficulties to which such fidelity could be exposed, and also in spite of the various symptoms of weakness and crisis in individual priests. We are all aware that "we have this treasure in earthen vessels"[33]; yet we know very well that it is precisely a treasure.

Why is it a treasure? Do we wish thereby to reduce the value of marriage and the vocation to family life? Or are we succumbing to a Manichean contempt for the human body and its functions? Do we wish in some way to devalue love, which leads a man and a woman to marriage and the wedded unity of the body, thus forming "one flesh"[34]? How could we think and reason like that, if we know, believe and proclaim, following St. Paul, that marriage is a "great mystery" in reference to Christ and the Church?[35] However, none of the reasons whereby people sometimes try to "convince us" of the inopportuneness of celibacy corresponds to the truth, the truth that the Church proclaims and seeks to realize in life through the commitment to which priests oblige themselves before ordination. The essential, proper and adequate reason, in fact, is contained in the truth that Christ declared when He spoke about the renunciation of marriage for the sake of the kingdom of heaven, and which St. Paul proclaimed when he wrote that each person in the Church has his or her own particular gifts.[36] Celibacy is precisely a "gift of the Spirit." A similar though different gift is contained in the vocation to true and faithful married love, directed towards procreation according to the flesh, in the very lofty context of the sacrament of Matrimony. It is obvious that this gift is fundamental for the building up of the great community of the Church, the People of God. But if this community wishes to respond fully to its vocation in Jesus Christ, there will also have to be realized in it, in the correct proportion, that other "gift," the gift of celibacy "for the sake of the kingdom of heaven."[37]

---

33. Cf. 2 Cor. 4:7.
34. Gn. 2:24; cf. Mt. 19:6.
35. Cf. Eph. 5:32.
36. Cf. 1 Cor. 7:7.
37. Mt. 19:12.

Why does the Latin Catholic Church link this gift not only with the life of those who accept the strict program of the evangelical counsels in religious institutes but also with the vocation to the hierarchical and ministerial priesthood? She does it because celibacy "for the sake of the kingdom" is not only an eschatological sign; it also has a great social meaning, in the present life, for the service of the People of God. Through his celibacy, the priest becomes the "man for others," in a different way from the man who, by binding himself in conjugal union with a woman, also becomes, as husband and father, a man "for others," especially in the radius of his own family: for his wife, and, together with her, for the children, to whom he gives life. The priest, by renouncing this fatherhood proper to married men, seeks another fatherhood and, as it were, even another motherhood, recalling the words of the Apostle about the children whom he begets in suffering.[38] These are children of his spirit, people entrusted to his solicitude by the Good Shepherd. These people are many, more numerous than an ordinary human family can embrace. The pastoral vocation of priests is great, and the Council teaches that it is universal: it is directed towards the whole Church,[39] and therefore it is of a missionary character. Normally, it is linked to the service of a particular community of the People of God, in which each individual expects attention, care and love. The heart of the priest, in order that it may be available for this service, must be free. Celibacy is a sign of a freedom that exists for the sake of service. According to this sign, the hierarchical or "ministerial" priesthood is, according to the tradition of our Church, more strictly "ordered" to the common priesthood of the faithful.

Test and Responsibility

9 The often widespread view that priestly celibacy in the Catholic Church is an institution imposed by law on those who receive the sacrament of Orders is the result of a misunderstanding, if not of downright bad faith. We all know that it is not so. Every Christian who receives the sacrament of Orders commits himself to

---

38. Cf. 1 Cor. 4:15; Gal. 4:19.
39. Cf. Decree *Presbyterorum ordinis*, 3, 6, 10, 12.

celibacy with full awareness and freedom, after a training lasting a number of years, and after profound reflection and assiduous prayer. He decides upon a life of celibacy only after he has reached a firm conviction that Christ is giving him this "gift" for the good of the Church and the service of others. Only then does he commit himself to observe celibacy for his entire life. It is obvious that such a decision obliges not only by virtue of a law laid down by the Church but also by virtue of personal responsibility. It is a matter here of *keeping one's word to Christ and the Church*. Keeping one's word is, at one and the same time, a duty and a proof of the priest's inner maturity; it is the expression of his personal dignity. It is shown in all its clarity when this keeping one's promise to Christ, made through a conscious and free commitment to celibacy for the whole of one's life, encounters difficulties, is put to the test, or is exposed to temptation—all things that do not spare the priest, any more than they spare any other Christian. At such a moment, the individual must seek support in more fervent prayer. Through prayer, he must find within himself that attitude of humility and sincerity before God and his own conscience; prayer is indeed the source of strength for sustaining what is wavering. Then it is that there is born a confidence like the confidence expressed by St. Paul in the words: "There is nothing that I cannot master with the help of the One who gives me strength."[40] These truths are confirmed by the experience of many priests and proved by the reality of life. The acceptance of these truths constitutes the basis of fidelity to the promise made to Christ and the Church, and that promise is at the same time the proof of genuine fidelity to oneself, one's own conscience, and one's own humanity and dignity. One must think of all these things especially at moments of crisis, and not have recourse to a dispensation, understood as an "administrative intervention," as though in fact it were not, on the contrary, a matter of a profound question of conscience and a test of humanity. God has a right to test each one of us in this way, since this earthly life is a time of testing for every human being. But God also wishes us all to emerge victorious from such tests, and He gives us adequate help for this.

---

40. Phil. 4:13.

Perhaps, not without good reason, one should add at this point that the commitment to married fidelity, which derives from the sacrament of Matrimony, creates similar obligations in its own sphere; this married commitment sometimes becomes a source of similar trials and experiences for husbands and wives, who also have a way of proving the value of their love in these "trials by fire." Love, in fact, in all its dimensions, is not only a call but also a duty. Finally, we should add that our brothers and sisters joined by the marriage bond *have the right to expect from us*, priests and pastors, good example and *the witness of fidelity to one's vocation until death*, a fidelity to the vocation that we choose through the sacrament of Orders just as they choose it through the sacrament of Matrimony. Also in this sphere and in this sense we should understand our ministerial priesthood as "subordination" to the common priesthood of all the faithful, of the laity, especially of those who live in marriage and form a family. In this way, we serve in "building up the body of Christ"[41]; otherwise, instead of cooperating in the building up of that body we weaken its spiritual structure. Closely linked to this building up of the body of Christ is the authentic development of the human personality of each Christian—as also of each priest—a development that takes place according to the measure of the gift of Christ. The disorganization of the spiritual structure of the Church certainly does not favor the development of the human personality and does not constitute its proper testing.

Every Day We Have To Be Converted Anew

10 "What must we do, then?"[42]: dear brothers, this seems to be your question, just as the disciples and those who listened to Christ the Lord asked Him so often. What must the Church do, when it seems that there is a lack of priests, when their absence makes itself felt especially in certain countries and regions of the world? How are we to respond to the immense needs of evangelization, and how can we satisfy the hunger for the Word and the Body of the Lord? The Church, which commits herself to maintaining

---

41. Eph. 4:12.
42. Lk. 3:10.

priestly celibacy as a particular gift for the kingdom of God, *professes faith in and expresses hope in* her Teacher, Redeemer and Spouse, and at the same time in Him who is "Lord of the harvest" and "giver of the gift."[43] In fact, "every perfect gift is from above, coming down from the Father of lights."[44] We, for our part, cannot weaken this faith and confidence with our human doubting or our timidity.

In consequence, we must all be converted anew every day. We know that this is a fundamental exigency of the Gospel, addressed to everyone,[45] and all the more do we have to consider it as addressed to us. If we have the duty of helping others to be converted we have to do the same continuously in our own lives. Being converted means returning to the very grace of our vocation; it means meditating upon the infinite goodness and love of Christ, who has addressed each of us and, calling us by name, has said: "Follow me." Being converted means continually "giving an account" before the Lord of our hearts about our service, our zeal and our fidelity, for we are "Christ's servants, stewards entrusted with the mysteries of God."[46] Being converted also means "giving an account" of our negligencies and sins, of our timidity, of our lack of faith and hope, of our thinking only "in a human way" and not "in a divine way." Let us recall, in this regard, the warning that Christ gave to Peter himself.[47] Being converted means, for us, seeking again the pardon and strength of God in the sacrament of Reconciliation, and thus always beginning anew, and every day progressing, overcoming ourselves, making spiritual conquests, giving cheerfully, for "God loves a cheerful giver."[48]

Being converted means "to pray continually and never lose heart."[49] *In a certain way prayer is the first and last condition for conversion*, spiritual progress and holiness. Perhaps in these recent years—at least in certain quarters—there has been too much discussion about the priesthood, the priest's "identity," the value of his

---

43. Mt. 9:38; cf. 1 Cor. 7:7.
44. Jas. 1:17.
45. Cf. Mt. 4:17; Mk. 1:15.
46. 1 Cor. 4:1.
47. Cf. Mt. 16:23.
48. 2 Cor. 9:7.
49. Lk. 18:1.

presence in the modern world, etc., and on the other hand there has been too little praying. There has not been enough enthusiasm for actuating the priesthood itself through prayer, in order to make its authentic evangelical dynamism effective, in order to confirm the priestly identity. It is prayer that shows the essential style of the priest; without prayer this style becomes deformed. Prayer helps us always to find the light that has led us since the beginning of our priestly vocation, and which never ceases to lead us, even though it seems at times to disappear in the darkness. Prayer enables us to be converted continually, to remain in a state of continuous reaching out to God, which is essential if we wish to lead others to Him. Prayer helps us to believe, to hope and to love, even when our human weakness hinders us.

Prayer likewise enables us continually to rediscover the dimensions of that kingdom for whose coming we pray every day, when we repeat the words that Christ taught us. Then we realize *what our place is in the realization of the petition:* "Thy kingdom come," and we see how necessary we are in its realization. And perhaps, when we pray, we shall see more easily those "fields...already white for harvest"[50] and we shall understand the meaning of Christ's words as He looked at them: "So ask the Lord of the harvest to send laborers to his harvest."[51]

We must link prayer with continuous work upon ourselves: this is the *formatio permanens.* As is rightly pointed out by the Document on this theme issued by the Sacred Congregation for the Clergy,[52] this formation must be both interior, that is to say, directed towards the deepening of the priest's spiritual life, and must also be pastoral and intellectual (philosophical and theological). Therefore, since our pastoral activity, the proclamation of the Word and the whole of the priestly ministry depend upon the intensity of our interior life, that activity must also find sustenance in assiduous study. It is not enough for us to stop at what we once learned in the seminary, even in cases where those studies were done at university level, which the Sacred Congregation for Catholic Education resolutely recommends. This process of

---

50. Jn. 4:35.
51. Mt. 9:38.
52. Cf. Circular Letter of November 4, 1969: *AAS* 62 (1970), pp. 123ff.

intellectual formation must last all one's life, especially in modern times, which are marked—at least in many parts of the world—by the widespread development of education and culture. To the people who enjoy the benefits of this development we must be *witnesses* to Jesus Christ, and properly qualified ones. As teachers of truth and morality, we must tell them, convincingly and effectively, of the hope that gives us life.[53] And this also forms part of the process of daily conversion to love, through the truth.

Dear brothers: you who have borne "the burden of the day and the heat,"[54] who have put your hand to the plough and do not turn back,[55] and perhaps even more those of you who are doubtful of the meaning of your vocation or of the value of your service: think of the places where people anxiously await a priest, and where for many years, feeling the lack of such a priest, they do not cease to hope for his presence. And sometimes it happens that they meet in an abandoned shrine, and place on the altar a stole which they still keep, and recite all the prayers of the Eucharistic liturgy; and then, at the moment that corresponds to the transubstantiation a deep silence comes down upon them, a silence sometimes broken by a sob...so ardently do they desire to hear the words that only the lips of a priest can efficaciously utter. So much do they desire Eucharistic Communion, in which they can share only through the ministry of a priest, just as they also so eagerly wait to hear the divine words of pardon: *Ego te absolvo a peccatis tuis!* So deeply do they feel the absence of a priest among them!... Such places are not lacking in the world. So if one of you doubts the meaning of his priesthood, if he thinks it is "socially" fruitless or useless, reflect on this!

We must be converted every day, we must rediscover every day the gift obtained from Christ Himself in the sacrament of Orders, by penetrating the importance of the salvific mission of the Church and by reflecting on the great meaning of our vocation in the light of that mission.

---

53. Cf. 1 Pt. 3:15.
54. Mt. 20:12.
55. Cf. Lk. 9:62.

Mother of Priests

11 Dear brothers, at the beginning of my ministry I entrust all of you to the Mother of Christ, who in a special way is our Mother: the Mother of priests. In fact, the beloved disciple, who, as one of the Twelve, had heard in the Upper Room the words "Do this in memory of me,"[56] was given by Christ on the cross to His Mother, with the words: "Behold your son."[57] The man who on Holy Thursday received the power to celebrate the Eucharist was, by these words of the dying Redeemer, given to His Mother as her "son." All of us, therefore, who receive the same power through priestly Ordination have in a certain sense a prior right to see her as our Mother. And so I desire that all of you, together with me, should find in Mary the Mother of the priesthood which we have received from Christ. I also desire that you should entrust your priesthood to her in a special way. Allow me to do it myself, *entrusting to the Mother of Christ* each one of you—without any exception—in a solemn and at the same time simple and humble way. And I ask each of you, dear brothers, to do it yourselves, in the way dictated to you by your own heart, especially by your love for Christ the Priest, and also by your own weakness, which goes hand in hand with your desire for service and holiness. I ask you to do this.

The Church of today speaks of herself especially in the Dogmatic Constitution *Lumen gentium*. Here too, in the last chapter, she proclaims that she looks to Mary as to the Mother of Christ, because she calls herself a mother and wishes to be a mother, begetting people for God to a new life.[58] Now, dear brothers: How near you are to this cause of God! How deeply it is imprinted upon your vocation, ministry and mission. In consequence, in the midst of the People of God, that looks to Mary with immense love and hope, you must look to her with exceptional hope and love. Indeed, you must proclaim Christ who is her Son; and who will better communicate to you the truth about Him than His Mother? You must nourish human hearts with Christ: And

---

56. Lk. 22:19.
57. Jn. 19:26.
58. Cf. Dogmatic Constitution *Lumen gentium*, Chapter VIII.

who can make you more aware of what you are doing than she who nourished Him? "Hail, true Body, born of the Virgin Mary." In our "ministerial" priesthood there is *the wonderful and penetrating dimension of nearness to the Mother of Christ*. So let us try to live in that dimension. If I may be permitted to speak here of my own experience, I will say to you that in writing to you I am referring especially to my own personal experience.

As I communicate all this to you, at the beginning of my service to the universal Church, I do not cease to ask God to fill you, priests of Jesus Christ, with every blessing and grace, and as a token of this communion in prayer I bless you with all my heart, in the name of the Father and of the Son and of the Holy Spirit.

Accept this blessing. Accept the words of the new Successor of Peter, that Peter whom the Lord commanded: "And once you have recovered, you in your turn must strengthen your brothers."[59] Do not cease to pray for me together with the whole Church, so that I may respond to that exigency of a primacy of love that the Lord made the foundation of the mission of Peter, when He said to him: "Feed my lambs."[60] Amen.

From the Vatican, April 8, Passion Sunday (Palm Sunday), in the year 1979, the first of the pontificate.

POPE JOHN PAUL II

---

59. Lk. 22:32.
60. Jn. 21:16.

HOLY THURSDAY, 1980

The Mystery and Worship of the Eucharist

My venerable and dear brothers, bishops of the Church,

1 Again this year, for Holy Thursday, I am writing a letter to all of you. This letter has an immediate connection with the one which you received last year on the same occasion, together with the letter to the priests. I wish *in the first place to thank you cordially* for having accepted my previous letters with that spirit of unity which the Lord established between us, and also for having transmitted to your priests the thoughts that I desired to express at the beginning of my pontificate.

During the Eucharistic Liturgy of Holy Thursday, you renewed, together with your priests, the promises and commitments undertaken at the moment of ordination. Many of you, venerable and dear brothers, told me about it later, also adding words of personal thanks, and indeed often sending those expressed by your priests. Furthermore, many priests expressed their joy, both because of the profound and solemn character of Holy Thursday as the annual "feast of priests" and also because of the importance of the subjects dealt with in the letter addressed to them.

Those replies form a rich collection which once more indicates how dear to the vast majority of priests of the Catholic Church is the path of the priestly life, the path along which this Church has been journeying for centuries: How much they love and esteem it, and how much they desire to follow it for the future.

At this point I must add that *only a certain number of matters were dealt with in the letter to priests,* as was in fact emphasized at the beginning of the document.[1] Furthermore, the main stress was laid upon the pastoral character of the priestly ministry; but this certainly does not mean that those groups of priests who are not engaged in direct pastoral activity were not also taken into con-

---

1. Cf. Chapter 2: *AAS* 71 (1979), pp. 395f.

sideration. In this regard I would refer once more to the teaching of the Second Vatican Council, and also to the declarations of the 1971 Synod of Bishops.

The pastoral character of the priestly ministry does not cease to mark the life of every priest, even if the daily tasks that he carries out are not explicitly directed to the pastoral administration of the sacraments. In this sense, the letter written to the priests on Holy Thursday was addressed to them all, without any exception, even though, as I said above, it did not deal with all the aspects of the life and activity of priests. I think this clarification is useful and opportune at the beginning of the present letter.

I

THE EUCHARISTIC MYSTERY
IN THE LIFE OF THE CHURCH
AND OF THE PRIEST

Eucharist and Priesthood

2 The present letter that I am addressing to you, my venerable and dear brothers in the episcopate—and which is, as I have said, in a certain way a continuation of the previous one—is also closely linked with the mystery of Holy Thursday, and is related to the priesthood. In fact I intend to devote it to the Eucharist, and in particular *to certain aspects of the Eucharistic Mystery and its impact on the lives of those who are the ministers of it:* and so those to whom this letter is directly addressed are you, the bishops of the Church; together with you, all the priests; and, in their own rank, the deacons too.

In reality, the ministerial and hierarchical priesthood, the priesthood of the bishops and the priests, and, at their side, the ministry of the deacons—ministries which normally begin with the proclamation of the Gospel—are in the closest relationship with the Eucharist. The Eucharist is the principal and central *raison d'être* of the sacrament of the priesthood, which effectively came into being at the moment of the institution of the Eucharist, and together with it.[2] Not without reason the words "Do this in memory of me" are said immediately after the words of Eucharistic consecration, and we repeat them every time we celebrate the holy Sacrifice.[3]

Through our ordination—the celebration of which is linked to the holy Mass from the very first liturgical evidence[4]—we are united in a singular and exceptional way to the Eucharist. In a certain way we derive *from* it and exist *for* it. We are also, and in a special way, responsible for it—each priest in his own community and each bishop by virtue of the care of all the communities entrusted to him, on the basis of the *sollicitudo omnium ecclesiarum* that St. Paul speaks of.[5] Thus we bishops and priests are entrusted with the great "Mystery of Faith," and while it is also given to the whole People of God, to all believers in Christ, yet to us has been entrusted the Eucharist also "for" others, who expect from us a particular witness of veneration and love towards this sacrament, so that they too may be able to be built up and vivified "to offer spiritual sacrifices."[6]

In this way our Eucharistic worship, both in the celebration of Mass and in our devotion to the Blessed Sacrament, is like a life-giving current that links our ministerial or hierarchical priesthood to the common priesthood of the faithful, and presents it in its vertical dimension and with its central value. The priest fulfills his principal mission and is manifested in all his fullness when he celebrates the Eucharist,[7] and this manifestation is more complete when he himself allows the depth of that mystery to become visible, so that it alone shines forth in people's hearts and minds, through his

---

2. Cf. Ecumenical Council of Trent, Session XXII, Can. 2: *Conciliorum Oecumenicorum Decreta*, ed. 3, Bologna 1973, p. 735.

3. Because of this precept of the Lord, an Ethiopian Eucharistic Liturgy recalls that the Apostles "established for us patriarchs, archbishops, priests and deacons to celebrate the ritual of your holy Church": *Anaphora Sancti Athanasii: Prex Eucharistica*, Haenggi-Pahl, Fribourg (Switzerland) 1968, p. 183.

4. Cf. *La Tradition apostolique de saint Hippolyte*, nos. 2-4, ed. Botte, Munster-Westfalen 1963, pp. 5-17.

5. 2 Cor. 11:28.

6. 1 Pt. 2:5.

7. Cf. Second Vatican Ecumenical Council, Dogmatic Constitution on the Church *Lumen gentium*, 28; *AAS* 57 (1965), pp. 33f.; Decree on the Ministry and Life of Priests *Presbyterorum ordinis*, 2, 5: *AAS* 58 (1966), pp. 993, 998; Decree on the Missionary Activity of the Church *Ad gentes*, 39: *AAS* 58 (1966), p. 986.

ministry. This is the supreme exercise of the "kingly priesthood," "the source and summit of all Christian life."[8]

Worship of the Eucharistic Mystery

3 This worship is directed towards God the Father through Jesus Christ in the Holy Spirit. In the first place towards the Father, who, as St. John's Gospel says, "loved the world so much that he gave his only Son, so that everyone who believes in him may not be lost but may have eternal life."[9]

It is also directed, in the Holy Spirit, to the incarnate Son, in the economy of salvation, especially at that moment of supreme dedication and total abandonment of Himself to which the words uttered in the Upper Room refer: "This is my body given up for you.... This is the cup of my blood shed for you...."[10] The liturgical acclamation: "We proclaim your death, Lord Jesus" takes us back precisely to that moment; and with the proclamation of His resurrection we embrace in the same act of veneration Christ risen and glorified "at the right hand of the Father," as also the expectation of His "coming in glory." *Yet it is the voluntary emptying of Himself, accepted by the Father and glorified with the resurrection,* which, sacramentally celebrated together with the resurrection, brings us to adore the Redeemer who "became obedient unto death, even death on a cross."[11]

And this adoration of ours contains yet another special characteristic. It is compenetrated by the greatness of that human death, in which the world, that is to say, each one of us, has been loved "to the end."[12] Thus it is also a response that tries to repay that love immolated even to the death on the cross: it is our "Eucharist," that

---

8. Second Vatican Ecumenical Council, Dogmatic Constitution on the Church *Lumen gentium*, 11: *AAS* 57 (1965), p. 15.

9. Jn. 3:16. It is interesting to note how these words are taken up by the liturgy of St. John Chrysostom immediately before the words of consecration and introduce the latter: cf. *La divina Liturgia del nostro Padre Giovanni Crisostomo*, Roma-Grottaferrata 1967, pp. 104f.

10. Cf. Mt. 26:26-28; Mk. 14:22-25; Lk. 22:18-20; 1 Cor. 11:23-25; cf. also the Eucharistic Prayers.

11. Phil. 2:8.

12. Jn. 13:1.

is to say our giving Him thanks, our praise of Him for having redeemed us by His death and made us sharers in immortal life through His resurrection.

This worship, given therefore to the Trinity of the Father and of the Son and of the Holy Spirit, above all accompanies and permeates the celebration of the Eucharistic Liturgy. But it must fill our churches also outside the timetable of Masses. Indeed, since the Eucharistic Mystery was instituted out of love, and makes Christ sacramentally present, it is worthy of thanksgiving and worship. And this worship must be prominent in all our encounters with the Blessed Sacrament, both when we visit our churches and when the sacred Species are taken to the sick and administered to them.

Adoration of Christ in this sacrament of love must also find expression *in various forms of Eucharistic devotion:* personal prayer before the Blessed Sacrament, Hours of Adoration, periods of exposition—short, prolonged and annual (Forty Hours)—Eucharistic benediction, Eucharistic processions, Eucharistic congresses.[13] A particular mention should be made at this point of the Solemnity of the Body and Blood of Christ as an act of public worship rendered to Christ present in the Eucharist, a feast instituted by my Predecessor Urban IV in memory of the institution of this great Mystery.[14] All this therefore corresponds to the general principles and particular norms already long in existence but newly formulated during or after the Second Vatican Council.[15]

---

13. Cf. John Paul II, Homily in Phoenix Park, Dublin, 7: *AAS* 71 (1979), pp. 1074ff.; Sacred Congregation of Rites, instruction *Eucharisticum mysterium: AAS* 59 (1967), pp. 539-573; *Rituale Romanum, De sacra communione et de cultu Mysterii eucharistici extra Missam,* ed. *typica,* 1973. It should be noted that the value of the worship and the sanctifying power of these forms of devotion to the Eucharist depend not so much upon the forms themselves as upon interior attitudes.

14. Cf. *Bull Transiturus de hoc mundo* (Aug. 11, 1264): *Aemilii Friedberg, Corpus Iuris Canonici,* Pars II. *Decretalium Collectiones,* Leipzig 1881, pp. 1174-1177; *Studi eucharistici,* VII Centenario della Bolla 'Transiturus,' 1264-1964, Orvieto 1966, pp. 302-317.

15. Cf. Paul VI, encyclical letter *Mysterium fidei: AAS* 57 (1965), pp. 753-774; Sacred Congregation of Rites, Instruction *Eucharisticum Mysterium: AAS* 59 (1967), pp. 539-573; *Rituale Romanum, De sacra communione et de cultu Mysterii eucharistici extra Missam,* ed. *typica,* 1973.

The encouragement and the deepening of Eucharistic worship are *proofs of that authentic renewal* which the Council set itself as an aim and of which they are *the central point*. And this, venerable and dear brothers, deserves separate reflection. The Church and the world have a great need of Eucharistic worship. Jesus waits for us in this sacrament of love. Let us be generous with our time in going to meet Him in adoration and in contemplation that is full of faith and ready to make reparation for the great faults and crimes of the world. May our adoration never cease.

Eucharist and Church

4 Thanks to the Council we have realized with renewed force the following truth: Just as the Church "makes the Eucharist" so "the Eucharist builds up" the Church[16]; and this truth is closely bound up with the mystery of Holy Thursday. The Church was founded, as the new community of the People of God, in the apostolic community of those Twelve who, at the Last Supper, became partakers of the body and blood of the Lord under the species of bread and wine. Christ had said to them: "Take and eat.... Take and drink." And carrying out this command of His, they entered for the first time into sacramental communion with the Son of God, a communion that is a pledge of eternal life. From that moment until the end of time, *the Church is being built up through that same communion with the Son of God, a communion which is a pledge of the eternal Passover.*

Dear and venerable brothers in the episcopate, as teachers and custodians of the salvific truth of the Eucharist, we must always and everywhere preserve this meaning and this dimension of the sacramental encounter and intimacy with Christ. It is precisely these elements which constitute the very substance of Eucharistic worship. The meaning of the truth expounded above in no way

---

16. John Paul II, encyclical letter *Redemptor hominis*, 20: *AAS* 71 (1979), p. 311; cf. Second Vatican Ecumenical Council, Dogmatic Constitution on the Church *Lumen gentium*, 11: *AAS* 57 (1965), pp. 15f.; also, note 57 to Schema II of the same dogmatic constitution, in *Acta Synodalia Sacrosancti Concilii Oecumenici Vaticani II*, vol. II, periodus 2a, pars I, public session II, pp. 251f.; Paul VI, Address at the general audience of September 15, 1965: *Insegnamenti di Paolo VI*, III (1965), p. 103; H. de Lubac, *Méditation sur l'Eglise*, 2 ed., Paris 1963, pp. 129-137.

diminishes—in fact, it facilitates—the Eucharistic character of spiritual drawing together and union between the people who share in the sacrifice, which then in Communion becomes for them the banquet. This drawing together and this union, the prototype of which is the union of the Apostles about Christ at the Last Supper, express the Church and bring her into being.

But the Church is not brought into being only through the union of people, through the experience of brotherhood to which the Eucharistic Banquet gives rise. The Church is brought into being when, in that fraternal union and communion, we celebrate the sacrifice of the cross of Christ, when we proclaim "the Lord's death until he comes,"[17] and later, when, being deeply compenetrated with the mystery of our salvation, we approach as a community the table of the Lord, in order to be nourished there, in a sacramental manner, by the fruits of the holy Sacrifice of propitiation. Therefore in Eucharistic Communion we receive Christ, Christ Himself; and our union with Him, which is a gift and grace for each individual, brings it about that in Him we are also associated in the unity of His Body which is the Church.

Only in this way, through that faith and that disposition of mind, is there brought about that building up of the Church, which in the Eucharist truly finds its "source and summit," according to the well-known expression of the Second Vatican Council.[18] This truth, which as a result of the same Council has received a new and vigorous emphasis,[19] must be a frequent theme of our reflection and teaching. Let all pastoral activity be nourished by it, and may it also be food for ourselves and for all the priests who collaborate with us, and likewise for the whole of the communities entrusted to us. In this practice there should thus be revealed, almost at every

---

17. 1 Cor. 11:26.

18. Cf. Second Vatican Ecumenical Council, Dogmatic Constitution on the Church *Lumen gentium*, 11: *AAS* 57 (1965) pp. 15f.; Constitution on the Sacred Liturgy *Sacrosanctum concilium*, 10: *AAS* 56 (1964), p. 102; Decree on the Ministry and Life of Priests *Presbyterorum ordinis*, 5: *AAS* 58 (1966), pp. 997f.; Decree on the Bishops' Pastoral Office in the Church *Christus Dominus*, 30: *AAS* 58 (1966), pp. 688f.; Decree on the Church's Missionary Activity *Ad gentes*, 9: *AAS* 58 (1966), pp. 957f.

19. Cf. Second Vatican Ecumenical Council, Dogmatic Constitution on the Church *Lumen gentium*, 26: *AAS* 57 (1965), pp. 31f., Decree on Ecumenism *Unitatis redintegratio*, 15: *AAS* 57 (1965), pp. 101f.

step, that *close relationship between the Church's spiritual and apostolic vitality* and *the Eucharist, understood in its profound significance* and from all points of view.[20]

Eucharist and Charity

5   Before proceeding to more detailed observations on the subject of the celebration of the Holy Sacrifice, I wish briefly to reaffirm the fact that Eucharistic worship constitutes the soul of all Christian life. In fact, Christian life is expressed in the fulfilling of the greatest commandment, that is to say, in the love of God and neighbor, and this love finds its source in the Blessed Sacrament, which is commonly called the sacrament of love.

The Eucharist signifies this charity, and therefore recalls it, makes it present *and at the same time brings it about*. Every time that we consciously share in it, there opens in our souls a real dimension of that unfathomable love that includes everything that God has done and continues to do for us human beings, as Christ says: "My Father goes on working, and so do I."[21] Together with this unfathomable and free gift, which is *charity* revealed in its fullest degree in the saving sacrifice of the Son of God, the sacrifice of which the Eucharist is the indelible sign, there also springs up within us a lively response of love. We not only know love; we ourselves *begin to love*. We enter, so to speak, upon the path of love and along this path make progress. Thanks to the Eucharist, the love that springs up within us from the Eucharist develops in us, becomes deeper and grows stronger.

Eucharistic worship is, therefore, precisely the expression of that love which is the authentic and deepest characteristic of the Christian vocation. This worship springs from the love and serves

---

20. This is what the Opening Prayer of Holy Thursday asks for: "We pray that in this Eucharist we may find the fullness of love and life": *Missale Romanum, ed. typica altera* 1975, p. 244; also the communion epiclesis of the Roman Missal: "May all of us who share in the body and blood of Christ be brought together in unity by the Holy Spirit. Lord, remember your Church throughout the world; make us grow in love": Eucharistic Prayer II: *ibid.*, pp. 458f.; Eucharistic Prayer III, p. 463.

21. Jn. 5:17.

the love to which we are all called in Jesus Christ.[22] A living fruit of this worship is the perfecting of the image of God that we bear within us, an image that corresponds to the one that Christ has revealed in us. As we thus become adorers of the Father "in spirit and truth,"[23] we mature in an ever fuller union with Christ, we are ever more united to Him, and—if one may use the expression—we are ever more in harmony with Him.

The doctrine of the Eucharist, sign of unity and bond of charity, taught by St. Paul,[24] has been in subsequent times deepened by the writings of very many saints who are living examples for us of Eucharistic worship. We must always have this reality before our eyes, and at the same time we must continually try to bring it about that our own generation too may add new examples to those marvelous examples of the past, new examples no less living and eloquent, that will reflect the age to which we belong.

Eucharist and Neighbor

6 *The authentic sense of the Eucharist becomes of itself the school of active love for neighbor.* We know that this is the true and full order of love that the Lord has taught us: "By this love you have for one another, everyone will know that you are my disciples."[25] The Eucharist educates us to this love in a deeper way; it shows us, in fact, what value each person, our brother or sister, has in God's eyes, if Christ offers Himself equally to each one, under the species of bread and wine. If our Eucharistic worship is authentic, it must make us grow in awareness of the dignity of each person. The awareness of that dignity becomes the *deepest motive of our relationship with our neighbor.*

---

22. Cf. Prayer after communion of the Mass for the Twenty-second Sunday in Ordinary Time: "Lord, you renew us at your table with the bread of life. May this food strengthen us in love and help us to serve you in each other": *Missale Romanum, ed. cit.,* p. 361.

23. Jn. 4:23.

24. Cf. 1 Cor. 10:17; commented upon by St. Augustine: *In Evangelium Ioannis* tract. 31, 13; *PL* 35, 1613; also commented upon by the Ecumenical Council of Trent, Session XIII, can. 8; *Conciliorum Oecumenicorum Decreta,* ed. 3, Bologna 1973, p. 697, 7; cf. Second Vatican Ecumenical Council, Dogmatic Constitution on the Church *Lumen gentium,* 7: *AAS* 57 (1965), p. 9.

25. Jn. 13:35.

We must also become particularly sensitive to all human suffering and misery, to all injustice and wrong, and seek the way to redress them effectively. Let us learn to discover with respect the truth about the inner self that becomes the dwelling place of God present in the Eucharist. Christ comes into the hearts of our brothers and sisters and visits their consciences. How the image of each and every one changes, when we become aware of this reality, when we make it the subject of our reflections! The sense of the Eucharistic Mystery leads us to a love for our neighbor, to a love for every human being.[26]

Eucharist and Life

7   Since, therefore, the Eucharist is the source of charity, it has always been at the center of the life of Christ's disciples. It has the appearance of bread and wine, that is to say of food and drink; it is, therefore, as familiar to people, as closely linked to their life, as food and drink. The veneration of God, who is love, springs, in Eucharistic worship, from that kind of intimacy in which *He Himself, by analogy with food and drink, fills our spiritual being*, ensuring its life, as food and drink do. This "Eucharistic" veneration of God, therefore, strictly corresponds to His saving plan. He Himself, the Father, wants the "true worshipers"[27] to worship Him precisely in this way, and it is Christ who expresses this desire, both with His words and likewise with this sacrament in which He makes possible worship of the Father in the way most in conformity with the Father's will.

From this concept of Eucharistic worship there then stems the whole *sacramental style of the Christian's life*. In fact, leading a life based on the sacraments and animated by the common priesthood

---

26. This is expressed by many prayers of the Roman Missal: the Prayer over the Gifts from the Common, "For those who work for the underprivileged"; "May we who celebrate the love of your Son also follow the example of your saints and grow in love for you and for one another": *Missale Romanum, ed. cit.*, p. 721; also the Prayer after Communion of the Mass "For Teachers": "May this holy meal help us to follow the example of your saints by showing in our lives the light of truth and love for our brothers": *ibid.*, p. 723; cf. also the Prayer after Communion of the Mass for the Twenty-second Sunday in Ordinary Time, quoted in note 22.

27. Jn. 4:23.

means in the first place that Christians desire God to act in them in order to enable them to attain, in the Spirit, "the fullness of Christ himself."[28] God, on His part, does not touch them only through events and by this inner grace; He also acts in them with greater certainty and power through the sacraments. The sacraments give the lives of Christians a sacramental style.

Now, of all the sacraments it is the Holy Eucharist that brings to fullness their initiation as Christians and confers upon the exercise of the common priesthood that sacramental and ecclesial form that links it—as we mentioned before[29]—to the exercise of the ministerial priesthood. In this way Eucharistic worship is the *center and goal of all sacramental life.*[30] In the depths of Eucharistic worship we find a continual echo of the sacraments of Christian initiation: Baptism and Confirmation. Where better is there expressed the truth that we are not only "called God's children" but "that is what we are"[31] by virtue of the sacrament of Baptism, if not precisely in the fact that in the Eucharist we become partakers of the body and blood of God's only Son? And what predisposes us more to be "true witnesses of Christ"[32] before the world—as we are enabled to be by the sacrament of Confirmation—than Eucharistic Communion, in which Christ bears witness to us, and we to Him?

It is impossible to analyze here in greater detail the links between the Eucharist and the other sacraments, in particular with the sacrament of family life and the sacrament of the sick. In the encyclical *Redemptor hominis*[33] I have already drawn attention to the close link between the sacrament of Penance and the sacrament of the Eucharist. *It is not only that Penance leads to the Eucharist, but that the Eucharist also leads to Penance.* For when we realize who it is that we receive in Eucharistic Communion, there springs

---

28. Eph. 4:13.
29. Cf. above, no. 2.
30. Cf. Second Vatican Ecumenical Council, Decree on the Missionary Activity of the Church *Ad gentes,* 9, 12: *AAS* 58 (1966), pp. 958-961f.; Decree on the Ministry and Life of Priests *Presbyterorum ordinis,* 5: *AAS* 58 (1966), p. 997.
31. 1 Jn. 3:1.
32. Second Vatican Ecumenical Council, Dogmatic Constitution on the Church *Lumen gentium,* 11: *AAS* 57 (1965), p. 15.
33. Cf. no. 20: *AAS* 71 (1979), pp. 313f.

up in us almost spontaneously a sense of unworthiness, together with sorrow for our sins and an interior need for purification.

But we must always take care that this great meeting with Christ in the Eucharist does not become a mere habit, and that we do not receive Him unworthily, that is to say, in a state of mortal sin. The practice of the virtue of penance and the sacrament of Penance are essential for sustaining in us and continually deepening that spirit of veneration which man owes to God Himself and to His love so marvelously revealed. The purpose of these words is to put forward some general reflections on worship of the Eucharistic Mystery, and they could be developed at greater length and more fully. In particular, it would be possible to link what has been said about the effects of the Eucharist on love for others with what we have just noted about commitments undertaken towards humanity and the Church in Eucharistic Communion, and then outline the picture of that "new earth"[34] that springs from the Eucharist through every "new self."[35] *In this sacrament* of bread and wine, of food and drink, *everything that is human really undergoes a singular transformation and elevation.* Eucharistic worship is not so much worship of the inaccessible transcendence as worship of the divine condescension, and it is also the merciful and redeeming transformation of the world in the human heart.

Recalling all this only very briefly, I wish, notwithstanding this brevity, to create a wider context for the questions that I shall subsequently have to deal with: These questions are closely linked with the celebration of the Holy Sacrifice. In fact, in that celebration there is expressed in a more direct way the worship of the Eucharist. This worship comes from the heart, as a most precious homage inspired by the faith, hope and charity which were infused into us at Baptism. And it is precisely about this that I wish to write to you in this letter, venerable and dear brothers in the episcopate, and with you to the priests and deacons. It will be followed by detailed indications from the Sacred Congregation for the Sacraments and Divine Worship.

---

34. 2 Pt. 3:13.
35. Col. 3:10.

II

THE SACRED CHARACTER
OF THE EUCHARIST AND SACRIFICE

Sacred Character

8   Beginning with the Upper Room and Holy Thursday, the celebration of the Eucharist has a long history, a history as long as that of the Church. In the course of this history the secondary elements have undergone certain changes, *but there has been no change in the essence of the "Mysterium"* instituted by the Redeemer of the world at the Last Supper. The Second Vatican Council too brought alterations, as a result of which the present liturgy of the Mass is different in some ways from the one known before the Council. We do not intend to speak of these differences: It is better that we should now concentrate on what is essential and immutable in the Eucharistic liturgy.

There is a close link between this element of the Eucharist and its sacredness, that is to say, its being a holy and sacred action. Holy and sacred, because in it are the continual presence and action of Christ, "the Holy One" of God,[36] "anointed with the Holy Spirit,"[37] "consecrated by the Father"[38] to lay down His life of His own accord and to take it up again,[39] and the High Priest of the New Covenant.[40] For it is He who, represented by the celebrant, makes His entrance into the sanctuary and proclaims His Gospel. It is He who is "the offerer and the offered, the consecrator and the consecrated."[41] The Eucharist is a holy and sacred action, because it constitutes the sacred species, the *Sancta sanctis*, that is to say,

---

36. Lk. 1:34; Jn. 6:69; Acts 3:14; Rev. 3:7.
37. Acts 10:38; Lk. 4:18.
38. Jn. 10:36.
39. Cf. Jn. 10:17.
40. Heb. 3:1; 4:15, etc.
41. As was stated in the ninth-century Byzantine liturgy, according to the most ancient codex, known formerly as *Barberino di San Marco* (Florence), and, now that it is kept in the Vatican Apostolic Library, as *Barberini Greco* 366f. 8 verso, lines 17-20. This part has been published by F.E. Brightman, *Liturgies Eastern and Western*, I. *Eastern Liturgies*, Oxford 1896, p. 318, 34-35.

the "holy things (Christ, the Holy One) given to the Holy," as all the Eastern liturgies sing at the moment when the Eucharistic Bread is raised in order to invite the faithful to the Lord's Supper.

The sacredness of the Mass, therefore, is not a "sacralization," that is to say, something that man adds to Christ's action in the Upper Room, for the Holy Thursday supper was a sacred rite, a primary and constitutive liturgy, through which Christ, by pledging to give His life for us, Himself celebrated sacramentally the mystery of His passion and resurrection, the heart of every Mass. Our Masses, being derived from this liturgy, possess of themselves a complete liturgical form, which, in spite of its variations in line with the families of rites, remains substantially the same. The sacred character of the Mass is a sacredness instituted by Christ. The words and actions of every priest, answered by the conscious active participation of the whole Eucharistic assembly, echo the words and actions of Holy Thursday.

The priest offers the Holy Sacrifice *in persona Christi;* this means more than offering "in the name of" or "in place of" Christ. *In persona* means in specific sacramental identification with "the eternal High Priest"[42] who is the author and principal subject of this sacrifice of His, a sacrifice in which, in truth, nobody can take His place. Only He—only Christ—was able and is always able to be the true and effective "expiation for our sins and...for the sins of the whole world."[43] Only His sacrifice—and no one else's—was able and is able to have a "propitiatory power" before God, the Trinity, and the transcendent holiness. Awareness of this reality throws a certain light on the character and significance of the priest celebrant who, *by confecting the Holy Sacrifice and acting "in persona Christi,"* is sacramentally (and ineffably) brought into that most profound *sacredness,* and made part of it, spiritually linking with it in turn all those participating in the Eucharistic assembly.

This sacred Rite, which is actuated in different liturgical forms, may lack some secondary elements, but it can in no way lack its essential sacred character and sacramentality, since these are willed by Christ and transmitted and regulated by the Church. Neither

---

42. Opening Prayer of the Second Votive Mass of the Holy Eucharist: *Missale Romanum, ed. cit.,* p. 858.

43. 1 Jn. 2:2; cf. *ibid.,* 4:10.

can this sacred Rite be utilized for other ends. If separated from its distinctive sacrificial and sacramental nature, the Eucharistic Mystery simply ceases to be. It admits of no "profane" imitation, an imitation that would very easily (indeed regularly) become a profanation. This must always be remembered, perhaps above all in our time, when we see a tendency to do away with the distinction between the "sacred" and "profane," given the widespread tendency, at least in some places, to desacralize everything.

In view of this fact, *the Church has a special duty to safeguard and strengthen the sacredness of the Eucharist.* In our pluralistic and often deliberately secularized society, *the living faith* of the Christian community—a faith always aware of its rights vis-à-vis those who do not share that faith—ensures respect for this sacredness. The duty to respect each person's faith is the complement of the natural and civil right to freedom of conscience and of religion.

The sacred character of the Eucharist has found and continues to find expression in the terminology of theology and the liturgy.[44] This sense of the objective sacred character of the Eucharistic Mystery is so much part of the faith of the People of God that their faith is enriched and strengthened by it.[45] Therefore the ministers of

---

44. We speak of the *divinum Mysterium*, the *Sanctissimum*, the *Sacrosanctum*, meaning what is *sacred* and *holy* par excellence. For their part, the Eastern Churches call the Mass *raza* or *mysterion, hagiasmos, quddasa, qedasse*, that is to say "consecration" par excellence. Furthermore there are the liturgical rites, which, in order to inspire a sense of the sacred, prescribe silence, and standing or kneeling, and likewise professions of faith, and the incensation of the Gospel Book, the altar, the celebrant and the sacred species. They even recall the assistance of the angelic beings created to serve the Holy God, i.e., with the *Sanctus* of our Latin Churches and the *Trisagion* and *Sancta Sanctis* of the Eastern liturgies.

45. For instance, in the invitation to receive Communion, this faith has been so formed as to reveal complementary aspects of the presence of Christ the Holy One: the epiphanic aspect noted by the Byzantines ("Blessed is he who comes in the name of the Lord: The Lord is God and *has appeared to us*": La divina Liturgia del santo nostro Padre Giovanni Crisostomo, Roma-Grottaferrata 1967, pp. 136f.); the aspect of relation and union sung of by the Armenians (Liturgy of St. Ignatius of Antioch: "*Unus Pater sanctus nobiscum, unus Filius sanctus nobiscum, unus Spiritus sanctus nobiscum*": Die Anaphora des heiligen Ignatius von Antiochien, ubersetzt von A. Rucker, Oriens Christianus, 3ª ser., 5 [1930], p. 76); and the hidden heavenly aspect celebrated by the Chaldeans and Malabars (cf. the antiphonal hymn sung by the priest and the assembly after Communion: F.E. Brightman, *op. cit.*, p. 299.

the Eucharist must, especially today, be illumined by the fullness of this living faith, and in its light they must understand and perform all that is part, by Christ's will and the will of His Church, of their priestly ministry.

Sacrifice

9 The Eucharist is above all else a sacrifice. It is the sacrifice of the redemption and also the sacrifice of the New Covenant,[46] as we believe and as the Eastern Churches clearly profess: "Today's sacrifice," the Greek Church stated centuries ago, "is like that offered once by the Only-begotten Incarnate Word; it is offered by Him (now as then), since it is one and the same sacrifice."[47] Accordingly, precisely by making this single sacrifice of our salvation present, man and the world are restored to God through the paschal newness of redemption. This restoration cannot cease to be: it is the foundation of the "new and eternal covenant" of God with man and of man with God. If it were missing, one would have to question both the excellence of the sacrifice of the redemption, which in fact was perfect and definitive, and also the sacrificial value of the Mass. In fact, the Eucharist, being a true sacrifice, brings about this restoration to God.

Consequently, the celebrant, as minister of this sacrifice, is the authentic *priest*, performing—in virtue of the specific power of sacred ordination—a true sacrificial act that brings creation back to God. Although all those who participate in the Eucharist do not confect the sacrifice as He does, they offer with Him, by virtue of

---

46. Cf. Second Vatican Ecumenical Council, Constitution on the Sacred Liturgy *Sacrosanctum concilium*, 2, 47: *AAS* 56 (1964), pp. 83f.; 113; Dogmatic Constitution on the Church *Lumen gentium*, 3 and 28: *AAS* 57 (1965), pp. 6, 33f.; Decree on Ecumenism *Unitatis redintegratio* 2: *AAS* 57 (1965), p. 91; Decree on the Ministry and Life of Priests *Presbyterorum ordinis*, 13: *AAS* 58 (1966), pp. 1011f.; Ecumenical Council of Trent, Session XXII, chap. I and II: *Conciliorum Oecumenicorum Decreta*, ed. 3, Bologna 1973, pp. 732f. especially: *una eademque est hostia, idem nunc offerens sacerdotum ministerio, qui se ipsum tunc in cruce obtulit, sola offerendi ratione diversa* (ibid., p. 733).

47. *Synodus Constantinopolita adversus Sotericum* (January 1156 and May 1157): Angelo Mai, *Spicilegium romanum*, t. X, Rome 1844, p. 77; *PG* 140, 190; cf. Martin Jugie, Dict. Theol. Cath., t. X, 1338; *Theologia dogmatica christianorum orientalium*, Paris, 1930, pp. 317-320.

the common priesthood, their own *spiritual sacrifices* represented by the bread and wine from the moment of their presentation at the altar. For this liturgical action, which takes a solemn form in almost all liturgies, has a "spiritual value and meaning."[48] The bread and wine become in a sense a symbol of all that the eucharistic assembly brings, on its own part, as an offering to God and offers spiritually.

It is important that this first moment of the Liturgy of the Eucharist in the strict sense should find expression in the attitude of the participants. There is a link between this and the offertory "procession" provided for in the recent liturgical reform[49] and accompanied, in keeping with ancient tradition, by a psalm or song. A certain length of time must be allowed, so that all can become aware of this act, which is given expression at the same time by the words of the celebrant.

Awareness of the act of presenting the offerings should be maintained throughout the Mass. Indeed, it should be brought to fullness at the moment of the consecration and of the anamnesis offering, as is demanded by the fundamental value of the moment of the sacrifice. This is shown by the words of the Eucharistic Prayer said aloud by the priest. It seems worthwhile repeating here some expressions in the third Eucharistic Prayer that show in particular the sacrificial character of the Eucharist and link the offering of our persons with Christ's offering: "Look with favor on your Church's offering, and see the Victim whose death has reconciled us to yourself. Grant that we, who are nourished by his body and blood, may be filled with his Holy Spirit, and become one body, one spirit in Christ. May he make us an everlasting gift to you."

This sacrificial value is expressed earlier in every celebration by the words with which the priest concludes the presentation of the gifts, asking the faithful to pray "that my sacrifice and yours may be acceptable to God, the almighty Father." These words are binding, since they express the character of the entire Eucharistic Liturgy and the fullness of its divine and ecclesial content.

---

48. *Instituto Generalis Missalis Romani*, 49c: *Missale Romanum, ed. cit.*, p. 39; cf. Second Vatican Ecumenical Council, Decree on the Ministry and Life of Priests *Presbyterorum ordinis*, 5: *AAS* 58 (1966), pp. 997f.

49. *Ordo Missae cum populo*, 18: *Missale Romanum, ed. cit.*, p. 390.

All who participate with faith in the Eucharist become aware that it is a "sacrifice," that is to say, a "consecrated Offering." For the bread and wine presented at the altar and accompanied by the devotion and the spiritual sacrifices of the participants are finally consecrated, so as to become *truly, really and substantially* Christ's own body that is given up and His blood that is shed. Thus, by virtue of the consecration, the species of bread and wine re-present[50] in a sacramental, unbloody manner the bloody propitiatory Sacrifice offered by Him on the cross to His Father for the salvation of the world. Indeed, He alone, giving Himself as a propitiatory Victim in an act of supreme surrender and immolation, has reconciled humanity with the Father, solely through His sacrifice, "having cancelled the bond which stood against us."[51]

To this sacrifice, which is renewed in a sacramental form on the altar, the offerings of bread and wine, united with the devotion of the faithful, nevertheless bring their unique contribution, since by means of the consecration by the priest they become sacred species. This is made clear by the way in which the priest acts during the Eucharistic Prayer, especially at the consecration, and when the celebration of the Holy Sacrifice and participation in it are accompanied by awareness that "the Teacher is here and is calling for you."[52] This call of the Lord to us through His sacrifice opens our hearts, so that, purified in the mystery of our redemption, they may be united to Him in Eucharistic Communion, which confers upon participation at Mass a value that is mature, complete and binding on human life: "The Church's intention is that the faithful not only offer the spotless victim but also learn to offer themselves and daily to be drawn into ever more perfect union, through Christ the Mediator, with the Father and with each other, so that at last God may be all in all."[53]

It is therefore very opportune and necessary to continue to actuate a new and intense education, in order to discover all the richness contained in the new liturgy. Indeed, the liturgical renewal

---

50. Cf. Ecumenical Council of Trent, Session 22, chap I, *Conciliorum Oecumenicorum Decreta*, ed. 3, Bologna 1973, pp. 732f.
51. Col. 2:14.
52. Jn. 11:28.
53. *Instituto Generalis Missalis Romani*, 55f.: *Missale Romanum, ed. cit.*, p. 40.

that has taken place since the Second Vatican Council has given, so to speak, greater visibility to *the Eucharistic Sacrifice*. One factor contributing to this is that the words of the Eucharistic Prayer are said aloud by the celebrant, particularly the words of consecration, with the acclamation by the assembly immediately after the elevation.

All this should fill us with joy, but we should also remember that *these changes demand new spiritual awareness and maturity*, both on the part of the celebrant—especially now that he celebrates "facing the people"—and by the faithful. Eucharistic worship matures and grows when the words of the Eucharistic Prayer, especially the words of consecration, are spoken with great humility and simplicity, in a worthy and fitting way, which is understandable and in keeping with their holiness; when this essential act of the Eucharistic Liturgy is performed unhurriedly; and when it brings about in us such recollection and devotion that the participants become aware of the greatness of the mystery being accomplished and show it by their attitude.

III

THE TWO TABLES OF THE LORD AND THE COMMON POSSESSION OF THE CHURCH

The Table of the Word of God

10 We are well aware that from the earliest times the celebration of the Eucharist has been linked not only with prayer but also with the reading of Sacred Scripture and with singing by the whole assembly. As a result, it has long been possible to apply to the Mass the comparison, made by the Fathers, with the two tables, at which the Church prepares for her children the Word of God and the Eucharist, that is, the bread of the Lord. We must therefore go back to the first part of the sacred mystery, the part that at present is most often called the *Liturgy of the Word*, and devote some attention to it.

The reading of the passages of Sacred Scripture chosen for each day *has been subjected by the Council* to new criteria and requirements.[54] As a result of these norms of the Council a new collection of readings has been made, in which there has been applied to some extent the principle of continuity of texts and the principle of making all the sacred books accessible. The insertion of the Psalms with responses into the liturgy makes the participants familiar with the great wealth of Old Testament prayer and poetry. The fact that these texts are read and sung in the vernacular enables everyone to participate with fuller understanding.

Nevertheless, there are also those people who, having been educated on the basis of the old liturgy in Latin, experience the lack of this "one language," which in all the world was an expression of the unity of the Church and through its dignified character elicited a profound sense of the Eucharistic Mystery. It is therefore necessary to show not only understanding but also full respect towards these sentiments and desires. As far as possible these sentiments and desires are to be accommodated, as is moreover provided for in the new dispositions.[55] The Roman Church has special obligations towards Latin, the splendid language of ancient Rome, and she must manifest them whenever the occasion presents itself.

The possibilities that the post-conciliar renewal has introduced in this respect are indeed often utilized so as to make us *witnesses of and sharers in the authentic celebration of the Word of God.* There is also an increase in the number of people taking an active part in this celebration. Groups of readers and cantors, and still more often choirs of men or women, are being set up and are devoting themselves with great enthusiasm to this aspect. The Word of God, Sacred Scripture, is beginning to take on new life in many Christian communities. The faithful gathered for the liturgy prepare with song for listening to the Gospel, which is proclaimed with the devotion and love due to it.

---

54. Cf. Constitution on the Sacred Liturgy *Sacrosanctum concilium*, 35, 51: *AAS* 56 (1964), pp. 109, 114.

55. Cf. Sacred Congregation of Rites, Instruction *In edicendis normis*, VI, 17-18; VII, 19-20: *AAS* 57 (1965), pp. 1012f.; Instruction *Musicam sacram*, IV, 48: *AAS* 59 (1967), p. 314; Decree *De Titulo Basilicae Minoris*, II, 8: *AAS* 60 (1968), p. 538; Sacred Congregation for Divine Worship, Notif. *De Missali Romano, Liturgia Horarum et Calendario*, I, 4: *AAS* 63 (1971), p. 714.

All this is noted with great esteem and gratitude, but it must not be forgotten that complete renewal makes yet other demands. These demands consist in *a new sense of responsibility towards the Word of God* transmitted through the liturgy in various languages, something that is certainly in keeping with the universality of the Gospel and its purposes. The same sense of responsibility also involves the performance of the corresponding liturgical actions (reading or singing), which must accord with the principles of art. To preserve these actions from all artificiality, they should express such capacity, simplicity and dignity as to highlight the special character of the sacred text, even by the very manner of reading or singing.

Accordingly, these demands, which spring from a new responsibility for the Word of God in the liturgy,[56] go yet deeper and *concern the inner attitude* with which the ministers of the Word perform their function in the liturgical assembly.[57] This responsibility also concerns *the choice of texts.* The choice has already been made by the competent ecclesiastical authority, which has also made provision for the cases in which readings more suited to a particular situation may be chosen.[58] Furthermore, it must always be remembered that only the Word of God can be used for Mass readings. The reading of Scripture cannot be replaced by the reading of other texts, however much they may be endowed with undoubted religious and moral values. On the other hand, such texts can be used very profitably in the homily. Indeed the homily is supremely suitable for the use of such texts, provided that their content corresponds to the required conditions, since it is one of the tasks that belong to the nature of the homily to show the points of convergence between revealed divine wisdom and noble human thought seeking the truth by various paths.

---

56. Cf. Paul VI, Apostolic Constitution *Missale Romanum:* "We are fully confident that both priests and faithful will prepare their minds and hearts more devoutly for the Lord's Supper, meditating on the scriptures, nourished day by day with the words of the Lord": *AAS* 61 (1969), pp. 220f.; *Missale Romanum, ed. cit.,* p. 15.

57. Cf. *Pontificale Romanum. De Institutione Lectorum et Acolythorum,* 4, *ed. typica,* 1972, pp. 19f.

58. Cf. *Instituto Generalis Missalis Romani,* 319-320; *Missale Romanum, ed. cit.,* p. 87.

The Table of the Bread of the Lord

11 The other table of the Eucharistic Mystery, that of the Bread of the Lord, also requires reflection from the viewpoint of the present-day liturgical renewal. This is a question of the greatest importance, since it concerns a special act of living faith, and indeed, as has been attested since the earliest centuries,[59] it is a manifestation of *worship of Christ, who in Eucharistic Communion entrusts Himself to each one of us,* to our hearts, our consciences, our lips and our mouths, in the form of food. Therefore there is special need, with regard to this question, for the watchfulness spoken of by the Gospel, on the part of the pastors who have charge of Eucharistic worship and on the part of the People of God, whose "sense of faith"[60] must be very alert and acute particularly in this area.

I therefore wish to entrust this question to the heart of each one of you, venerable and dear brothers in the episcopate. You must above all make it part of your care for all the churches entrusted to you. I ask this of you in the name of the unity that we have received from the Apostles as our heritage, collegial unity. This unity came to birth, in a sense, at the table of the Bread of the Lord on Holy Thursday. With the help of your brothers in the priesthood, do all you can to *safeguard the sacred dignity of the Eucharistic ministry and that deep spirit of Eucharistic Communion* which belongs in a special way to the Church as the People of God, and which is also a particular heritage transmitted to us from the Apostles, by various liturgical traditions, and by unnumbered generations of the faithful, who were often heroic witnesses to Christ, educated in "the school of the cross" (redemption) and of the Eucharist.

It must be remembered that the Eucharist as the table of the Bread of the Lord is a continuous invitation. This is *shown in the*

---

59. Cf. Fr. J. Dölger, *Das Segnen der Sinne mit der Eucharistie. Eine altchristliche Kommunionsitte: Antike und Christentum*, t. 3 (1932), pp. 231-244; *Das Kultvergehen der Donatistin Lucilla von Karthago. Reliquienkuss vor dem Kuss der Eucharistie*, ibid., pp. 245-252.

60. Cf. Second Vatican Ecumenical Council, Dogmatic Constitution on the Church *Lumen gentium*, 12, 35; *AAS* 57 (1965), pp. 16, 40.

liturgy when the celebrant says: "This is the Lamb of God. Happy are those who are called to his supper"[61]; it is also shown by the familiar Gospel parable about the guests invited to the marriage banquet.[62] Let us remember that in this parable there are many who excuse themselves from accepting the invitation for various reasons.

Moreover, our Catholic communities certainly do not lack people who *could participate* in Eucharistic Communion *and do not*, even though they have no serious sin on their conscience as an obstacle. To tell the truth, this attitude, which in some people is linked with an exaggerated severity, has changed in the present century, though it is still to be found here and there. In fact, what one finds most often is not so much a feeling of unworthiness, as a certain lack of interior willingness, if one may use this expression, a lack of Eucharistic "hunger" and "thirst," which is also a sign of lack of adequate sensitivity towards the great sacrament of love and a lack of understanding of its nature.

However, we also find in recent years another phenomenon. Sometimes, indeed quite frequently, everybody participating in the Eucharistic assembly goes to Communion; and on some such occasions, as experienced pastors confirm, there has not been due care to approach the sacrament of Penance so as to purify one's conscience. This can of course mean that those approaching the Lord's table find nothing on their conscience, according to the objective law of God, to keep them from this sublime and joyful act of being sacramentally united with Christ. But there can also be, at least at times, another idea behind this: the idea of the Mass as *only* a banquet[63] in which one shares by *receiving the body of Christ in order to manifest, above all else, fraternal communion.* It is not hard to add to these reasons a certain human respect and mere "conformity."

This phenomenon demands from us watchful attention and a theological and pastoral analysis guided by a sense of great responsibility. We cannot allow the life of our communities to lose the

---

61. Cf. Jn. 1:29; Rv. 19:9.
62. Cf. Lk. 14:16ff.
63. Cf. *Instituto Generalis Missalis Romani*, 7-8: *Missale Romanum*, ed. cit., p. 29.

good quality of sensitiveness of Christian conscience, guided solely by respect for Christ, who, when He is received in the Eucharist, should find in the heart of each of us a worthy abode. This question is closely linked not only with the practice of the sacrament of Penance but also with a correct sense of responsibility for the whole deposit of moral teaching and for the precise distinction between good and evil, a distinction which then becomes for each person sharing in the Eucharist the basis for a correct judgment of self to be made in the depths of the personal conscience. St. Paul's words, "Let a man examine himself,"[64] are well known; this judgment is an indispensable condition for a personal decision whether to approach Eucharistic Communion or to abstain.

Celebration of the Eucharist places before us many other requirements regarding the ministry of the Eucharistic table. Some of these requirements concern only priests and deacons, others concern all who participate in the Eucharistic liturgy. Priests and deacons must remember that the service of the table of the bread of the Lord imposes on them special obligations which refer in the first place to Christ Himself *present in the Eucharist* and secondly to all who actually participate in the Eucharist or who might do so. With regard to the first, perhaps it will not be superfluous to recall the words of the *Pontificale* which on the day of ordination the bishop addresses to the new priest as he hands to him on the paten and in the chalice the bread and wine offered by the faithful and prepared by the deacon: *"Accipe oblationem plebis sanctae Deo offerendam. Agnosce quod agis, imitare quod tractabis, et vitam tuam mysterio dominicae crucis conforma."*[65] This last admonition made to him by the bishop should remain as one of the most precious norms of his Eucharistic ministry.

It is from this admonition that the priest's attitude in handling the bread and wine which have become the body and blood of the Redeemer should draw its inspiration. Thus it is necessary for all of us who are ministers of the Eucharist to examine carefully our actions at the altar, in particular the way in which we handle that food and drink which are the body and blood of the Lord our God

---

64. 1 Cor. 11:28.
65. *Pontificale Romanum. De Ordinatione Diaconi, Presbyteri et Episcopi*, ed. typica, 1968, p. 93.

in our hands: the way in which we distribute Holy Communion; the way in which we perform the purification.

All these actions have a meaning of their own. Naturally, scrupulosity must be avoided, but God preserve us from behaving in a way that lacks respect, from undue hurry, from an impatience that causes scandal. Over and above our commitment to the evangelical mission, our greatest commitment consists in exercising this mysterious power over the body of the Redeemer, and all that is within us should be decisively ordered to this. We should also always remember that to this ministerial power we have been sacramentally consecrated, that we have been chosen from among men "for the good of men."[66] We especially, the priests of the Latin Church, whose ordination rite added in the course of the centuries the custom of anointing the priest's hands, should think about this.

In some countries *the practice of receiving Communion in the hand* has been introduced. This practice has been requested by individual episcopal conferences and has received approval from the Apostolic See. However, cases of a deplorable lack of respect towards the Eucharistic species have been reported, cases which are imputable not only to the individuals guilty of such behavior but also to the pastors of the church who have not been vigilant enough regarding the attitude of the faithful towards the Eucharist. It also happens, on occasion, that the free choice of those who prefer to continue the practice of receiving the Eucharist on the tongue is not taken into account in those places where the distribution of Communion in the hand has been authorized. It is therefore difficult in the context of this present letter not to mention the sad phenomena previously referred to. This is in no way meant to refer to those who, receiving the Lord Jesus in the hand, do so with profound reverence and devotion, in those countries where this practice has been authorized.

But one must not forget the primary office of priests, who have been consecrated by their ordination to represent Christ the Priest: For this reason their hands, like their words and their will, have become the direct instruments of Christ. Through this fact, that is, as ministers of the Holy Eucharist, they have a primary responsibility for the sacred species, because it is a total responsibility:

---

66. Heb. 5:1.

They offer the bread and wine, they consecrate it, and then distribute the sacred species to the participants in the assembly who wish to receive them. Deacons can only bring to the altar the offerings of the faithful and, once they have been consecrated by the priest, distribute them. How eloquent therefore, even if not of ancient custom, is the rite of the anointing of the hands in our Latin ordination, as though precisely for these hands a special grace and power of the Holy Spirit is necessary!

To touch the sacred species and *to distribute them with their own hands* is a privilege of the ordained, one which indicates an active participation *in the ministry of the Eucharist.* It is obvious that the Church can grant this faculty to those who are neither priests nor deacons, as is the case with acolytes in the exercise of their ministry, especially if they are destined for future ordination, or with other lay people who are chosen for this to meet a just need, but always after an adequate preparation.

A Common Possession of the Church

12 We cannot, even for a moment, forget that the Eucharist is a special possession belonging to the whole Church. It is the *greatest gift* in the order of grace and of sacrament that the divine Spouse has offered and unceasingly offers to His spouse. And precisely because it is such a gift, all of us should in a spirit of profound faith let ourselves be guided by a sense of truly Christian responsibility. A gift obliges us ever more profoundly because it speaks to us not so much with the force of a strict right as with the force of personal confidence, and thus—without legal obligations—it calls for *trust and gratitude.* The Eucharist is just such a gift and such a possession. We should remain faithful in every detail to what it expresses in itself and to what it asks of us, namely, thanksgiving.

The Eucharist is a common possession of the whole Church as the sacrament of her unity. And thus the Church has the strict duty to specify everything which concerns participation in it and its celebration. We should, therefore, act according to the principles laid down by the last Council, which, in the Constitution on the Sacred Liturgy, defined the authorizations and obligations of individual bishops in their dioceses and of the episcopal conferences, given the fact that both act in collegial unity with the Apostolic See.

Furthermore we should follow the directives issued by the various departments of the Holy See in this field: be it in liturgical matters, in the rules established by the liturgical books in what concerns the Eucharistic Mystery,[67] and in the Instructions devoted to this Mystery, be it with regard to *communicatio in sacris*, in the norms of the *Directorium de re oecumenica*[68] and in the *Instructio de peculiaribus casibus admittendi alios christianos ad communionem eucharisticam in Ecclesia catholica*.[69] And although at this stage of renewal the possibility of a certain "creative" freedom has been permitted, nevertheless this freedom must strictly respect the requirements of substantial unity. We can follow the path of this pluralism (which arises in part from the introduction itself of the various languages into the liturgy) only as long as the essential characteristics of the celebration of the Eucharist are preserved, and the norms prescribed by the recent liturgical reform are respected.

Indispensable effort is required everywhere to ensure that within the pluralism of Eucharistic worship envisioned by the Second Vatican Council the unity of which the Eucharist is the sign and cause is clearly manifested.

This task, over which in the nature of things the Apostolic See must keep careful watch, should be assumed not only by each *episcopal conference* but by every minister of the Eucharist, without exception. Each one should also remember that he is responsible for the common good of the whole Church. The *priest as minister*, as celebrant, as the one who presides over the Eucharistic assembly of the faithful, should have a special *sense of the common good of the Church*, which he represents through his

---

67. Sacred Congregation of Rites, Instruction *Eucharisticum Mysterium: AAS* 59 (1967), pp. 539-573; *Rituale Romanum. De sacra communione et de cultu Mysterii eucharistici extra Missam*, ed. typica, 1973; Sacred Congregation for Divine Worship, *Litterae circulares ad Conferentiarum Episcopalium Praesides de precibus eucharisticis: AAS* 65 (1973), pp. 340-347.

68. Nos. 38-63: *AAS* 59 (1967), pp. 586-592.

69. *AAS* 64 (1972), pp. 518-525. Cf. also the *Communicatio* published the following year for the correct application of the above-mentioned Instruction: *AAS* 65 (1973), pp. 616-619.

ministry, but to which he must also be subordinate, according to a correct discipline of faith. He cannot consider himself a "proprietor" who can make free use of the liturgical text and of the sacred rite as if it were his own property, in such a way as to stamp it with his own arbitrary personal style. At times this latter might seem more effective, and it may better correspond to subjective piety; nevertheless, objectively it is always a betrayal of that union which should find its proper expression in the sacrament of unity.

Every priest who offers the Holy Sacrifice should recall that during this Sacrifice it is not *only* he with his community that is praying but the whole Church, which is thus expressing in this sacrament her spiritual unity, among other ways by the use of the approved liturgical text. To call this position "mere insistence on uniformity" would only show ignorance of the objective requirements of authentic unity, and would be a symptom of harmful individualism.

This subordination of the minister, of the celebrant, to the *Mysterium* which has been entrusted to him by the Church for the good of the whole People of God, should also find expression in the observance of the liturgical requirements concerning the celebration of the Holy Sacrifice. These refer, for example, to dress, and in particular to the vestments worn by the celebrant. Circumstances have of course existed and continue to exist in which the prescriptions do not oblige. We have been greatly moved when reading books written by priests who had been prisoners in extermination camps, with descriptions of Eucharistic Celebrations without the above-mentioned rules, that is to say, without an altar and without vestments. But although in those conditions this was a proof of heroism and deserved profound admiration, nevertheless in *normal conditions* to ignore the liturgical directives can be interpreted as a lack of respect towards the Eucharist, dictated perhaps by individualism or by an absence of a critical sense concerning current opinions, or by a certain *lack of a spirit of faith.*

Upon all of us who, through the *grace* of God, are ministers of the Eucharist, there weighs a particular responsibility for the ideas and attitudes of our brothers and sisters who have been entrusted to our pastoral care. It is our vocation to nurture, above all by personal example, every healthy manifestation of worship towards Christ present and operative in that sacrament of love. May God preserve us from acting otherwise and weakening that worship by "becoming unaccustomed" to various manifestations and forms of Eucharistic worship which express a perhaps "traditional" but healthy piety, and which express above all that "sense of the faith" possessed by the whole People of God, as the Second Vatican Council recalled.[70]

As I bring these considerations to an end, I would like to ask forgiveness—in my own name and in the name of all of you, venerable and dear brothers in the episcopate—for everything which, for whatever reason, through whatever human weakness, impatience or negligence, and also through the at times partial, one-sided and erroneous application of the directives of the Second Vatican Council, may have caused scandal and disturbance concerning the interpretation of the doctrine and the veneration due to this great sacrament. And I pray the Lord Jesus that in the future we may avoid in our manner of dealing with this sacred Mystery anything which could weaken or disorient in any way the sense of reverence and love that exists in our faithful people.

May Christ Himself help us to follow the path of true renewal towards that fullness of life and of Eucharistic worship whereby the Church is built up in that unity that she already possesses, and which she desires to bring to ever greater perfection for the glory of the living God and for the salvation of all humanity.

CONCLUSION

13 Permit me, venerable and dear brothers, to end these reflections of mine, which have been restricted to a detailed examination of only a few questions. In undertaking these reflections, I have had before my eyes all the work carried out by the Second Vatican Council, and have kept in mind Paul VI's encyclical *Mysterium Fidei*, promulgated during that Council, and all the documents issued after the same Council for the purpose of implementing the post-conciliar liturgical renewal. A very close and organic *bond exists between the renewal of the liturgy and the renewal of the whole life of the Church.*

---

70. Cf. Second Vatican Ecumenical Council, Dogmatic Constitution on the Church *Lumen gentium*, 12: *AAS* 57 (1965), pp. 16f.

The Church not only acts but also expresses herself in the liturgy, lives by the liturgy and draws from the liturgy the strength for her life. For this reason liturgical renewal carried out correctly in the spirit of the Second Vatican Council is, in a certain sense, the measure and the condition for putting into effect the teaching of that Council which we wish to accept with profound faith, convinced as we are that by means of this Council the Holy Spirit "has spoken to the Church" the truths and given the indications for carrying out her mission among the people of today and tomorrow.

We shall continue in the future to take special care to promote and follow the renewal of the Church according to the teaching of the Second Vatican Council, *in the spirit of an ever-living Tradition.* In fact, to the substance of Tradition properly understood belongs also a correct re-reading of the "signs of the times," which require us to draw from the rich treasure of Revelation "things both new and old."[71] Acting in this spirit, in accordance with this counsel of the Gospel, the Second Vatican Council carried out a providential effort to renew the face of the Church in the sacred liturgy, most often having recourse to what is "ancient," what comes from the heritage of the Fathers and is the expression of the faith and doctrine of a Church which has remained united for so many centuries.

In order to be able to continue in the future to put into practice the directives of the Council in the field of liturgy, and in particular in the field of Eucharistic worship, *close collaboration is necessary* between the competent department of the Holy See and each episcopal conference, a collaboration which must be *at the same time vigilant and creative.* We must keep our sights fixed on the greatness of the most holy Mystery and at the same time on spiritual movements and social changes, which are so significant for our times, since they not only sometimes create difficulties but also prepare us for a new way of participating in that great Mystery of Faith.

Above all I wish to emphasize that the problems of the liturgy, and in particular of the Eucharistic Liturgy, must not be *an occasion for dividing Catholics and for threatening the unity of the Church.* This is demanded by an elementary understanding of that sacra-

---

71. Mt. 13:52.

ment which Christ has left us as the source of spiritual unity. And how could the Eucharist, which in the Church is the *sacramentum pietatis, signum unitatis, vinculum caritatis*,[72] form between us at this time a point of division and a source of distortion of thought and of behavior, instead of being the focal point and constitutive center, which it truly is in its essence, of the unity of the Church herself?

We are all equally indebted to our Redeemer. We should all listen together to that Spirit of truth and of love whom He has promised to the Church and who is operative in her. In the name of this truth and of this love, in the name of the crucified Christ and of His Mother, I ask you, and beg you: Let us abandon all opposition and division, and let us all unite in this great mission of salvation which is the price and at the same time the fruit of our redemption. The Apostolic See will continue to do all that is possible to provide the means of ensuring that unity of which we speak. Let everyone avoid anything in his own way of acting which could "grieve the Holy Spirit."[73]

In order that this unity and the constant and systematic collaboration which leads to it may be perseveringly continued, I beg on my knees that, through the intercession of Mary, holy spouse of the Holy Spirit and Mother of the Church, we may all receive the light of the Holy Spirit. And blessing everyone, with all my heart I once more address myself to you, my venerable and dear brothers in the episcopate, with a fraternal greeting and with full trust. In this collegial unity in which we share, let us do all we can to ensure that the Eucharist may become an ever greater source of life and light for the consciences of all our brothers and sisters of all the communities in the universal unity of Christ's Church on earth.

In a spirit of fraternal charity, to you and to all our confreres in the priesthood I cordially impart the apostolic blessing.

From the Vatican, February 24, First Sunday of Lent, in the year 1980, the second of the Pontificate.

POPE JOHN PAUL II

---

72. Cf. St. Augustine, *In Evangelium Ioannis tract.* 26, 13: *PL* 35, 1612f.
73. Eph. 4:30.

INAESTIMABILE DONUM, APRIL 17, 1980

Instruction on Worship of the Eucharistic Mystery

FOREWORD

Following the letter that Pope John Paul II addressed on February 24, 1980, to the bishops and, through them, to the priests, and in which he again considered the priceless gift of the Holy Eucharist, the Sacred Congregation for the Sacraments and Divine Worship is calling to the bishops' attention certain norms concerning worship of this great Mystery.

These indications are not a summary of everything already stated by the Holy See in the documents concerning the Eucharist promulgated since the Second Vatican Council and still in force, particularly in the *Missale Romanum*,[1] the Ritual *De Sacra Communione et de Cultu Mysterii Eucharistici Extra Missam*,[2] and the Instructions *Eucharisticum Mysterium*,[3] *Memoriale Domini*,[4] *Immensae caritatis*,[5] and *Liturgicae instaurationes*.[6]

This Sacred Congregation notes with great joy the many positive results of the liturgical reform: a more active and conscious participation by the faithful in the liturgical mysteries, doctrinal and catechetical enrichment through the use of the vernacular, and the wealth of readings from the Bible, a growth in the community sense of liturgical life, and successful efforts to close the gap between life and worship, between liturgical piety and personal piety, and between liturgy and popular piety.

---

1. Ed. Typica Altera, Rome, 1975.
2. Ed. Typica, Rome, 1973.
3. Sacred Congregation of Rites, May 25, 1967: *AAS* 59 (1967), pp. 539-573.
4. Sacred Congregation for Divine Worship, May 29, 1969: *AAS* 61 (1969), pp. 541-545.
5. Sacred Congregation for the Discipline of the Sacraments, January 29, 1973: *AAS* 65 (1973), pp. 264-271.
6. Sacred Congregation for Divine Worship, September 5, 1970: *AAS* 62 (1970), pp. 692-704.

But these encouraging and positive aspects cannot suppress concern at the varied and frequent abuses being reported from different parts of the Catholic world: the confusion of roles, especially regarding the priestly ministry and the role of the laity (indiscriminate shared recitation of the Eucharistic Prayer, homilies given by lay people, lay people distributing Communion while the priests refrain from doing so); an increasing loss of the sense of the sacred (abandonment of liturgical vestments, the Eucharist celebrated outside church without real need, lack of reverence and respect for the Blessed Sacrament, etc.); misunderstanding of the ecclesial character of the liturgy (the use of private texts, the proliferation of unapproved Eucharistic Prayers, the manipulation of the liturgical texts for social and political ends). In these cases we are face to face with a real falsification of the Catholic liturgy: "One who offers worship to God on the Church's behalf in a way contrary to that which is laid down by the Church with God-given authority and which is customary in the Church is guilty of falsification."[7]

None of these things can bring good results. The consequences are—and cannot fail to be—the impairing of the unity of Faith and worship in the Church, doctrinal uncertainty, scandal and bewilderment among the People of God, and the near inevitability of violent reactions.

The faithful have a right to a true liturgy, which means the liturgy desired and laid down by the Church, which has in fact indicated where adaptations may be made as called for by pastoral requirements in different places or by different groups of people. Undue experimentation, changes and creativity bewilder the faithful. The use of unauthorized texts means a loss of the necessary connection between the *lex orandi* and the *lex credendi*. The Second Vatican Council's admonition in this regard must be remembered: "No person, even if he be a priest, may add, remove or change anything in the liturgy on his own authority."[8] And

---

7. St. Thomas, *Summa Theologiae*, 2-2, Q. 93, A. 1.
8. Second Vatican Council, Constitution on the Sacred Liturgy *Sacrosanctum concilium*, nos. 22, 3.

Paul VI of venerable memory stated that: "Anyone who takes advantage of the reform to indulge in arbitrary experiments is wasting energy and offending the ecclesial sense."[9]

I

THE MASS

1 "The two parts which in a sense go to make up the Mass, namely the Liturgy of the Word and the Eucharistic Liturgy, are so closely connected that they form but one single act of worship."[10] A person should not approach the table of the bread of the Lord without having first been at the table of His Word.[11] Sacred Scripture is therefore of the highest importance in the celebration of Mass. Consequently there can be no disregarding what the Church has laid down in order to insure that "in sacred celebrations there should be a more ample, more varied and more suitable reading from Sacred Scripture."[12] The norms laid down in the Lectionary concerning the number of readings, and the directives given for special occasions are to be observed. It would be a serious abuse to replace the Word of God with the word of man, no matter who the author may be.[13]

2 The reading of the Gospel passage is reserved to the ordained minister, namely the deacon or the priest. When possible, the other readings should be entrusted to a reader who has been instituted as such, or to other spiritually and technically trained lay people. The first reading is followed by a responsorial psalm, which is an integral part of the Liturgy of the Word.[14]

---

9. Paul VI, address of August 22, 1973: *L'Osservatore Romano*, August 23, 1973.

10. Second Vatican Council, Constitution on the Sacred Liturgy *Sacrosanctum concilium*, no. 56.

11. Cf. *ibid.*, 56; cf. also Second Vatican Council, Dogmatic Constitution on Divine Revelation *Dei Verbum*, no. 21.

12. Second Vatican Council, Constitution on the Sacred Liturgy *Sacrosanctum concilium*, no. 35.

13. Cf. Sacred Congregation for Divine Worship, Instruction *Liturgicae instaurationes*, no. 2, a.

14. Cf. *Institutio Generalis Missalis Romani*, no. 36.

3 The purpose of the homily is to explain to the faithful the Word of God proclaimed in the readings, and to apply its message to the present. Accordingly the homily is to be given by the priest or the deacon.[15]

4 It is reserved to the priest, by virtue of his ordination, to proclaim the Eucharistic Prayer, which of its nature is the high point of the whole celebration. It is therefore an abuse to have some parts of the Eucharistic Prayer said by the deacon, by a lower minister, or by the faithful.[16] On the other hand the assembly does not remain passive and inert; it unites itself to the priest in faith and silence and shows its concurrence by the various interventions provided for in the course of the Eucharistic Prayer: the responses to the Preface dialogue, the *Sanctus*, the acclamation after the Consecration, and the final *Amen* after the *Per Ipsum*. The *Per Ipsum* itself is reserved to the priest. This *Amen* especially should be emphasized by being sung, since it is the most important in the whole Mass.

5 Only the Eucharistic Prayers included in the Roman Missal or those that the Apostolic See has by law admitted, in the manner and within the limits laid down by the Holy See, are to be used. To modify the Eucharistic Prayers approved by the Church or to adopt others privately composed is a most serious abuse.

6 It should be remembered that the Eucharistic Prayer must not be overlaid with other prayers or songs.[17] When proclaiming the Eucharistic Prayer, the priest is to pronounce the text clearly, so as to make it easy for the faithful to understand it, and so as to foster the formation of a true assembly entirely intent upon the celebration of the memorial of the Lord.

7 *Concelebration*, which has been restored in the Western Liturgy, manifests in an exceptional manner the unity of the priesthood. Concelebrants must, therefore, pay careful attention to the signs that indicate that unity. For example, they are to be present

---

15. Cf. Sacred Congregation for Divine Worship, Instruction *Liturgicae instaurationes*, no. 2, a.

16. Cf. Sacred Congregation for Divine Worship, circular letter *Eucharistiae participationem*, April 27, 1973: *AAS* 65 (1973), pp. 340-347, 8; Instruction *Liturgicae instaurationes*, no. 4.

17. *Institutio Generalis Missalis Romani*, no. 12.

from the beginning of the celebration, they are to wear the prescribed vestments, they are to occupy the place appropriate to their ministry as concelebrants, and they are to observe faithfully the other norms for the seemly performance of the rite.[18]

8 *Matter of the Eucharist.* Faithful to Christ's example, the Church has constantly used bread and wine mixed with water to celebrate the Lord's Supper. The bread for the celebration of the Eucharist, in accordance with the tradition of the whole Church, must be made solely of wheat, and, in accordance with the tradition proper to the Latin Church, it must be unleavened. By reason of the sign, the matter of the Eucharistic celebration "should appear as actual food." This is to be understood as linked to the consistency of the bread, and not to its form, which remains the traditional one. No other ingredients are to be added to the wheaten flour and water. The preparation of the bread requires attentive care to ensure that the product does not detract from the dignity due to the Eucharistic bread, can be broken in a dignified way, does not give rise to excessive fragments, and does not offend the sensibilities of the faithful when they eat it. The wine for the Eucharistic celebration must be of "the fruit of the vine" (Lk. 22:18) and be natural and genuine, that is to say not mixed with other substances.[19]

9 *Eucharistic Communion.* Communion is a gift of the Lord, given to the faithful through the minister appointed for this purpose. It is not permitted that the faithful should themselves pick up the consecrated bread and the sacred chalice, still less that they should hand them from one to another.

10 The faithful, whether religious or lay, who are authorized as extraordinary ministers of the Eucharist can distribute Communion only when there is no priest, deacon or acolyte, when the priest is impeded by illness or advanced age, or when the number of the faithful going to Communion is so large as to make the celebration of Mass excessively long.[20] Accordingly, a reprehensible

---

18. Cf. *ibid.*, nos. 156, 161-163.
19. Cf. *ibid.*, nos. 281-284; Sacred Congregation for Divine Worship, Instruction *Liturgicae instaurationes*, no. 5; *Notitiae* 6 (1970), no. 37.
20. Cf. Sacred Congregation for the Discipline of the Sacraments, Instruction *Immensae caritatis*, no. 1.

attitude is shown by those priests who, though present at the celebration, refrain from distributing Communion and leave this task to the laity.

11 The Church has always required from the faithful respect and reverence for the Eucharist at the moment of receiving it.

With regard to the manner of going to Communion, the faithful can receive it either kneeling or standing, in accordance with the norms laid down by the episcopal conference: "When the faithful communicate kneeling, no other sign of reverence towards the Blessed Sacrament is required, since kneeling is itself a sign of adoration. When they receive Communion standing, it is strongly recommended that, coming up in procession, they should make a sign of reverence before receiving the Sacrament. This should be done at the right time and place, so that the order of people going to and from Communion is not disrupted."[21]

The *Amen* said by the faithful when receiving Communion is an act of personal faith in the presence of Christ.

12 With regard to Communion under both kinds, the norms laid down by the Church must be observed, both by reason of the reverence due to the Sacrament and for the good of those receiving the Eucharist, in accordance with variations in circumstances, times and places.[22]

Episcopal conferences and ordinaries also are not to go beyond what is laid down in the present discipline: the granting of permission for Communion under both kinds is not to be indiscriminate, and the celebrations in question are to be specified precisely; the groups that use this faculty are to be clearly defined, well disciplined, and homogeneous.[23]

13 Even after Communion the Lord remains present under the species. Accordingly, when Communion has been distributed, the sacred particles remaining are to be consumed or taken by the competent minister to the place where the Eucharist is reserved.

---

21. Sacred Congregation of Rites, Instruction *Eucharisticum Mysterium*, no. 34. Cf. *Institutio Generalis Missalis Romani*, nos. 244 c, 246 b, 247 b.
22. Cf. *Institutio Generalis Missalis Romani*, nos. 241-242.
23. Cf. *ibid.*, end of no. 242.

14   On the other hand, the consecrated wine is to be consumed immediately after Communion and may not be kept. Care must be taken to consecrate only the amount of wine needed for Communion.

15   The rules laid down for the purification of the chalice and the other sacred vessels that have contained the Eucharistic species must be observed.[24]

16   Particular respect and care are due to the sacred vessels, both the chalice and paten for the celebration of the Eucharist, and the ciboria for the Communion of the faithful. The form of the vessels must be appropriate for the liturgical use for which they are meant. The material must be noble, durable, and in every case adapted to sacred use. In this sphere, judgment belongs to the episcopal conference of the individual regions.

Use is not to be made of simple baskets or other recipients meant for ordinary use outside the sacred celebrations, nor are the sacred vessels to be of poor quality or lacking any artistic style.

Before being used, chalices and patens must be blessed by the bishop or by a priest.[25]

17   The faithful are to be recommended not to omit to make a proper thanksgiving after Communion. They may do this during the celebration with a period of silence, with a hymn, psalm or other song of praise,[26] or also after the celebration, if possible by staying behind to pray for a suitable time.

18   There are, of course, various roles that women can perform in the liturgical assembly: these include reading the Word of God and proclaiming the intentions of the Prayer of the Faithful. Women are not, however, permitted to act as altar servers.[27]

---

24. Cf. *ibid.*, no. 238.
25. Cf. *Institutio Generalis Missalis Romani*, nos. 288, 289, 292, 295; Sacred Congregation for Divine Worship, Instruction *Liturgicae instaurationes*, no. 8; *Pontificale Romanum, ordo dedicationis ecclesiae et altaris*, p. 125, no. 3.
26. Cf. *Institutio Generalis Missalis Romani*, no. 56 j.
27. Cf. Sacred Congregation for Divine Worship, Instruction *Liturgicae instaurationes*, no. 7.

19   Particular vigilance and special care are recommended with regard to Masses transmitted by the audio-visual media. Given their very wide diffusion, their celebration must be of exemplary quality.[28]

In the case of celebrations that are held in private houses, the norms of the Instruction *Actio pastoralis* of May 15, 1969, are to be observed.[29]

II

EUCHARISTIC WORSHIP OUTSIDE MASS

20   Public and private devotion to the Holy Eucharist outside Mass also is highly recommended: for the presence of Christ, who is adored by the faithful in the Sacrament, derives from the sacrifice and is directed towards sacramental and spiritual Communion.

21   When Eucharistic devotions are arranged, account should be taken of the liturgical season, so that they harmonize with the liturgy, draw inspiration from it in some way, and lead the Christian people toward it.[30]

22   With regard to exposition of the Holy Eucharist, either prolonged or brief, and with regard to processions of the Blessed Sacrament, Eucharistic Congresses, and the whole ordering of Eucharistic piety, the pastoral indications and directives given in the Roman Ritual are to be observed.[31]

23   It must not be forgotten that "before the blessing with the Sacrament, an appropriate time should be devoted to the reading of the Word of God, to songs and prayers, and to some silent

---

28. Cf. Second Vatican Council, Constitution on the Sacred Liturgy, *Sacrosanctum concilium*, no. 20; Pontifical Commission for Social Communications, Instruction *Communio et progressio*, May 23, 1971: *AAS* 63 (1971), pp. 593-656, no. 151.

29. *AAS* 61 (1969), pp. 806-811.

30. Cf. *Rituale Romanum, De Sacra Communione et de Cultu Mysterii Eucharistici Extra Missam*, nos. 79-80.

31. Cf. *ibid.*, nos. 82-112.

prayer."³² At the end of the adoration, a hymn is sung, and a prayer chosen from among the many contained in the Roman Ritual is recited or sung.³³

24 The *tabernacle* in which the Eucharist is kept can be located on an altar, or away from it, in a spot in the church which is very prominent, truly noble, and duly decorated, or in a chapel suitable for private prayer and for adoration by the faithful.³⁴

25 The tabernacle should be solid, unbreakable, and not transparent.³⁵ The presence of the Eucharist is to be indicated by a tabernacle veil or by some other suitable means laid down by the competent authority, and a lamp must perpetually burn before it, as a sign of honor paid to the Lord.³⁶

26 The venerable practice of genuflecting before the Blessed Sacrament, whether enclosed in the tabernacle or publicly exposed, as a sign of adoration, is to be maintained.³⁷ This act requires that it be performed in a recollected way. In order that the heart may bow before God in profound reverence, the genuflection must be neither hurried nor careless.

27 If anything has been introduced that is at variance with these indications, it is to be corrected.

Most of the difficulties encountered in putting into practice the reform of the liturgy and especially the reform of the Mass stem from the fact that neither priests nor faithful have perhaps been sufficiently aware of the theological and spiritual reasons for which the changes have been made, in accordance with the principles laid down by the Council.

Priests must acquire an ever deeper understanding of the authentic way of looking at the Church,³⁸ of which the celebration

---

32. *Ibid.*, no. 89.
33. Cf. *ibid.*, no. 97.
34. Cf. *Institutio Generalis Missalis Romani*, no. 276.
35. Cf. *Rituale Romanum, De Sacra Communione et de Cultu Mysterii Eucharistici Extra Missam*, no. 10.
36. Cf. Sacred Congregation of Rites, Instruction *Eucharisticum Mysterium*, no. 57.
37. Cf. *Rituale Romanum, De Sacra Communione et de Cultu Mysterii Eucharistici Extra Missam*, no. 84.
38. Cf. Second Vatican Council, Dogmatic Constitution on the Church *Lumen gentium*.

of the liturgy and especially of the Mass is the living expression. Without an adequate biblical training, priests will not be able to present to the faithful the meaning of the liturgy as an enactment, in signs, of the history of salvation. Knowledge of the history of the liturgy will likewise contribute to an understanding of the changes which have been introduced, and introduced not for the sake of novelty but as a revival and adaptation of authentic and genuine tradition.

The liturgy also requires great balance, for, as the Constitution *Sacrosanctum concilium* says, it "is thus the outstanding means by which the faithful can express in their lives, and manifest to others, the mystery of Christ and the real nature of the true Church. It is of the essence of the Church that she be both human and divine, visible and yet invisibly endowed, eager to act and yet devoted to contemplation, present in this world and yet not at home in it. She is all these things in such a way that in her the human is directed and subordinated to the divine, the visible likewise to the invisible, action to contemplation, and this present world to that city yet to come, which we seek."[39] Without this balance, the true face of Christian liturgy becomes obscured.

In order to reach these ideals more easily it will be necessary to foster liturgical formation in seminaries and faculties[40] and to facilitate the participation of priests in courses, meetings, assemblies or liturgical weeks, in which study and reflection should be properly complemented by model celebrations. In this way priests will be able to devote themselves to more effective pastoral action, to liturgical catechesis of the faithful, to organizing groups of lectors, to giving altar servers spiritual and practical training, to training animators of the assembly, to enriching progressively the repertoire of songs, in a word to all the initiatives favoring an ever deeper understanding of the liturgy.

In the implementation of the liturgical reform, great responsibility falls upon national and diocesan liturgical commissions and

---

39. Second Vatican Council, Constitution on the Sacred Liturgy *Sacrosanctum concilium*, no. 2.

40. Cf. Sacred Congregation for Catholic Education, Instruction on Liturgical Formation in Seminaries *In Ecclesiasticam Futurorum Sacerdotum Formationem*, June 3, 1979.

liturgical institutes and centers, especially in the work of translating the liturgical books and training the clergy and faithful in the spirit of the reform desired by the Council.

The work of these bodies must be at the service of the ecclesiastical authority, which should be able to count upon their faithful collaboration. Such collaboration must be faithful to the Church's norms and directives, and free of arbitrary initiatives and particular ways of acting that could compromise the fruits of the liturgical renewal.

This document will come into the hands of God's ministers in the first decade of the life of the *Missale Romanum* promulgated by Pope Paul VI following the prescriptions of the Second Vatican Council.

It seems fitting to recall a remark made by that Pope concerning fidelity to the norms governing celebration: "It is a very serious thing when division is introduced precisely where *congregavit nos in unum Christi amor*, in the liturgy and the Eucharistic Sacrifice, by the refusing of obedience to the norms laid down in the liturgical sphere. It is in the name of tradition that we ask all our sons and daughters, all the Catholic communities, to celebrate with dignity and fervor the renewed liturgy."[41]

The bishops, "whose function it is to control, foster, and safeguard the entire liturgical life of the Church entrusted to them,"[42] will not fail to discover the most suitable means for ensuring a careful and firm application of these norms, for the glory of God and the good of the Church.

---

41. Consistorial address of May 24, 1976: *AAS* 68 (1976), p. 374.
42. Second Vatican Council, Decree *Christus Dominus*, no. 15.

Rome, April 3, 1980, Holy Thursday.

This instruction, prepared by the Sacred Congregation for the Sacraments and Divine Worship, was approved on April 17, 1980, by the Holy Father, John Paul II, who confirmed it with his own authority and ordered it to be published and to be observed by all concerned.

JAMES R. CARDINAL KNOX
Prefect

VIRGILIO NOE
Assistant Secretary

TOPICAL INDEX

The numbers refer to the pages of this book. Where applicable, the numbered paragraphs of particular documents are given within parentheses. The page references embrace entire numbered paragraphs, so as to draw attention to the context of each topic. The documents are denoted by the following abbreviations:

   G .... *General Catechetical Directory*
   A .... *Acerbo nimis*
   P .... *Provido sane consilio*
   C .... *Creed of the People of God*
   E .... *Evangelii nuntiandi*
 CT .... *Catechesi tradendae*
  M .... *Metanoia (Holy Thursday) Documents*

Citations as a rule are made first to the General Catechetical Directory and then to the other documents in the order given above. This has been done in order to facilitate comparative study in terms of the General Catechetical Directory as the most basic and comprehensive of the documents.

ACTIVITIES OF CATECHESIS
—G 60-69; 100-101 (Activity of the Catechumen)
—P 23-27
—E 175-196
—CT 245-248; 258-267
ADMINISTRATION AND SUPERVISION OF CATECHESIS
—G 117-138 (Part Six, nos. 98-134)
—A 10-11; 12-13
—P 17-25; 26-27 (Questionnaire for Supervision)
—CT 210; 221; 248; 258-267
—M 321-324; 327-337
—See: Catechetical Teachers, Formation of; Pastoral Care
ADOLESCENCE: see Secondary Level
ADULT CATECHESIS
—G 112-116
—CT 243; 254
—M 327-337

AGE LEVELS
  —G 103-116 (Part Five, nos. 77-97)
  —See: Elements; Secondary Level
ATHEISM
  —G 49-50; 80-81
  —A 3-5
  —P 18-19
  —E 178-181
  —CT 253-254; 264
  —See: Reality of the Problem; Indifferentism

BASICS OF THE FAITH: see Elements
BISHOPS; BISHOPS' CONFERENCES
  —G 41-43; 56-57; 68-69; 125; 133-134
  —P 17-19; 23-25
  —E 191
  —CT 258-259
  —M 271-274; 296-297; 332

CATECHESIS, HISTORICAL SURVEY OF
  —CT 216-222
CATECHESIS, NATURE OF
  —G 60-69
  —A 8-10
  —P 15-17
  —E 171-172
  —CT 209-210; 223
  —See: Norms or Criteria; Revelation; Methodology
CATECHETICAL LITERATURE AND TEACHING AIDS
  —G 129-134
  —E 171-172
  —CT 247-248
  —See: Textbooks, Evaluation of
CATECHETICAL REGULATIONS: see Administration and Supervision of Catechesis
CATECHETICAL TEACHERS, FORMATION OF
  —G 124-128
  —A 12-13
  —P 25
  —E 172; 194-196
  —CT 261; 264; 266-267
  —See: Witness; Magisterium; Norms or Criteria; Methodology, General Principles of and special topics
CATECHETICAL TEACHING: see Christian Doctrine and Instruction; Methodology
CATECHISM, CATECHISMS
  —G 63-64, 77-78, 99, 129-130, 138
  —A 8-10; 11
  —CT 219; 229; 248; 270
  —See: Formulated Doctrine; Creed
CHILDREN, CATECHETICAL INSTRUCTION OF
  —G 104-107
  —A 7-10
  —P 16-17
  —E 172
  —CT 238-240
  —See: Age Levels; Methodology

CHRISTIAN CULTURE
—G 115-116
—E 157-158; 186-189
—CT 255-258
—See: Rational Foundation of Faith; Secondary Level

CHRISTIAN DOCTRINE AND INSTRUCTION
—G 63-65, 67-71
—A 8-10; 12-13
—P 15-17; and *passim*
—E 171-172
—CT 226-227
—See: Formulated Doctrine; Revelation; Faith; Methodology

"CHRISTIAN" MARXISM: see Politicization of Catechesis

CHRISTIAN MESSAGE: see Revelation; Faith

CHRISTOCENTRISM
—G 59; 74-75; 81-84
—A 8-10
—P 15-17
—C 29-39; and *passim*
—E 149-152; 161-162
—CT 211-216; 225; 229-231; 233-234
—M 273; 308-311; and *passim*
—See: Jesus Christ; Revelation; Content of Catechesis; Methodology; Norms or Criteria

CHURCH
—G 48-53; 56-59; 67-69; 92-96
—C 35-37
—E 152-155; 167-168; 184-187; 200-201
—CT 216-222; 228
—M 275-277; 301-305; 335
—See: Church and the World

CHURCH AND THE WORLD
—G 47-48; 65; 80-81; 94-95; 115-116
—C 38
—E 157-158
—CT 249-250
—See: Liberation, Evangelical

COMMUNICATION MEDIA AND CATECHESIS
—G 131-132
—E 170; 172-173
—CT 221; 245

CONTENT OF CATECHESIS
—G 54-95
—A 1; 1-13
—P 15-17; 25; 26-27
—C 29-39; and *passim*
—E 161-168; 171-172; 187-189
—CT 222-224; 229-234; 255-258
—See: Jesus Christ; Christocentrism; Revelation; Faith; Deposit; Norms or Criteria; Methodology, Magisterial; Errors in Catechetics Today

CONVERSION
—G 49; 62-63; 72
—E 156-157; 166
—CT 224-225; 249-250
—M 290-293

CREED
—G 63-64; 76-77
—C 29-39; and *passim*
—CT 230-231; 255
—See: Revelation; Formulated Doctrine

CRISIS OF FAITH
—G 48-50; 80
—C 30
—See: Errors in Catechetics Today

DEPOSIT OF REVELATION, DEPOSIT OF FAITH
—G 56-57; 67
—P 15-17
—C 29
—E 147; 154-155; 161-168; 179; 189
—CT 230; 233-235; 247-248
—See: Revelation; Faith; Magisterium; Creed; Content of Catechesis

DICHOTOMIES: see Politicization of Catechesis

DOCTRINE: see Christian Doctrine; Formulated Doctrine; Revelation; Faith; Content of Catechesis; Catechisms

ECUMENISM
—G 65
—E 200-206
—CT 235-238

EDUCATION IN FAITH: see Formation for Christian Living; Prayer and Catechesis

ELEMENTS OF DOCTRINE, ELEMENTARY LEVEL
—G 103-108; 125-126
—A 7
—CT 229; 239-240; 252-253; 256
—See: Methodology; Catechisms

ERRORS IN CATECHETICS TODAY
—G 42; 51-53; 70-71
—A 8-10
—C 30
—E 155; 165; 167-168; 182
—CT 214; 222; 226-227; 232; 233-234; 246; 247; 249-250; 252-253; 255-258
—M 323; 325; 328-329

ESCHATOLOGY
—G 96
—C 38-39
—E 162-163

EUCHARIST, EUCHARISTIC SACRIFICE
—G 60; 64; 84-87; 139-143
—C 37-38
—E 161-164
—CT 210-211; 225; 227-228; 233-234
—M 277-282; 296-314; 327-337
—See: Jesus Christ; Christocentrism; Liturgy and Catechesis; Sacraments

EVANGELIZATION AND CATECHESIS
—G 60-61
—E 149-152; 159; 171-172
—CT 222-225; 229-230

Topical Index

EVANGELIZATION, NATURE OF
—G 45-49; 60-61; 104-105; 119; 133
—E 145-161; and *passim*
—See: Jesus Christ; Revelation; Reality of the Problem; Re-evangelization

EXPERIENCE APPROACH
—G 63-64
—E 159
—CT 226-227
—See: Activities of Catechesis; Reality of the Problem

EXPERIENCE, ROLE OF
—G 99-100; 125-126

EXTREMISM IN CATECHETICS: see Politicization of Catechetics; Errors in Catechetics Today

FAITH
—G 58-59; 62-64; 70-71; 79-80; 130
—A 9
—C 31-39; and *passim*
—E 147; 170; 188-189
—CT 211; 221; 228-229; 253-254; 255-258
—M 310-315
—See: Revelation; Formulated Doctrine

FAITH, RATIONAL FOUNDATION OF
—G 110, 115-116
—C 30
—CT 255-256
—See: Secondary Level

FAMILY CATECHETICS
—G 87; 103-109; 121-122; 127-128; 131
—E 172; 193-194
—CT 221; 239-240; 263-264

FORMATION FOR CHRISTIAN LIVING
—G 59; 62-66; 72-77; 86-92 97-98; 104-115
—A 4-5
—P 20-21
—E 171-172
—CT 211; 237; 252-253
—M 305-307
—See: Prayer and Catechesis; Sacraments

FORMULATED DOCTRINE
—G 67-71; 72-74; 85-87; 99
—C 31-39; and *passim*
—CT 229; 233-234; 252-253
—See: Christian Doctrine; Revelation; Faith; Creed; Catechisms

GOD THE FATHER
—G 48-50; 54; 58-59; 73-75; 79-83; 85; 91-93; 122-123
—C 31-32
—E 161
—CT 221
—M 300; 311

GOD THE SON: see Jesus Christ, Incarnate Redeemer

GOD THE HOLY SPIRIT
—G 56-57; 62-63; 66; 74-77; 79-80; 85-86; 88; 89-91; 95-96; 127
—A 10
—C 33

—E 161; 196-198; 206
—CT 235; 267-269
—M 300
HOLY SEE
—G 137-138; 142-143
—P 17-21
—C 36
—E 190-191
—CT 221
—M 327-337
—See: Magisterium
HORIZONTALISM: see Errors in Catechetics Today; Politicization of Catechesis
HUMAN ADVANCEMENT: see Liberation, Evangelical; Church and the World; Formation for Christian Living
HUMAN RIGHTS: see Liberation, Evangelical; Church and the World

IGNORANCE, RELIGIOUS
—G 51-53
—A 2-4; 5-7; 9; 13
—See: Reality of the Problem
ILLITERACY, RELIGIOUS: see Ignorance, Religious; Elements; Methodology
INCARNATION: see Jesus Christ
INDIFFERENTISM
—G 49-50
—A 2-4; 13
—E 180-181
—CT 253-254; 264
—See: Reality of the Problem; Atheism

INITIATION, CHRISTIAN
—G 84-87; 104-108; 139-143
—M 305-307
—See: Sacraments; Age Levels

JESUS CHRIST, INCARNATE REDEEMER AND TEACHER
—G 50-53; 55-56; 58-59; 73-84; 88-89; 92-93; 122-123
—C 32-33; 37-38
—E 148-152; 161-168
—CT 211-216; 225; 226-227; 232-233; 240
—M 300; and *passim*
—See: Methodology; Christocentrism; Revelation; Content of Catechesis; Creed; Deposit
JOY AND MORALE IN CATECHESIS
—G 82-83; 105-106
—E 196-206
—CT 253-258

LAY CATECHISTS
—P 24
—E 171-172; 192-193
—CT 261-264
—See: Family Catechetics; Catechetical Teachers, Formation of
LIBERATION, EVANGELICAL
—E 156-158; 162-168; 181-184
—CT 233
—M 304-305
—See: Church and the World
LIFE OF FAITH
—G 51-52; 62-69

—E 158-159; 169; 196-206
—CT 222-225; 253-255; 267-269
—M 290-293; and *passim*
—See: Formation for Christian Living; Prayer and Catechetics; Witness

LITURGY AND CATECHETICS
—G 60; 64; 77; 80; 127-128
—A 7
—E 170-171
—CT 227-228; 246-247; 263
—M 277-285; 327-337
—See: Eucharist, Eucharistic Sacrifice

MAGISTERIUM
—G 41-43; 56-57; 59; 70-73; 79-80; 87; 90-91; 100-101
—C 35-36
—E 171; 183; 188-189
—CT 212; 230; 247; 249-250
—See: Norms or Criteria; Methodology, Magisterial

MARY, THE EVER-VIRGIN MOTHER
—G 76; 95-96; 104-105
—C 34
—E 206
—CT 269-270
—M 294-295

METANOIA: see Conversion

METHODOLOGY, GENERAL PRINCIPLES OF
—G 70-71; 77-78; 97-102; 125-126
—A 7; 8-10

—E 168-175
—CT 226-227; 233-235; 238-244; 249-250; 255
—See: Norms or Criteria; Methodology, Magisterial; Methodology, Didactic; Elements of Doctrine; Elementary Level; Secondary Level

METHODOLOGY, MAGISTERIAL (OR SUPERNATURAL)
—G 47-69; 72-78 (Applications of Magisterial Methodology)
—CT 249-250
—See: Magisterium; Norms or Criteria

METHODOLOGY, DIDACTIC (OR NATURAL)
—G 97-102; 103-116 (Applications)
—A 7; 8-9; 12-13
—P 20-21
—E 159; 169-170
—CT 220; 226; 251-253
—See: Age Levels; Catechetical Literature and Teaching Aids

METHODOLOGY: ART OF CATECHETICAL TEACHING
—G 126-127
—A 12-13
—CT 225; 254
—M 282-283
—See: Catechetical Teacher, Formation of

METHODOLOGY: CULTURES AND CATECHETICS
—G 45-46; 48; 50-51; 72; 82-

83; 94-95; 115-116; 125-126
—C 38
—E 157-158; 164-168
—CT 250-251; 264-266
METHODOLOGY: LANGUAGE IN CATECHETICS
—G 67-68
—C 30
—E 187-188
—CT 233-235; 255
METHODOLOGY, MEMORIZATION IN CATECHETICS
—G 99
—CT 252-253
METHODOLOGY: TEACHING APPROACH IN CATECHESIS
—G 97; 125-126; and *passim*
—A 4-10; 12-13
—P 16-27; and *passim*
—E 149-150; 159; 171-172
—CT 211-212; 220; 226-227; 252-253
—See: Experience Approach; Revelation; Faith; Deposit; Methodology, Didactic
MINISTRY OF THE WORD
—G 54-69 (Part Two, nos. 10-35); and *passim*.
—E 155
—M 271-274
—See: Methodology, General Principles of; and special topics
MORALITY AND CATECHESIS
—G 88-92
—A 8-9
—P 20

—CT 233; 250
—See: Sin, Original and Personal; Formation for Christian Living
MYSTERIES: see Revelation; Jesus Christ
MYSTERY OF CHRIST: see Jesus Christ

NATIONAL CATECHETICAL DIRECTORIES
—G 45; 103-104; 107-108; 138
NORMS OR CRITERIA
—G 70-78 (Part Three, Chapter 1, nos. 36-46)
—See: Magisterium; Content of Catechesis; Methodology; Christocentrism; Deposit

ORGANIZATION OF CATECHESIS: see Administration and Supervision of Catechesis

PASTORAL CARE, PASTORAL THEOLOGY
—G 41-43; 61-62; 68-69; 135; 136
—A 5-7; 12-13
—P 20-25
—E 169; 174-175; 181-184
—CT 221-229; 238-244; 255-267
—M 271-337; and *passim*
—See: Administration and Supervision of Catechesis; Theology and Catechetics

PERSONALITY, DEVELOPMENT OF
—G 113
—E 161-168
—CT 228-229; 232-233
—See: Age Levels; Sacraments

POLITICIZATION OF CATECHESIS
—G 94-95
—C 38
—E 165-168
—CT 226-227; 233-235; 249-251
—See: Errors in Catechetics Today

POPULAR PIETY
—E 174-175
—CT 251-252

PRAYER AND CATECHESIS
—G 62-63; 64; 68; 97-99; 104-106; 127
—M 290-293
—See: Formation for Christian Living

PRIESTS AND CATECHESIS: see Pastoral Care

PROBLEMS IN CONTEMPORARY CATECHETICS: see Reality of the Problem; Errors in Catechetics Today; Politicization of Catechesis

PROFESSION OF FAITH: see Creed

PURPOSE OF CATECHESIS
—G 60-69
—P 15-17
—E 171-172
—CT 211-214; 225; 228-229
—M 296-326; and *passim*

REALITY OF THE PROBLEM
—G 45-53 (Part One, nos. 1-9)
—A 1-4
—P 17-19
—C 30
—E 145-146; 158; 175-176
—CT 224-225; 243-244; 255-258
—M 328; 335-336
—See: Errors in Catechetics Today; Atheism; Crisis of Faith; Conversion; Evangelization; Ignorance, Religious; Illiteracy, Religious; Methodology: Culture and Catechesis

REDEMPTION: see Jesus Christ

RE-EVANGELIZATION
—G 46; 49
—E 176-177
—CT 224
—See: Reality of the Problem

RELIGIOUS
—E 192
—CT 260

RENEWAL OF CATECHESIS
—G 50-53
—A 5-10; and *passim*
—P 19-25
—CT 212
—M 327-329

REVELATION, CONCEPT OF
—G 54-59; 72
—A 4-5
—P 15-17
—C 31

—E 149-155; 176-184; 202; 205
—CT 216; 227; 230; 249-250; 254-255
—M 314-316

REVELATION, CONTENT OF
—G 63-64; 70-96; 129-131
—C 31-39; and *passim*
—E 161-168; 179
—CT 229-238; 241
—See: Faith; Deposit; Norms or Criteria

SACRAMENTS AND CATECHESIS
—G 84-88
—P 21-23
—C 37-38
—E 159-160; 173-174
—CT 227-228; 237; 263
—M 283-285; 297-301; 306; 317-321; 327-337
—See: Liturgy and Catechesis; Formation for Christian Living

SACREDNESS OF EUCHARISTIC WORSHIP
—M 308-311; 327-337
—See: Jesus Christ; Christocentrism

SALVATION HISTORY
—G 75-77; 79-82
—CT 252; 254

SCIENTIFIC STUDY OF CATECHESIS: see Pastoral Theology

SCRIPTURE
—G 58; 67-68; 79-80
—C 33-34
—E 149-152
—CT 214-216; 230; 257; 269
—M 314-316; 329

SECONDARY LEVEL
—G 108-112
—CT 240-243
—See: Young People; Methodology; Age Levels

SIN, ORIGINAL AND PERSONAL
—G 79-80; 85-86; 89-91
—C 34-35
—E 165-168
—CT 232; 233-234
—M 307
—See: Morality and Catechesis

SPIRITUAL DEVELOPMENT: see Age Levels; Initiation, Christian; Sacraments; Prayer and Catechesis

TEXTBOOKS, EVALUATION OF
—G 130-131
—CT 237-238; 247-248
—See: Norms or Criteria; Revelation; Faith; Deposit

THEOCENTRISM: see Christocentrism; Norms or Criteria; Revelation; Jesus Christ

THEOLOGY AND CATECHETICS
—G 41-43; 60-62; 68-69; 70-73; 125-126; 131
—C 29-31
—CT 257-258
—See: Pastoral Theology; Magisterium; Norms or Criteria

TRADITION, LIVING DIVINE
—G 56-57; 59; 77; 130
—C 30-31; 35-36

—E 189-190
—CT 216-222
—M 324-326; 337
—See: Revelation; Creed; Catechisms; Magisterium

VIOLENCE: see Liberation, Evangelical; Errors in Catechetics Today; Politicization of Catechetics

WITNESS, CATECHESIS AS
—G 49-50; 62-63; 67-69; 80-81; 93-95; 101-102; 114
—C 29; 31
—E 158-159; 169; 199-206
—CT 238-239
—M 283-293
—See: Catechetical Teachers, Formation of; Magisterium

WORD OF GOD: see Revelation; Faith; Jesus Christ; Scripture; Language, Use of in Catechetics

YOUNG PEOPLE
—G 107-112
—E 194
—C 224-225; 238-243; 245-246; 254
—See: Secondary Level; Methodology

GENERAL INDEX

Acerbo nimis 17, 22
Actio pastoralis 334
Ad gentes 156
Ambrose, St. 218, 233
Augustine, St. 185, 218, 255, 256, 258, 267, 269, 275

Bellarmine, St. Robert 219
Benedict XIV, Pope 3, 7, 10, 22, 23
Biblical Commission 250
Bishops' Catechetical Commission 134
Borromeo, St. Charles 219
Bosco, St. John 283

Canisius, St. Peter 219
Catechetical Bureau 26
Catechetical Day 24, 26
Catechism of the Council of Trent 11, 22
Catholic Action 24, 26
Chrysostom, St. John 218, 233
Clement of Rome, St. 218
Code of Canon Law 17
Colombia 167
Confraternity of Christian Doctrine 20, 21, 26
Confraternity of the Blessed Sacrament 21
Constitution on the Sacred Liturgy 321
Council of Trent 7, 34, 219

Course of Lectures on Religion 23
Creed of Nicea 30
Curé d'Ars 283
Cyril of Jerusalem, St. 218

De Catechizandis rudibus 255
de Paul, St. Vincent 283
De Sacra Communione et de Cultu Mysterii Eucharistici extra Missam 327
Declaration on Religious Freedom 52
Decree on the Bishops' Pastoral Office in the Church 41
Decree on the Missionary Activity of the Church 50, 51
Diocesan Catechetical Office 133, 134
Dogmatic Constitution on Divine Revelation 54

Ecclesiae sanctae 276
Etsi minime 7, 22
Eucharisticum Mysterium 327
Eusebius of Caesarea 177
Evangelii nuntiandi 210, 223, 231, 246, 269

Feast of Christian Doctrine 24
Fourth General Assembly of the Synod of Bishops 210ff., 223, 226, 249

Gaudium et spes 156, 157
General Catechetical Directory 210, 223
Gregory, Pope St. 12
Gregory the Great, St. 283

Ignatius of Antioch, St. 83, 276
Immensae caritatis 327
International Catechetical Congress 210
International Council for Catechesis 210

John of Avila, St. 283
John Paul I 211

Latin 315
Leo the Great, St. 190
Liturgicae instaurationes 327
Lumen gentium 156, 278-279, 294

Maximilian Kolbe, Bl. 283
Memoriale Domini 327
Missale Romanum 327, 337
Mysterium Fidei 324

National Catechetical Office 134

Optatam totius 282
Orbem catholicum 17, 25
Origen 218

Pastoral Constitution on the Church in the Modern World 52
Paul VI 210, 211, 226, 231, 238, 257, 267, 276, 277, 324, 329
Pius X, Pope St. 17, 22, 233
Provido sane 133

Redemptor hominis 306
Rerum novarum 233
Roman Catechism 11, 219
Roman Ritual 334

Sacerdotalis caelibatus 286
Sacred Congregation for Catholic Education 292
Sacred Congregation for the Clergy 41, 138, 292
Sacred Congregation for the Doctrine of the Faith 42
Sacred Congregation for the Evangelization of Peoples 261
Sacred Congregation for the Sacraments and Divine Worship 307
Sacrosanctum concilium 336
Sapieha, Cardinal Adam Stephen 275
Second Vatican Council 42, 45, 50, 62, 94, 146, 154, 156, 184, 210, 227, 230, 235, 272ff., 297, 302, 308, 324ff.
Social Communications Days 245
Solemn Profession of Faith 257

Third General Assembly of the Synod of Bishops 146

Urban IV, Pope 300

Year of Faith 29, 31

Daughters of St. Paul

IN MASSACHUSETTS
 50 St. Paul's Ave., Jamaica Plain, Boston, MA 02130; **617-522-8911.**
 172 Tremont Street, Boston, MA 02111; **617-426-5464; 617-426-4230.**

IN NEW YORK
 78 Fort Place, Staten Island, NY 10301; **212-447-5071; 212-447-5086.**
 59 East 43rd Street, New York, NY 10017; **212-986-7580.**
 625 East 187th Street, Bronx, NY 10458; **212-584-0440.**
 525 Main Street, Buffalo, NY 14203; **716-847-6044.**

IN NEW JERSEY
 Hudson Mall—Route 440 and Communipaw Ave.,
 Jersey City, NJ 07304; **201-433-7740.**

IN CONNECTICUT
 202 Fairfield Ave., Bridgeport, CT 06604; **203-335-9913.**

IN OHIO
 2105 Ontario Street (at Prospect Ave.), Cleveland, OH 44115;
 216-621-9427.
 25 E. Eighth Street, Cincinnati, OH 45202; **513-721-4838;
 513-421-5733.**

IN PENNSYLVANIA
 1719 Chestnut Street, Philadelphia, PA 19103; **215-568-2638.**

IN VIRGINIA
 1025 King Street, Alexandria, VA 22314; **703-683-1741; 703-549-3806.**

IN FLORIDA
 2700 Biscayne Blvd., Miami, FL 33137; **305-573-1618.**

IN LOUISIANA
 4403 Veterans Memorial Blvd., Metairie, LA 70002; **504-887-7631;
 504-887-0113.**
 1800 South Acadian Thruway, P.O. Box 2028, Baton Rouge, LA 70821;
 504-343-4057; 504-381-9485.

IN MISSOURI
 1001 Pine Street (at North 10th), St. Louis, MO 63101; **314-621-0346;
 314-231-1034.**

IN ILLINOIS
 172 North Michigan Ave., Chicago, IL 60601; **312-346-4228;
 312-346-3240.**

IN TEXAS
 114 Main Plaza, San Antonio, TX 78205; **512-224-8101; 512-224-0938.**

IN CALIFORNIA
 1570 Fifth Ave., San Diego, CA 92101; **619-232-1442.**
 46 Geary Street, San Francisco, CA 94108; **415-781-5180.**

IN WASHINGTON
 2301 Second Ave., Seattle, WA 98121.

IN HAWAII
 1143 Bishop Street, Honolulu, HI 96813; **808-521-2731.**

IN ALASKA
 750 West 5th Ave., Anchorage, AK 99501; **907-272-8183.**

IN CANADA
 3022 Dufferin Street, Toronto 395, Ontario, Canada.

IN ENGLAND
 199 Kensington High Street, London W8 63A, England.
 133 Corporation Street, Birmingham B4 6PH, England.
 5A-7 Royal Exchange Square, Glasgow G1 3AH, England.
 82 Bold Street, Liverpool L1 4HR, England.

IN AUSTRALIA
 58 Abbotsford Rd., Homebush, N.S.W. 2140, Australia.